Infrastructure Finance

Founded in 1807, John Wiley & Sons is the oldest independent publishing company in the United States. With offices in North America, Europe, Australia, and Asia, Wiley is globally committed to developing and marketing print and electronic products and services for our customers' professional and personal knowledge and understanding.

The Wiley Finance series contains books written specifically for finance and investment professionals as well as sophisticated individual investors and their financial advisors. Book topics range from portfolio management to e-commerce, risk management, financial engineering, valuation and financial instrument analysis, as well as much more.

For a list of available titles, visit our web site at www.WileyFinance.com.

Infrastructure Finance

*The Business of Infrastructure
for a Sustainable Future*

NEIL S. GRIGG

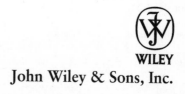

WILEY

John Wiley & Sons, Inc.

For general information on our other products and services or for technical support, please contact our Customer Care Department within the United States at (800) 762-2974, outside the United States at (317) 572-3993 or fax (317) 572-4002.

Wiley also publishes its books in a variety of electronic formats. Some content that appears in print may not be available in electronic books. For more information about Wiley products, visit our web site at www.wiley.com.

Library of Congress Cataloging-in-Publication Data:

Grigg, Neil S.
  Infrastructure finance : the business of infrastructure for a sustainable future / Neil S. Grigg.
       p.   cm. – (Wiley finance series)
  Includes bibliographical references and index.
  ISBN 978-0-470-48178-3 (cloth)
  1. Infrastructure (Economics)–United States–Finance.   2. Public works–United States–Finance.   3. Municipal services–United States–Finance.   I. Title.
  HC110.C3G75 2010
  363.6068′1–dc22   2009037063

Printed in the United States of America

10 9 8 7 6 5 4 3 2 1

To public works and utility leaders
around the world

Contents

Every society must work through its political system to decide how it will respond to the basic needs of its citizens. The needs begin with safety and security and extend to health, education, and opportunity for a good life. As a society becomes more affluent, the needs become open-ended and require public choices to avoid sinking under too much debt. Deciding how to meet it drives political debate about the allocation of resources and the roles of government, business, and individuals. While the debates proceed, it remains clear that infrastructure is a solid investment that is essential to meet human and environmental needs, whether they involve safe drinking water, effective transportation, pollution control, or public school buildings.

Now infrastructure finance is in the limelight because the nation is challenged to maintain its support systems during the financial crisis. Although the crisis is tough, it seems we have been here before, even if the problems were different, such as the oil embargo of the 1970s or the savings and loan debacle of the 1980s. Through these, our financial systems have held our economic system together.

The central issue in the debates involves shades of an old question: Does capitalism or socialism reign? If a society views infrastructure as purely a private good to be available only to those who can afford its services, life would be unfair and miserable for many, many people. If it views infrastructure-related services as purely tax-supported public goods, the result would be inefficiency, waste, and lack of public choice. So, the answer is somewhere in between: Infrastructure involves both private and public goods. The solutions are based on neither capitalism nor socialism but on a mixed approach.

Infrastructure decisions are not simple because, as society has become more complex, so have its infrastructure systems and the values and institutions that determine society's choices. Gone are the days when a community could get by with a few narrow streets and a basic water system. Today, complex networks of infrastructure systems traverse cities and regions to provide networks of energy, water, transportation, and more. These are connected by cybersystems, and their reliability affects everything from national defense to the health of newborns.

One obstacle to effective decisions is that the definition of *infrastructure* can be arbitrary and create confusion. In this book we define it in a clear way as the built environment and its essential support systems for transportation, communications, energy, water, and waste management. Other essential systems, such as food, criminal justice, and public hospitals, could be included, but the six categories we focus on are distinctive as interrelated physical systems with many common attributes. Communications is a little different from the others, but its infrastructure is often colocated with other public facilities.

The financial details of the infrastructure subsectors embrace a surprising range of topics of national importance that include, for example, effects of the housing bubble, effects of gas price rises on travel, electricity and global warming, the crisis in water, disposal of nuclear wastes, massive aging infrastructures, and the war on terror. Each of these issues adds cost to infrastructure and affects its bottom line in one way or another. These topics are the subjects of best-sellers about the problems the world faces today, such as melting icebergs, the ravages of poverty, and the need for clean energy.

Financing these systems requires a substantial portion of the nation's gross domestic product, somewhere around 10 percent if you define infrastructure as only basic support networks and around 20 percent if you include housing and commercial buildings in its definition. How these macroeconomic numbers are estimated is explained in Chapter 11 of the book.

Given the size and importance of infrastructure systems, it is natural that fierce debates will rage about how to pay for it. These debates focus on questions such as which systems to provide, how much to provide, and who will pay for them. Although these questions are debated at the policy level, they are mostly decided at the level of infrastructure management organizations, firms, and regulatory agencies.

The first part of the book explains the main infrastructure sectors, how they can be aggregated to form a composite sector, and how they offer investment opportunities. The second part presents a scorecard of statistics for the aggregated infrastructure sector and its constituents, introduces an overall financial model for the sector, explains its capital structure, and describes the sources of revenues for its subsectors. The final chapter explains current thinking about national policy, including public and private roles in improving infrastructure while dealing with an ongoing financial crisis.

Along the way, the book presents a number of brief profiles of public agencies, private infrastructure companies, and supplier firms. The profiles illustrate how the players participate in the infrastructure arena. They also illustrate how private sector players can work within the government-dominated infrastructure arena.

As a caveat, I would like to emphasize that the company profiles are not presented to give investment advice. They illustrate ranges of choice among large and small businesses with different financial strategies and positions within the infrastructure sectors.

As a note on the sources used, many notes are included in the chapters, and Appendix A provides a list of principal data sources. For the most part, these have been noted when used, but in some cases a general source such as "Yahoo Finance" was consulted to obtain a single number, such as annual revenues. As that number is available from a wide range of sources, these are not always noted because doing so would add too much clutter to the text. Appendix B is a listing of infrastructure companies that were discussed in the text and can help the reader navigate quickly to them. Appendix C provides a list of acronyms and will help clear up the mysteries of infrastructure's "alphabet soup."

NEIL S. GRIGG
January 2010

Acknowledgments

This book spun out of my long-term interest in infrastructure management, which is expressed through a course in the civil engineering department at Colorado State University. I would like to thank a number of people and institutions for the help I have received in the evolution of this course and the ideas behind this book. These begin with the professors at West Point, where as a cadet in about 1960 I discovered *American City* magazine, which sparked my interest in city and public works management.

Later, the seed of the course was inherited at the University of Denver from Dr. Ron Hensen, who focused on city planning and transportation. At that time, the United States was implementing Great Society programs, such as New Cities and the War on Poverty, and was in the grips of the Vietnam War. The course began to take on land development topics to explain how developers negotiated with cities on infrastructure finance. As a consultant, I worked on infrastructure financial studies and gained an appreciation for capital and operations budgets and accounting. About the same time, I witnessed the birth of Denver's transit system, which started with three small buses bought through a federal grant. It was interesting to see how transit required subsidies because of low ridership, even if people did not like to subsidize it.

My next eye-opener on infrastructure finance was in the North Carolina state government, where I had oversight responsibility for the Wastewater Construction Grants program, one of the largest public works financing programs of the day. I also witnessed the plight of small cities trying to finance their infrastructure without a tax base or the income to pay adequate fees.

By the 1980s, the "infrastructure crisis" had my attention. I participated in events organized by the American Society of Civil Engineers and the American Public Works Association on infrastructure policy and financing and I served as a consultant to the National Council on Public Works Improvement, which issued the first infrastructure report card. I also had several opportunities to work as an international consultant on infrastructure projects supported by development banks. These gave me a picture of the financial dilemmas facing developing countries, and I began to include development banking in the infrastructure course. Later, I noted that some countries had excellent financial and regulatory theories but could not implement them due to local politics, culture, and financial problems.

As the United Kingdom grappled with its infrastructure issues, I was impressed with how it imposed a regionalization scheme on the water industry. I thank Dr. Dan Okun, who was a leader at the University of North Carolina, for kindling my interest in this. With this scheme, the United Kingdom had created state water companies, which looked efficient to me at the time. However, the Thatcher government privatized them, as well as other state enterprises, and I was able to see sharp differences between public and private sector approaches. In a visit to one of the authorities, I noted how carefully they computed the condition of their buried assets as they prepared for their initial public offering.

After I returned to Colorado State in 1982 and reinitiated my course on infrastructure, I was appointed to the city's Water Board and later to the city's Transportation Board. These boards advise the City Council on policies and finance for utilities, street maintenance, transit finance, and related policy topics. I began to study financial modeling for utilities, rate studies, regulatory programs, and tools for financial analysis. Some of these topics were included in two 1980s books on urban water systems and on infrastructure management, both published by Wiley. I noted the divide between the financial approaches of engineer-managers and accountants, who did not seem to have a good handle on fixed asset management. Some of this problem was addressed in the 1990s by the Government Accounting Standards Board through its new statement GASB 34.

I had noticed the irony that engineers and rising infrastructure managers had much responsibility for finance, but as students they were taught next to nothing about it. In response, I increased the finance content in the infrastructure course to cover utility rates, taxes, and the bond market, among other topics. I was able to reach back in time to my economics professors at West Point, who required us to read the *Wall Street Journal* and to compile mock portfolios of stocks. This had sparked a lifelong interest in economics and finance, and I began using the *Wall Street Journal* as a teaching aid in my infrastructure course. A good share of the *Journal*'s content relates in one way or another to infrastructure.

By 2009, when the book was being prepared, the housing and economic crisis was in full bloom, and the government was applying infrastructure stimulus tools. Having studied the lessons of the Great Depression, this was like a living laboratory to give me insight into the differences between public sector and private sector infrastructure developments. The Obama administration initiated a number of Keynesian tools, and infrastructure investment was a core part of the package.

So, it is a long story as to how the book evolved, and I appreciate very much the valuable help I received along the way. I also benefited from the support from Wiley staff members Bill Falloon, Executive Editor, Finance and Investment, Meg Freeborn, who served as Development Editor during manuscript design and preparation, and Melissa Lopez, who handled production editing capably. I appreciate their counsel on the development of the book and moving it from concept to completion.

CHAPTER 1

An Introduction to Infrastructure Finance

The business of infrastructure will always be vibrant because without basic systems such as transportation, energy, and water, neither the economy nor society can function. No matter how you define it, infrastructure is a large and important business sector. When defined broadly, the infrastructure business includes buildings, transportation, energy, water, telecommunications, and waste management as well as the cross-cutting construction and environmental businesses. When it is defined narrowly, it focuses on the construction industry, which is a vital and important sector of the economy.

Two compelling issues drive the need to finance infrastructure systems. The first is that the systems provide the physical basis for life, whether safe drinking water, energy to stay warm, or other essential services. The second issue is the business of infrastructure, or the functioning of the private sector and government organizations that provide and sustain the essential structures, equipment, and services of infrastructure.

This chapter introduces infrastructure as a business and identifies its main issues. Chapter 2 explains how infrastructure is a composite sector and introduces its subsectors. After a chapter about each of the subsubsectors, a summary chapter presents a range of investment opportunities. The remaining chapters in the book explain the capital and operating finances of infrastructure and identify the driving forces and trends that will shape its sectors in the future.

WHAT IS INFRASTRUCTURE BUSINESS?

Having a clear definition is the key to analyzing the "infrastructure business." As the reader will see, people define *infrastructure* in different ways. To view it as a business, you must focus on its financials. The definition can be fuzzy, so it is even more important to specify what infrastructure includes.

Much of the interest in infrastructure is focused on the construction industry, but infrastructure involves more than construction. One business letter, the *Infrastructure Investor* (2009), wrote that infrastructure "covers the man-made facilities that ensure any economy can operate" and that it includes transportation (railways, roads, and airports), utilities (energy generation and distribution, water, and waste processing, and telecommunications), and social infrastructure (schools, hospitals, and state housing).

Our definition varies from this, but the idea is the same. Investments in infrastructure target basic facilities that meet the needs of society and the economy. One variation is the attention we give to the built environment itself, with its emphasis on residential and commercial buildings. If these are not included in the infrastructure sector, then a major share of construction spending is missed. Another important part of our approach is that we distinguish between infrastructure and operation of infrastructure-related services, which is important in analyzing the sector.

In the chapters that follow, the reader will see that infrastructure is a composite of sectors such as construction, transportation, energy, and water, among others. Why should anyone be interested in this composite sector when its parts, such as transportation or electric utilities, can be analyzed separately? Surely these parts are large and complex enough to deserve their own analysis. The answer is, of course, they are large and deserve their own analysis, but they have common attributes that lend themselves to analysis of the composite sector for the purposes of investors, public sector managers, and policy makers.

Investors are now being presented with new infrastructure stock funds and are told that infrastructure is an attractive sector because it is essential and solid at a time when other sectors are changing rapidly. This can seem like a new investment opportunity, and it does have new facets. However, much of what is offered comprises systems that have been around a long time.

Public sector managers are confronted with complex decisions, such as how to solve traffic congestion or when and how to renew aging infrastructure systems. Facing these issues, policy makers—such as local government elected leaders—face funding decisions that may dwarf their other financial decisions.

The general purpose of the book is to pose and answer questions that will help these three groups: investors, public sector managers, and policy makers. For the policy makers, the book opens a discussion of new forms of public-private cooperation and mechanisms to make government more efficient and responsive to public needs. For the public sector managers, it explains the financial structures and performances of the distinct infrastructure sectors. It ranges across public and private sector systems to explain how they obtain operating and capital revenues and how the balance between demand and supply is achieved. For investors, the book explains the structures of the industries that are in the infrastructure arena, how they obtain their capital and operating revenues, and how opportunities for private sector involvement arise in the capital markets, in equities of listed companies, and in private business start-ups.

INFRASTRUCTURE THEN AND NOW

Whereas the public side of infrastructure has a high profile, the fact is that infrastructure has always had a high level of private sector involvement. Just 100 years ago, the infrastructure business was strong in the United States, railroad stocks were hot on Wall Street, the electric utility industry was new, and the public demanded more roads for its new Model T automobiles. Go back 100 years earlier, and you see that change from a rural to an urban society gave birth to the technological age that drove the need for infrastructure.

This industrialization and urbanization that led to infrastructure development started around 1800, when a private banking venture led by Aaron Burr built a new water system for New York City. At that time and for another century, bankers were important players in financing infrastructure systems as well as other high-stakes national issues, even wars.

The steam engine had been invented, and it powered the Industrial Revolution. The privately owned Erie Canal created a boom for the Northeast, and people could see the close links between transportation and economic development. The growing nation required more and more politically charged internal improvements, and infrastructure issues moved to center stage in politics as well as business.

Now we live in a different world, but the infrastructure business remains important because the public still needs rail, electricity, roads, and many other infrastructure-related public services. If you include the Internet as part of infrastructure, then it rises even higher on the agenda. In any case, we are reminded of infrastructure constantly by the media. *Time* magazine, in its March 23, 2009, cover story, reported on 2 its top 10 national trends as related to infrastructure (Lacayo, 2009). One was the evolution of smart highways that serve to organize economic activity (see Chapter 4), and the other was recycling the suburbs with updated land uses (see Chapter 3).

Not only is the role of infrastructure in the economy large, it is growing in importance. This role was high on the agenda of many economists during the 1980s and 1990s, and they explained how infrastructure is essential to economic development, productivity, and employment (Gramlich, 2001). They also showed that infrastructure investments encourage innovation, competitiveness, and is the basis for a high standard of living (Infrastructure Australia, 2008).

During the recent financial crises, infrastructure figured prominently in national stimulus packages and the U.S. budget. Having learned from past recessions, cities have been competing to show how many "shovel-ready" projects they have on their books. Much of the response to the financial crisis has been about housing, public projects, and transportation systems, all of which are central to infrastructure policy.

America is under criticism for how it invests in infrastructure. Along with other policy questions, we as a society face decisions about how much to invest in infrastructure, even while we are confronted with tremendous "needs estimates" to rebuild highways and fix aging sewers. Some say that if the nation does not invest more, it risks having the infrastructure of a third-world country. Experts look back at past nation building and grand projects like the Interstate Highway System and ask, "Where is that vision today?" Investment analysts compare America's infrastructure investment of 2.4 percent of gross domestic product (GDP) to Europe's 5 percent and China's 9 percent and point to dysfunctional transportation, choked ports and airports, road congestion, and inadequate rail track systems.

One way to view this lack of investment is as a "third deficit," to go along with our national debt and social security deficit. On a more positive note, it is apparent that we are entering a period of massive investment to rebuild and reinvent our infrastructure, almost like the 1930s New Deal or 1950s Interstate Highway eras. In any case, the overall view among experts interviewed by the *Economist* (2008) was "It's time to think big again."

As we explain in the book, an important dimension of infrastructure finance is how it can be used to manage demand and raise efficiency of critical public systems and services. This challenge is aimed directly at a central question about infrastructure: Should it emphasize public or private purposes? Public purposes focus on the core needs of society, such as clean air and water and access to education and healthcare. Private purposes relate to more discretionary needs, such as housing choices and entertainment.

Infrastructure finance addresses the central questions of public versus private purposes and is thus in the crossfire of political debates about a fair society. Chapter 14 discusses how decisions about infrastructure finance align public and private purposes. It answers questions about the roles of government and the private sector and how to meet basic human needs, such as safe water, disposal of wastes, energy, and transportation to work.

Infrastructure is at the center of debates about the global problem of poverty. When basic needs are not met, *why* are they not met? Whose job is it to provide them? Should the poor pay the same for basic services as affluent people? If basic services are not provided, who should intervene?

On a broader scale, what are society's obligations to provide infrastructure for the many displaced and disenfranchised people around the world? Hundreds of millions of people displaced by war, climate change, or lack of opportunity do not have the basic support systems provided by infrastructure.

In more affluent societies, the more urgent problem is to find ways to sustain current levels of infrastructure-related services in the face of resource and environmental limits. Doing this requires more attention to managing demand rather than constantly ratcheting up supply. Closely related to demand management and efficiency of infrastructure is the subtle but important issue of trade-offs. You will read over and over in the book about how society and individuals can make choices about using public services, and the closer we can align these choices with the obligation to pay, the better our management will be.

The other focus in the book is on the attractiveness of infrastructure businesses, whether as an investment, such as purchase of municipal bonds or stocks of listed companies or direct equity stakes, or as a business line for entrepreneurs. The controversy over privatization and use of public-private partnerships is addressed with this topic. Chapter 10 provides examples of investment opportunities, including privatization.

While people have a general idea about infrastructure, measuring its financial performance is difficult because it is hard to define and classify and it has broad public purposes as well as well-defined private purposes. Infrastructure is not one unified system but a composite of systems involving utilities, transportation systems, and environmental services, among others. Also, reports about infrastructure tend to confuse the condition of government-owned physical assets and operating performance of the organizations that provide public services.

The definition of infrastructure can seem abstract and apply to different types of systems. To avoid a fuzzy definition, the book focuses on the constructed assets in six systems: the built environment itself, transportation, communications, energy, water, and waste management systems. This definition leaves out nonphysical categories, such as economic and social infrastructure systems. It emphasizes that infrastructure services are required for people and the economy, and they are not simply based on consumer choice.

To formalize this definition, we can say that infrastructure comprises the structural assets of the built environment and its physical support networks, and it includes a great deal of equipment, such as generators, motors, and actuators. In most cases, when accounting for infrastructure, we include both structures and equipment, which are the two types of fixed assets tracked by the U.S. Bureau of Economic Affairs.

Our definition of infrastructure distinguishes between the structures of infrastructure systems and the equipment of the organizations using the infrastructure to deliver public services, such as private motor vehicles and aircraft. In the case of rail companies, infrastructure includes structures and railcars. In the case of airlines, equipment is not considered part of infrastructure in our analysis but is part of the fixed assets of private companies using public infrastructure. You could, of course, make a case to include privately owned aircraft as infrastructure, but the definition of it would require adjustment.

The concept of public and private infrastructure systems can be confusing. There are many possibilities, but our main focus in the book is on infrastructure systems that provide public services, as distinguished from those that meet only private needs, such as the infrastructure that serves a manufacturing site. In some cases, the infrastructure that provides public services also serves broad public purposes that fall outside of the direct service. For example, a privately owned toll bridge could provide the public service of access across a river, but it might be required to remain open in case emergency vehicles needed to use it. Whether the bridge owner was compensated or not for the emergency access could be a matter for negotiation when rate-setting decisions are approved by regulators.

Some of the terms used can be confusing, and this list may help clarify them:

Public infrastructure	Infrastructure that meets public purposes
Publicly owned infrastructure	Infrastructure owned by governments
Private infrastructure	Infrastructure that meets private purposes only
Privately owned infrastructure	Infrastructure owned by private entities that might be used to provide public services and meet public purposes
Private company	A company whose ownership is private and not be share held by the public
Public company	A company that is owned by the public through issuance of traded stock shares
Public service	A service provided by government to the public
Public purposes	Goals of society that benefit all citizens

Given these variables, our focus is mainly on what is called public infrastructure, but it includes privately owned systems that provide public services. Although we focus on the public infrastructure, it is difficult to divorce the discussion from private infrastructure because it creates the main demands on public infrastructure. Private, residential, and commercial buildings are prime examples of private facilities that need public infrastructure systems.

Our definition is consistent with one used by the U.S. Congressional Budget Office (1983) and cited more recently by Dzierwa (2009) in his investment analysis of infrastructure as a sector. He emphasized that infrastructure has the common characteristics of capital intensity, high public investment by all levels of government, and criticality to the economy. The sectors included in the CBO study were about the same as ours, although we also include buildings as infrastructure because their financial needs are the largest among built facilities, and they drive needs for the other categories of infrastructure. How this is handled is explained in Chapter 2, which presents a conceptual model in which all building types form the core of the built environment, which drives demand for the other categories of infrastructure.

A SYSTEM OF SYSTEMS

In the broadest sense, infrastructure is everything in the built environment that is distinct from natural and human environments. Usually definitions are more specific and explain what infrastructure is and which categories of systems it includes. Here are a few examples of these definitions:

- The basic physical systems of a country's or community's population (InvestorWords, 2009)
- The functional modes of public works and combined infrastructure system (National Research Council, 1987)
- Physical assets that provide services used in production and final consumption (New Zealand Ministry of Economic Development, 2005)
- Assets that range from large-scale national networks to smaller community-based facilities (Infrastructure Australia, 2008)
- A collective term for services (refers to critical national infrastructure) (Parliamentary Information Management Committee, 2009)

The definitions are usually accompanied by explanations of why infrastructure is essential to the economy, to quality of life, to communities, to the environment, and to high standards of living.

In some cases, economic and social systems can be called infrastructures. For example, the U.S. Department of Homeland Security includes economic and government systems, such as emergency services, finance, food, and public safety, in its definition of "critical infrastructure" (2009). It is also not

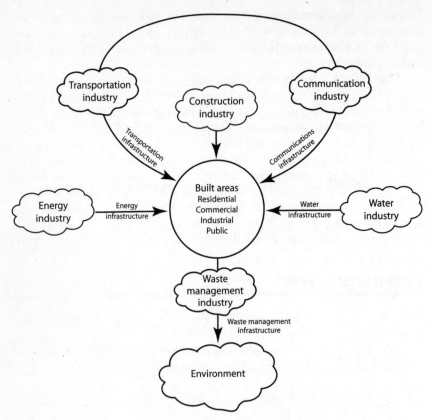

EXHIBIT 1.1   Built Environment and Infrastructure Support Systems

unusual to find social facilities, such as hospitals, schools and universities, museums, and libraries, in the definition. These definitions illustrate the dual nature of infrastructure: It can be explained as physical infrastructure or it can refer to operating sectors.

In our definition, infrastructure is limited to the buildings of the built environment and their support systems for transportation, communications, energy, water, and waste management. Exhibit 1.1 shows how these five infrastructure systems support the developed areas and corridors of the built environment.

As Exhibit 1.2 illustrates, all infrastructure systems utilize large-scale fixed assets, provide essential public services, involve both the public and private sectors, and are regulated by the government for health, safety, and performance. They include but are not limited to the services offered

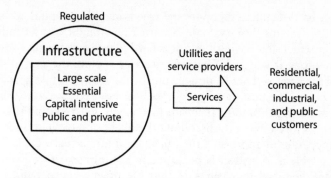

EXHIBIT 1.2 Distinctive Attributes of Infrastructure Systems

by public utilities for energy, water, and other utility services. Even with these attributes, it can be hard to say why one public service, such as road transportation, is based on infrastructure and another public service, such as police protection, is not.

The answer to this question comes through the arcane science of classification, which is explained for infrastructure systems in Chapter 2. Using a classification system, we can place police protection in a category of security services, which do not depend as much on physical assets as infrastructure-related services do.

The classification framework in Chapter 2 can be used to explain infrastructure investment needs and policies. At the highest level, the classification system starts with human systems, constructed systems, and natural systems. The classification can be taken to successively lower levels until the most basic components of the built environment are included, down to a streetlamp or water valve.

The terms *sector, industry,* and *system* are used interchangeably to explain infrastructure. When *sector* and *industry* are used, they generally refer to economic issues. The term *system* usually refers to physical components working together, such as a network of roads.

SECTOR STRUCTURE AND SIZE

Chapter 11 is about measuring the infrastructure sector, including both capital and operating costs. It is often difficult to separate these costs, but accounting for infrastructure must recognize that sometimes one organization provides the infrastructure (such as a roads department) and another one provides the operating services (such as transit services).

It can be difficult to compute the true annualized capital costs for infrastructure systems. For example, a buried pipe might cost $1 million per mile to construct, but its lifetime cost is hard to measure because you do not know how long it will last. Once debt service is paid, the capital-intensive nature of the asset will not be noticed much, and it may be taken for granted. This may continue until it fails, and lead to the need for sudden large expenditures for repair and/or renewal. Just as you must know the condition of a house before buying it, discerning the likelihood of these sudden costs can be important in appraising the full costs of infrastructure.

The problem of neglect is pervasive in the infrastructure management arena. One financial manager said that the practice is to build it, forget it, and rebuild it. Out of sight, out of mind is another slogan that applies. What should an elected city council member argue to rebuild a sewer that has not yet failed, when the funds can go for another community park that might even have the names of the elected council members on a placard?

No matter how you measure it, infrastructure activity is a major part of the economy. Although it is not measured directly in national economic accounts, the infrastructure sector's size can be approximated by statistics such as construction spending, government spending, and utility revenues. Construction is 4 to 5 percent of GDP on the basis of value added. Energy costs are on the order of 8 percent, and, while it is not accounted for in an integrated way, the transportation sector is huge. If you add utilities, real estate, waste management, professional services, and government activities related to infrastructure, the percentage rises. Taking all together, the costs to build, maintain, and operate infrastructure systems and all buildings rise to around 20 percent or more of the economy. Of course, the critical issue in measuring this is what infrastructure includes.

While it is difficult to measure infrastructure's economic impact, estimates in Chapter 11 show that the value of U.S. infrastructure assets is around $8.3 trillion for public structures and $28.0 trillion for private structures (2007 data). Most of the public asset value is in roads, streets, and other infrastructure networks, while the private asset value is heavily weighted toward residential housing.

Expanding, modernizing, and renewing public infrastructure place heavy burdens on state and local governments as well as rate payers and taxpayers. For example, the $8.3 trillion asset value for public infrastructure represents over $80,000 per household in the United States, and the number is heading up as systems become more complex and need replacing with new models. The residential housing cost per household is much larger and is a principal reason for the financial crisis that occurred with the housing bubble. New management approaches are needed to deal with these large obligations while not increasing taxes and fees to burdensome levels.

ESTIMATING THE PER CAPITA COST

Although the details are complex, the overall cost of infrastructure can be estimated from the capital and operating costs for each sector. For the built environment, these would be paid as rent or opportunity cost for residential, commercial, and industrial facilities. In the transportation sector, costs would include the upkeep and capital on roads and the subsidies and fares of transit, rail, and aviation systems. The energy and communications sector revenues would be added to all charges and subsidies for water, wastewater, and waste management. The sum of all these costs would cover all debt service and operations of the infrastructure categories.

Generally speaking, if the GDP is about $45,000 per capita and if all infrastructure costs are 10 percent of GDP, then the annual cost to provide infrastructure and related services is about $4,500 per capita in the United States. If infrastructure costs are greater, at 15 percent of GDP, then the cost is $6,750 per capita, or about $20,000 for a three-person household. The numbers appear low if you consider the full cost of housing and other buildings.

As the major factor in infrastructure cost, residential housing comprises a large percentage of the estimates. For example, for a $200,000 three-person home, the annual cost per capita is about $4,000 (assuming a 40-year life, cost of capital at 5 percent, and maintenance at 10 percent of annualized capital cost). That amounts to an estimate of $1,000 per month for housing for the family, which would be higher if the interest rate rose.

The costs of the other infrastructure categories add to the total cost of housing, but they cost less than the buildings themselves. For example, as Chapter 6 shows, the total national electric power and natural gas revenues for a year are around $500 billion, or a per capita cost of about $1,700. Adding all such related infrastructure costs to the costs of housing seems to corroborate the $20,000-per-family range (about 15 percent of GDP) for housing plus infrastructure. In the final analysis, the per capita cost to provide infrastructure depends on its definition and how the costs are allocated. Chapter 10 presents an overall picture of these costs in the form of a scorecard for infrastructure.

NEED FOR NEW APPROACHES

It is true that infrastructure was a driving force of the Industrial Revolution, but economic challenges have shifted. Now society and the economic system are more complex. There are close links between infrastructure and economic vitalization, and no one can afford command-and-control approaches to infrastructure development unless the systems can be financed and sustained.

Mandel (2009) saw a link between infrastructure challenges and our current need for more innovation:

> *Of course, no industrial revolution in the past has been based on a single technology. A combination of radio, television, flight, antibiotics, synthetic materials, and automobiles drove the productivity surge of the early and mid-20th century. The Industrial Revolution of the second half of the 19th century combined railroads, electricity, and the telegraph and telephone. (p. 34–40)*

So, what about innovation in infrastructure? Can we bring better services to more people at a reasonable cost and help the triple bottom line? The links between infrastructure and quality of life are undeniable. Developed and developing countries need sustainable infrastructure to support their citizens while not damaging the environment. Success for these countries will depend on their management approaches and financing methods.

New management approaches to achieve sustainable infrastructure systems must confront their capital intensity, which presents obstacles to performance improvement and cost reduction. New approaches, such as those described in Chapter 14, can feature different forms of ownership and financing as well as new technologies and management strategies.

While it is tempting to think that a market approach of pricing infrastructure services will solve the problem, this strategy suffers from market failure, a term that explains how the private market cannot fully deal with issues of public goods. This difficult issue draws in the economic problems of managing monopolies to protect the public interest as well as many newer business issues about social equity and environmental protection.

The opposite of market failure is government failure. The government cannot manage infrastructure fully by itself without spiraling into pure socialism and waste caused by pork-barrel approaches and other public sector problems. At its best, the issue becomes one of efficiency. At its worst, corruption and criminal activity are involved.

This combination of market failure and government failure leads to a principal theme of the book: the need for improved models for public-private cooperation, or a "middle way." In today's parlance, these are usually referred to as public-private partnerships. They are discussed in more detail in Chapter 12.

Embedded in the discussions in the book about infrastructure finance are many new management approaches. In addition to public-private cooperation, these include pursuit of efficiency and equity, environmental sustainability, and triple-bottom-line thinking to link infrastructure to objectives for energy conservation, environmental management, and security.

The next chapter provides an overview of the infrastructure sectors, including the built environment, transportation and communications, energy and water, and waste management. Separate chapters follow for each of these key infrastructure sectors. A chapter to summarize investment opportunities wraps up Part I of the book.

SUMMARY

Whereas infrastructure is often considered a technical sector, current issues point to the important roles of business and finance in improving the sector. Technology will continue to push new developments, but the most important changes will be organizational and financial. This section reviews important issues that confirm how these issues drive today's infrastructure sector.

Infrastructure as a Business

The infrastructure business evolved rapidly during the Industrial Revolution and is still in a period of change. The earliest public roads, railroads, water systems, electric power systems, and other facilities were private, for-profit ventures. Although it has changed, the infrastructure business will remain vibrant because it is essential to the economy, society, and the environment. Even during the Great Depression, electric power, transit, and other infrastructure services continued in operation. Although demands for infrastructure continue and grow, the nature of the business has changed so that the security of regulated returns is less certain than in the past.

Infrastructure as a Third Deficit

The large backlog of infrastructure needs comprises a third national deficit, along with the public debt and unmet future Social Security needs. Therefore, America will be challenged to invest enough in its infrastructure to meet the identified needs because it has other heavy financial obligations. Its dispersed population and standard of living create greater per capita infrastructure costs than other, more centralized nations face. The United States must develop new policies to respond to these challenges.

Infrastructure Is Not Just a Public Good or a Private Good

Infrastructure systems serve both public and private purposes, and it will always be difficult to draw a fine line between services that can be financed through consumer choice and those that require government mandates and subsidies. This juxtaposition presents a challenge to the political and economic systems: Can the U.S. political system adapt once again to show how a representative democracy can step up to the plate to make equitable choices that serve all the people?

Infrastructure Is a Core Issue in Overcoming Poverty

Around the world, poverty and deprivation are all about lack of basic infrastructure and related services. How can people escape poverty if they lack housing, safe water, affordable energy, transportation to a job, and a healthy way to dispose of wastes? If nations and the international community are serious about overcoming poverty, they must find ways to straddle the public and private purposes of infrastructure services and deliver workable and sustainable systems to everyone.

Trends and Driving Forces

Without exception, infrastructure systems are becoming more complex, costly, and vulnerable. These attributes pose danger and opportunity. The danger occurs because infrastructure may absorb more national resources and cause distress in society when it fails, but the opportunity is to create through the private sector new products and services to address these changes. Information technology, telecommunications, smart controls, new sensors, and other technologies can help ensure more reliable and responsive infrastructure systems at affordable costs.

Management Requires Keen Insight

While it is easy to agree on the need for infrastructure and public services, defining what is meant by this can be difficult. Without a fixed definition of infrastructure and clear demand signals from the marketplace, it can be difficult o measure the financial performance of infrastructure systems. Lacking performance indicators, politicians can refuse to invest or spend on the basis that they require more evidence of the results. This dilemma afflicts infrastructure systems and creates problems ranging from financing transit buses to preventing failures of aging infrastructure systems, such as buried water lines.

Choice in Services

Providing infrastructure and its public services is not only a matter of defining needs and meeting them. It is also about giving people choices so they can decide how much of the infrastructure services to use and how to pay for them. Infrastructure finance is the key tool to provide this choice by creating demand management systems that raise overall efficiency of infrastructure delivery systems. Infrastructure finance offers new ways to make government more effective in its management and oversight roles, including tools that have come through reinventing government and managing the price of government.

Sustainable and Attractive Infrastructure Businesses

Although the idyllic notion of a reliable investment in a regulated infrastructure service that pays unending dividends is a thing of the past, many infrastructure investments still hold attraction for stability, safety, and attractive returns. Some come with assurance of regulation, but even in the absence of regulation, municipal bonds, stocks of growing companies with strong and steady markets, and private equity investments can be very attractive. As in other arenas, picks of the most promising investments remain difficult, but infrastructure offers many opportunities for investors willing to analyze the sector in depth.

PART One

Infrastructure Sectors and Investments

CHAPTER 2

Models of the
Infrastructure Sectors

Once infrastructure is defined, the next step to understanding it in depth is to probe the organizational issues that explain roles of the public and private sectors, how managing structures may be different from delivering public services, and how different infrastructure sectors vary in their use of capital investments. These issues can be addressed by using a simple conceptual model of the infrastructure sector as a composite system of systems. This conceptual model shows us what the sector includes and how its elements interact. It provides insight to help evaluate the investment possibilities of the overall sector or its subindustries. Without a model like this, every situation is different, and we lack the ability to make a rigorous analysis that compares forces across the industry.

Using the model introduced in this chapter, we classify infrastructure systems and their operating sectors. In the model, the built environment creates demand for transportation and communication systems, energy and water system inputs, and waste management systems. Each part of the composite sector of infrastructure operates differently, and the model explains how they work individually and together. It provides an overall classification system and explains how fixed assets in each subsector support operating organizations, which provide essential public services. Starting with the macro-view, you can use the classification system to see infrastructure as a supersector and drill down to see its tiniest parts.

CLASSIFICATION SYSTEM

The classification system provides a way to compare infrastructure sectors, such as roads and energy, and to understand the nuances of business that takes place at different levels of organizations and government. It is based on infrastructure as a composite of subsectors, each of which has different characteristics for asset types, functions, ownership, and type of service delivered. Classifying industries this way involves finding common attributes and placing objects into categories. While this might not seem very interesting, it is important in the analysis of business activities in industries.

Exhibit 2.1 illustrates a view of the infrastructure sector with four levels. It begins at the macro-level, drills down to sectors and then industries, and then drills to physical systems. This shows at a glance how any physical system fits into the big picture of infrastructure. The example shown is from the water sector.

Exhibit 2.1 creates a basis to classify infrastructure system by levels. As you see on the exhibit, infrastructure at the top level is a sector of a bigger system, perhaps the economy, which is a sector of all national life. You can classify these big-picture systems in different ways. At the lower end, you can drill down to lower and lower levels of detail.

Exhibit 2.2 shows how, at the first level down, the names of the sectors align with government departments, such as transportation and energy. We interpret this to mean that infrastructure as a composite sector cuts across several important government departments (or ministries, as they are called in some countries). This makes sense because so many aspects of government affairs relate to infrastructure in one way or another. In some developing or fast-growing countries, there may be a ministry of infrastructure to group similar development and construction activities.

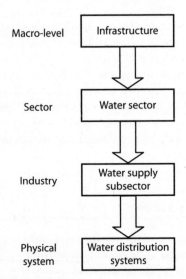

EXHIBIT 2.1   Infrastructure by Levels (Water Sector Example)

EXHIBIT 2.2 Classification System for Infrastructure Sector Levels

Sector	System	Examples of Subsystems
Transportation	Roads and bridges	Highways/streets
	Transit	Bus
	Rail	Passenger/freight
	Air	Airports
	Water transport	Docks
Communication	Wired	Fiber cable
	Wireless	Cellular phone
Energy	Electric power	Generation
	Natural gas	Transmission
Water	Water supply	Distribution
	Wastewater	Treatment
	Irrigation	Sprinkler
	Flood control	Structural
	Dams	Federal
Waste	Solid wastes	Collection/disposal
	Hazardous wastes	Chemical

At the next level down, the names align with industries, such as electric power, which is part of the energy sector. Each of these infrastructure industries is important by itself, and some of them, such as electric power, involve annual expenditures of hundreds of billions of dollars. Electric power also consumes more capital than any other single industrial sector. These industries are often the basis of economic groups, and investment indices have been developed for utilities, transportation, and construction, for example.

At the next level down, subsystems take on technical and management characteristics, such as local streets as part of the roads and bridges system. As you drill deeper into the classification system, more classifiers are available. For example, roads are classified by ownership (state, local, etc.), service level (arterial, freeway, etc.), and pavement type (asphalt, concrete). At the higher levels, only a few variables serve to classify infrastructure, but lower in the system, the numbers of variables increase sharply.

It is at this level where infrastructure names such as lifelines and networks make the most sense because they are subsystems that perform physically based functions within infrastructure systems, such as to convey water or energy.

The classification system can go deeper than the levels shown in Exhibit 2.2. For example, street pavements of asphalt or concrete can be classified by service levels and quality. You can have a six-level sequence of infrastructure-transportation-roads and bridges-streets-pavements-asphalt, for example. If you add type of asphalt, that makes a seventh level. Another example could be water pipes of different sizes and materials. A 12-inch ductile iron water pipe can be lined or unlined, and it can be of different ages. This increase of number of variables with depth in the system is an inherent characteristic of classification frameworks.

As you move deeper and deeper into infrastructure levels, you finally reach the point at which every bolt or piece of wire can be classified. This might seem way too low. However, as information technology is used more and more to manage infrastructure systems, the emerging asset management systems will demand more and more data. At present, however, these systems are catching up with decades in which infrastructure was buried and forgotten, and often it is a challenge merely to locate major buried facilities. The information technologies being used to solve this problem are the basis for some of the fastest-growing infrastructure sector companies (see Chapter 10).

The classification system explains why the concept of infrastructure creates confusion among different groups. Policy analysts lump the sectors and discuss infrastructure at the higher levels. When they discuss infrastructure, they are seeking general principles to set policy, and their discussions may seem abstract to people working on specific issues within the subsectors.

Industry analysts study the middle levels and seek to find patterns of economic activity to explain supply and demand for goods and services, financial flows, movement of prices, and other economic trends.

Technical professionals work at the more specific levels and are not as comfortable with the general and abstract language used at the higher levels. When the term *infrastructure* became popular in the 1980s, many civil engineers were not familiar with it, for example.

The point is, with a complex system like infrastructure with many levels, even at the lower levels of classification there is enough clustering to create subindustries and require separate trade associations. Take the field of road transportation, for example. There are separate trade associations for asphalt, concrete pavement, aggregates, traffic engineers, and other niche groups. As another example, in the case of water and wastewater, there are separate associations for ductile iron pipe, plastic pipe, and pumps. To understand what is happening in these sectors, sometimes you have to drill down to those levels.

INFRASTRUCTURE AND SERVICE ORGANIZATIONS

Accounting for infrastructure and analyzing its financial performance requires a distinction between its fixed assets (such as a bridge) and the operating entities (such as a roads department). Operating entities draw on the fixed assets to deliver services that support economic and social activity in each sector.

In some cases, the fixed assets are owned and operated by the same entity that provides the public services. For example, electric utilities mostly use their own energy infrastructures (generating plants, transmission lines, etc.) to provide energy to customers. In other cases, the operating entity does not own the infrastructure but relies on it to provide the service. An example of this arrangement is a waste management company using a government-owned landfill.

Ideally, standard financial reports, such as income statements and balance sheets, would be used to show the health and condition of the infrastructure sector as a whole. Realistically, however, the reports mix the financial situation in private sector and government infrastructure organizations and may create a confusing picture. While it is not possible to sort this out completely, we provide in Exhibit 2.3 a view of the physical assets and the owner/operators for each sector. In the exhibit, the sector of transportation has been broken into road, air, transit, and rail subgroups.

EXHIBIT 2.3 Infrastructure Owners and Operating Sectors

Sectors	Physical Assets	Operators/Users
Built environment	Residential Commercial Industrial	Owners Users
Roads	Roads Bridges	Cars Trucks Buses
Transit	Rail Bus Rapid Transit	Transit agencies
Rail	Rail	Rail companies
Air	Airports Air Traffic Control System	Airlines Civil aviation
Energy	Generation Transmission Distribution	Electric and gas utilities
Water and wastewater	Production Treatment Piping	Water and wastewater utilities
Waste management	Landfills Processing	Waste management companies

For some systems (such as electric power utilities), the assets and operations of infrastructure organizations can be reported together on integrated financial statements. In those cases, their ability to provide energy can be assessed fairly well, although externalities such as the cost of fuel and environmental regulations will complicate the picture. In other cases (such as for the transportation services provided by roads), mobility is not determined solely by the fixed assets but also involves a fleet of vehicles that are not owned by the roads sector.

Exhibit 2.3 shows how operating entities for road travel, aviation, and waste management provide public services by using infrastructures of roads, airports, and landfills owned by government. Operating entities that mostly own their infrastructures are transit, rail, energy, and water/wastewater. This latter group comprises public utilities, whereas those in the first group (such as local streets) are usually not defined as utilities. Some in the utilities group operate on an interstate basis, whereas others are local. Regulatory structures will vary accordingly.

BUSINESS MODELS OF INFRASTRUCTURE SUBSECTORS

The business models of the infrastructure operating sectors differ between public or private ownership and with several other variables. Examples of business models include:

- State transportation department
- Local government streets department
- Private regulated monopoly utility (energy and water sectors)
- Private regulated company, nonmonopoly (telecom)
- Toll road authority
- Mass transit provider
- Railroad
- Airline
- Waste management company

Some of these are government enterprises, and others are privately owned companies, either listed (public companies) or unlisted and in completely private ownership, such as by a private equity group. A private sector utility company might own and/or operate systems across different industries, such as electric power, natural gas, and perhaps water supply. It might have a subsidiary to also offer nonregulated construction and/or operating and maintenance services. Engineering firms offer a wide range of professional services and might enter the "build-operate-transfer" business. A wide range of companies offer equipment-related services, including sales, leasing, training, and other support.

In Chapters 3 to 8, the business models for the sectors will explain how operating entities own or do not own the infrastructures they depend on to offer services. Ownership of infrastructure is an important variable to measure the degree of integration of a service industry. The concept of industrial integration illustrates how infrastructure organizations gain vertical or horizontal control of their supply chains or markets. When the concept is applied at the level of an industry, it generally relates to the coherence of the industry and the degree to which its participants deal with each other.

Industry integration is the opposite of industry fragmentation. One facet of integration is the extent to which an industry comprises firms that are dedicated to it as opposed to being involved with multiple industries. If many part-time players make up an industry, it is not as coherent as an industry that has many dedicated players. Another dimension of industry integration is whether it comprises thousands or even millions of small, unrelated players, or whether it has only a few integrated firms.

Exhibit 2.4 shows variables to illustrate the concept of industry integration. It illustrates the owners of infrastructure, the operating entities, the public services provided, the beneficiaries of services, the flow of payments, and the use of government payments to assist in the operations of the infrastructure.

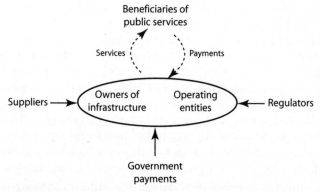

EXHIBIT 2.4   Industry integration for infrastructure sectors

Although Exhibit 2.4 illustrates a simple model, it actually shows eight variables. Once you assign names and attributes to these variables for the organizational forms within the infrastructure sectors, the model becomes much more complex and is the basis for the management and financial models shown in Chapter 12.

The next section is a preview of the subsequent chapters, which explain industry organization in these sectors and how they relate to each other.

HOW INFRASTRUCTURE SYSTEMS SERVE THE BUILT ENVIRONMENT

The function of infrastructure systems is to support flows and activities of people, goods, materials, and information in the built environment. Built areas are created by the construction industry and its partners in real estate, banking, and development. Transportation and communications systems provide for flows of people, goods, and information. Water and energy sustain the economic and human sides of the built environment, and the waste management system handles its residuals. The next few paragraphs provide further detail on how the sectors and systems of infrastructure support the built environment.

> **Built environment.** As explained in Chapter 1, the built environment provides infrastructure in the form of buildings and drives demand for other network services. Residential, commercial, and other buildings require services from infrastructure systems and provide public services themselves. The networks that provide transportation, communications, water, energy, and waste management are integral parts of the built environment, but their fixed assets are accounted for within separate sectors.

> **Transportation.** The transportation industry is not very integrated. Highways and streets are mostly operated by state and local governments and toll authorities, but transportation service and parking providers usually are separate. Transit bus and rail systems are operated mostly by local authorities. Intercity rail for passengers and freight is mostly in the private sector. Air transportation involves mostly government airports and private airline companies and general aviation. Other modes include ports, harbors, and waterways; pipeline freight transport; and intermodal transportation.

> **Communication.** Service providers in this rapidly changing sector are mostly private businesses. The sector includes wired and wireless communications.

Energy sector. Electric power is provided by public and private utilities, including the federal government. Natural gas is conveyed by transmission companies and distributed by local utilities and companies. The utilities in the energy sector are mostly integrated in the sense that they own their own supply chains and distribution outlets, and the industry is integrated in the sense that it comprises mostly players devoted to their core businesses. Liquefied natural gas and propane are also significant energy supply sources for the built environment. Transportation relies heavily on petroleum.

Water systems. Water supply is provided by public and private utilities, whereas wastewater service is provided mostly by government utilities. Water and wastewater utilities usually own their own process chains, and the industry is integrated in that it comprises mostly players devoted to the water business. The water industry also includes stormwater, irrigation and drainage, flood control, and hydropower.

Waste management. The waste management business is not very integrated. Waste collection companies and agencies do not always own transfer and disposal facilities. Solid and hazardous wastes involve both public and private sector organizations, and nuclear wastes involve national political issues.

MATRIX OF OWNERS AND USERS OF INFRASTRUCTURE SYSTEMS

To assess investment needs of infrastructure, it is important to distinguish the owners of the structures and the users of the systems. The infrastructure–industry matrix shown in Exhibit 2.5 illustrates the sectors, the infrastructures, and the owner/operator entities of infrastructure service organizations. The owner/operators column illustrates the division of responsibility between the public and private sectors and also indicates when infrastructure and equipment are separated, such as private vehicles operating over public road infrastructure. Note that transportation is divided into four categories because it is the largest and most diverse of our six basic groups. The matrix includes most categories rated by the American Society of Civil Engineers in its Infrastructure Report Card. The omissions are dams, inland waterways, levees, public parks and recreation, and schools. The Infrastructure Report Card is discussed in more detail in Chapter 11.

EXHIBIT 2.5 Matrix of Infrastructure Industries

Sector	Infrastructures	Owners/Operators
Built environment	Public and private buildings and facilities	Property owners/managers
Highways and streets	Road and bridge systems	State and local governments, road and bridge authorities (Vehicles are owned separately)
Mass transit	Light and heavy rail systems, bus rapid transit systems	Transit agencies and companies (also own vehicles)
Rail transportation	Rail infrastructure systems	Rail companies (also own vehicles)
Aviation	Airports	Air Traffic Control system (federal); airlines (own/operate aircraft)
Communications	Cables, wireless systems	Telecom companies
Energy	Electric power and natural gas infrastructures	Generators, transmission, and distribution companies/utilities
Water and wastewater	Source, treatment, distribution, collection, and disposal systems	Utilities and private water companies
Waste management	Landfills, incinerators, processing plants	Local governments, waste companies (most equipment)

INFRASTRUCTURE AND SERVICES: STRUCTURES AND EQUIPMENT

In some ways, infrastructure challenges the basic paradigm that shows land, labor, and capital as inputs to the economic system. A clue to the challenge lies in the definition of capital, which can be expanded to distinguish roles and responsibilities in infrastructure management. Distinguishing these roles and responsibilities is a recurrent theme in this book, and much of it boils down to distinguishing structural capital and equipment capital.

For example, in the case of delivering road-based transportation, the structures are roads and bridges and the equipment comprises privately owned vehicles. In the case of rail transportation, the structures are rails and the equipment comprises rail cars, but in this case they have the same owners, as opposed to the roads case, in which the structures and equipment have different owners.

Accounting for these structures and equipment poses a challenge to us, but it is important to look at this topic in enough detail to identify the flows of funds. Exhibit 2.6 presents a view to illustrate structures and equipment as separate inputs. On the figure, you see the structural components and one set of equipment to operate them. An example of this equipment would be traffic signals to operate a road system. In fact, these signals comprise a complex control system already, and the system will become more complex with the emergence of "smart roads" (see Chapter 4).

Another set of equipment shown on the figure is that of the operating entities. In the case of road transportation, the equipment comprises the vehicles that provide transportation. If the service was electric energy, the equipment to operate the infrastructure and to deliver the services would be the same because electric power service is more integrated than road transportation.

This electric power example also illustrates another facet of integration of infrastructure systems. In the case of road transportation, the vehicle owners themselves provide the equipment to deliver the service (transportation). In the case of electric power, the utilities provide the equipment to deliver the service (electric power). However, in the case of electric power, the

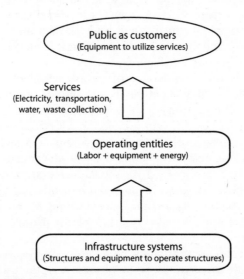

EXHIBIT 2.6 Infrastructure systems and equipment

privately owned equipment of the public as customers would be the systems in individual homes and places where electricity is used.

Viewing the different owners of equipment to operate structures, to deliver services, and to utilize services offers us another dimension by which to classify infrastructure systems. The issues may seem like fine points, but they are essential to defining and classifying infrastructure as a sector in a rigorous manner. They are also fundamental to the business models of companies seeking new ways to deliver services. In the case of the communications sector, for example, telecom companies often must subsidize the consumers' equipment to get them to enter into long-term contracts. This is actually a substitute mechanism for the monopoly franchise telecom companies used to have that provided security for adequate rates of return on infrastructure investments.

INFRASTRUCTURE SUPPORT SECTOR

One way to view infrastructure as a sector is the top-down classification system presented earlier that emphasizes its sectors. Another way is to view how the array of support businesses sells equipment and services in the infrastructure industries. This array comprises a large set of business that include, for example, engineering and construction services, construction equipment, materials, process equipment and assemblies, control systems and computers, business and legal services, and financial support.

A prism to see these supplier inputs is provided through professional and trade associations, the media, and trade show promoters. These show niches in the sector and unveil new products, new management trends, new policies, and new investment channels.

We can study how this bazaar of infrastructure support goods and services is arranged by looking at the sectors and the products and services. Sectors, such as electric power, are where customers with similar needs congregate. They require different products and services, which are tailored for them by the companies that choose to participate in each sector.

Products and services are organized by producer groups that market those products and services across the industry sectors. For example, electronic instruments or meter reading and bill collecting systems are used in several infrastructure industries. Once a company becomes successful with these product lines, it will naturally look for markets in other sectors for its sales.

The infrastructure sectors and product groups are served by many professional and trade associations. Some of these are pure trade associations, and some mix professional and commercial goals. Examples of trade associations might include those in the asphalt and pump businesses. Examples of the mostly professional associations include the American Society of Civil Engineers and the American Institute of Architects. Compared to the larger trade or hybrid trade-professional associations, these will have small trade shows, but they may exercise great influence in infrastructure policies and standards. These differences may seem subtle, but they explain many of the dynamics of the convention, trade show, and media marketplaces related to infrastructure. A few examples of the associations, trade shows, and media may help our understanding of the infrastructure business arena.

Road construction and operation is such a large industry that you must follow several professional and trade groups to look for new products, management trends, policies, and investment channels. For example, new products such as pavement materials and traffic signals might be exhibited at a hybrid association, such as the American Public Works Association, which has a membership of influential local public works managers. Management trends and policies are more likely to be discussed at the meetings of the American Association of State Highway and Transportation Officials and the Transportation Research Board, which is a unit of the National Research Council. In the case of private investments in roads, the discussions seem to be occurring at meetings and in media related to capital investments, such as special workshops organized by financial magazines and information services.

Transit and rail are much smaller industries than road transportation. Scheduled transit is highly focused, but a large number of paratransit and other nonscheduled groups operate. This divergence of interests between scheduled and nonscheduled systems is evident in the program of the American Public Transportation Association (APTA), which hosts an annual meeting to attract officials of the transit industry. APTA also hosts a number of smaller meetings where the interests of the niche groups can be discussed. It even offers special workshops on fare collection, for example, a surprisingly important topic in public transportation. Other meetings concern new products and systems, such as rail cars and operating systems, and management trends and policies. Given the social importance of transit, there are frequent interactions between transit officials and the Federal Transit Administration.

Rail transportation is offered by relatively few large companies, and even when smaller ones are counted, the total numbers are much smaller than road or transit. Passenger rail is mostly restricted to the quasi-government company Amtrak. More freight rail companies are in operation, and the Association of American Railroads (AAR) represents their interests. AAR focuses more on policy work than on bringing the industry and the vendors together. Given the small number of large companies in the rail industry, there is no apparent compelling need for a large trade association, as vendors can pitch their products directly to the companies in smaller venues. Also, given the close connection between rail and government actions, there are frequent interactions between AAR members and the Federal Rail Administration.

The air transportation industry divides into the airports and the airline companies and, of course, the Federal Aviation Administration is closely involved in air traffic control and many safety and security issues. After the terrorist attacks of 9/11, the Transportation Security Administration became a component of the Department of Homeland Security. It employs some 50,000 people and is a large and important agency, especially to air travel.

On the public infrastructure side, the American Association of Airport Executives hosts an annual conference that attracts airport and aviation professionals and vendors, airline employees, and government representatives. The Air Transport Association of America (ATA) is the trade association for the larger U.S. airlines. Like the AAR, the ATA works closely with federal agencies, but does not host a large annual trade show. IATA is an international air transportation association that hosts an annual general meeting and globally creates a network of airline companies and support groups.

Water supply and wastewater are diverse industries and have a large group of associations, trade groups, and media outlets. The largest meetings to view products are those of the American Water Works Association (AWWA) and the Water Environment Federation (WEF). Management trends and policies are discussed at those meetings, but many more water groups are involved. An example is the National Association of Water Companies (NAWC), which represents the interests of private water companies. U.S. Environmental Protection Agency (USEPA) policies have more impact on this sector than other government agencies, so utilities follow their policies closely.

The National Solid Waste Management Association is the core trade association for waste management companies, and the Waste Equipment Technology Association represents the vendors for the industry. It is a sponsor of WasteExpo, the largest trade show for waste management and recycling. In 2009, a medical waste conference was held simultaneously with WasteExpo. Waste Age magazine is a principal source of industry news. USEPA is the main federal agency regulating the waste management industry.

The telecom industry is large and diverse that it defies any attempt to identify one group or trade show to cover the industry. The Institute of Electrical and Electronics Engineers is a place to look for technological developments, especially its International Communications Society.

The public-private split in the electric power industry results in division into categories according to ownership. The Edison Electric Institute (EEI) represents shareholder-owned utilities, and the American Public Power Association (APPA) represents publicly-owned ones. EEI hosts an annual meeting with an exposition, and the program focuses on general issues such as the future of electricity, environmental concerns, and electric-powered automobiles. The attraction of the meeting to industry executives is shown by the critical issues discussed, such as renewables, low-carbon strategies, energy efficiency, smart grid, electric automobiles, and a nuclear energy renaissance.

APPA is the association for community-owned electric utilities. It also has an annual conference and exposition with similar topics but more focus on government ownership. The National Rural Electric Cooperative Association represents consumer-owned cooperative electric utilities and some public power districts.

The electric power industry is so large that it requires many additional meetings to showcase all products and organize training needed for different functions. For example, a trade show named "DistribuTECH" focuses on electricity transmission and distribution with sessions that cover automation and control, efficiency, engineering, demand response, renewables integration, and power delivery equipment. It has recently focused more on water utility technology as well.

A number of other trade shows help us to follow infrastructure business developments. For example, the CONEXPO-CON/AGG show is gigantic, with some 140,000 attendees 2,000 exhibitors of construction equipment, materials, and products (see Chapter 9).

In addition to the associations and trade shows, many magazines and newletters cover the infrastructure business from top to bottom. The classification system presented in this chapter provides a good way to see how these trade media are organized.

SUMMARY

The definition, classification, and descriptions above comprise a macro-level model of the business of infrastructure. Chapter 12 presents a general management model and a financing model. These three models—one to characterize the sector, one to show management functions in an organization, and one to show financial flows—provide a detailed picture of how infrastructure systems are managed. Exhibit 2.7 shows these in a comparative form.

From the exhibit, you can see how, in the top-level model, the structure of the infrastructure sector is characterized. Then, at the next level, the management model shows characteristics of the organizations in the infrastructure sector. This is followed by the financing model, which illustrates issues of capital finance versus operations, debt and ownership, and other financial variables.

The model of the composite infrastructure sector leads to business models that help explain the differences among the separate infrastructure

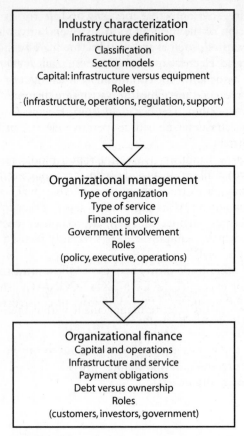

EXHIBIT 2.7 Models of Sectors, Organizations, Finance

services. The model requires a classification of infrastructure systems and operating sectors, an explanation of how they work together, and ways to examine the levels of infrastructure within the systems and how they are financed.

The Systems Serve the Built Environment

In a big-picture view, the world is organized into natural, constructed, and human systems, which are explained by science, engineering, and social studies. Constructed infrastructure needs the needs of human systems while protecting the natural environment. These basic facts lead to systems to define and classify infrastructure so its characteristics can be studied.

It Is a Composite System with Operating Sectors

At the macro-level, infrastructure is a composite group with sectors, industries, and physical systems. Sectors have broad and inclusive names, such as energy, transportation, and water. Infrastructure industries are identified with the economic organization of services, such as electric power. Physical systems are the purview of engineers and constructors and include tangible elements such as pipelines, roads, and bridges.

Management Involves System Owners and System Users

To characterize an infrastructure service completely, you must consider both the physical system and the equipment that uses it to deliver services. These are different kinds of fixed assets and may have different owners. To explain infrastructure services, you must correctly identify the distinct roles of infrastructure owners and service providers.

Owners and Service Organizations Can Be Public or Private

Public or private infrastructure owners and service provider groups coexist in the infrastructure sector. Each sector has unique arrangements, and infrastructure management within the sectors requires unique approaches to public-private partnerships. Effectively organizing these partnerships will be the key to overcoming future challenges of infrastructure management and require a vigorous private sector working with nimble and responsive governments that shares their governance responsibilities.

CHAPTER 3

Infrastructure and the Constructed Environment

A limited view of what infrastructure includes masks its strong connection with trade, transportation, and all economic activity. A better view shows how infrastructure supports the built environment, which enables economic activity to take place.

This chapter explains how the built environment stimulates demand for its supporting infrastructure. It covers financing strategies and investment outlooks for the structures in built areas and their associated infrastructure systems. This chapter addresses types of buildings and facilities; subsequent chapters explain the support systems (water, energy, and wastes) and the linking networks (transportation and communications). Special attention is given in this chapter to the Housing Finance System because it is important in supporting healthy growth of residential housing, which drives demand for infrastructure.

LAND USES IN THE BUILT ENVIRONMENT

The tight link between the built environment and infrastructure systems is caused by their interdependence—infrastructure supports business, which provides its funding and rationale. Infrastructure is so "inextricably linked to the world of business and to our real estate industry that we ignore it at our own peril" (Urban Land Institute and Ernst & Young, 2009).

The built environment is a metaphor for the cities where people live, work, shop, and play. It drives the demand for infrastructure and public services in and between urban areas, including demand for intercity passenger and freight travel. It provides facilities for residential living, business, and social activities, and managing it engages a real estate industry, which itself is about 10 percent of the economy.

While the built environment is synonymous with cities, technically it includes all urbanized areas and urban clusters, along with the infrastructure links that support them. These generally consist of a central place and adjacent densely settled census blocks with a total population of at least 50,000 for urbanized areas and 2,500 for urban clusters. Any area not classified as an urbanized area or cluster is a rural area, which also requires infrastructure systems (U.S. Census Bureau, 2009a).

Urbanization has proceeded from the time of original settlement in the United States. From the colonial period, the United States experienced a long period of farm-to-city migration. By 1900, urban population was still under 40 percent, in spite of large farm-to-city migrations. As the nation grew, it passed through successive eras of development, such as the postwar housing boom of the 1950s. Shopping centers followed, and now the earliest ones are over 50 years old. Many are past their prime, and decisions about their futures will drive the shape of many urban areas.

This obsolescence of commercial facilities and the need for renewal will be a dominant force in twenty-first-century urbanization. In its March 23, 2009 cover story, *Time* magazine predicted that recycling the suburbs and their aging malls is a top trend for the nation (Lacayo, 2009). Infilling, rebuilding, and renovation of facilities are consistent with other infrastructure trends, such as energy conservation, emphasis on alternative transportation, and urban gardening to promote local food supplies.

In recent years, urban population as a percent of total population has been increasing slowly. In 2000 it was 79 percent, up from 75.2 percent in 1990. While urban population as a percentage is not increasing rapidly now, urban areas continue to change at a rapid pace. Cities in fast-growth areas such as in the Southwest expect continued rapid growth, once the recession is over. In declining areas, cities may see depopulation, such as in older manufacturing areas where plants have closed.

The built environment has the familiar look of a city, a neighborhood, or a built-up area with homes, shops, and perhaps factories. Its land uses are classified as residential areas; office, commercial, and government buildings; hospitals, schools and churches; industrial areas; public safety facilities; and transportation, communication, and utility facilities. These categories create an information system used to plan and control urban development.

Residential housing comprises the majority of fixed assets and construction spending in the built environment, and is a strong driver of demand for infrastructure services, such as utility services and transportation trips. This is why a collapse of housing prices can cause so much havoc in the financial markets and other parts of the economy.

Residential housing includes single-family and multifamily homes and varies widely by price. Homes are built by the private sector, while the public sector regulates housing and supports it with infrastructure. Providing affordable housing is an important issue in communities, and public housing and homelessness programs are important social issues in communities.

Office, commercial, and government buildings provide centers of economic and social activity for built areas. Retail areas, such as downtowns and shopping centers, attract concentrations of people and create demand for infrastructure and services. Amusement and sports centers are diverse and also create needs for infrastructure, including for peak loads such as large events. Infrastructure security is a particular concern in these venues where large numbers of people congregate.

Demand for healthcare facilities increases as the population ages. These facilities require special attention in infrastructure planning due to their loads on services, their needs for security, and the tax-exempt status of some. Schools and churches have similar attributes as public service facilities and may require special protection and utility services.

Industrial areas and warehouse districts are often located in special zones and can have their own infrastructures, comprising roads, utilities, and energy systems, which need to be coordinated with public systems. Manufacturing plants may also have large environmental impacts.

Essential public safety facilities, including firehouses, police, and emergency response centers, require special coordination with transportation and communication systems. While the facilities normally do not have special needs for infrastructure services, they must be secure because they provide protection for the rest of the area and facilities.

Like public safety centers, transportation, communication, and utility centers must be secure. These include facilities for water supply and treatment, wastewater treatment, electric power generation, natural gas relay stations, transportation hubs, communication nodes, and solid waste transfer stations.

GROWTH AND CHANGE IN URBAN AREAS

While the nineteenth and twentieth centuries saw great change in urban areas and their supporting infrastructure, this century promises dramatic change as well. The dominant paradigm in the nineteenth century was technological advancement that created railroads, utilities, automobiles, and other improvements that required infrastructure systems to support them. During the twentieth century, great corporations were created and massive urbanization led to the megalopolis and the unending settlements of cities and conurbations. Construction of the Interstate Highway System knitted urban areas into the patterns we see today. During the twenty-first century, new patterns of growth will emerge in response to the information economy, immigration, and resource-based development.

As Exhibit 3.1 shows, the total national population increased steadily from around 5 million in 1800 to nearly 300 million by the year 2000. The Census Bureau projection for the year 2010 was to reach 310 million, a figure that will require confirmation in the 2010 Census. In 2010, current rates of increase hover around 0.98 percent and are projected to decrease to 0.79 percent by 2050, reflecting a slowing of the rate of growth. All of the estimates are subject to change with variables such as longevity, birth rate, and net international migration. In fact, even the official projections change from year to year as new data become available.

Even with a middle-range estimate for the year 2100, the population will be double that of 2000, meaning that a nation the size of today's United States will be added to our numbers over the next 100 years. In the year 2050, which seems closer and closer all the time, we will have added some 140 million to the 2000 population, the equivalent of adding the combined populations of today's Mexico and California to the nation. If the estimates

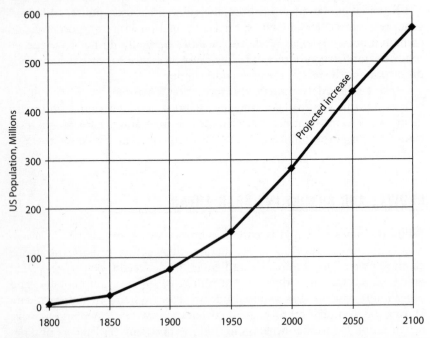

EXHIBIT 3.1   U.S. Population with Projections to 2100
Source: U.S. Census Bureau, 2009b

on Exhibit 3.1 seem unrealistic, consider the boom in China, which increased its 1900 population from some 400 million to about 1.3 billion today. A high-range population projection for the United States shows a 2100 population of over 1 billion, a level that would move us into the population range of today's China and India and present massive problems to the nation. Regardless of the population numbers, meeting the infrastructure needs of the future and its increasing population will be a formidable challenge.

To present a picture of where the population will increase the most, Exhibit 3.2 shows the states with the greatest projected percentage growth to the year 2030. These increases will place large demands on infrastructure systems, such as to find the water for Nevada's and Arizona's increases, to solve transportation problems in Florida and Texas, and to provide for a California population nearing 50 million people.

If the states shown are to grow more rapidly than the average, then other states will grow at a slower rate. States with low rates of projected growth include populated areas of the East and Northeast (e.g., New York, Pennsylvania, and Connecticut); industrial areas of the Midwest (e.g., Michigan, Ohio, and Illinois); some southeastern states (Alabama, Mississippi, and Louisiana); and farm states (Kansas, Nebraska, Iowa, and

EXHIBIT 3.2 Projected State Population Increases to the Year 2030

Rank by Population Gain	State	Projected Increase 2004–2030	Percent Gain
1	Florida	12,703,391	79.5
2	California	12,573,213	37.1
3	Texas	12,465,924	59.8
4	Arizona	5,581,765	108.8
5	North Carolina	4,178,426	51.9
6	Georgia	3,831,385	46.8
7	Virginia	2,746,504	38.8
8	Washington	2,730,680	46.3
9	Nevada	2,283,845	114.3
10	Colorado	1,491,096	34.7
11	Oregon	1,412,519	41.3
12	Utah	1,252,198	56.1
13	Idaho	675,671	52.2
14	New Hampshire	410,685	33.2
15	Alaska	240,742	38.4
	United States	82,162,529	29.2

Source: U.S. Census Bureau, 2009b

South Dakota). Also, Wyoming will grow very slowly, and West Virginia and North Dakota are projected to lose population, as is the District of Columbia, which is expected to experience some depopulation.

The recession has had identifiable impacts on urban population growth. Cities that were losing population to the suburbs held onto populations with people who have fewer options and do not want long commutes. For example, Chicago grew at 0.73 percent in the 12 months ending in July 2008, which is a reversal from lower and negative growth for the previous five years. It seems to be a combination of added interest in central cities, difficulty in selling houses, and transportation. Cities that are declining saw the declines slow down, and growing cities saw faster growth. Big cities of more than a million population grew at 0.97 percent for the year ending July 2008, an increase that seems to reflect a cooling of the robust real estate and job market in the suburbs. All of this means slower growth in the suburbs, which is being seen in the suburbs of big cities. These changes can mean pressure for infrastructure systems, such as public schools. Fast-growing Sunbelt cities, such as Tucson and Las Vegas, saw slower growth beginning in 2008 than during the housing boom.

To accommodate this growth and change, land use controls are mostly in the hands of local governments, which generally follow a process such as shown in Exhibit 3.3. The process is expensive and requires deep pockets on the part of developers. For that reason, project finance is a critical element in moving a development ahead. The process begins with the concept for a sub-division, a shopping center, an industrial park, or some other development. The preliminary planning and deals phase may require real estate, architecture, engineering, financial, and legal inputs, among others. This leads to the developer's proposal, which undergoes scrutiny by local regulators and may elicit protest from interest groups during the review and negotiation phase. The approval decision is labeled political because the local political process determines whether the project can proceed or not. Of course, there is a big difference in the political approval for a downtown Manhattan development and a new retail store in a small town. After approval, the development enters the construction and sales phases, followed by operation and maintenance. Subdivisions and malls that were developed as recently as the 1970s now seem old in some places, and those developed during the 1950s are among the ones identified by *Time* magazine as needing "recycling."

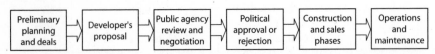

EXHIBIT 3.3   Steps in the Development Process

Local governments plan their infrastructure improvements through the process of comprehensive planning, and it would be very helpful to know the directions and pace of growth. That would provide a rational approach to capital planning and investment. Unfortunately, land use changes have proved tricky to predict, and they depend on the decisions of private developers as much as they do on the plans of local governments. Planners have several tools, however, to help in detecting the need for new infrastructure. One is population forecasting itself. Another is economic forecasting, which relates jobs to population growth. Land use modeling has taken on a new life with the increased sophistication of geographic information system (GIS) models (see discussion in Chapter 9 about information technology in the construction industry). Prior to the development of GIS models, planners were searching for ways to direct growth toward the most productive and least disruptive paths in terms of natural resource impacts.

While many urban land use models have been developed, an early one called "Urban Dynamics" serves to illustrate the close connections between population, economic development, and infrastructure. The model developer, Jay Forrester (1969) of the Massachusetts Institute of Technology, applied a model tool called "industrial dynamics" to the forces of growth within cities. The form of the model shown in Exhibit 3.4 illustrates how new population growth comes with different skill levels, such as managers and professionals, laborers, and underemployed people. The population growth generates demand for housing, which will also be arrayed according to ability to pay and will be correlated with labor skill levels. Finally, the job-creation system would be arrayed in terms of new enterprises, mature businesses, and declining businesses.

While simple conceptually, the model offers powerful options for simulating urban policies, changes in housing markets, economic change, immigration, and other forces that will affect urban growth and demand for infrastructure. At Colorado State University, we used the model as the basis for a course on urban dynamics and published a paper showing how it could be used to predict the need for water supply infrastructure (Grigg and Bryson, 1975). It would be used as well to show forces on housing markets, transportation, energy, and other infrastructure categories. In fact, Forrester's model became the focus of the emerging field of systems dynamics, which forms a quantitative core of systems thinking as it applies to the business world. Several powerful software packages are available to facilitate systems modeling, including land use models.

Green building is a strong transformative force on residential, commercial, and industrial buildings, including public buildings. The attributes of a green building depend on a number of factors, such as type of building and stage of life. One set of attributes is presented by the U.S. Green Building

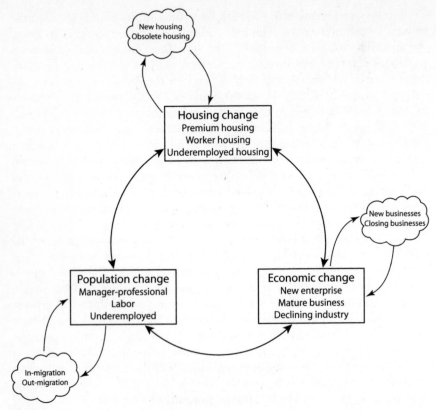

EXHIBIT 3.4 Urban Growth Model

Council (2009), and are generally defined through its LEED (Leadership in Energy and Environmental Design) certification process. Attributes are defined for sustainable sites, water efficiency, energy and atmosphere, materials and resources, indoor environmental quality, innovation in design, and regional priority.

Urban Land Institute

The Urban Land Institute (2009) has more than 40,000 members from the land use and real estate communities. It is a multidisciplinary real estate forum with a focus on responsible use of land and sustaining communities. To get an idea of its diverse membership, its councils include those on affordable Housing, Community Development, Commercial and Retail Development, corporate real estate, entertainment and hotel development, industrial and office parks, inner city, manufactured housing, recreation, residential neighborhoods, senior housing, and sustainable development.

FINANCIAL ASSETS IN THE BUILT ENVIRONMENT

The capital stock in the built environment is a measure of wealth as vested in constructed facilities. Other wealth includes financial assets, natural resources, cultural resources, intellectual resources, and so on. The wealth category that measures infrastructure is, however, in fixed assets.

To assess the capital stock of the built environment, fixed asset data published by the U.S. Bureau of Economic Affairs (2009a) and data from the U.S. Census Bureau's (2009c) tabulation of construction spending can be used. The fixed asset data are based on replacement cost less depreciation. Construction spending measures the rate of increase of fixed assets and represents a source of data that is independent from fixed assets themselves.

As of December 31, 2007, total fixed assets in the United States were $42.6 trillion, of which $33.4 trillion were private and $9.2 were public. These figures illustrate the dominance of private fixed assets (78 percent) over government fixed assets (22 percent) in the economy.

Fixed assets increased from 2002 through 2007 at annual rates from 5 to 10 percent, reflecting a period of high investment and growth. Due to the financial downturn in 2008, the rate of growth will slow down. Fixed asset data are based on original cost less depreciation and do not reflect market value. The decline in market value of some fixed assets is measured by the Flow of Funds accounts of the Federal Reserve Bank.

Of the private fixed assets, residential structures accounted for $17.8 trillion (53.4 percent) and nonresidential structures accounted for $10.2 trillion (30.6 percent). The rest ($5.3 trillion, or 16.0 percent) was in the category of equipment and software. The residential structures category includes $14.5 trillion in residential housing, $55.8 billion in other housing such as dormitories, and $3.3 trillion in improvements. Thus, when residential housing starts fall, the rest of the fixed assets are affected in a big way.

Private nonresidential structures, valued at about $10.3 trillion at the end of 2007, include commercial, office, medical, and manufacturing facilities as major categories. Hotels, private schools, and churches are other significant categories. The private infrastructure facilities required by electric utilities, petroleum and natural gas, communication, and railroads are included in these data.

Government fixed assets in 2007 totaled $9.2 trillion, of which $8.3 trillion (90.2 percent) were structures and $897 billion was in equipment and software. Public infrastructure is found in this category; its major group is highways and streets at $2.7 trillion of the total. Public schools are also large, at $1.6 trillion, and other public infrastructure, including categories such as water plants, totals just under $1.0 trillion.

These data on fixed assets in the built environment can be summarized as shown in Exhibit 3.5:

- Total national fixed assets were $42.6 trillion (78 percent private, 22 percent public).
- Residential structures were $17.8 trillion (42 percent) of all fixed assets ($14.5 trillion in housing and the rest in improvements).
- Of the $10.3 trillion in private nonresidential structures, 34 percent was in commercial, office, and medical buildings, the rest in manufacturing, hotels, hospitals, schools, churches, and private utility structures.
- When you add private and government data, the size of the schools subsector becomes $2.0 trillion, or larger than the private commercial subsector.
- Of the $9.2 trillion in government fixed assets, 29.8 percent was highways and streets and 18 percent in schools. The rest is in miscellaneous categories totaling less than 10 percent.
- Public and private electric power assets totaled about $1.1 trillion.

Fixed assets increase through construction and capital spending, which are discussed in Chapter 11. The basic difference between accumulated construction spending and current levels of fixed assets is depreciation, after inflation is accounted for.

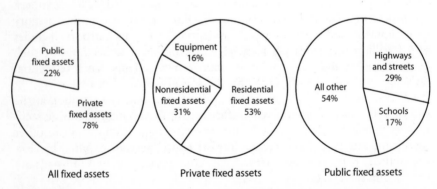

EXHIBIT 3.5   Distribution of Fixed Assets in the United States (December 31, 2007, data)

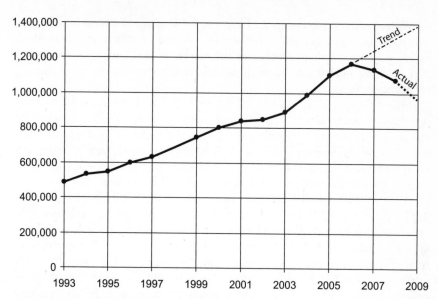

EXHIBIT 3.6   Total Construction Spending, $ Millions
Source: U.S. Census Bureau, 2009c data as of April 2009

As shown in Exhibit 3.6, construction spending rose rapidly during the late 1990s and slowed in 2002 after the dot-com boom was over. Then it rose again through 2006 and started to fall in 2007. By early 2009, spending levels were below $1 trillion per year, nearly back to 2003 levels in current dollars. By comparing what could have been if the trend continued with the actual levels, you see that construction spending could have been near $1.4 trillion, but it is actually less than $1 trillion in 2009, a difference of 40 percent.

HOUSING FINANCE AS AN ENGINE OF DEVELOPMENT

Because most financial value of the built environment is in residential housing, the Housing Finance System takes on major importance.* The financing systems for other types of structures, such as commercial and office buildings, industrial facilities, and government buildings and facilities, operate

---

*Sources for this section are U.S. Housing and Urban Development (2008a and b); Lui and Emrath (2008); and McDonald and Thornton (2008).

through more diverse channels. Commercial lending is a core business for many banks and other lenders that focus on the commercial sector. Businesses also have other avenues to finance their buildings and structures, such as funding from cash flow, issuing stock for expansion, or issuing corporate bonds.

The financial crisis has offered dramatic proof that residential housing is a major component in the national financial picture and an engine for infrastructure demand. Housing starts stimulate activity in the labor market; demand for commodities, such as lumber and concrete; and housing equipment, such as lighting fixtures and heating systems. They also generate income for services such as real estate, legal, and brokerage.

One estimate is that building each new single-family home generates 3.05 jobs and $89,216 in taxes; each multifamily rental unit generates 1.16 jobs and $33,494 in taxes; and each $100,000 spent on remodeling generates 1.11 jobs and $30,217 in taxes. These taxes include all construction-related and other fees imposed by local governments. The estimated average value of a new home sold in 2008 was $302,000, a figure that declined sharply during the financial crisis that punctured the housing bubble (Liu and Emrath, 2008).

The total housing stock in the United States in 2007 was about 128 million units. About 110.7 million were occupied, with some 75.6 million of these owner occupied (one in three of which is owned free and clear). The median home value in 2007 was $191,471 (U.S. Census Bureau, 2008). These data include apartments, single-family homes, manufactured housing, new construction, and vacant housing units.

Multifamily housing starts are on the order of 20 percent of total housing starts. Exhibit 3.7 shows housing start data since 2000 and illustrates how total starts fluctuate up and down, and how the distribution among

EXHIBIT 3.7   Single- and Multifamily Housing Starts

	Single Family	Multifamily	Total	Multifamily %
2007	1,045,900	309,200	1,355,200	0.23
2006	1,465,400	335,500	1,800,900	0.19
2005	1,715,800	352,500	2,068,300	0.17
2004	1,610,500	345,300	1,955,800	0.18
2003	1,499,000	348,700	1,847,700	0.19
2002	1,358,600	346,400	1,704,900	0.20
2001	1,273,300	329,400	1,602,700	0.21
2000	1,230,900	337,800	1,568,700	0.22

National Association of Homebuilders, 2009a

single-family and multifamily units shifts (National Association of Home-builders, 2009a).

Until the United States developed a system for housing finance, it was a nation of renters. In 1934, in the depths of the Great Depression, only 4 in 10 U.S. households owned homes. Since then, a number of actions have been taken to make housing more affordable; homeownership has risen in the United States to its current level of nearly 70 percent.

The goal of the Housing Finance System is to deliver affordable mortgages to homeowners and attractive mortgage securities to investors. The system includes funding, lending, and servicing and is based on loans called mortgages. Mortgages carry risks to lenders for default and changing interest rates.

The system evolved through trial and error. Prior to the 1930s, a common solution was for people to pool their money to help each other out. Most loans in this era were for 6 to 10 years with no amortization and maximum loan to value ratios were of about 50 percent. During the 1870s, mortgage banks were formed in the Midwest and West and raised funds by selling mortgage-backed bonds. Many of these banks defaulted during the financial crisis of the 1890s. The efforts over the years evolved into more formal lending institutions, such as savings and loans (S&Ls).

From the 1930s to the 1960s, new experiments were tried. The 1920s had seen increases in credit, only to slam to a halt in the Great Depression with its many defaults and deflation of almost 50 percent in home values. The federal government organized the Homeowners Loan Corporation and the Reconstruction Finance Corporation to liquidate bad loans in bank portfolios and to bail out insolvent lending institutions. These programs had some success but created some moral hazard, in which people might benefit by defaulting when they did not have to. Congress passed the Federal Home Loan Bank Act in 1932 to create the FHLBank System and the Federal Home Loan Banks. The purpose was to regulate and offer liquidity to existing S&Ls.

After 1932, the Roosevelt Administration created the Federal Housing Administration (FHA), which introduced long-term, low–down payment loans that were amortized with fixed rates. It also authorized private mortgage associations. Created by the National Housing Act of 1934, FHA provides mortgage insurance on loans on single-family and multifamily homes, including manufactured homes and hospitals, made by FHA-approved lenders. FHA is the largest insurer of mortgages in the world. FHA-insured loans require less cash to close a loan than conventional mortgages, and there is more flexibility in calculating payment ratios. The homeowner pays the cost of the mortgage insurance in monthly payment. FHA operates entirely from self-generated income. Private mortgage insurance increased in the 1960s and 1970s, and FHA's market share declined. S&Ls initially thought that FHA was a competitor but learned that they could work it on a cooperative basis.

Mortgage associations were authorized to issue bonds and buy mortgages from primary market lenders. Fannie Mae was started in 1938 as a government agency called the Federal National Mortgage Association. The Federal Deposit Insurance Corporation and Federal Savings and Loan Insurance Corporation for S&Ls were also established in the 1930s.

In 1968 Congress converted Fannie Mae to a private shareholder-owned company. Fannie Mae works in the secondary mortgage market to help mortgage bankers, brokers, and other primary mortgage players to provide funds for homebuyers at affordable rates. It obtains its funds by issuing debt securities.

When Fannie Mae was privatized, the Government National Mortgage Association (Ginnie Mae) was spun out of the original Federal National Mortgage Association. Its mission is to guarantee repayment of securities backed by mortgages of government employees or veterans (FHA and Veterans Administration loans).

Because Fannie Mae had a monopoly on government-guaranteed mortgage loads, Freddie Mac was created by Congress as the Federal Home Loan Mortgage Corporation through the Emergency Home Finance Act of 1970. Freddie Mac's mission is essentially the same as Fannie Mae's: to expand the secondary market for mortgages and mortgage-backed securities by buying mortgages made by primary lenders.

From the early 1970s to the early 1980s, new forms of mortgage-backed securities were introduced to consolidate loans or other debt instruments into single assets or securities. These take on different forms and can be sold to financial companies that include S&Ls, pension funds, trusts, mutual funds, life insurance companies, and foreign investors.

The high interest rates of the early 1980s led to new hedging instruments in the form of options, futures, and others and increased volatility of the financial markets. The government had deregulated S&Ls on both the asset side (mortgages) and the liability side (money market deposits). Financial pressures led to the S&L debacle and creation of the Resolution Trust Corporation in 1989.

After about 1990, information technology applications such as automated underwriting systems increased greatly. This improves access to information but also carries risk of fraud. As this system evolved, mortgage characteristics changed greatly. Now the mortgage features of assumability and prepayment penalties are mostly gone. Most mortgages are fixed rate (about 70 percent), but adjustable-rate mortgages (ARMs) have increased in use. The interest rates for ARMs are based on common indices such as the Eleventh Federal Home Loan Bank Board District Cost of Funds Index and National Cost of Funds Index.

Freddie Mac and Fannie Mae increased the size of the secondary markets, where mortgages are bought and sold, and many other private operators now operate in this market. Now it is common for banks or S&Ls to originate mortgage loans and sell them quickly.

These developments set the stage for the housing crisis that hit beginning about 2006. The causes of the housing bubble and associated financial crisis are complex, but two factors seemed strong in causing them. First, there was a residential real estate boom from 1996 to 2005 with homeownership increasing from 65.4 percent to 68.9 percent. In this period, the Standard & Poor's/Case-Schiller Home Price Index rose at 8.5 percent, more than four times the rate of inflation. This rate of increase can be seen on Exhibit 3.8, which illustrates how home price levels curved sharply upward after 1995. Beginning in the first quarter of 2006, prices slowed, then began to fall sharply.

To illustrate the dramatic and sudden switch in house price changes, Exhibit 3.9 shows the quarterly percentage changes and how dramatically the situation changed after 2006. These data are for the house price index, which was started by the Office of Federal Housing Enterprise Oversight (OFHEO) in 1995 and taken over by the U.S. Federal Housing Finance Agency (Federal Home Loan Financing Agency, 2009).

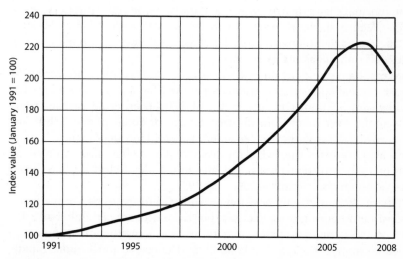

EXHIBIT 3.8 Monthly U.S. House Price Index (Purchase only, seasonally adjusted index)
Source: FHFA, 2009

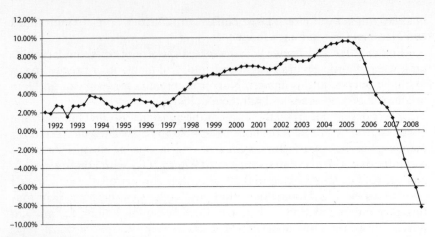

EXHIBIT 3.9   Quarterly House Price Changes in Percent
Source: FHFA, 2008

The underlying factor in causing these rises was the subprime mortgage market. Seeing the rapid rise in home prices, lenders sensed that they could lend without much risk because home values were rising above the balances owed. Thus, if a borrower defaulted, the home could be sold without a loss to the lender. As credit eased, demand for housing and prices rose. This rise in mortgage lending can be seen in data from the Federal Reserve Bank (2009a), which shows rises of 13 percent in total lending for 2004–2005 and 12 percent the following year. These were followed by declines to zero from 2007 to 2008 as reality set in.

Many banks and lending institutions became vulnerable, especially the government-sponsored enterprises Fannie Mae and Freddie Mac. The Housing and Economic Recovery Act of 2008 transferred regulatory responsibilities over them from the Department of Housing and Urban Development (HUD) to a new independent Federal Housing Finance Agency, which also regulates the FHLBank System. The FHFA also assumed responsibility for affordable housing goals of the Federal Housing Enterprises Financial Safety and Soundness Act of 1992.

No one knows exactly how long it will take to recover from the financial crisis and housing price declines, but these declines certainly had a big effect on infrastructure-related activity, such as construction spending on residential homes. Because home-building declined so much more rapidly than other construction, the percentage of public construction to total construction rose significantly (see Chapter 12).

A financial crisis creates a decline in economic security for people losing jobs or facing other setbacks. This increases the need for affordable housing where there is an apparent nationwide shortage (U.S. Department of Housing and Urban Development, 2008c). The definition of affordable housing is based on a household paying 30 percent or less of its income on housing. A full-time worker earning the minimum wage cannot afford a two-bedroom apartment in the United States; HUD estimates that 12 million renter and homeowner households pay more than 50 percent of their incomes for housing and may have difficulty buying food, clothing, transportation, and medical care. Lack of affordable housing can increase demands on transportation systems, decrease enrollment in schools, and affect the supply of labor. Policies to increase affordable housing might include zoning, land use regulations, and tax and fiscal measures.

The National Low Income Housing Coalition (2009) publishes information about affordability of homes. Some of the most expensive or out-of-reach places to live include Hawaii, New York City, California, and several states of the Northeast. The coalition promotes 30 percent of household income as the limit of affordability.

Pulte Homes Inc.

After World War II, subdivisions and large-scale homebuilding altered the landscape of U.S. cities. Today, large and small homebuilders supply a mix of housing to meet a diversity of needs and wishes. The largest homebuilder in the United States, Pulte Homes Inc. (2009), started in 1950 when 18-year old William Pulte built his first house near Detroit. The company was incorporated in 1956, and its first subdivision was developed in 1959. It expanded its markets and went public in 1969, and during the 1970s, Pulte was in 10 major markets and became listed on the American Stock Exchange. In 1983, the stock became listed on the New York Stock Exchange. In 1995, Pulte reached its current status as the largest homebuilder in the United States. In 1999, Pulte became a Fortune 500 company, and by 2007, the company had delivered over 500,000 homes and was number 170 on the Fortune 500 list. In 2008, Pulte Homes had revenues of $6.3 billion, down from $14.3 billion in 2006. In 2009, it announced a merger with Centex Corporation in a stock-for- stock transaction. When the merger is completed, the combined company will operate in 29 states (Pulte Homes History, 2009; Yahoo Finance, 2009). In 2009, Pulte experienced a rare rebuke of its directors when three failed to receive majority votes in a stockholder election. Reasons are not entirely clear but relate to shareholder activism about methods of electing boards and stock performance (Corkery, 2009). Two other large homebuilders are Toll Brothers Inc. with $3.2 billion revenue in 2008, down from $6.1 billion in 2006, and Hovnanian Enterprises Inc., which dropped about the same, from $6.1 billion in 2006 to $3.3 billion in 2008.

Fannie Mae and Freddie Mac

Fannie Mae and Freddie Mac are government-sponsored enterprises that provide liquidity and stability in the secondary mortgage market by securitizing mortgages in the primary market. They have single-family, multifamily, and investment departments that securitize single-family and multifamily mortgage loans, invest in rental and other housing projects, and manage investment activity and capital positions. Customers include mortgage banks, S&Ls, savings banks, commercial banks, credit unions, community banks, insurance companies, and finance agencies. Fannie Mae had revenue of $52 billion in 2008, but losses totaled $60 billion and the company is in government receivership. Freddie Mac's financials are about the same, with revenue and losses both at $51 billion and the company in receivership. Their histories were explained earlier and their investment prospects are summarized in Chapter 9 (Yahoo Finance, 2009).

National Association of Homebuilders

The homebuilding industry is represented by the National Association of Homebuilders (NAHB; 2009b), which is a powerful trade organization that speaks for policies favoring urban development and home finance. NAHB was formed in 1942 to promote housing policies during the war. It broke away from the National Association of Real Estate Boards, and by 1952, it had a membership of over 15,000. The postwar housing boom fueled interest in homebuilding, and in 1979, the NAHB membership topped 100,000, increasing again to around 200,000 by the year 2000. NAHB sponsors the International Builder's Show. Even in a down year, the show attracted over 60,000 attendees and 1,600 exhibitors in 2009.

Public Housing

Public housing is part of the affordable housing mix but owned by public agencies. It is actually a large part of built environments, and some 1,900 housing authorities across the US are coordinated through the Public Housing Authorities Director's Association (2009). It works with Congress on public housing legislation and funding and works closely with HUD on regulations. The New York City Housing Authority is the largest public housing authority in the United States. It has some 178,000 apartments in 338 developments, and some 680,000 people are served by its programs. As another example of local programs, the District of Columbia Housing Authority provides low-income housing for families, seniors, and disabled people. Its programs serve about 10 percent of residents through ownership of some 8,000 rental units, a voucher program (formerly Section 8) working with some 3,000 landlords, and development of mixed-income communities.

COMMERCIAL AND CENTRAL CITY DEVELOPMENT

Although residential housing and the housing finance system dominate the built environment's economic picture, commercial, industrial, and government facilities also drive demand for infrastructure. In the late nineteenth and early twentieth centuries, commercial development emphasized development of central cities. Innovations such as skyscrapers and mass transit determined the shape of cities, and most retail activity was in downtown areas. Commercial lending financed some construction, but companies usually provided their own financing. For example, the Chrysler Building in Manhattan was financed by Walter Chrysler through the Chrysler car company. Leasing office space in the building was a strategy to recover part of the investment. Developers speculated with their own money or with corporate money. Banks and other lenders began to see real estate developers and contractors as safe investments and offered financing that led to megaprojects, such as the Rockefeller Center, the Empire State Building, and the Sears Tower in Chicago (Real Estate Developer.com, 2009).

The automobile and mass transit systems began to force decentralization of cities and created opportunities for developers and commercial contractors. After World War II, suburbanization and creation of shopping malls and highway bypasses reshaped American cities. This led to decline in many central cities, causing older warehouses and office buildings to fall into disrepair and disuse. Now a growing sector of real estate is renovation, rehabilitation, and conversion of uses. Revitalization of city centers through major sports complexes is another trend, and we are seeing more public-private partnerships as developers bring project ideas for shopping areas, downtown revitalization, and innovative housing to local governments.

Shopping centers and malls led and followed development of residential areas. Today, demand for infrastructure is driven by combinations of land uses that are negotiated by developers and local officials. Big-box shopping centers have replaced many of the older malls, which are struggling to find new identities, especially after the housing crash beginning in 2006.

As central cities rebuild, demand for capital to finance commercial properties may increase. For example, in 2009, developers of a New York City skyscraper obtained a loan of nearly $1.3 billion for refinancing a 945-foot structure. The developer had already leased 98 percent of the building, and most of it to the Bank of America Corporation, which teamed with four other banks to provide the financing. The financing will replace

$650 million in tax-exempt bonds that were issued to spur construction after 9/11 (Peltz, 2009).

Commercial property will undergo transitions at least as painful as those that hit residential housing. For example, during the financial crisis, recreational property developers (along with airlines and the overall travel industry) experienced hard times because economic problems caused declines in tourism. For example, in 2009, casino developer Fontainebleau Las Vegas LLC filed for Chapter 11 bankruptcy protection when it failed to get about $800 million in construction funding for a $2.9 billion property in Las Vegas. It had already filed a $3 billion lawsuit against a group of lenders to pay construction workers and finish the project. Bank of America was considering "restructured financing," and the developer was hoping for a fast track resolution of its legal claims (ENR.com, 2009a).

Simon Property Group, Inc. and General Growth Properties

Commercial developers and builders provide shopping centers, office complexes, and other developments to serve the economic and social needs in cities. Simon Property Group, Inc. (2009) is the largest public U.S. real estate company and a real estate investment trust (REIT) that focuses on regional malls, outlets, and community/lifestyle centers. At the end of 2007, it owned interests in 168 regional malls, 38 premium outlet centers, 67 community/lifestyle centers, and other properties, shopping centers, or outlet centers. Its 2008 revenue was $3.8 billion, and it had total assets of $23.4 billion of which $19 billion was property, plant, and equipment (Yahoo Finance, 2009).

General Growth Properties, Inc. (GGP) is the second largest U.S. mall owner/operator with ownership or management responsibility for more than 150 regional shopping malls in 41 states. The company was started by the Bucksbaum family, who financed their first shopping center in Cedar Rapids, Iowa, in 1954. In the 1960s, they began building enclosed malls, and in 1970 they merged their interests into General Growth Properties as a REIT, a business form established by law in 1960 as a way for small investors to become involved in real estate. In 2004, GGP bought the Rouse Company, developer of the new city Columbia, Maryland, and a number of famous shopping malls, such as Harborplace in Baltimore. Recent shifts in the prospects for malls have created challenges for GGP. In response, it has focused on new big-box designs and Internet shopping. As of 2009, it is having a hard time servicing debt due to lack of sufficient cash flow in the midst of a strong recession, and the company entered bankruptcy (General Growth Properties, Inc., 2009; Yahoo Finance, 2009).

School Districts

Although commercial developers garner most attention, public property developers and owners also impact infrastructure, and in many cases they pay less for it than private developers. Public buildings are owned by local, state, and federal governments. For example, the nation's some 14,000 school districts provide facilities for a growing school-age population. Two school districts in growing areas illustrate the infrastructure challenges. In Fort Collins, Colorado, the Poudre School District (2009) serves some 25,600 students. It issued a $175 million bond offering in 2000 and built six schools, including a comprehensive and modern new high school. It also performed repairs and/or expansion in all its other schools, for activity and media centers, flex rooms, classrooms, theaters, roof repairs, flooring, lighting, pavement, hallway "bridges," lunchrooms, lockers, Americans with Disabilities Act compliance, and restroom remodeling. In addition to structural changes, it funded educational upgrades to include computers, software, labs, wireless network upgrades, telephones in classrooms, technical equipment, and instructional television. The district is growing and plans another bond issue in 2010.

As a very large school district, Chicago Public Schools (CPS; 2009) serves over 400,000 students in more than 600 schools. It has a $5.1 billion capital program. In fiscal year 2008, it obtained $250 million in bond proceeds to renovate and build 27 schools. Financing is heavily weighted toward local property taxes, and the state government has not contributed to capital financing in the last four years. As of 2008, capital investments had reached $7.1 billion, including land, improvements, and equipment. The focus in 2008 was on renovations, new labs, and meeting disability requirements. Six new replacement high schools are scheduled to be completed by 2012. CPS has a debt load of $5.1 billion.

GSA and Military Construction

The U.S. General Services Administration (GSA; 2009) manages thousands of government properties. Established in 1949, it currently has revenues of $17.7 billion and almost 12,000 employees. Its top customers are the Departments of Defense, Justice, Homeland Security, Judiciary, and Treasury.

Military construction is a multibillion-dollar enterprise. For example, the U.S. Army's (2009) budget for fiscal year 2009 includes $15 billion for military construction and base realignment and closure. The work is focused on basic infrastructure for barracks, family housing, dining, chapels, physical fitness facilities, child development centers, fire stations and emergency services, medical facilities, and commissaries.

IMPACT FEES AND THE
GROWTH-PAYS-ITS-OWN-WAY PHILOSOPHY

A model for infrastructure demand as a function of development shows systems for transportation, energy, water, communications, and waste management as functions of the structures they serve: the residential housing, commercial centers, offices, and the other types of structures required by the population. Ultimately, the population determines the required infrastructure to serve its economic and social needs as well as to protect the environment.

The demand for infrastructure to serve new developments can be estimated through the growth-pays-its-own-way philosophy. A national model would show how infrastructure cost is related to the number and distribution of structures in the built environment. At the community level, estimates can be made to set infrastructure impact fees. These fees benefit existing residents because they reduce pressure to raise taxes and fees for facility maintenance and rehabilitation.

A national calculation of infrastructure value per person or housing unit is not precise, but we can estimate that all fixed assets at $42.6 trillion work out to about $142,000 per capita or about $387,000 for each of some 110 million occupied housing units. This shows the high financing load for infrastructure and housing, which amounts to about $400,000 for a family of three. The public side of this calculation shows fixed assets of $9.2 trillion, or about $90,000 per occupied house. This number includes federal assets and assets of program areas that normally do not charge impact fees (such as school districts) as well as infrastructure-related fixed assets.

Usually impact fees—one-time charges to finance infrastructure improvements to serve new growth—limited to basic services such as water, wastewater, roads, and drainage; however, in home rule states, impact fees can be expanded to other facilities as long as they can be justified. When they are applied, they are levied against new building projects and computed according to the cost of the new growth. They can be spent only on capacity-enhancing capital facilities; they cannot be spent on ongoing operational expenses.

Impact fees take into account different land uses and demands on infrastructure. To address housing affordability, impact fees can recognize differences in residential units. They can also take into account areas without growth potential, such as central cities, and cost differentials, such as distance and density of development. Variable rates can be based on unit size and recognize the differences in impact of smaller units on facilities. Local government can choose to pay impact fees from other funds.

The usual procedure to compute an impact fee is to estimate the infrastructure capital cost required to serve a development and to compute the unit cost for each type of new facility that will use the infrastructure system. Doing this requires estimates of demand-to-capacity ratios for capital facilities and estimates of the number and cost of facilities to meet a prescribed level of service for a growing population. A financial study must be prepared to allocate the costs of infrastructure to the development that requires it (Duncan Associates, 2009a).

Regulation of impact fees is imposed by legislation in some states. For example, Wisconsin's comprehensive 1993 legislation sets forth rules of how fees are to be set and administered. The legislation delineates these types of public facilities:

- Highways and other transportation facilities
- Sewage and storm runoff collection and treatment
- Water distribution
- Parks and other recreational facilities
- Solid waste and recycling facilities
- Fire protection
- Law enforcement
- Emergency medical
- Libraries

Presumably, water source and treatment are included under "water distribution." Facilities owned by a school district are not defined as public facilities.

The fees must bear a rational relationship to the need for public facilities to serve land development and not exceed a proportional share of the costs of the facilities. Fees must be reduced by other assessments or funds from the federal or state governments. Fees cannot be used to address existing deficiencies and must be applied to new facilities.

Developers must pay fees before a building permit is issued. Local governments must deposit fees in separate accounts, and unused fees are to be refunded to the developer after a specified time period. Local governments can exempt low-cost housing from impact fees, but fees cannot be shifted to other developments. Different impact fees may be imposed on different types of land development. Also, fees may vary among zones in the municipality (US Housing and Urban Development, Regulatory Barriers Clearinghouse, 2009).

Approximately 60 percent of U.S. cities with more than 25,000 residents now impose impact fees to fund infrastructure needed to service new housing and other development. Fast-growing states such as in the South or Southwest make use of them the most. Impact fees can add substantial costs to residential housing. In 2008, the national average was $11,239. In some states, the fees are much higher. For example, in California, where impact fees are most heavily used, the fees range up to $50,000 with the average in the $20,000 range (Duncan Associates, 2009b).

In Fort Collins, Colorado, the fees for a typical residential dwelling unit with lot size of 8,600 square feet as of early 2009 were:

Electric power	$ 2,537
Water supply	$ 9,029
Wastewater	$ 3,194
Stormwater	$ 436
Street oversizing	$ 2,534
Total	$17,730

The water charge includes a raw water charge, which is $5,203 of the total shown for water. This occurs because in Colorado, water supplies must be purchased as water rights. In water-short areas this charge can be much higher, in some cases over $25,000 per house connection. Other states may face comparable charges to develop water supply infrastructure facilities.

FUTURE CITIES AND INFRASTRUCTURE

What requirements will the future built environment place on infrastructure? City planners and futurists probe how urban areas will change, and part of the answer lies in development patterns. The other part of the answer lies in trade-offs among choices about how we use and pay for resources and the emergence of new technologies. These are likely to shape future demands on infrastructure as much or more than the shape and appearance of future cities.

Futuristic urban patterns are already on the horizon. The locations of urban activity are mostly fixed by past investments in infrastructure, such as the Interstate Highway System and energy grids, but changes occur around the edges and in redevelopment zones. Additionally, there will be spreading of development into rural zones as more people become liberated from cities by telecommuting and taking advantage of dispersed job availability in the information economy. These patterns suggest three changes in urban shape: the edge city, the intensification of development in urban areas, and the dispersal of population into rural and small city zones. Earlier in the chapter the states with the greatest projected population growth were identified, and they will exhibit these types of growth. For example, Florida, California, and Texas are each expected to add over 12 million in population by 2030, and edge city development, intensification, and dispersal will be the mechanisms to accommodate the growth. Arizona's population growth of over 6 million will encounter similar patterns, but entire new retirement communities may be developed as well. In the case of Colorado, growth is expected to spread along the Front Range in already established patterns that will become denser.

No single pattern will explain all of the growth, but their combinations will require new and expanded infrastructure along with renewals of existing systems. How the new, expanded, or renewed systems will be provided will depend on choices about resource use and application of technologies. These are shown on Exhibit 3.10, along with the driving forces of population, economic, and technological change.

The diagram shows the five infrastructure sectors that serve the changing built environment and its residential, commercial, and industrial land uses. The built environment changes in response to the population, economic, and

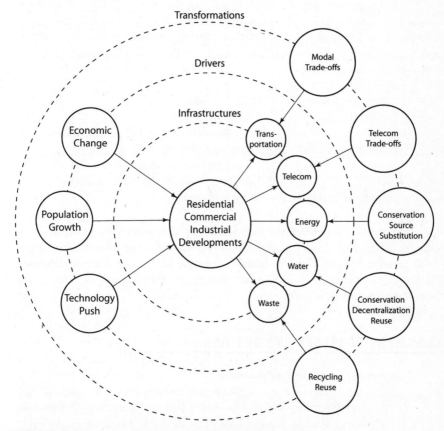

EXHIBIT 3.10 Future Infrastructure Demands and Choices

technological drivers and creates shifting demands on the infrastructures. How the infrastructures respond depends on the transformational and trade-off choices, such as modal split among transportation, telecom trade-offs such as between wired and wireless, energy shifts, water conservation and decentralization of systems, and waste recycling and reuse. The bottom line of the demand for future infrastructure: You would not simply see linear increases in demand for commodities such as pavement and buried pipe, but the demands would depend on all the forces shown in the exhibit.

The built environment will continue to adapt to new forces, such as the financial crisis, climate change, and the cost of energy. Information technology has accelerated the trend toward decentralization, and today's push for renewable energy, taking structures off-grid, and greater security will force new changes. The interest in green construction will create demand for new types of buildings and land uses and for renovation of the old. Green building will also be a driving force of transformation for buildings, to go along with the transformational forces that impact the five infrastructure categories. A summary of these forces shows strong forces of environmentalism, economy, energy efficiency, resource conservation, recycling and reuse, and changing social choices:

Built environment	Green building
Transportation	Modal trade-offs
Energy	Conservation and source substitution
Telecommunications	Trade-offs among devices/ communication patterns
Water	Conservation, decentralization, reuse
Waste management	Recycling, reuse

In the financial arena, the jury is out for how changes that result from the bursting of the housing bubble will play out. No one knows how long it will take for home prices and housing starts to recover, and the weaknesses of lending institutions must be addressed before the shape of new financing mechanisms will be known.

SUMMARY OF ISSUES AND OUTLOOK

Support for the Built Environment

The built environment and its real estate industry are tightly linked to infrastructure, which supports all types of buildings. Residential housing is by far the largest component by value in the built environment, so fluctuations in housing starts create waves across the economy and in demand for and use of infrastructure. Construction spending rose rapidly during the late 1990s but slowed after the dot-com boom ended and slowed again during the financial crisis.

Commercial Building and Renovation as Top Trends

The postwar housing boom was accompanied by new malls and commercial buildings, which will require replacements or substitutes due to depreciation and obsolescence. The outcome of decisions about these commercial facilities will have large impacts on infrastructure, on REITs, and on the capital requirements for commercial lending.

Transformation of Industrial Areas in the New Economy

Globalization will affect existing industrial areas dramatically, and cities will be looking for ways to renew them and create industrial parks and redevelopments to create jobs and revitalize urban areas. Their success or failure will lead to needs for renewed infrastructure or to new problems created by older infrastructures that must function without the resource base they had in the past.

Public Safety: A Local Version of Critical Infrastructure

Public safety facilities, such as police stations, firehouses, emergency medical, and other control centers, can be located in strategic positions in urban areas and serve as anchors to community stability during turbulent times. These infrastructures are not financed by fees but by tax rolls and require corresponding political support.

The New Economy Driving Change in Infrastructure

The new economy will be shaped by global forces as well as local population shifts, which depend on migration more than on natural growth. The top 10 states for forecast growth are in the Southeast and Mid-Atlantic (Florida, North Carolina, Georgia, Virginia); the Southwest (Texas, Arizona); and the West (California, Washington, Nevada, and Colorado). This leaves the Northeast, the Midwest and Plains, and the North Central regions as more stagnant areas for infrastructure growth.

Local Planning

Although it is affected by national policy and financial controls, the local planning process is inherently political. As residential housing is dominant in driving infrastructure decisions, most infrastructure decisions are in the hands of local political leaders. Large, regional facilities, such as interchanges and city-wide water facilities, require regional cooperation, an inherently difficult political process. Other large-scale infrastructures, such as electricity generation plants, are controversial to national groups.

The Emergence of Green Building

Green building seems to be the leading wave of a new emphasis on conservation. This emphasis can affect practically every aspect of infrastructure and can cause large changes in infrastructure financial systems. Examples include revenue decreases in water and electric systems, conversion of roads through traffic calming (to slow traffic deliberately), and reduced waste streams through recycling.

Housing Finance: The Key to Healthy Cities

Sustaining a vibrant residential housing market and opportunities for homeownership will require a viable housing finance system. Many lessons are being learned during the financial crisis. Along with the prospects for economic growth, these lessons will determine the shape of housing policy for the future. Social needs such as affordable and public housing will suffer unless local and national leaders find ways to balance financial recovery with responsive public programs.

Impact Fees Depend on Growth

Rapid growth led to significant infrastructure finance through impact fees, which rose to become significant parts of total housing cost. With the fall in housing costs and starts, impact fee revenues have dropped and jeopardize the capacity of local governments to meet expansion and renewal needs of vital infrastructure facilities, especially the lifeline categories of water and wastewater and renewal of transportation facilities.

Transformational Forces and the Future of Infrastructure

The transformational forces at play, such as the Internet economy, global warming, social networking, conservation, source substitution, and recycling, have the capacity to change infrastructure demand radically. They will be of greater influence on future infrastructure needs than linear projections of population growth and responses in the form of traditional planning.

CHAPTER 4

Transportation Sector

Measured by its investment and expenditures, the transportation industry is the largest and most diverse of the public infrastructure sectors. Its importance in undergirding national life—from daily commerce to preparing for war—is unquestioned.

This chapter explains the transportation sector's overall structure, financial framework, and issues. Financing mechanisms for transportation infrastructure are diverse because of the mixed nature of the industry. Its three components—public infrastructure, public/private services, and private vehicles—provide a way to classify the financing systems, however. The chapter provides details on the main categories of infrastructure and services, which include roads, airports, ports and waterways, rail, mass transit, and pipelines. Each subsector has its own financial structure, and these are explained individually. The common elements and cross-cutting themes of transportation are also summarized in the chapter.

SECTOR STRUCTURE AND SIZE

The transportation sector is difficult to characterize because aggregated financial information about its nature and performance requires many statistics. In national economic statistics, what is labeled "transportation" does not even include the biggest transportation infrastructure sector of roads and bridges. The Dow Jones Transportation Average is mostly about transportation of freight rather than passenger travel. The Bureau of Transportation Statistics of the U.S. Department of Transportation maintains detailed statistics on many of the transportation subsectors, but the overall sector ranges far and wide in its scope.

Transportation requires many types of organizations, infrastructures, equipment, and vehicles to facilitate mobility of people and goods. It is closely connected to the volatile energy sector and to large-scale environmental problems. Transportation is an essential industry for all freight and passenger travel and to service the modern just-in-time manufacturing system and the logistics-based Internet economy.

Manufacturing of transportation vehicles draws giant automobile, aircraft, and other manufacturing industries into the transportation sector. In addition to passenger travel, the transportation industry undergirds trade from the local to global scale.

The publicly provided transportation infrastructure comprises roads, airports, ports, and waterways. Rail infrastructure is mostly in the private sector, but it has many interfaces with publicly owned roads and airports. Services that mix public and private providers—such as mass transit and airline travel—require publicly provided infrastructure and public/private partnerships to ensure functionality of the transportation systems. As of 2009, the automotive part of the sector is in turmoil with historical bankruptcies, including giant General Motors.

One way to think about the transportation sector is as a combination of all related infrastructures (roads, bridges, airports, ports, waterways, rail lines, transit hubs, and pipelines) and all transportation service organizations, such as those listed in the Dow Jones Transportation Average. To characterize the sector fully, you would add the industries that provide vehicles and support services. To go further, you would add the part of the energy sector that provides the petroleum to fuel most transportation. Clearly, transportation is a giant sector when all of these components are included.

As Exhibit 4.1 shows, the transportation infrastructure systems support the public service providers and the vehicles owned by private parties and/or firms. This requires public-private cooperation or a social contract in which the government provides most of the roads, airports, and infrastructure and the private sector provides most of the automobiles, airlines, fuel, and other support. Continuing renegotiation of this social contract occurs, as the government faces large bills and uncertain conditions to maintain the massive transportation network.

Most infrastructures, especially the capital-intensive road system, are publicly owned, but some parts, such as rail lines, are owned by the private sector. Equipment—such as trucks, aircraft, and rail cars—is a large part of the fixed assets of the transportation industry and is almost entirely in the private sector, with the exception of transit equipment. Later we show how, in the case of roads, it appears that the private side of transportation expenditures are about 10 times the public side.

The sector structure of transportation is usually classified by modes and by cargo (passenger, freight, or commodity). The modes include roads and

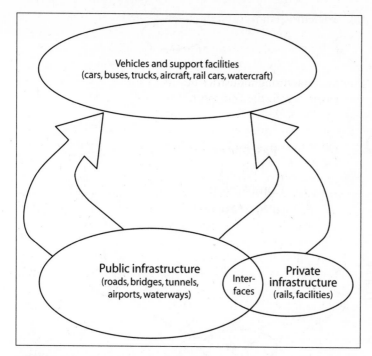

EXHIBIT 4.1 Transportation Infrastructures and Service Providers

highways, air, mass transit, rail, water, and pipeline. The types of vehicles can be added to this classification, and even bike and pedestrian travel can be included. Intermodal transportation systems are also classified, and the movement of information over the Internet can be added to the list as well.

Each of the transportation modal sectors has its own infrastructure and investment needs, but many trade-offs are available. As Exhibit 4.2 shows, movement of passengers, freight, commodities, and information can be handled by various services and their supporting infrastructures. These trade-offs affect the finances of the service organizations dramatically, as evinced by the increase in use of transit, decline of gasoline use with rising prices, or shifts of freight from air to rail. Another important trade-off is transportation of information instead of passengers or freight. Examples from infrastructure categories include telecommuting, shipment of digital files over the Internet instead of sending paper copies, and even scheduling of water and energy use by trading information rather than shipping commodities over physical networks.

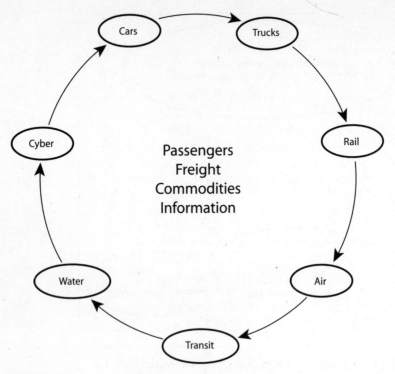

EXHIBIT 4.2   Transportation Trade-Offs

The overall statistics of transportation system extent and use are maintained by the U.S. Bureau of Transportation Statistics (2009a), which compiles information on passenger and freight travel by mode. Systems included are (based on 2006 statistics):

- 4,033,007 miles of public road
- 5,233 public-use airports
- 1,171 airports serving enplaned passengers (includes 26 large hub areas)
- 161,842 miles or rail line (Class I, regional, and local freight, and Amtrak)
- 168,255 directional miles of bus transit (also trolley and rail)
- 26,000 miles of navigable channels (also 620 miles of ferry directional miles)
- 169,346 miles of oil pipe
- 300,400 miles of gas transmission pipe

Other statistics include ports (Great Lakes, inland, ocean), locks, and natural gas distribution miles (1.2 million miles).

Statistics on use of the transportation modes are complex and not especially meaningful, unless you want to note trends, such as a reduction in vehicle-miles traveled, which would be important information for highway planning. For example, all rural travel by all types of vehicles increased from 1.032 to 1.037 trillion miles from 2005 to 2006. All urban travel by all types of vehicles increased in the same period from 1.957 to 1.977 trillion miles. These data indicate an annual increase of 1.0 percent for all urban travel, compared to 0.45 percent for rural travel. The data can be examined in great detail. For example, the increases in rural and urban travel seem to show most growth in use of vans, pickup trucks, and sport/utility vehicles, as compared to passenger cars and truck travel, which was flat in the period.

In the case of airline travel, the data show a decline from 681 million to 633 million passengers for the 12 months ending March 31, 2009. Freight mail also dropped, by 6.3 percent in the same period. Top domestic routes were Atlanta–Orlando, New York–Chicago, Atlanta–New York, Los Angeles–San Francisco, and Atlanta–Washington. It is evident that these statistics are important economic indicators as well as measures of use of infrastructure systems.

ROAD AND HIGHWAY SYSTEMS

It is no wonder that financing roads is such a challenge because the investment required to maintain roads and bridges is the largest among all infrastructure categories. The sheer scale of the system explains why such a large investment is required. The U.S. system includes over 4 million miles of intercity highways, roads, and urban streets as well as some 600,000 bridges, including some 47,000 miles of Interstate Highways. A large share of the some $9 trillion in U.S. public fixed assets (see Chapter 1) is in roads, and most of these are owned by state and local governments.

For perspective, the United States has far and away more miles of roads to maintain than other large countries. Exhibit 4.3 shows a comparison with several European, Asian, and Latin American countries and illustrates how extensive the U.S. system is (Economist, 2007).

The cost of the U.S. system seems to be much greater on a per capita basis than the other nations shown in Exhibit 4.3. By computing road miles per 10,000 in population, we see that the United States has over twice the per capita mileage of Germany and Japan and over 10 times that of Indonesia. To be fair, Germany and Japan are more urbanized, and the United States

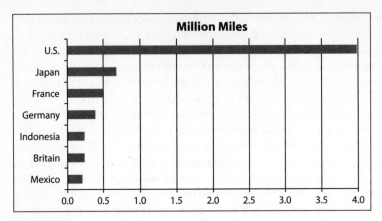

EXHIBIT 4.3   Road Network Lengths in Million Miles

has a more extensive system of low-cost rural roads; still, the total mileage and maintenance obligations are quite different.

	Road miles per 10,000 population
U.S.	133.0
France	91.7
Japan	54.0
Germany	47.9
Britain	40.1
Mexico	20.0
Indonesia	10.7

To gain a financial perspective on the costs of road travel, if each of the 4 million miles of U.S. roads had a replacement value of $1 million, the total would be $4 trillion, which is in the ballpark of the depreciated value of $2.7 trillion reported in Chapter 2. Of course, the 4 million miles contains some with hundreds of millions of dollars per mile in costs and others with much below $1 million. Building and maintaining this vast network requires an industry with a broad array of heavy construction companies, engineers, paving contractors, and equipment companies.

Roads and bridges are mostly financed from dedicated funds at the three levels of government. In 2006, when total expenditures were $161 billion, sources of funding were 21 percent, 51 percent, and 29 percent for federal, state, and local governments (U.S. Federal Highway Administration, 2009a). Normally, capital expenditures are around half of total expenditures. For example, data from 2004 showed capital outlay at 47.6 percent of total spending. Additionally, bond retirement and interest on debt were 9.3 percent of the total, so all capital-related items totaled 56.9 percent. If you consider that some of the administrative costs were associated with capital expenditures, the real total might be some 60 percent of total spending. A round number of half would indicate a 2006 level of some $80 billion in capital spending, a number that is close to the construction spending statistics of that year.

Taking as estimates for total road expenditures some $80 billion each for operating and capital, and using the numbers given earlier of about 3 trillion miles of vehicle travel per year, the indication is that road costs are about $0.027 per mile for operations and $0.027 per mile for capital. This yields an order-of-magnitude total of $0.054 per vehicle-mile traveled. Of course, the number would be much higher for an 18-wheeler than for a small car. Using the 2009 Internal Revenue Service (IRS) mileage rate for cars of $0.55 per mile indicates that the road cost is about 10 percent of the vehicle operating cost. This is an inexact figure, but it does give us an order-of-magnitude idea of the public-private split of costs for road transportation.

Another snapshot of these costs is available from the operation of a toll road, for example, the New Jersey Turnpike (2009). It had a 2007 annual budget of $863 million and vehicle-miles traveled of 12.5 billion. This works out at about $0.07 per vehicle-mile, and the authority's budget is split between operating and capital. It is interesting that in its budget, the authority spends some $60 million on police protection and another $78 million on toll collection. These costs are absorbed into other budgets for non–toll roads. If they are removed, the per-mile figure drops to $0.058, about the same as the national average cited earlier. Bear in mind that these estimates are overall averages. More exact computations would require analysis of road types, levels of service, and other complex variables.

Another conclusion from the data presented about the cost of road travel is that annual expenditures for road transportation are much, much greater than the some $160 billion reported. If the road infrastructure cost is 10 percent of the vehicle operating cost, then vehicle travel costs are some $1.6 trillion annually. The order of magnitude of this estimate is verified by an annual gasoline bill in the United States of about $400 billion, which is a fraction of total vehicle operating costs that include capital, maintenance, and insurance. Using a national total of about 3 trillion vehicle-miles driven, along with an approximate per mile cost of $0.75 for both cars and trucks, you would arrive at an estimate of $2.25 trillion for all vehicle operating costs. Although these numbers are approximate, they illustrate the large scale of the motor vehicle industry and how its costs dominate road transportation costs.

Most national press about road financing is about federal sources, but combined state and local funding exceeds federal contributions. Federal funding is mostly from the Highway Trust Fund, which was created in 1956 to finance the Interstate and federal-aid highway system. The idea was to create a system of user charges, which are collected indirectly by assessing gasoline use. The fund receives excise tax revenues from sales of fuel, truck tires, trucks, and trailers, and heavy vehicle use. Most of the taxes are paid to the IRS by the producer, retailer, or heavy vehicle owner. The federal funding comes via a series of authorization bills, which normally occur every five years. The first Transportation Equity Act was the 1991 Intermodal Surface Transportation Efficiency Act, which President George H.W. Bush called a "jobs bill." This was followed by the Transportation Equity Act for the 21st Century (TEA-21) and then the Safe, Accountable, Flexible, Efficient Transportation Equity Act: A Legacy for Users (SAFETEA-LU) in 2005 (U.S. Federal Highway Administration, 2009b). SAFETEA-LU authorized $244 billion over five years, and the 2009 stimulus package also included $27.5 billion for transportation.

A mass transit account was started in 1983 to divert some funds to transit and create a cross-subsidy from road use to transit. As discussed later in the chapter, this diversion of funds from roads to transit is a major issue in promoting use of transit and in offering the public options in their transportation choices.

Most state governments also levy gas taxes to help finance their roads and bridges. For example, in Colorado the Department of Transportation's (2008) fiscal year (FY) 2009–10 budget of $869 million was financed through $420 million from state funds, including the gas tax, vehicle registrations, and other funds. Federal funds expected were $330 million, and the other $105 million was from miscellaneous sources, such as transit, aeronautics, and gaming funds. Expenditures were $239 million on system quality (bridges, pavement maintenance, etc.); $186 million on mobility (other maintenance, metro projects, etc); $179 million on administration and other categories; $169 million on strategic projects and debt service; and $95 million on safety.

Most local governments use property taxes and fees to finance their roads, but they struggle to find enough money to maintain them. For example, in the City of Fort Collins, Colorado, financing the street system is a funding challenge, both for capital and for maintenance. The city has a dedicated sales tax for street maintenance, but it falls short of the annual needs so there is a constant search for funds to maintain the system. In addition, the city has a long list of capital improvements that goes way beyond its ability to finance them. They include intersection improvements, bike lanes, overpasses, and safety upgrades, among others. An example of an issue facing the city is to create "quiet zones" to solve a bothersome train noise problem in the city.

Trends in road use include an apparent plateau in vehicles miles traveled, a statistic that has been flat since 2004, even before the large rise in oil prices in 2008. The drop in traffic with the rise in gas prices and 2009 recession was the largest since World War II. Also, the traffic is shifting to larger-capacity urban roadways, where passenger cars and trucks dominate. The greatest growth in traffic is in the southeastern and intermountain West states. The total traffic is largest on principal arterials in the largest 100 metro areas, but the most miles per capita are in low-density southeastern and southwestern metro areas.

Road infrastructure faces challenging financial issues that include projections of continuing increases in regional traffic demand, in spite of the flat national trend. These are expected to resume their upward trend after the current recession ends. The problem of financing such a complex system with continually increasing demands is at the top of the political agendas in Washington and many state capitals, especially those in fast-growing states.

The levels of investment needs are reported in U.S. Federal Highway Administration's (2009c) periodic Conditions and Performance Report, which reports costs to maintain systems to prevent increases in highway user costs and to cover pavement and bridge preservation and required system expansion. The scenarios take into account new technologies, such as intelligent transportation systems, but not operational improvements, such as congestion pricing. The Federal Highway Administration's (FHWA) two levels of annual cost estimates for 2003 to 2022 are $73.8 billion for the "cost to maintain" scenario and $118.9 billion for the "cost to improve" scenario, which would address the backlog of highway ($398 billion) and bridge ($63 billion) deficiencies.

Comparing these numbers to the average annual road capital expenditures of about $80 billion shows that we just about maintain the existing system but do not improve it. As we show in Chapter 10, the American Society of Civil Engineers grades the existing system as D–; unless the funding increases, no overall improvements will occur.

The National Surface Transportation Infrastructure Financing Commission (2008) identified three problems:

1. Revenue is not enough to maintain the existing network and take care of needed expansion.
2. Current funding mechanisms and levels of revenue are not linked closely enough to system use, thus allowing demand and costs to grow faster than revenue.
3. Effectiveness of existing revenue is dissipated because investments are not directed at cost-effective projects.

It reached these tentative conclusions:

- System demands are outpacing investment.
- System maintenance costs are competing with necessary expansion of the system.
- The fuel tax, which has been the key federal funding source for our system, is no longer sufficient at current rates.
- More direct user charges should be explored.
- We need not only more investment in our system but more intelligent investment complemented by better operation of the system.

In addition to the large burden of financing operations and maintenance on the vast roads infrastructure network, other pressures include congestion and mobility; reliance on freight and trucks to service the Internet economy; and environmental impacts on air quality, water quality, and greenhouse gases.

With an increasing population and rising demand for travel, the road transportation system will be stressed. However, with greater fuel economy, the inevitable decline in revenues from the gas tax must be faced if the nation is to maintain and improve its roads infrastructure. This decline, both in current dollars and in purchasing power, is caused by the federal government being unwilling to increase the current 18.4 cent per gallon tax as gasoline use is declining. At the same time, increased construction costs degrade the ability of the fund to pay for needed upgrades.

In 2009, the Obama administration predicted that the Highway Trust Fund would be short $17 billion over the next two years due to the recession and gas tax increases. In 2008, Congress transferred $8 billion from the government's general fund to meet the shortfall, and it may have to do so again. This transfer represents a transfer of funding from gas tax to income tax and a willingness by the government to take on debt to finance highways. Meanwhile, state governments are facing severe funding limits due to revenue shortages, so the near-term prospects for funding for highways and bridges look very limited (Conkey, 2009a).

Given the writing on the wall about public highway funding, it is natural that interest in toll roads would rise. Toll roads are used in a number of European and Asian countries to provide private answers to public problems, and interest in the United States has been increasing. A high-profile example is the Texas experiment with toll roads. Under Governor Rick Perry, Texas has developed an active toll road program, especially in Dallas.

In July 2009, the Texas state legislature refused the governor's request to extend the state's authority to contract with private toll road developers. Although this does not appear to end the Texas experiment with private toll road operations, it shows how fickle the politics of privatization can be. The Texas experiments featured competition between the public and private sectors, such as for concessions in North Texas, where two contracts went to the North Texas Tollway Authority, which had to take on high debt and agree to escalating toll rates and large up-front payments to the state. Rates increased from 10 cents a mile to 14.5 cents per mile, and rates on managed-lane projects might go to 50 to 75 cents a mile during rush hour.

The North Texas Tollway Authority plans to build more toll roads in the next 5 to 10 years. In the Dallas and Fort Worth areas, the Spanish firm Cintra will rebuild LBJ Freeway in Dallas and construct the North Tarrant Express near Fort Worth. Both will mix tax dollars and private funds (Lindenberger, 2009).

Other states with expanded authority for private toll roads are New York, Florida, Virginia, Georgia, Pennsylvania, and California. Other related privatization deals involve private contracts for city parking in Chicago and Pittsburgh and in California, even public courthouses.

Toll roads have pluses and minuses. People who use toll roads contribute more in capital cost per mile because they are paying for roads they use and those they do not use (in gas taxes). To build and finance toll roads may cost more than raising gas taxes to finance expansion of the existing road networks. Opposition may come from rural areas, where roads can be adequate and landowners are wary of state takeovers of land. Anti-toll activists may choose to push modest increases in gas taxes, which states have been reluctant to raise. Texas's last increase was 1991, at 20 cents per gallon. As toll roads proliferate and free roads become more jammed, the notion that toll roads are optional will be seen as wrong. I saw this firsthand in Asia, where you can zip along on an expensive toll road, right next to a free road that is essentially a parking lot, filled with all types of vehicles.

Currently, the toll road boom seems to have cooled, as lenders are cautious during this economy and worry that the public-private deals involve too much leverage.

While developments in toll experiments and in smart roads may hold at least part of the answer for the future (see Chapter 14), the nation still has a gigantic roads and bridges infrastructure to maintain. Therefore, the future promises to be one of searching for funds while, at the same time, looking at alternative management strategies and to technology-induced productivity increases in transportation.

Intelligent Transportation Systems

One trend to watch in road transportation is emergence of "smart roads." *Time* magazine in its March 23, 2009, cover story predicted that highways, especially the interstate system, would change dramatically with smart technologies. The changes will involve traffic management and vehicle operations. Some of the issues in traffic management are traffic monitoring, electronic tolling, and traveler information services. Vehicle operations include technologies such as global positioning systems (GPS) and accident avoidance.

Smart traffic systems involve complex plans and technologies and require a combination of new products and services and advice by system planners to help agencies implement the new systems. Transportation consulting firms are adapting the new methods. and the top 20 listed by ENR (2009b) had $10.1 billion in 2008 revenue. The top five of these were: AECOM Technology Corporation, Jacobs, URS Corporation, Parsons Brinkerhoff, Inc., and HNTB Companies.

AECOM is a broad-based firm providing services to transportation, facilities, environmental, and energy markets. It has 43,000 employees and works in more than 100 countries. AECOM (2009) has transportation projects that include the largest construction project in Europe, the Crossrail project in the United Kingdom; New York City's Second Avenue Subway; Minneapolis–St. Paul's Central Corridor Light Rail; the Miami Intermodal Center; I-95 improvement in South Florida; and program management for capital improvement at Los Angeles International Airport. Its services span the range of planning and engineering work, including corridor studies, environmental studies, design, traffic management planning, and design-build. Revenue for the year ended March 31, 2009 was $5.9 billion (Yahoo Finance, 2009).

On the technology side, a number of companies are developing products for use in smart transportation systems. For example, Telvent Farradyne, a subsidiary of the Spanish firm Telvent, provides smart transportation technologies for traffic and freeway management, travel information, electronic toll collection, parking management, traffic enforcement, traffic signal, transit fare payment, and tunnel control system. Iteris Inc. is another company that develops technologies to reduce traffic congestion and improve safety of transportation systems. Its intelligent transportation technologies combine image processing and traffic engineering technology. Iteris had $65.2 million in revenue in the year ending March 31, 2008 (Yahoo Finance, 2009).

URS Corporation

URS Corporation (2009) is another large consulting firm with emphasis in transportation. Originally incorporated in 1957 and named URS in 1976, it began military work in the 1960s at overseas military bases. By the mid-1980s, it had 40 U.S. offices with emphasis on infrastructure, waste management, and pollution control. Transportation provided its best growth opportunities, and by 1997 through acquisitions, URS became the fifth largest U.S. engineering company. It has participated in many projects across the nation, covering every type of transportation problem. URS had $10.1 billion in revenue in 2008 (Yahoo Finance, 2009).

Abertis Infrastructure

Almost all roads and bridges are publicly owned, but the private sector is taking increasing interest. For example, Abertis Infraestructuras, S.A. (2009), based in Barcelona, Spain, traces its origins to the 1960s, when it built Spain's first toll road. It evolved from being an operator of toll roads in Spain to become an international transportation player. After a period of growth, it became Spain's largest and Europe's third largest toll road operator. Today, Abertis manages transportation and communications infrastructures with five divisions: highway concessions, car parks, logistics services, telecommunications, and airports. The highway division constructs and operates highways under concession agreements.

In 2008, Abertis teamed up with Citigroup, Inc., to make an offer to privatize the Pennsylvania Turnpike, but it withdrew after the state legislature seemed to balk. The Spanish-led ACS Group owns a large stake in Abertis and has signed a deal to build and operate a nearly $1.8 billion toll lane project in South Florida. The 35-year deal will use funding from an international consortium of financing institutions. The I-95 Express LLC organization was formed by ACS Infrastructure Development (ASCID), which will fund 12 percent of the project. Ten banks are lending $780 million, and the project received $655 million in a federal Transportation Infrastructure Finance and Innovation Act loan. The Florida Department of Transportation will regulate rates for use of the toll road and collect the revenue. ACSID will receive an annual availability payment of $65.9 million in 2009 dollars. ACS can get 12 percent return on investment if it meets every performance goal for operations and maintenance. Florida is shielded from cost overruns on $1.8 billion deal over 35 years (Wood, 2009).

Vulcan Materials Company and CEMEX, S.A.B. de C.V.

Vulcan Materials Company (2009) produces and sells basic construction materials in the form of aggregates, asphalt, and cement. Vulcan is the nation's largest producer of aggregates, which include crushed stone, sand and gravel, and rock. The company's asphalt, and recycled concrete products are used primarily in construction of highways, streets, and other public works.

The asphalt and concrete group produces asphalt mix and ready-mixed concrete and other concrete products. The cement group sells Portland and masonry cement as well as calcium products for several industries. Vulcan Materials was founded in 1909 in Birmingham, Alabama. Its 2008 revenues were \$3.7 billion, and it has struggled with a large decline in demand for its principal product of aggregates. Its total assets at the end of 2008 were \$8.9 billion, of which \$4.2 billion were in plant, property, and equipment.

One of Vulcan's competitors is CEMEX, a Mexico-based worldwide materials operator with a focus on cement and related materials. Its revenues increased from \$15.1 billion in 2005 to \$21.6 billion in 2007 (Yahoo Finance, 2009).

Caltrans

The California Department of Transportation (Caltrans) is the largest state transportation department in the United States as measured by expenditure and population served. Caltrans manages more than 50,000 miles of highway lanes and provides intercity rail services. It has some 22,000 employees and a budget on the order of \$13 billion from diverse sources. Of this budget, most is for highways (\$11.8 billion). One wrinkle in Caltrans' operation, as compared to some other state departments, is the influence of a union (the Professional Employees in California Government) on Caltrans' policy to do most of its infrastructure design work in-house. Texas's transportation budget is the second largest one, and all state transportation budgets vary year by year on the basis of construction activities. Florida is another fast-growing state with a large transportation budget (California Legislative Analysts Office, 2009).

New Jersey Turnpike Authority

Turnpike authorities are usually independent government enterprises that exist solely to develop and operate toll roads. The 148-mile New Jersey Turnpike Authority (2009) was completed in 1951 and thus predates the Interstate Highway System. It has 29 interchanges and several extensions and spurs. It has been modernized with electronic toll collection and high-occupancy vehicle (HOV) lanes. Financial statistics for the Authority were given earlier.

City of Dallas Streets Program

Management of streets by local government is usually within a public works department or a variation of it. These departments manage public works for local governments and handle large capital and operating budgets. Public works expenditures, including utilities, can be the major part of the budgets for many local governments. For example, in the City of Dallas, Texas (2007), the capital improvement needs inventory for 2007 shows $3.2 billion in needed street and transportation improvements, which are about 35 percent of all infrastructure-related needs in the city. This is about $2,700 for each of the some 1.2 million residents in the city.

Local government streets programs fall into the category of public works that can be used to cut budgets and defer maintenance, and they also are good targets for shovel-ready stimulus funding. This up-and-down approach to street maintenance will not be popular with city engineers, contractors, or the public, but it does meet a need for a flexible construction category that helps to smooth financial turbulence.

MASS TRANSIT SYSTEMS

Mass transit includes multiple modes, mainly intracity bus and rail. Commuter rail is a form of mass transit, but as distances increase, it becomes intercity passenger rail. However, other than Amtrak, the United States has little intercity passenger rail now. This seems poised to change, as a number of state-based systems are in the planning stages.

Transit is an essential service and is becoming more so with the rising cost of automobile travel and pressure on petroleum supplies, the main fuel for automobiles. The challenge is to finance transit, because its cost exceeds its revenues in almost every situation. To meet the economic and social needs of the population, however, transit systems must be sustained.

Transit involves a diverse collection of modes. Most transit trips are by bus (almost 60 percent), then heavy rail (almost 30 percent), with the other modes accounting for the rest. Ferryboats, paratransit, vanpools, shuttle buses, and even taxicabs can be considered as transit services as well. In addition to fixed route transit, flexible and paratransit systems operate to meet many needs. These include shuttle buses, Dial-a-Ride service, taxicabs, and other arrangements. Many of these are regulated by state public utility commissions and granted licenses to certain services in exchange for submission to rate regulation. For example, Veolia's SuperShuttle International operates a shuttle from Fort Collins, Colorado, to Denver International Airport. In 2009, another applicant was denied a license for an alternative service to serve the same route.

Given this diversity in modes, it is not easy to characterize the transit sector, although the statistics of the public transit agencies are readily available from government transportation statistics.

Transit use was higher early in the twentieth century than it is today. It fell sharply as road networks improved and automobile use increased. In the last few decades, transit ridership has been steady and increased gradually to 10 billion trips in 2007 (American Public Transit Association, 2009). The financial and energy crisis that began in 2007 increased ridership by more than 5 percent, the greatest increase in 25 years. Time will tell whether these increases will continue.

Compared to road travel, transit is a much smaller sector. To compare transit and road travel, you would have to consider all operating expenses of automobiles, trucks, and support facilities, even including service stations and repair shops. That would total a big share of the gross domestic product and dwarf transit expenditures. Still, transit was about a $45 billion industry in 2006. Capital expenses were $13.3 billion and operating expenses were $32.0 billion, reflecting the heavy emphasis on operation of equipment, as opposed to structures. Passengers paid 33 percent of the total, with local and state governments paying 44 percent and the federal government paying just under 8 percent. The remaining 15 percent of revenue came from taxes, advertising, interest, and other categories (see Exhibit 4.4). (U.S. Federal Highway Administration, 2009a).

Transit investment needs are reported in the same U.S. Department of Transportation Condition and Performance Report that reports these needs for roads and bridges. For 2005 to 2024, average annual investments

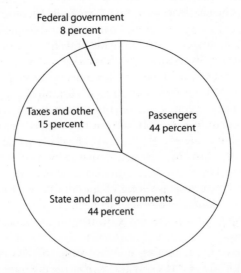

EXHIBIT 4.4   Funding Distribution for Transit

required were $15.8 billion for the maintain scenario and $21.8 billion for the improve scenario. Most needs are for large urban areas of over 1 million in population because most passenger miles are there (U.S. Federal Highway Administration, 2009c). Federal appropriations for capital and operating were only $9.5 billion in 2008, showing that deferred maintenance is increasing for transit systems, just as it is for roads.

Transit systems vary from very large, such as in New York City and Chicago, to the many smaller systems, such as the Transfort system in Fort Collins, Colorado. The five largest transit agencies, ranked by trips, are MTA New York City transit; Chicago Transit Authority; Los Angeles County Metropolitan Transportation Authority; Washington Metropolitan Area Transportation Authority; and the Massachusetts Bay Metropolitan Transportation Authority. They accounted for about 45 percent of all trips in the nation during 2006. The rest of the top 25 are mainly big-city systems, including five more New York area systems. This includes commuter rail as well as transit for intracity travel.

The challenging issues with transit are financial and sociopolitical. Transit services serve both economic and social purposes, for which they receive subsidies. They are efficient from a collective standpoint but are not always the most convenient individual choice. You see this conundrum for transit playing out in many places. For example, when the bus system started during the 1970s in Fort Collins, it initially had three small buses, which were purchased with federal grant funds. The buses ran with light loads most of the time, causing many citizens to complain about the apparent waste. The city persevered, however, and has built a fixed route system that now serves a much larger portion of the population, including university students. The system still requires subsidies from the general fund and it still has its detractors, who see light loads as indicators of money wasted. These people are not convinced by the arguments about the social necessity of transit and how a viable system must be maintained as an alternative to the automobile. Although this dilemma is not felt so much in cities that depend on transit, such as New York City, it is felt in many smaller and more dispersed communities.

Transit systems also face challenges due to their dependence on labor for operations. For this reason, they can be vulnerable to strikes, unless prohibited by law. The vulnerability of monopoly transit to labor strikes was shown by the 2005 New York subway strike. Gelinas (2005) explained how union members at Jamaica Buses Incorporated and the Triboro Coach Corporation struck, inconveniencing many New Yorkers and sparking a general New York City transit strike. The Transport Worker's Union reasoned that privately owned Jamaica and Triboro were to be merged into the Metropolitan Transportation Authority (MTA) in 2006, and the workers could strike without violating the state law that prohibits public workers from striking. New York had seven private bus lines (holding monopoly franchises with subsidies), but Mayor Michael Bloomberg started buying their assets and merging them into the MTA. London, England, has also seen crippling subway strikes, such as the one in 2009 by the Rail, Maritime and Transport Union that shut down the system for 48 hours.

Transit also faces security issues that were highlighted by the Madrid and London bombings and the Tokyo subway nerve gas attack. Growth in heavy rail in New York saw a decline in use after the September 11 terrorist attacks that destroyed parts of the subway system.

Transit works best when a city has captive constituencies without many cars, but it faces obstacles of acceptance, finance, and operations. New technologies, such as bus rapid transit and light rail offer promise for greater convenience and mobility. There are also models for effective bus service. For example, in London the government plans bus routes and fares and invites bids to provide the service for a fixed subsidy during a three- to five-year period. London has contracted out its bus services this way for two decades and cut its costs by up to one-half during the first decade (Gelinas, 2005).

Investment in transit continues to raise controversy. Whereas a strong claim is that lower-income people need mass transit, a counterargument is that mass transit causes the urbanization of poverty. Glaeser et al. (2008) reported research to show that demand for land and preference for suburban living explain how the poor are packed into urban areas because transit is available. While the findings are not definitive, they do indicate that travel modes are big factors in shaping cities.

Prospects for transit seem to be improving, even in sprawling cities like Los Angeles and Denver that have implemented light-rail systems. Denver is now considering heavy rail, including a line to Denver International Airport. If the public gets disenchanted with automobiles, which seems unlikely, and turns to transit, then transit-oriented development will blossom. You can already see many instances in which transit has stimulated retail operations near travel nodes. In a large city, such as Washington D.C., you might see at a Metro stop a constant flow of buses and vans, a large park-and-ride facility, many bike racks, taxi stands, pedestrians, and heavy traffic where cars drop off commuters.

In the Washington area, another high-profile transit project is unfolding in the form of the Dulles (Airport) Metrorail, which is to be a 23-mile line, extending from the terminus of the existing metro system in Fairfax County, Virginia to the airport and to serve several activity centers along the way. This $4 billion project has a timeline dating back to 1964, when the airport opened. In 1998, Raytheon Engineers proposed a Dulles line and in 1999, Bechtel submitted a competing proposal. Then, in 2000 WGI bought Ratheon's construction arm, and WGI and Bechtel formed a team and submitted a detailed proposal to the State of Virginia in 2001. They formed Dulles Transit Partners and signed a contract with Virginia in 2004. Phase I construction was scheduled to start in 2005, but has been delayed 4 years. Dulles Transit Partners did not receive a development fee and invested $25 million for preliminary engineering, but they are to be reimbursed after successful negotiation of a design-build contract. The program is receiving some federal subsidies through the Federal Transit Administration. The first 11-mile phase is scheduled to open in 2014 and the line to the airport to open in 2015. In addition to federal funding, other sources include county tax districts, airport fees from Washington Dulles International Airport, and revenues from the Dulles Toll Road. The Metropolitan Washington Airports Authority will continue to operate the toll road (Rubin, 2004; Dulles Corridor Rail, 2009).

Metropolitan Transit Authority

To illustrate a very large transit system, the Metropolitan Transit Authority (2009) of New York (MTA) is a public-benefit corporation chartered in 1965. Members of its 17-member Board represent the state, New York City, and county executives. Non-voting seats represent the Permanent Citizens Advisory Committee and organized labor. All members are confirmed by the state Senate. MTA serves North America's largest transportation network in a 5,000 square mile area with 14.6 million people in New York City, Long Island, southeastern New York State, and Connecticut. In 2008, its budget was $10.8 billion and it had some 69,000 employees for its rail, subway, and bus systems. Average weekday ridership was about 8.5 million.

Rail Car Manufacturer, Siemens

Siemens (2009) is an example of a large firm, like General Electric, that is implementing a broad range of transportation solutions, including rail cars for mass transit. Siemens has 68,000 employees in the United States and focuses on energy, transportation, and smart infrastructure solutions as well as other information technology applications, such as medical records. In the transportation sector, it focuses on "complete mobility" by networking systems for urban and interurban mobility and logistics. Production of rail vehicles is one of its product lines, and Siemens produced the rail cars for new light rail systems in Charlotte and Denver. The Charlotte Area Transit System is named the "Lynx" system (to fit the family of animals like the Carolina Panthers football team and also sound like "links") and will have

16 articulated Avanto light-rail vehicles built by Siemens, the same as in Houston and Portland, Oregon. Siemens sees light rail requirements in the United States and Europe as similar and has developed a common platform for them. Siemens had $112 billion in revenue in the year ended September 30, 2008 (Yahoo Finance, 2009).

AIR TRAVEL AND AIRPORTS

The infrastructure for air transportation comprises airports and air traffic control systems for commercial, military, and civil aviation. Exhibit 4.5 illustrates how this public-private and multipurpose system is configured.

Like road transportation, air travel infrastructure is mostly public, and the operating entities are mostly private. Principal players in the air travel system are airline companies that provide the travel, local governments that operate airports, and the federal government to handle air traffic control and air security. The airlines provide equipment and infrastructure, in the form of hangers and other maintenance facilities.

The airline industry was heavily regulated until the Airline Deregulation Act of 1978, which removed many controls from fares, routes, and other market conditions. The deregulation caused shakeouts, mergers, failures, and other changes in services. Now air travel seems more like a commodity than it did in the past. Competition and deregulation have lowered the

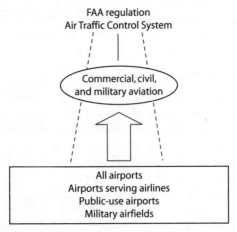

EXHIBIT 4.5   Air Travel Infrastructure and Operators

cost of a seat-mile, but low-margin airlines are sensitive to fuel cost, labor disruptions, and setbacks from security incidents or weather. In some countries, the main airline was owned by the government (such as British Air or Air France) but has been privatized.

After the terrorist attacks of September 11, 2001, Congress created the Transportation Security Administration (TSA) to take over civil aviation security from the Federal Aviation Administration (FAA). Congestion and delays remain a concern, and the industry still faces many challenges. No one is exactly sure how future paradigms for air travel will unfold, whether through today's hub-and-spoke system or new approaches with more travel between small hubs with smaller aircraft.

Airports in the United States are mostly owned by local governments and financed as enterprises. Revenues are from ticket taxes, landing fees, concessions, and other use charges. Infrastructure for expansion, equipment, facilities, and operations is required due to the growth of air travel; some financial assistance is provided through the FAA, which has a National Plan of Integrated Airport Systems.

The nation's first privately owned commercial airport has been opened in Branson, Missouri. The developer-owner-operator is Branson Airport LLC. The company transferred the land to the county in exchange for a 45-year lease. The county formed a state Transportation Development District that issued $114 million in municipal bonds to go with $41 million in equity funds. The plan is to serve some 8 million annual travelers, or a daily average of some 22,000 travelers (ENR, 2009).

The U.S. airline industry had large losses between the years 2000 and 2006, but in 2007 it made a $5.8 billion profit from rising load factors and fare increases. With the high cost of fuel in 2008 and the financial crisis in 2009, it experienced new challenges, and future profitability must be determined. Full-time employees in 2009 were at 392,000, down from 416,000 in 2005 (U.S. Federal Aviation Administration, 2008).

According to the International Air Transport Association (2009), based in Geneva, Switzerland, revenues of the global air transport industry will fall by 12.0 percent to $467 billion in 2009. This will result in a combined loss of $4.7 billion. Passenger traffic was expected to fall by 5.7 percent and cargo demand by 13.0 percent. Falling fuel prices help to cushion the losses. Asia Pacific carriers were hardest hit. North American carriers were expected to deliver the best performance, even with a small profit that is achieved by cutting capacity. Carriers in Europe, Latin America, and Africa were expected to post losses. The only region with demand growth was expected to be the Middle East. The association said that the historical margin of the fragmented industry is only 0.3 percent and to return to health it needs access to capital, the ability to merge and consolidate, and the freedom to access markets.

United Airlines

UAL Corporation is the holding company for the operating company of United Air Lines, Inc. The company was formed in 1934 with the merger of three airlines with Boeing. It has had periods of growth and difficulty, and in 1994, it reached an agreement where employees took a 55 percent stake in the company in exchange for pay cuts. United entered bankruptcy in 2002 and emerged in 2006 to make the longest airline bankruptcy case in the history of the industry. United's stock is now listed on the Nasdaq Stock Market under the ticker symbol UAUA and began trading on February 2, 2006. UAL had $20.2 billion in revenue in 2008 (Yahoo Finance, 2009).

Boeing

The airline industry is closely aligned with manufacturers of aircraft, and the Boeing Company (2009), which dates back to 1916, sells commercial jetliners and a broad array of other aircraft and aerospace products. Its Commercial Airplanes division produces the 747, 767, 777, and 787 aircraft, along with a 737 next-generation narrow-body model plane. The Boeing forecast is that in the next two decades, air passenger travel will grow at 5.0 percent and cargo at 5.8 percent, led by the fastest-growing economies. This is based on the record of the last 20 years, where air travel grew by 4.8 percent each year, despite major recessions, terrorism, the Asian financial crisis, the SARS outbreak, and two Gulf wars. Boeing had $60.9 billion in revenue in 2008 (Yahoo Finance, 2009). UAL announced a huge jet order in 2009 and asked competing manufacturers Boeing and Airbus to bid on a potential $10 billion order (Carey, 2009).

Allegiant Travel Co.

Allegiant Travel Company is interesting to profile because it bundles leisure travel, charter air, and scheduled services from small cities to destinations in the United States such as Las Vegas, Phoenix, and Ft. Lauderdale. Some experts predict that the direction of the air travel industry will be toward niche markets, such as the ones Allegiant serves, and away from the giant carriers' hub-and-spoke travelers. As of early 2009, Allegiant had 44 aircraft and provided service to 61 cities in 33 states. Allegiant's 2008 revenues were $504 million (Yahoo Finance, 2009). It was profiled in 2009 in the *Wall Street Journal* as the most profitable U.S. airline (Carey, 2009).

INTERCITY RAIL SYSTEMS

Intercity rail systems in the United States are active in freight transport, especially commodities, but the passenger rail system is limited to a few high-density corridors. Given the many forces and changes that transportation systems are experiencing, it seems likely that both freight rail and passenger rail are poised for expansion. The United States is behind on high-speed rail but is developing a national plan for it.

U.S. rail systems date back to the 1830s, when improvements in steam engines enabled new and faster forms of transportation. By 1870, a transcontinental line had been completed, and in 1900, railroad stocks were among the hottest on Wall Street. At that time, trains carried almost all intercity traffic, having taken over from stagecoaches and wagons. During World War I, the government nationalized the rail lines and used them to transport military goods and personnel, causing a decline in passenger traffic. With the postwar increase in automobile traffic, intercity train traffic continued its decline, and by 1929, it had fallen by 18 percent from its peak in 1920 (Boyd and Pritcher, 2007). By 1970, airlines were carrying 73 percent of intercity passenger travel, and the railroad share had dropped to 7.2 percent.

In the United States, use of passenger rail remains at low levels, but freight rail, which hauls more on the basis of bulk than it does in value, has been profitable for some companies. Europe's freight rail can haul a much greater percentage of all freight than in the United States. Because freight rail is important to the economy, problems with it can cause costly disruptions, which occurred after the post–dot-com recovery, when rail lines had cut staff too far. To avoid a repetition of those problems, rail lines are planning for a smoother post–financial crisis recovery by using mechanisms to make sure that employees can return to work quickly. In a sense, this is a contingency planning process applied to the recession.

Union Pacific Corporation kept one-third of its 5,000 furloughed employees (of 50,000 total employees) on a retainer with full benefits and partial pay, at a cost of $50 million per year. In 2004, it experienced 10 to 12 percent increases in volume within six months when the post–dot-com recovery started. It is believed that increased freight rail volumes presage a recovery because companies start ordering ahead of anticipated needs. This rapid change in business volume is an important parameter of the freight rail business, which must absorb shocks and not be paralyzed by unexpected events. In addition to the 2004 problems, Union Pacific had problems in 1997 and 1998 on the West Coast after its merger with Southern Pacific Rail Corporation.

The other main freight rail companies are taking different approaches to contingency planning. For example, Norfolk Southern has furloughed fewer of its 31,500 employees. Burlington Northern, with 41,000 employees, has furloughed some 7 percent, and CSX, with 37,400 employees, has furloughed 6 percent (Roth, 2009a).

President Obama announced a strategic rail plan in April 2009. The plan is to select from competitive state proposals to invest $8 billion from the stimulus package in high-speed rail, along with an additional $1 billion per year for five years. The vision was to emulate the Interstate Highway System and U.S. aviation system to inject federal leadership and stimulate public-private partnerships (U.S. Federal Rail Administration, 2009).

Potential rail projects are being considered in a number of states. For example, groups in Colorado are considering options to use rail to solve transportation problems along the Front Range and into the mountains. They are considering technologies ranging from conventional diesel to ultra-high-speed maglev and are evaluating ridership, revenue, capital cost, operating cost, and technical feasibility. One estimate is that $11.5 billion would be required to build rail lines in the corridors along the Front Range and from Denver into the mountains. Planning by the Rocky Mountain Rail Authority has been fueled by a $1.25 million grant from the state transportation department and involves 50 cities, counties, and other groups in the corridors (Leib, 2008).

Short-haul rail companies are also considering expansion. These are represented by the American Shortline and Regional Railroad Associations. Pennsylvania is the state with the most short haul lines, some 55 of them. The most commonly shipped commodity is coal, at 20 percent. The total 2004 revenue of this industry was about $3 billion, and it employed 12,463 people in 2006 (Matthews, 2007).

Today, trucks and rail each carry about 40 percent of domestic U.S. freight as measured in ton-miles, but when value is considered, rail drops to 3.7 percent and the truck share rises to 74 percent, because most rail traffic is in lower value commodities (U.S. Bureau of Transportation Statistics, 2009a).

In densely populated countries, passenger rail remains essential. The U.S. passenger rail system is used much less than those in Europe and Japan. In Europe, the Eurotunnel has connected England to the continent via rail. Developing countries see rail as a strategic investment option.

Internationally, fast-developing countries such as China are considering rail options. China's rail sector is very active and has opened several new lines, including a long-distance train that passes over 16,000-foot elevations on its way to Tibet. China plans to spend $730 billion on rail through 2020 to add 25,000 miles to its rail network. Part of the plan is in China's stimulus package, and new rail lines will link major cities and transport coal from producer regions (Digital Wire, 2008).

Amtrak

The federal government could see that new policies were needed if passenger rail was to survive, and it created the National Railroad Passenger Corporation (Amtrak) in 1971 to provide a balance in travel options and to reduce automobile congestion. In fact, no country now operates a passenger rail system without government support, even in Europe and Japan.

Amtrak's preferred stock is owned by the federal government, which appoints and confirms its board members. Common stock was issued in 1971 to railroads that contributed capital and equipment. FY 2007 revenue was $2.15 billion and expenses were $3.18 billion. To meet these losses, Amtrak gets annual subsidies from the federal government. Fourteen states pay Amtrak for extending routes or increasing frequencies of service, and transit agencies in seven states assist them by paying for use of track for their commuter trains (Amtrak, 2008).

Amtrak employs about 19,000 people, has passenger service on 21,000 miles of track (mainly owned by freight railroads), and serves 500 destinations in 46 states. Its Northeast Corridor is the busiest with more than 2,600 trains operating over some portion of the Washington-Boston route each day. In FY 2008, it served 28.7 million passengers, a fifth straight year of increases. When you compare this statistic to airline boardings of about 750 million in the same year, you see that Amtrak passengers are only about 4 percent of airline traffic. However, if you add in intercity commuter rail, the percentage increases.

Commuter Rail: Canadian National Railway

As an example of commuter rail, in 2008 Canadian National Railway (CNR) was seeking to buy a suburban Chicago rail line owned by Elgin, Joliet & Eastern, which is owned by U.S. Steel Corporation. This line would enable CNR to bypass congested Chicago rail facilities. There was big opposition from people who thought this would mean a lot more rail traffic through their areas. CNR would spend $300 million to buy it, $100 million on upgrades, and $60 million on noise and traffic mitigation (Roth, 2008).

Conrail, CSX, Norfolk Southern Corporation

To stabilize freight rail, Congress created the Consolidated Rail Corporation (Conrail), which began operations in 1976. Later, it was freed from operating commuter rail services. By 1981, Conrail no longer required federal subsidies. In 1987, the federal government sold its interest in Conrail in the largest initial public stock offering in history to that time. This returned the system to the private sector as a for-profit corporation (Conrail, 2009). Conrail is owned by CSX Corporation and Norfolk Southern Corporation. In 2008, revenues were $11.3 billion for CSX and $10.7 billion for Norfolk Southern (Yahoo Finance, 2009).

Burlington Northern Santa Fe Corporation

Burlington Northern Santa Fe Corporation is a large freight rail company, with 2008 revenues of $18 billion. The company today is a merger of some 390 different railroads over 150 years. These feature names such as the Chicago, Burlington & Quincy Railroad, the Northern Pacific Railway, and the Santa Fe. As of December 31, 2008, it operated a system with approximately 32,000 route miles in 28 states and 2 Canadian provinces (Yahoo Finance, 2009).

Equipment Manufacturers

European rail car manufacturers see the U.S. market as ripe for development. With $13 billion in stimulus funding to upgrade intercity rail, manufacturers such as Patentes Talgo SA (Spain) and Siemens AG (Germany) have a shot at supplying the market. Competitors include companies such as Canada's Bombardier, Inc. Also, contractors such as Actividades y Servicios de Construcción SA are interested in building the lines. Even state-owned companies, such as Spain's Renfe and France's Société Nationale des Chemins de Fer, are interested in operating contracts (Catan and Gautheier-Villars, 2009).

INTERCITY BUS TRANSPORTATION

In the early decades of the twentieth century, scheduled bus service was a major mode for intercity travel. Movies from the 1930s through the 1960s show many dramatic scenes that take place in bus stations or on buses. In 1961, the Freedom Riders used bus travel to highlight the segregated travel facilities that remained in the nation.

Today, some 3,500 motorcoach businesses in the United States and Canada offer scheduled intercity bus service. These include large players, such as Greyhound Lines, and many smaller bus lines. The level of service is much smaller today than in the past because buses have lost passengers to airlines and automobiles (American Bus Association, 2009).

Greyhound Lines is the largest intercity bus company in North America, serving 2,200 destinations in the United States. Founded in 1914, it began making transcontinental trips by 1926. The company suffered in the Great Depression, but it recovered and by World War II, it had 4,750 stations and nearly 10,000 employees. After the war and completion of the Interstate Highway System, ridership on Greyhound and the parallel system of Trailways Bus Company declined (Greyhound Lines, 2009).

Continued competition from airlines has caused further consolidation in long-distance intercity bus transportation. Large passenger buses continue to meet important needs in the overall mix of transportation, but scheduled service has been hard to sustain on a large-scale basis. Given the ongoing dispersal of population in suburbs and rural areas, there will be many opportunities for new intercity service on a microscale, however.

During the financial crisis, it was apparent that bus travel was increasing, even while demand for air travel and passenger rail decreased. Lower fares on buses are attractive, and now some are providing wireless Internet connections and power outlets in each row. Greyhound Lines is improving its buses, and Megabus, a unit of Stagecoach Group PLC, has been expanding and adding capacity to its systems (Chaker, 2009).

WATER-BASED TRANSPORTATION

The water transportation system comprises ocean shipping, ports and harbors, the Intracoastal Waterway, and navigation along river systems. Increasing international trade requires ports and harbors as intermodal nodes where goods can pass to rail or truck systems. Ports are important for military and economic reasons, and cities compete for traffic. Ports require infrastructure for berthing of ships, loading and unloading, and transportation of goods inland. Rail networks leading into ports handle substantial traffic and create the need for smooth intermodal handling systems. Most of the infrastructure management work at ports is done through public management agencies, such as port authorities.

The Atlantic and Pacific ports handle mostly container freight, while gulf coast ports handle mostly tanker and dry bulk freight. In 2000, the busiest port was at Los Angeles/Long Beach, California. In 2000, it handled 5,326 vessel calls for tanker, dry bulk, and cargo freight shipments. In terms of vessel calls, the next nine U.S. ports were Houston, New Orleans, New York, San Francisco, Philadelphia, Hampton Roads, Charleston, Columbia River, and Savannah (U.S. Bureau of Transportation Statistics, 2009b).

Dubai World

Security at ports has become a much greater issue than in the past. Terrorists might try to slip a weapon of mass destruction past a port in a container, and some shipments are attractive targets for terrorist attacks. Sensitivity about port operation was shown in a proposal by DP World, a subsidiary of Dubai World, to take over operation of several U.S. ports. In 2006, DP World purchased the Peninsular and Oriental Steam Navigation Company, which operated major U.S. ports in New York, Philadelphia, and several other cities. This raised concerns because the 9/11 attackers included nationals from the United Arab Emirates, and al Qaeda had funneled money through that country. After a long controversy, Dubai Ports World sold P&O's American operations to the Global Investment Group of AIG (Weisman and Graham, 2006).

PIPELINES

Pipeline transportation is also one of the freight categories maintained by the U.S. Bureau of Transportation Statistics, which catalogs trucking, railroad freight, inland waterways, and air freight. Pipeline transportation is mainly for petroleum, petroleum products, and natural gas. Their industries are discussed in Chapter 6, which is about the energy sector.

Pipeline statistics for oil and natural gas are maintained by the Office of Pipeline Safety of the U.S. Department of Transportation. On a local basis, industrial pipelines also carry chemical products, water, steam, slurries, and other liquids and gases used in manufacturing.

SECTOR ISSUES AND OUTLOOK

Transportation Infrastructure and Services Are Distinct

Analyzing the transportation sector requires us to view infrastructure and services apart from each other. This enables us to understand what the Dow Jones Transportation Average does measure (services) and does not measure (infrastructure investments) and to gain insight into the public-private nature of the sector. It can also help inform the public debate about how much tax revenue to invest in the roads system.

Transportation Is the Backbone of the Economy

The transportation sector is the backbone of the economy because it handles freight and passenger travel and is the basis for the modern just-in-time manufacturing system as well as the logistics-based

Internet economy. It undergoes continuing change in response to technological, social, and economic forces.

Transportation Is the Largest Infrastructure Sector

Whether measured by investment and expenditures, modes, or organizations, transportation is the largest infrastructure sector. It spans a broad range of industries that provide systems and equipment to keep it running. It is too complex to be used in its entirety for industrial policy, but some aspects—such as homeland security and sustaining the automobile industry—are being used as policy tools.

Maintaining Roads and Bridges Is a Major National Challenge

The sheer magnitude of the cost to maintain 4 million miles of roads and 600,000 bridges is a formidable national policy challenge. Funds are required to maintain, operate, renew, and expand the system while adapting new smart technologies. Think of the 47,000 mile Interstate Highway System and imagine the flows of people and goods it handles daily. The cost of the U.S. system seems to be much greater on a per capita basis than the cost of the roads and bridges of other nations.

Transit Can Shape Cities While Responding to Social Needs

Transit offers opportunities to continue to shape cities to efficient and sustainable forms while responding to social needs. Automation, bus, rapid transit, and light rail can help overcome problems of high labor and energy costs. Still, paying for transit and balancing the need for subsidies with social needs in cities remains a challenge. Americans are moving to the suburbs, exurban areas, and increasing their needs for commuter services and other travel that falls outside of corridors. An aging population requires many forms of informal and paratransit to handle social requirements that range from shopping to medical visits.

Air Transportation System Is Critical and Challenging

Aviation remains a system under stress with its increasing air traffic and security concerns. Airline companies have struggled with high fuel and labor costs, and paying for airport operation, maintenance, and expansion places burdens on local governments. New nimble forms of airline route selection may alter flight schedules, but it seems certain that rising demand for travel will keep the system under stress.

Intercity Rail Systems Are an Important Backbone and Will See Surprising Change

Rail systems are due for emphasis to adapt fuel-efficient transport to today's needs and pressures and to introduce new technologies and superfast trains to help rail become more competitive with air travel. Paying for commuter rail remains a large issue, although as new systems are built and payloads increase along crowded corridors, this problem may become more manageable.

Intercity Bus Transportation Has Many Facets

While the bygone era of the Greyhound or Trailways bus linking America's cities is gone, intercity buses will have many roles in the decades to come. Probably their biggest advantage over fixed route and scheduled rail and air systems is flexibility and ability to adapt to changed demands and surprises.

Smart Transportation Systems Will Continue to Evolve and Drive Innovation

While all infrastructures are adapting smart management systems, transportation, with its massive infrastructures and demands, is the focal point for implementation of information-based solutions to overcome capacity bottlenecks and improve efficiency.

Smart Roads Are a Trend to Watch

Application of information technology to automate transportation has been increasing steadily for many years. Now, with more fiber and wireless systems in place and with better control systems for signage, traffic metering and monitoring, and other transportation engineering purposes, it seems certain that smart roads will be a growing business category for years to come. The same increases will be seen in other infrastructure categories for smart grids, control systems for water supplies, and security monitoring of buried assets, among others.

Energy and Environmental Policies Will Impact Transportation Policy

Overreliance on vulnerable petroleum supplies and the need to re-spond to environmental pressures such as air quality and greenhouse gases will drive much of the agenda for transportation, as they will the energy sector. The geopolitical implications of continued re-liance on foreign oil are clear, and transportation uses so much energy that it is implicated in global warming as well as air quality issues, such as carbon monoxide and ozone.

Information Technology Offers Many Solutions for Transportation

Computers and information technology–based control systems have already infiltrated all sectors of transportation, everywhere from computers replacing electric systems in automobiles to the emer-gence of smart highways. These trends are certain to continue as vehicles and infrastructures get smarter and more reliant on infor-mation technology.

Innovative Finance Is a Transportation Management Tool

Traditional sources of funding are not adequate to finance a twentieth-century transportation system, and the twenty-first-century system will be not only smarter but financed in different ways. In 2009, the Obama administration predicted that the Highway Trust Fund would be $17 billion short over two years due to the recession and losses in gas tax revenues. Innovative transportation finance solutions are needed to bridge the gaps. The American Association of State Highway & Transportation Officials (2009) sponsors a site to exchange ideas about innovative finance. Examples include to convert roads to toll roads, privatize, and use pricing to manage demand. Other mechanisms include state infrastructure banks and grant anticipation revenue vehicles under the Transportation Infrastructure Finance and Innovation Act, which was passed to enable transportation agencies to borrow ahead of their needs to initiate construction.

Public-Private Partnerships Are Needed More than Ever

The number and variety of public-private partnerships have increased in response to funding difficulties with purely government highway operations. Examples include privately financed high-occupancy toll lanes and other public-private partnerships (Reason Foundation, 2009). These focus on toll roads such as Dulles Greenway (VA); 91 Express Lanes (CA); South Bay Expressway (CA); Chicago Skyway; Indiana Toll Road; SH 130 (TX); Northwest Parkway (CO); Pocahontas Parkway (VA); and Capitol Beltway (VA). Florida, Texas, and Virginia are active in road privatization programs. One disincentive is that private equity is the last to be paid after all other costs are deducted from gross revenues. Other costs include operations and maintenance, senior debt service, debt service reserves, subordinated debt service, major maintenance reserve, and equity distributions (see Conkey, 2009b).

Trade-offs Are Integral to Planning the Future of Transportation

Trade-offs between modes, between public and private systems, between times of travel, and many other areas in which choice can be linked to payment for transportation will influence the future of systems. A saying about transportation planning is that when you plan a road conventionally, you have a self-fulfilling prophecy because the traffic will appear. Avoiding this fallacy requires us to look realistically at trade-offs.

Workable Political Solutions Are Required to Advance Transportation

Above all, achieving a successful future for transportation requires the nation to find workable political solutions so it can overcome the barriers to improvement. Unless solutions can be found, the negative impacts of traffic congestion and failing infrastructures will keep getting worse, and everyone will lose. These solutions are intergovernmental and regional, and require planning and cooperation that go beyond single-issue and divisive politics. The more the market can be used, the less chance for political gridlock to impede progress.

The Future of Transportation

The future of transportation is exciting to imagine if society can overcome the barriers to system improvement. While indicators of strain include traffic congestion, high infrastructure cost, energy consumption, environmental impacts, and security concerns, the opportunity to use new technologies and methods to create better cities and social systems is a riveting one. The future may see corridors carrying rail, transit, Internet, and other networks. The theme "reinventing the highway" was selected by *Time* magazine selection of as one of 10 ideas changing the world now (Lacayo, 2009). The vehicles on future highways may be much different from those of today. The automobile industry is undergoing rapid change as it struggles to adapt to global overcapacity, overreliance on vulnerable petroleum supplies, and environmental pressures, such as air quality and greenhouse gases. New sources of energy and vehicle designs (such as hydrogen and hybrid vehicles), use of information technology, and emphasis on bike and pedestrian transportation are promising trends. More important than technologies are management systems and organization to overcome political barriers, develop financing methods, embrace new public-private roles, regulate effectively, and build a new social contract for transportation.

CHAPTER 5

Telecommunications Sector

Telecommunications (telecom) infrastructure is different from the other networks because it involves more private ownership and changes more rapidly than the other sectors. With deregulation and new technologies, telecom also presents consumers with more choices. Whereas 50 years ago, telecom was a stable monopoly business, after its deregulation in the 1980s, it changed dramatically and became much more diverse in structure. In the past, telecom and electric power were identified as the main public utilities, but now that has changed. Although both sectors are still subject to regulation, they have experienced a lot of unbundling and deregulation, especially telecom.

Although the telecommunications business is much different from other infrastructure-related businesses, it offers valuable lessons for the other services, particularly about deregulation and unbundling of business processes and about implementation of new technologies. This chapter summarizes the organization of the telecommunications sector and presents a brief overview of its major corporations, with emphasis on those that grew from the seeds planted in the 1980s breakup of the AT&T monopoly. Details of the telecommunication business go well beyond the scope of the book, which focuses on its infrastructure issues.

WHY TELECOMMUNICATIONS IS AN INFRASTRUCTURE SECTOR

Telecom resembles other networked infrastructures because it is a critical support system for the built environment, it requires physical systems that are sometimes colocated with other public facilities, and it is subject to regulation. Other than these attributes, it resembles other consumer services with its constant introduction of trendy new products and close connections with the media and entertainment businesses.

In many ways, these dual aspects of telecom—similar to a networked utility but linked to the media and entertainment industries—define it in its twenty-first-century form. In fact, the infrastructure-related sector of telecom is often bundled with the media sector in economic reports because of the way they go hand in hand. For example, in the U.S. system of economic statistics, telecom is lumped in a category labeled "Information," which contains as major groups publishing, motion pictures and sound recording, broadcasting, telecommunications, data services, and other information services, such as libraries. These statistics are contained in the North American Industry Classification System (NAICS), which covers all U.S. industries. This bundling of telecommunications carriers with businesses involved in the transport and delivery of information underscores how different today's telecom is from the monopoly phone companies of the past.

The telecommunications infrastructure is the pathway for the flow of information, so it is analogous to transportation, which is the pathway for flow of people and goods. Therefore, there is a trade-off between flow of people and information, such as through telecommuting. Also, in the emerging logistics economy, the flow of goods and even commodities is controlled by flow of information. A few examples of instances within the infrastructure sector in which transportation of people and goods can be traded off with transportation of information include telecommuting, teleconferencing, smart electric grids, and wheeling "paper" water from one place to another by exchanging information about its availability at points of demand.

Telecommunications systems have many interfaces with other infrastructures. Wires and cables are buried in the public rights-of-way. Energy and water utilities use dedicated communication systems to operate their far-flung facilities. The built environment is increasingly wired for Internet access. Telecom has public purposes that mimic other infrastructure categories and has been identified as a critical national infrastructure by the Department of Homeland Security. Emergency services are highly dependent on telecommunications infrastructure.

Notwithstanding these interfaces between infrastructures, telecommunications has become very different from a public utility, and it has little direct support from government, compared to other infrastructure categories. Local governments are at least partially involved in all other categories of public infrastructure, but they are not involved much in provision of telecommunications infrastructure. They might be involved in regulating cable television, but with the availability of satellite services, even that role has diminished. Although fiber cables might be buried in public rights-of-way beside water and electric lines, the business of telecommunications runs outside of the other infrastructure categories.

THEN AND NOW

Telecommunications technologies have evolved along a number of paths, but a series of key events shows the timeline: inventions of telegraph and telephone, installation of submarine cables, invention of wireless communication, breakup of the AT&T or Bell System, development of fiber optics, and development of the Internet. These events did not happen at just one time. A series of approximate dates for them is shown in Exhibit 5.1 to illustrate how the technologies and methods evolved.

The telegraph became commercially viable after the 1830s, followed by the telephone at the end of the nineteenth century. Transoceanic submarine cables had been laid after about 1870, and commercial wireless telecommunications began by the 1920s. These infrastructure-related developments were part of the continuing technological revolution we have experienced.

Many developments occurred between introduction of wireless and today's technologies, especially during World War II. Later, fiber optics evolved and became feasible for commercial telecommunications during the 1970s. The Bell System had a long-standing monopoly until its breakup in 1982. Then, during the 1980s, the Internet began to dominate telecommunications in an increasingly wired world. Since the development of the Internet, fiber optic cables, and wireless systems, telecom has exploded with new products and services for cell phone service, entertainment, and diverse business services.

Early telephone service comprised a monopoly that provided a phone, a wire, a switchboard, and land-line connections to other people with phone service. You had local service, and expensive long-distance service was available. The Bell System monopoly did research, built systems, sold equipment, and provided the full range of service at regulated prices. Once the Bell System was broken apart, telecommunications became more competitive with mobile phones, wireless services, and even cable television.

Although telecom services remain regulated, the rules adapt to new technologies and business systems. The telecommunications industry now involves much more than land-line telephones.

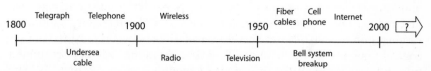

EXHIBIT 5.1   Timeline of Key Telecommunications Developments

SECTOR STRUCTURE AND SIZE

Telecom is a giant industry and seems poised to continue its rapid growth. Globally, the industry was about $1.7 trillion in 2008, and the U.S. share was a big percentage of this (Insight Research Corporation, 2009). Therefore, depending on what is included in it, the U.S. telecom industry is probably larger than electric power and natural gas combined.

While the physical characteristics of the telecommunications industry have similarities to those of other networked infrastructure industries, the business operations of telecommunications are much different, and the sector requires a different policy approach from government than other public infrastructure systems.

In the United States, the industry structure of telecommunications was shaped by the 1980s breakup of AT&T and by the following advancements in communication technologies. The 1980s breakup of AT&T was one of the most important business developments of the twentieth century. The breakup was inevitable because technologies and business organization had made the old model of a regulated monopoly obsolete. Things were simply moving too fast. The government-forced breakup occurred as a result of a Department of Justice lawsuit filed in 1974 and settled in 1982 with a consent order in the Federal District Court of the District of Columbia. The presiding judge was Harold H. Greene, who became famous for his role in overseeing the divesture process.

After the 1982 settlement, AT&T agreed to spin off its local phone companies into seven Baby Bells, which is the popular name given to the regional phone companies. Long-distance service was unbundled and partially deregulated. Since the breakup, there have been a number of divestures and acquisitions in the local service and long-distance markets. Now cell phone and wireless services are ascendant. Internet usage has increased greatly. Use of wired land lines for telecommunications has fallen.

The subsectors within the NAICS category 51 that relate most to infrastructure are wired telecommunications carriers, cellular telephone telecommunications carriers, and Internet service providers using their own wired infrastructure. Other aspects of the telecom business are spread across several NAICS categories.

Regulation in the telecommunications industry is by the Federal Communication Commission (FCC) and state public utility commissions. The first federal law placed regulatory authority in the Interstate Commerce Commission in 1910. States and cities had already begun local franchising control rates and service quality. Congress created the Federal Communications Commission in 1934 through the Communications Act of 1934. This locked in AT&T's monopoly until the 1970s Justice Department antitrust lawsuit, which was based on complaints by long-distance service providers.

The 1982 settlement created a need to develop new regulatory mechanisms, and the Telecommunications Act of 1996 ended the monopoly franchise system of local calling. After 1996, the FCC began to prepare new regulations to govern access to telecom infrastructure systems, but a series of challenges led to court cases and disagreements about the role of the FCC itself (Katz and Bolema, 2003).

Several bureaus of the U.S. Federal Communications Commission. (2009) regulate telecom. One regulates wireless and oversees cell phones, pagers, and use of the radio spectrum. Another bureau regulates wired telecommunications of interstate telephone companies and in some cases intrastate services. The Public Safety & Homeland Security Bureau addresses various security, emergency preparedness, and disaster management issues.

The structure of the telecommunications sector is shown by Exhibit 5.2, which illustrates the infrastructures used by wired and wireless service

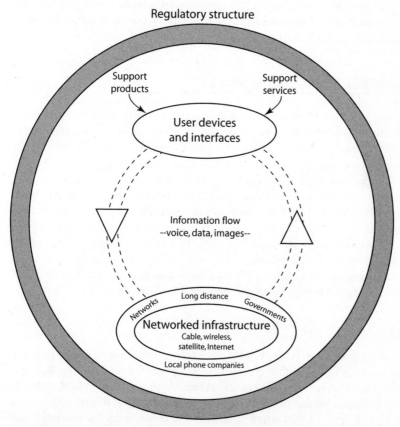

EXHIBIT 5.2   Telecom Infrastructure and Information Flow

providers. Some services, such as Voice over Internet Protocol (VoIP), require service providers to use infrastructure owned by others. In other cases, it is logical for service providers to contract with infrastructure owners to carry information. Regulation is exercised, but the telecom industry operates much more as a nonmonopoly business than other categories of infrastructure, and there is little direct government support to the industry.

INTERNET

The Internet is the core infrastructure for the cybereconomy. Its original backbone was a network known as the ARPANET, which was sponsored by the Department of Defense. This was taken over by the National Science Foundation in 1989 and run as NSFNet until 1995. Now the Internet is a private network of cabled systems owned by private providers, such as Level 3 Communications and AT&T, among others. In effect, the Internet comprises millions of networks that are linked by copper wires, fiber optic cables, wireless connections, and other means.

TELECOMMUNICATION COMPANIES

Investment outlooks in the telecommunications industry have changed along with technologies and business systems. At one time, many people owned "telephone" stock—meaning AT&T—and expected steady dividends; the investment environment has changed drastically since then.

After the Bell System breakup, the Baby Bells were organized to form Ameritech, Bell Atlantic, BellSouth, NYNEX, Pacific Telesis, Southwestern Bell, and U S West. In 1995, Southwestern Bell changed its name to SBC Corporation. It acquired AT&T in 2005 and took that name for the entire company. Subsequently, it acquired Pacific Telesis, Ameritech, and BellSouth as well as some smaller operating companies and now has the stock symbol "T." Bell Atlantic acquired NYNEX in 1996 and became Verizon in 2000, after acquiring GTE. U S West was acquired by Qwest in 2000.

Qwest

Qwest is an integrated telecommunications company that has at its core the former Baby Bell U S West. It currently offers phone, cell phone, VoIP, Internet/DSL, and DirectTV service in 14 states. After recovering from accounting and insider-trading problems a few years back, Qwest had revenues of $13.5 billion and 33,000 employees in 2008, when it had a market value of about $6.5 billion, about $14 billion in debt, and $575 million in cash (Yahoo Finance, 2009). Qwest has a nationwide fiber optic network that carries long distance, Internet, and data communications. The network was rumored to be for sale in 2009, potentially to competitors such as AT&T, Verizon, Level 3 Communications, Inc., or TW Telecom, Inc. This would strip the company of its long-haul capability and leave local service in place, thus restoring the semblance of the former Baby Bell. Another rumored option was to use Qwest to acquire other local service companies. These possible moves foreshadow continued change and competition in the telecom business (Raabe, 2009; Sharma and Cimilluca, 2009).

AT&T

Today's AT&T Inc. is a communications holding company with subsidiaries that offer wireless and long-distance services, including calling card, 800 numbers, conference calls, caller identification, call waiting, and voice mail services. It also provides data services, such as transport, Internet access, and various network services. It provides a range of telecommunications-related services, such as directory and operator assistance and satellite video services. It publishes yellow and white page directories, sells advertising, and offers related business services for retail, financial services, manufacturing, healthcare, and telecom companies. It evolved from the former SBC Communications Inc., which changed its name to AT&T Inc. in 2005 as a result of merger with the AT&T Corporation, which was founded in 1983. This enabled the new company to reclaim both the corporate name and the stock symbol "T." AT&T had $124 billion in revenue in 2008 (Yahoo Finance, 2009). With such a large revenue base, AT&T is having trouble growing its revenue. It is looking for growth through a business model that emphasizes mobile broadband, which enables users to connect devices to the Internet. One such device might be a smart parking meter, which would join other devices such as digital cameras and other consumer devices in using the Internet to share information. Such mobile broadband computing might have other infrastructure applications, such as meter reading.

Level 3 Communications, Inc.

Level 3 Communications, Inc. (2009) provides network and Internet services. It was founded in 1985 as a subsidiary of Peter Kiewit Sons, Inc., a construction company in Omaha, Nebraska. It began trading on the Nasdaq in 1998. Products and services include content delivery, media delivery, fiber optic use, and satellite video transport services. It offers VoIP services and various protocols to facilitate network-to-network communications. During

1998, the company raised $14 billion, and by the end of 2000, it provided service to 2,700 customers. It made several acquisitions and is currently one of only six Tier 1 Internet providers in the world, meaning that it offers access to the Internet without paying others for transit. It is a highly connected Internet Service Provider and is a major player in the Internet Protocol (IP) transit business (providing access to others) in North America and Europe. At the end of 2008, its networks included some 67,000 route miles in North America and 10,000 miles in Europe. It also is engaged in sales of coal. Level 3 had $4.3 billion in revenue in 2008 (Yahoo Finance, 2009).

SECTOR ISSUES AND OUTLOOK

It is evident that new technologies drive telecom more than they do the other networked infrastructures and produce ongoing rapid change in a sector that is the backbone of the information economy. Whereas it might seem that wireless communications are bringing the days of the land line to an end, other aspects of telecom—such as government and utility communications—still require dedicated infrastructures. In fact, automatic infrastructure controls and data collection devices are making other infrastructures more and more dependent on telecom. Telecom is characterized by dualities, such as wired and wireless, government and business, local and global scales, and these will assure that the industry continues to grow larger, more complex, and more difficult to regulate.

Telecom Is a Different Infrastructure

Although telecommunications is an infrastructure sector, it has important differences from the other networked systems. It is a critical support system for the built environment, it requires physical systems that sometimes are colocated with other public facilities, and it is subject to regulation. Notwithstanding these interfaces between infrastructures, telecommunications has become very different from a public utility, and it has little direct support from government compared to other infrastructure categories. Due to its rapid change, investments in telecommunications are not like those in other infrastructure categories. For example, in the dot-com crash of 2000, communication stocks fell more than those in other infrastructure categories.

Telecom Is the Backbone for the Information Economy

Telecommunications infrastructure provides the pathway for information flow, so it is analogous to transportation, which is the pathway for flow of people and goods. There are, in fact, trade-offs among flow of information, people, and goods. Perhaps the most important attribute of telecom as an infrastructure is its possibilities to transform other infrastructures through use of these smart technologies and trade-offs between movement of people and goods with movement of information. These technological frontiers open exciting possibilities for the future of telecom infrastructure and service organizations.

Telecom Is a Giant Industry

Globally, the telecom industry was about $1.7 trillion in 2008, and the U.S. share was a big percentage of this (Insight Research Corporation, 2009). Telecom has global implications and is linked tightly to the global economy. Although it changes rapidly, its trends indicate an industry that continues to expand in coverage and become more competitive. Depending on what is included in it, the U.S. telecom industry is probably larger than electric power and natural gas combined. Telecom seems poised to continue its rapid growth and will continue to develop new services as companies discover how people use information in different ways.

Telecom Is Technology Driven and a Test Bed for Innovation

The finances of the telecom industry resemble those of other tech sectors more than the infrastructure does. Tech sectors include electronics, optics, computers, and biotechnology, among others. Telecom uses technologies from several of these sectors, and changes its forms as it does so. For example, when there was an apparent need to have more fiber cable for the upcoming Internet boom, telecom companies invested in many new buried cable networks, only to learn that an overcapacity existed. Then, with exploding content such as movies on demand, all of a sudden more capacity was needed. These demand-push and supply-pull aspects of telecom seem destined to continue, along with the movement toward more smart devices and social networking in society. Internet usage is still increasing rapidly, and use of wired land lines for telecommunications is still falling.

Telecom Is Sorting Out Relationships among Carriers and Devices

How telecom is linked to other tech industries is illustrated by the ongoing change in the relationships between carriers, such as fiber cable, and devices, such as hand-held computers or personal computers. Telecom company carriers must find ways to capture use of devices so as to ensure subscriptions to their services. These subscription services are in ways a replacement strategy for the lost monopoly franchise that ensured a return on investment and continued business expansion with population growth. If carriers make infrastructure investments but lose business to competitors that cherry-pick the best customers, the prospects for growth are bleak. However, if they can capture customers through contracts, then they are assured of continued business. This need to capture customers is being played out with the current near-saturation of cell phones (at about 90%) and the emergence of netbooks, which are smaller laptops that promise to be a new way to surf the web, engage in social networking, and increase use of communication channels (Einhorn, 2009).

Telecom Regulation Undergoes Continuous Change

Whereas telecom was dominated for many years by the Bell Telephone monopoly, it has moved into a new era with much more diverse and competitive private sector services. Compared to the other infrastructure sectors, telecommunications is dominated much more by the private sector. It is subject to government regulation, but government does not invest much in telecommunications compared to other infrastructure categories, such as roads or water systems. Telecommunications is, however, designated as a critical infrastructure, and parts of it include networked infrastructure with buried lines, similar to water, electricity, wastewater, and natural gas. Given its uniqueness, the financial structure and flows of the telecommunications sector will remain different from those of other infrastructure sectors. Except for regulation, government agencies will be involved much less in telecommunications than they are in other infrastructure sectors. Still, telecommunications has many similarities to and cross-connections with other infrastructure sectors, such as electric power and water systems, and there is much to learn from studying it.

Telecom Infrastructure Is Shared, and Market-Driven Cooperation Is Required

Many players must share the infrastructures used by wired and wireless service providers. Some services require providers to use infrastructure that is owned by others. Innovation in contracting and regulation is required, and it can offer lessons for unbundling of other infrastructures, especially electric power.

Telecom Has Many Interfaces and Interdependences with Other Infrastructures

Telecommunications systems have many interfaces with other infrastructures. Wires and cables are buried in public rights-of-way. Energy and water utilities use dedicated communication systems to operate their far-flung facilities. The built environment is increasingly wired for Internet access. Telecom has public purposes that mimic other infrastructure categories and has been identified as a critical national infrastructure by the Department of Homeland Security. Emergency services are highly dependent on telecommunications infrastructure.

Telecom Involves Many Security Issues

Because communications are so vital, the vulnerability of the telecom sector takes on special importance. Whereas the energy sector is critical to life support and functioning of the economy, telecom keeps the information flow going. Security concerns begin with low-level activities, such as e-mail spam, and extend to global concerns, such as the effect an atmospheric electromagnetic pulse would have in knocking out the whole national telecom system, a disastrous event.

Telecom Can Transform Other Infrastructures

Perhaps the most important attribute of telecom as an infrastructure is its possibilities to transform other systems through use of smart technologies and trade-offs between movement of people and goods with movement of information. These technological frontiers open exciting possibilities for the future of telecom infrastructure and service organizations.

CHAPTER 6

Energy Sector

The importance of energy to the economy is evident in daily news about oil prices, global warming, and energy-related national security issues. The energy infrastructure supports the energy sector of the economy, which ranges across high-profile issues such as oil and gas supplies, coal mining, and the geopolitics of natural resources as well as the management of electric power and natural gas utilities. Energy is linked tightly to the other infrastructure categories, especially transportation and the heating, cooling, and powering of buildings.

Energy has been designated by the U.S. Department of Homeland Security (2009) as a critical infrastructure system because it provides essential inputs to our economy and social systems and is important to national security. In ways, if energy fails, the rest of the infrastructure systems go down and so do other sectors of the economy. For example, in a power outage, critical systems such as traffic signals and water supplies will fail unless they have backup power.

The focus of the chapter is on the energy utilities that supply electric power and natural gas. These have extensive fixed assets and have similar characteristics to other infrastructure systems. The chapter also addresses how trends in transportation, the built environment, and the petroleum and coal industries affect electric power and natural gas utilities. In that sense, the chapter spans the range of energy issues—from solar-powered homes to nuclear waste—but its focus is on utility issues and management. In the electric power and natural gas industries, the functions of generation, production, transmission, and distribution can involve government utilities and many different types of private companies.

SECTOR STRUCTURE AND SIZE

The structure of the energy sector includes providers, regulators, and support organizations. Providers include basic energy producers such as coal and renewables, along with energy carriers in the form of electric utilities and natural gas transmission companies. Regulators are in the Federal Energy Regulatory Commission, state public utility commissions, and other places, such as the Department of Transportation, which regulates natural gas pipelines.

The sector usually is classified by basic sources, which include petroleum, natural gas, coal, renewables, and nuclear energy. The primary energy industries of petroleum and coal include a number of large and powerful international companies.

Electric power is an energy carrier rather than a basic source because it uses basic sources to generate the energy delivered to end users. In other words, energy is converted from its basic forms, such as coal or natural gas, to electric power, which is transported over wires and then converted again by end use devices into mechanical or heat energy.

Natural gas is a basic source itself and can be used directly at some end points, such as to generate heat energy for cooking or hot water. In other cases, natural gas is converted into mechanical energy by burning and then turning of turbines, as in its use to generate electricity. Natural gas is transported through pipes to points of end use. While the transport infrastructures of electricity and natural gas (wires and pipes) are quite different, they serve similar functions. Natural gas competes with electricity at many points of end use as well as a source to generate electric power.

Petroleum is the main fuel for the transportation sector, and coal is the main fuel for electric power. These sources are implicated in global warming and other environmental issues. The supply of basic energy from petroleum and natural gas involves extensive operations of oil and gas companies that compete on a worldwide playing field. The international linkages of these operations make oil and gas one of nation's most sensitive national security issues. The coal industry is more secure because of extensive domestic supplies, but it creates its own issues of environment, safety, and health. Nuclear power as a basic energy source, mainly to generate electricity, could be poised for a comeback after recovering from decades of neglect that began with the 1979 Three Mile Island nuclear accident in Pennsylvania.

Renewables are the fastest-moving and most attractive sources of basic energy, but they draw in new issues, even opposition to wind power in some areas. Even beyond questions of supply, energy utilities face important issues that affect their financial results. For example, electricity deregulation and aging assets are large concerns, as they are in other infrastructure sectors.

The total energy economy of the United States is a significant fraction of gross domestic product (GDP). For example, crude oil at a use rate of 20 million barrels per day and price of $50 a barrel would total $365 billion per year, even before refining and distribution added to that commodity cost. Moreover, in 2008, oil prices spiked at well above $100 per bbl and daily use can exceed 20,000 bbl/day.

Annual sales of 3,700 billion kilowatts (KWH) electric power (2006 levels) at $0.08 would bring in $293 billion in revenue. Sales of 21.7 trillion cubic feet of natural gas at $10 per 1000 cubic feet (also 2006 levels) would cost $217 billion.

Adding the cost of oil and revenues for electric power and natural gas at these levels would total $875 billion, and could easily top $ one trillion as energy costs rise. In fact, the U.S. Energy Information Administration (USEIA) (2009a) reported total energy costs of $1.1 trillion in 2006, or some 8.6 percent of GDP.

The overall picture is captured in an energy balance diagram showing the sources and users of energy (Exhibit 6.1). The data shown are from 2008.

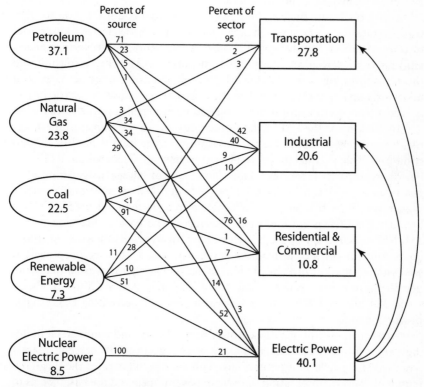

EXHIBIT 6.1 Sources and Uses of Basic Energy
Source: U.S. Energy Information Administration, 2009a

In the energy balance diagram, basic sources are petroleum, natural gas, coal, renewables, and nuclear power. The user sectors are transportation, industry, residential and commercial, and electric power. These aggregations mask many important details of the energy sector, but they do illustrate the overall energy situation.

Using the data shown on Exhibit 6.1, it is evident that electric power uses 40.1 percent of basic energy, transportation uses 27.8 percent, industry uses 20.6 percent, and residential and commercial buildings use 10.8 percent. These numbers vary significantly from year to year with trends in the economy, energy prices, environmental pressures, and other influences.

These numbers illustrate the large consumption of basic energy by electric power generators. However, these generators distribute the electric energy to the other energy-consuming sectors. As an energy carrier, electric power can be reallocated to industry, residential, and commercial uses to show the overall percentages of use by primary source (petroleum, natural gas, coal, renewables, and nuclear).

If you reallocate the electric power to the other end users, you see that transportation use of energy changes little because little electric power goes to transportation, but this could change in the future with plug-in vehicles. Currently, 95 percent of energy for transportation is from petroleum, and the transportation sector uses 27.8 percent of basic energy. However, it takes little imagination to visualize the large change in use of electric power if even a fraction of transportation moved from petroleum to electricity.

By looking at the USEIA data on energy use in the transportation sector, we see that in 2007, the transportation sector used a total of 29,026 trillion British thermal units (BTUs). Of this, 27,729 trillion BTUs, or 95.5 percent, was from petroleum. Total use of energy to generate electric power was 40,567 trillion BTUs, and total U.S. generation of electric power was 4.16 trillions of KWH. Therefore, it required 9,752 BTU to produce 1 KWH, according to these figures. The basic conversion rate is 1 KWH = 3,412 BTU, so the data show an average efficiency of about 35 percent in converting from basic energy sources to electric power. If we assumed that 10 percent of transportation energy use was shifted from petroleum to electric power, then it would require 2,773 trillion BTUs, or some 284 billion KWH. That would add almost 7 percent to U.S. electric power demands.

After reallocation of electric power to residential and commercial buildings, their use of all energy rises from 10.8 percent to 40 percent, mainly from electric power and natural gas. This number illustrates the large potential of energy conservation in reducing overall demand for basic forms of energy and shows why green building has so much potential to lower overall energy demands.

When electric power is added, use of energy by industry rises from 20.6 percent to 31 percent of all energy, drawing from all sources. This number illustrates that a large potential for energy savings also exists through conservation by industry and that the conversion from basic industries to information-based businesses will affect energy use significantly. However, it may simply shift energy problems to nations with larger manufacturing bases, principally China.

Exhibit 6.2 summarizes U.S. energy use in a different way to show how the economy requires 40 percent of its basic energy for residential and commercial buildings, 32 percent for industry, and 28 percent for transportation. Electric power is shown on the diagram as an energy carrier, not a source.

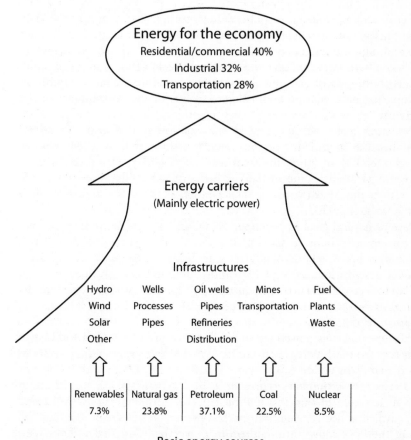

EXHIBIT 6.2   Energy Infrastructure for the Economy

At the bottom of the diagram are shown the five basic sources of energy, with petroleum the largest, followed by natural gas and coal, then nuclear and renewables.

The diagram shows the different infrastructures of the basic sources, ranging from generation facilities, through transmission, processing, and distribution. If use of energy was shown, the number of facilities would increase considerably. When you combine all of the infrastructures shown on the diagram with the facilities of energy utilities, it becomes a gigantic network, as you can see.

ENERGY TRENDS

Energy is a high-profile industry because its stakes and impacts are so high. Trends include flat demand for petroleum and pressures to shift from reliance on it and high interest in efficient and convenient vehicles, such as plug-in electrics, in renewable energy, and in energy conservation and green build-ings. Technologies, costs, and flows of energy sources change rapidly as globalization proceeds and the world grapples with environmental effects of energy use.

Statistics from the U.S. Energy Information Administration (2009a) show that U.S. petroleum use has been flat since at least 2004. For the five years ending in 2008, the total uses in mbbl/day, including liquefied petroleum gas, fuel oil, motor fuel, jet fuel, and other oils were: 20.7, 20.8, 20.7, 20.7, and 19.6 (forecast). The prediction is for 0.4 percent annual growth through 2030.

Use of natural gas has been increasing, and it is currently favored over coal for new electric generation plants. For the four years ending in 2008, total annual use in trillion cubic feet was 22.01, 21.66, 22.90, and 23.12. For perspective, annual use of 25 trillion cubic feet is equivalent to about 230 cubic feet per day for each of our 300 million citizens. The forecast is for an annual increase of 0.2 percent to 2030 (U.S. Energy Information Administration, 2009).

Electric power is poised for higher rates of growth, with a forecast of 1.1 percent annual increases to 2030. For the four years ending in 2008, total demands in billion KWH were: 3,815, 3,814, 3,903, and 3,934. For perspective, these numbers represent a 24/7 average power use of about 1.5 KW for each of our 300 million citizens. Although the overall trend is upward, it is not a given that electric power must increase continually. During the 2008 downturn, a drop in power use surprised utilities with falling revenues (Smith, 2008). The reasons are complex and can be due to economics, weather changes, and other factors.

Wild cards for the future seem to be use of electric power for buildings and computers and the extent that electricity is required for future plug-in vehicles. Although green building is trendy, the existing stock of buildings will be with us for a long time. Many of them are not very amenable to green retrofits, but occupants demand greater comfort. With global warming, there could be an increase in air conditioning, as is evident at my university, where large increases in electric power use are explained mostly by building upgrades rather than by new computing facilities. It may be that power-hungry computer facilities have already been installed and that newer ones, such as hand-held devices, will not place great new demands on the electric grid. Plug-in vehicles will, of course, require large amounts of energy as well as new battery technologies.

Demand for coal is also projected to increase annually at 1.4 percent, although why the projected coal increase is greater than the projected electricity increase is not explained (U.S. Energy Information Administration, 2009).

Coal use for the four years ending in 2008 in million short tons was 1,125, 1,114, 1,127, and 1,126. Finding ways to make coal cleaner is a critical issue for this industry, and it would seem that the proposed carbon caps would suppress increases in use of coal. Currently, we are seeing flat and declining demand, but the forces of change, such as increased demand for electric power and rising standards of living in other nations, might change the picture, even in the short run.

Use of renewables is growing, and their forecasted rate of increase is higher than the other sources, at 2.0 percent through 2030. Uses in billion KWH for the four years ending in 2008 were: 323.2, 350.6, 340.7, and 363.3. Exhibit 6.3 shows the production in KWH and the projected increases by category:

EXHIBIT 6.3 Energy Production and Trends

	2008	Annual Increases to 2030 (%)
Conventional Hydropower	267.99	0.2
Wind	49.91	6.7
Geothermal	16.82	3.1
Biogenic Municipal Waste	14.53	1.6
Wood and Other Biomass	12.84	8.8
Solar Thermal	1.13	6.4
Solar Photovoltaic	0.11	19.6

ELECTRIC POWER INDUSTRY

Among the infrastructure sectors, the electric power industry is the largest utility sector and places giant demands on capital expenditures every year. While not changing as rapidly as telecom, it still is experiencing many forces of change, and it involves many investment opportunities as well as dead ends.

The industry has changed from its 1880s start with Thomas Edison's street lighting business to a giant global industry that affects everyone and has enormous economic and environmental impacts. After Edison's beginning, spinoffs from his company led to large electric power utilities and formation of the General Electric Corporation. By the 1920s, utility barons had created large businesses, and electric power was a focal point in the national struggle against monopolies and abuse of utility businesses. In this period, the nation was learning needed lessons about the need for regulation, both to ensure equity in service and to prevent abuse of monopoly franchises.

During the 1930s, the nation learned new lessons about public power, and the public-private split in the electricity industry is still with us today. During the New Deal, the government organized the Tennessee Valley Authority (TVA) as a centerpiece of Franklin Roosevelt's recovery program. While it has undergone much change, TVA remains in public ownership as one of the nation's largest utility programs.

After 1930, the electric power industry passed through phases of rural electrification, growth, and decline of nuclear power, and increasing demand. During the 1990s, deregulation and unbundling of generation from transmission and distribution infrastructures was promoted. This shook up the industry and created many new players.

Today's electric power industry receives about $300 billion per year in revenues and employs some 400,000 workers (Edison Electric Institute, 2008). It has 203 shareholder-owned utilities, 1,874 municipal government–owned utilities, 133 public power districts, and 870 cooperatives that are subsidized by the Rural Utilities Service of the U.S. Department of Agriculture.

Another 1,688 nonutility generators provide cogeneration, small and independent power production, and merchant production, and these produced 35 percent of all power in 2005. A category of energy service providers includes 143 corporations, generators, brokers, and utility generation subsidiaries that are licensed to sell electricity in the competitive market using transmission and/or distribution facilities of electric distribution companies. Finally, another 31 state projects and 9 federal utilities market power to utilities.

On the basis of customers served, the industry is dominated by the shareholder-owned utilities, which serve 72.2 percent of all customers. Next are the cooperatives, at 12.3 percent, and then municipal systems, at 11.1 percent. Other political subdivisions, energy service providers, state systems, and federal systems serve the rest.

Financial Structure

The financial presence of electric power in the economy is huge. The industry places a large call on capital to expand and maintain their production, transmission, and distribution facilities. It accounts for a large share of new industrial construction, corporate financing, and common stock issuance among industrial companies.

On the basis of energy production and revenues, the industry is dominated by investor-owned utilities, but publicly owned utilities and power marketers have significant shares of production and revenues (see Exhibit 6.4).

The 2007 financials of the investor-owned utilities showed (Edison Electric Institute, 2009):

- Revenue: $406 billion (includes some gas revenue)
- Capital spending: $69 billion
- One-year growth in output: 2.8 percent
- One-year revenue increase: 6.2 percent

Taxes paid by investor-owned utilities amounted to $30 billion in 2006, including $14.8 billion in federal, state, and local income taxes. Most cooperatives are exempt from income taxes but pay other taxes. Government-owned utilities pay in-lieu-of fees instead of taxes. Federal-owned utilities are exempt from all income taxes.

EXHIBIT 6.4 Electric Power Production and Revenues

	Production, MWH, 000s	Percent of Total (%)	Sales, $ millions	Percent of Total (%)
Investor owned	2,265,365	61.9	207,475	63.7
Publicly owned	564,123	15.4	45,506	14.0
Cooperatives	371,278	10.2	31,456	9.7
Power marketers	414,240	11.3	39,701	12.2
Federal power agencies	42,517	1.2	1,500	0.5

Source: American Public Power Association, 2009

Investor-owned electric utilities pay out more in dividends than any other industrial category, usually over 60 percent of earnings. More than 90 percent of electric companies pay dividends. The reduced dividend tax rate that was created by the Jobs and Growth Tax Reconciliation Act of 2003 (currently extended through 2010) attracted more investment to electric utility stocks, raised stock prices, and lowered cost of capital.

Investor-owned utilities are regulated by state public utility commissions, a practice that dates back to the 1920s (Wasik, 2006). Regulation is split between the federal role, centered in the Federal Energy Regulatory Commission, and state regulation through public utility commissions, in which the rate of return is controlled.

The level of capital spending by electric utilities may rise. According to an industry-funded study by the Brattle Group, capital investment for electric utilities will be $1.5 to $2 trillion by 2030 (Smith, 2008).

Investor-Owned Electric Utilities

The investor-owned utilities include a range of utility sizes. Samples from different states and of different sizes are presented next.

Pacific Gas and Electric   Pacific Gas and Electric (2009) serves 5.1 million electric accounts and 4.2 million natural gas accounts or some 15 million people in a 70,000-square-mile service area. The company had 20,000 employees and revenues of $13.2 billion in 2007.

Exelon   Exelon (2009) serves 5.4 million electric customers in Illinois and Pennsylvania and 485,000 gas customers in Philadelphia. It owns Commonwealth Edison, PECO, and power generation and marketing subsidiaries. It had $18.9 billion in revenue in 2007.

Southern Company   Southern Company (2009) operates in four states and serves nearly 4.4 million customers. It had $15.4 billion in revenues in 2007. It owns Alabama Power, Georgia Power, Gulf Power, and Mississippi Power and sells power through its generation business via Southern Power.

Pepco Holdings Inc.   Pepco Holdings (2009) operates in the Mid-Atlantic region, with about 1.9 million customers. Its electric subsidiaries are Pepco, Delmarva Power, and Atlantic City Electric. Delmarva Power also provides natural gas. Pepco sells wholesale power through Conectiv Energy. It had revenue of $10.7 billion in 2007.

Duke Energy   Duke Energy (2009) has about 4 million U.S. customers. It operates electric generating capacity in the Midwest and the Carolinas and has natural gas distribution in Ohio and Kentucky. It also has more than 4,000 megawatts of electric generation in Latin America. It had revenues of $12.7 billion in 2007.

NATURAL GAS INDUSTRY

As an energy industry, natural gas competes with electric power in several markets. Natural gas supplies about 22 percent of primary energy in the United States and serves many residential, commercial, and industrial energy needs. It can also fuel vehicles. If that use of natural gas increases and plug-in vehicles become a reality, we may see electricity and natural gas competing again as a transportation fuel. Use of natural gas to generate electricity is also increasing because of its price and the environmental opposition to coal.

The natural gas industry dates back to its first use for street lighting, which started soon after 1800. It has grown to a global industry with exploration, production, transmission, and distribution arms. Energy companies are constantly on the lookout for new sources of supply.

The core of the natural gas industry is in its exploration and production companies, transportation pipeline companies, and local distribution utilities. In the United States, some 6,300 producers work with about 160 transmission pipeline companies and another 1,200 local distribution companies. Of the producers, some 21 are "majors," or companies that report to the USEIA's Financial Reporting System. Local distribution prices are regulated by state public utility commissions and transmission is regulated by the federal government. After the mid-1980s, wellhead prices were deregulated. Pipeline ownership was unbundled, and interstate pipeline companies may provide transportation only. There are also more options for distribution of gas.

U.S. consumption of natural gas in 2007 was 23.1 trillion cubic feet, which was some 22 percent of world consumption. The average price delivered to residential customers was $13.01 per thousand cubic feet (US Energy Information Administration, 2009b). If one-fifth of natural gas is used for residential buildings, some 4.5 trillion cubic feet would sell for $58 billion at this price and work out to a monthly bill of about $45 for each of the some 110 million occupied homes in the United States.

Residential revenues in 2007 were close to this estimate. Based on total 2007 revenues, the gas industry is about one-third the size of the electricity sector. However, the price of natural gas can fluctuate sharply, so this comparison can change quickly. Natural gas revenues in billions of dollars for 2007 were, according to the American Gas Association (2009):

Residential	$55.0
Commercial	21.2
Industrial	11.3
Electric power generation	4.1
Other	0.5
Total	$92.1

Natural Gas Companies

The largest natural gas production companies also produce oil, and include companies such as Exxon Mobil and Texaco. Large transmission companies include El Paso Natural Gas Company, Columbia Gas Transmission Corporation, Tennessee Gas Transmission Co., and the Natural Gas Pipeline Company. Large distribution companies are often in the electric power business along with gas.

Next are selected examples of large natural gas companies that are listed in the USEIA Financial Reporting System.

El Paso Corporation   El Paso (2009) has businesses for pipeline transmission and exploration and production. It owns the largest interstate natural gas pipeline system in the United States at about 42,000 miles and transports more than 25 percent of the gas consumed in the nation daily. Its production ranks in the top 10 among U.S. domestic independent producers. It had $4.7 billion in revenues in 2007.

Energen   Energen's (2009) regulated business is Alabama Gas Corporation, the largest natural gas distributor in Alabama with about 450,000 customers. It has an oil and gas subsidiary, which earns about 85 percent of its net income. Its revenues were $309 million in 2007.

Sempra Energy   Sempra Energy (2009) has 13,600 employees in all of its businesses, and had 2007 revenue of about $11 billion. Its San Diego Gas & Electric Co. and Southern California Gas Co. subsidiaries serve more than 20 million customers. Its other businesses develop energy infrastructure and products and services internationally.

Xcel Energy   Xcel Energy (2009) operates in eight western and midwestern states. It has 1.8 million natural gas customers (and 3.3 million electricity customers). It had 2008 revenues of $10 billion, which include both electricity and natural gas operations.

Energy East Corporation Energy East (2009) has been acquired by Iberdrola (IBE.MC), one of the world's four largest energy companies by market capitalization. It delivers natural gas and electricity to nearly 3 million customers in five states. For example, New York State Electric and Gas serves 871,000 customers, and Connecticut Natural Gas Corporation serves 155,000 customers with gas. Revenues were $5.1 billion in 2007.

PETROLEUM INDUSTRY

Although the petroleum industry is not analyzed directly in the book as an infrastructure sector, it is interdependent with the other infrastructure systems that are analyzed, especially transportation. In some countries, where the petroleum industry is controlled by the government and state companies, policies for it might be developed by national policy in a similar way as electric power sector policy. The main difference might be in the greater possibility to export petroleum. The price of gasoline has significant effects on transportation and other infrastructures. The future availability of supplies, along with environmental concerns, signals us to watch the petroleum industry for clues about trends in use of infrastructure systems.

Petroleum, or crude oil and refined products, provides about 40 percent of total U.S. energy needs, including 97 percent of transportation demand. Gasoline accounts for more than 44 percent of total demand for petroleum products, and diesel fuel accounts for 75 percent of refinery sales of distillate fuel oils. Petroleum also provides for 21 percent of residential and commercial needs from propane and related fuels. Water and waste management infrastructure systems also use significant quantities of petroleum-based inputs. (U.S. Energy Information Administration, 2009a).

Trends to watch in the petroleum industry include oil consumption, price, and the development of substitute energy stocks that will affect infrastructure systems. Exhibit 6.5 shows the changes in the annual price of oil and illustrates a rising trend toward record prices over $140 per barrel in summer of 2008, followed by a sharp decline in 2009. Volatility in the prices is shown by the overlay that illustrates a broad trading range of maximum and minimum prices of 2008. Due to cost, supply, and security issues, the auto industry is looking at greater fuel efficiency, plug-in electric vehicles, and new fuel cell technologies. All of these factors point toward flat or

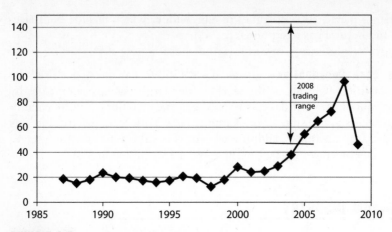

EXHIBIT 6.5   Oil Price Fluctuations
Source: Annual Europe Brent spot prices, U.S. Energy Information Administration (2009c)

decreasing petroleum consumption, but perhaps more pressure on natural gas and electric sources)(U.S. Energy Information Administration, 2009c).

Exxon Mobil Corporation

Although the petroleum industry is not included as an infrastructure sector per se, its large players have a presence in the energy sector, especially natural gas. They also see themselves as energy companies as opposed to only oil and gas companies, so their profiles may rise in the future. After all, we are seeing coal companies take positions as electric power generators; what is to prevent an oil and gas company from moving, for example, into renewables and then into electric power generation?

Exxon Mobil Corporation is the largest petroleum company in the world and operates in the crude oil and natural gas industries. It also markets petrochemicals and has interests in electric power generation facilities. The company's gross revenue in 2008 was some $477 billion, up from $378 billion in 2006 (Yahoo Finance, 2009).

COAL INDUSTRY

Coal is the fuel produced in greatest quantity in the United States. About 90 percent of it is used to generate about half of the nation's electric power, so is important to electric power infrastructure and to heating and cooling of buildings. It is also a basic energy source for industries that require large energy inputs, such as steel, cement, and paper.

The United States is reported to have the largest coal reserves in the world, some 267.6 billion short tons of economically recoverable reserves, or enough to last over 200 years at current production levels. With so much coal, we are sometimes labeled the Saudi Arabia of coal. However, these estimates may be overblown, according to a 2009 report by the U.S. Geological Survey, which assesses mineral deposits in the nation. The survey's analysis showed that less of the coal may be recoverable with today's costs than has been thought (Smith, 2009). Since 1949, U.S. coal production has increased from about 480 million short tons to 1,146 million short tons in 2007. It has been mostly flat since about 1990 (U.S. Energy Information Administration, 2009d).

It can cost more to ship coal than to mine it. To lower costs, coal-fired electric power plants may be located near coal mines. Some 68 percent of coal in the United States is transported by train, with the rest by barge, ship, truck, and slurry pipeline. Shipping of coal is an important business for railroads, which increase profits with longer runs and larger unit trains with high-capacity cars. American Electric Power, the nation's largest user of coal, has 9,100 railroad cars and 2,480 river barges to handle transport of coal. In 2009, along with a partner Cleco Corporation, it bought a Louisiana coal mine (Smith, 2009).

Coal prices are highly variable. They surged around 1980 due to inflation, anticipation of rising oil prices, and demand for electric power. This spurred coal producers to look for new reserves and to open mines; utilities entered into long-term contracts to guarantee prices. By 1985, the industry was changing and now it is now bigger, more competitive, and more integrated than in the past, making it difficult for smaller players to enter the market. Natural gas has captured some of the market for electric-generating capacity from coal-fired units.

The main obstacle to increased use of coal is its environmental impacts, which are extensive. Currently, global warming and emission of carbon dioxide is the highest-profile issue, but coal production and use are also implicated in water and air pollution as well as land use impacts. The coal industry is working on its environmental problems and tries to clean coal before it leaves mines and to find low-sulfur coal. New technologies are sought to remove sulfur and nitrogen oxides from coal or to convert coal to a gas or liquid fuel.

The main issues for the coal industry lie in solving environmental problems so that coal can be used to generate more electric power. Should transportation infrastructure see more electric vehicles, the demand for electricity and for coal could increase.

Peabody Energy Company

The Peabody Energy Company is the largest coal producer in the United States, based on its 2007 production of 192 million short tons, or nearly 17 percent of national production (U.S. Energy Information Administration, 2009d). The company reported that it is the world's largest private-sector coal company, with 2008 sales of 256 million tons. It also claimed to fuel some 10 percent of U.S. electricity production. In some countries—China, for example—coal production is a government monopoly. Peabody Energy owns interests in 30 coal operations in the United States and Australia and has interests in a Venezuelan mine. It also coal-fueled generating plants and develops technologies to convert coal to natural gas and transportation fuels. As of 2008, it had 9.2 billion tons of proven and probable coal reserves. In 2008, Peabody earned $953 million on $6.6 billion in revenues. It has total assets of $9.8 billion of which $7.3 billion is in property, plant, and equipment. Total shareholder's equity is $2.9 billion (Yahoo Finance, 2009).

NUCLEAR POWER INDUSTRY

Given concern over the environment and the increase in energy costs, it is logical that nuclear energy would get another look in the United States. In France, some 59 nuclear power plants generate the majority of the nation's electric power. According to the USEIA (2009d), as of 2007, the U.S. Nuclear Regulatory Commission (NRC) had licensed 104 commercial nuclear generating units totaling 87,400 net megawatts of capacity. As of March 31, 2008, the NRC was reviewing nine applications for construction permits and licenses.

The United States has some 104 nuclear power plants that generate some 8 percent of all electric energy, so why is it that France, with fewer plants, generates such a large percentage? Based on statistics of the USEIA and the World Nuclear Association (U.S. Nuclear Energy Institute, 2009), the United States has some 97.5 gigawatts of capacity and France has some 63.2 gigawatts, or about 65 percent of the U.S. total. France generates around 430 billion KWH per year with nuclear power, compared to about 810 billion KWH in the United States (2007 statistics). France exports over 10 percent of its production to other European countries. Its total electric power production is about 14 percent of that in the United States, but its population is some 20 percent of the U.S. total. It is apparent that France generates relatively more energy from its nuclear power plants and has lower per capita electric power use than in the United States.

Of the existing U.S. plants, practically all are owned and/or operated by private sector companies. The only exceptions are the plants owned by the Tennessee Valley Authority and the Omaha Public Power District. Twenty-three companies are listed as operators of plants, showing that operating capacity in the nuclear industry is concentrated in a relatively few players. The companies are: (U.S. Nuclear Energy Institute. 2009)

AmerenUE

American Electric Power Co. Inc.

Arizona Public Service Co.

Constellation Generation

Detroit Edison Co.

Dominion Generation

Duke Energy Corp.

Energy Northwest

Entergy Nuclear

Exelon Generation Co., LLC

FirstEnergy Nuclear Operating Co.

Florida Power & Light Co.

Luminant Generation

Nuclear Management Co., LLC

Pacific Gas & Electric Co.

PPL Susquehanna, LLC

Progress Energy

PSEG Nuclear, LLC

South Carolina Electric & Gas Co.

Southern California Edison Co.

Southern Nuclear Operating Co.

STP Nuclear Operating Co.

Wolf Creek Nuclear Operations Corp.

Time will tell whether a resurgence in U.S. nuclear power will occur. Cost, safety, security, public perception, and waste management are factors in the policy decisions that will determine the future of the nuclear industry in the nation.

RENEWABLES

Data presented earlier in the chapter showed that use of renewables is growing faster than other energy sources, and government policies in many countries are promoting their use. Hydropower and wind energy are the largest sources among renewables. Use of wind energy is increasing at a rapid rate, while hydropower is not. While wind power is not free from problems, it does seem to promise to generate a significant percentage of electric energy in the future.

Business in the wind energy industry is changing rapidly, and new players are emerging. Membership in the American Wind Energy Association (2009) shows a diverse group of companies that include manufacturers of wind turbines, wind farm developers, venture capitalists, utilities seeking to enter the wind business, and suppliers of goods and services to the industry.

Clipper Windpower, Vestas, GE Energy, Earth Turbines, Inc., and John Deere Renewables LLC manufacture wind turbines and in some cases develop wind farms.

Renewables Companies

Companies that develop wind generation systems include AES Wind Generation, Edison Mission Energy, and Mesa Power LP. DNV Global Energy Concepts provides consulting and other services.

Wind Capital Group   The Wind Capital Group (2009) is a privately owned development company based in Missouri that builds wind farms. It has a partnership with NTR plc, a toll road operator, which is also a player in the waste management business. NTR plc is an Irish company whose shares may be traded over-the-counter with the company's stockbrokers. It was founded in 1978 to develop and operate Ireland's first toll road and is now the leading toll road operator in Ireland. It has evolved to invest in renewable energy and sustainable waste management. Its main interests are in recycling, solar, wind, and ethanol.

Broadwind Energy   Broadwind Energy (2009) has a vision to become the "premier source of comprehensive supply-chain solutions for energy- and infrastructure-related industries in North America." It has four "platforms" for energy services, gears and bearings, heavy manufacturing and transportation platforms, and towers and monopolies. It is another example of a company seeking to enter the infrastructure market across a range of industries.

ENERGY STORAGE

Hidden behind the giant scope of the energy sector are many subtle details that affect its infrastructure. For example, the generic terms *generation, transmission, storage,* and *distribution* have important implications when applied to specific situations. In the case of generation, issues ranging from choice of fuels to environmental impacts must be considered. Transmission brings in issues of aging transmission grids and natural gas pipelines as well as opportunities for new technologies, such as smart electric grids.

Of these generic processes, storage may have the greatest potential to change how energy is managed. It includes technologies that range from using stored water for hydroelectricity, to new lithium-ion batteries for small devices and even automobiles, to use of compressed air to store wind energy. Control strategies, such as use of smart electric grids, can be employed to even out the flow of electric energy.

Hydroelectricity

Earlier, hydropower was shown as one of the renewables, with annual generation of about 268 billion KWH in 2008 and a projected rate of increase of 0.2 percent. At this rate of generation, hydropower generates some 7 percent of national electric power needs, and the percentage will drop as other sources increase.

Hydropower's value goes beyond its generation because it is ideal for peak power. That is, as electric demand fluctuates over a day, steam plants are slow to increase or decrease their production, but hydropower can be turned off or on with the flip of a switch. This same ability to change rapidly may play havoc with rivers, as they experience water surges that may not be good for fish and wildlife. Still, hydropower will continue to play important roles in electric power portfolios.

The infrastructure for hydropower includes dams, tunnels, penstocks, surge tanks, powerhouses, and transmission lines. Pumped storage is a variation of hydropower; here surplus steam power is used to pump water uphill, to be released later when needed due to increased demand.

While U.S. hydropower production will remain near 7 percent of electric power, some nations rely much more on hydro. For example, the Latin American countries of Colombia, Venezuela, and Brazil may generate three-fourths of their power from hydroelectricity, and in the developing world, a number of attractive sites remain to be exploited. China's massive Three Gorges Dam, which came on line in 2006, is planned to have a capacity of 22,500 megawatts, by far the world's largest. By comparison, total installed hydropower capacity in the U.S. is about 77,600 megawatts (U.S. Energy Information Administration, 2009a).

Compressed Air or Smart Grids

Because wind energy cannot be stored directly, utilities are searching for ways to use it effectively. Two general methods are being discussed: use of compressed air and rapid transfer across smart grids from point of supply to point of use.

The idea of using compressed air is to pump air into underground chambers when excess energy is available and to release it later when energy is needed. This idea has been tested only on a small scale. It remains to be seen whether it will add much to the national energy portfolio.

Smart grid transfer of wind energy generation is still to be tested as well, and its effectiveness will depend on the adequacy of transmission networks, the effective use of information to move energy from one place to another, and the ability of the energy market to accommodate the technologies.

Batteries

Battery technology is the key to energy use in the new economy for devices ranging from cell phones to plug-in vehicles. Successive improvements in small batteries have already enabled devices such as laptop computers to be used much more widely, and the technology developers are working hard to improve the batteries.

If battery technology can be developed and sustained for vehicles, it will be a game changer for transportation infrastructure. Prospects appear good, as auto manufacturers have already announced vehicles such as the Chevrolet Volt, which would depend on the new technologies. The key variable will be the financial feasibility of battery-operated vehicles, and a number of questions remain to be answered. Among these are how to establish the infrastructure of plug-in receptacles, how to service the vehicles, and the lifetime of the batteries.

Johnson Controls, Inc.   Johnson Controls, Inc. operates in building efficiency, automobiles, and power solutions. As such, it straddles several areas of the infrastructure business. Its building efficiency business focuses on integrated building management systems, including controls, security, and mechanical equipment. Its power business division produces lead-acid batteries and other types, including nickel-metal-hydride and lithium-ion batteries for hybrid vehicles. The company's 2008 revenue was $5.5 billion, up from $4.4 billion in 2006(Yahoo Finance, 2009).

HYDROGEN ENERGY

As the search for energy solutions continues, hydrogen has seemed to some people to be the ultimate source. On one hand, hydrogen seems to be a basic source of energy because it burns like natural gas. On the other hand, because it requires other basic sources to produce it, it seems more like an energy carrier. These attributes make hydrogen somewhat attractive as an energy carrier and storage medium. If transient processes, such as wind energy, can be used to produce hydrogen, then a new possibility for energy storage exists.

Hydrogen-based energy would require new infrastructure systems to support supply lines and all ancillary facilities. The dominant issue about this new infrastructure would be the policy design for the right mixture of public and private roles. With technology being changeable and uncertain, a government-run system would seem to be too rigid to succeed. But it is not reasonable to expect the private sector to plan and develop the infrastructure needed. Advocates of particular technological designs would need a mixed public-private approach. Utilizing existing infrastructure and service networks to the extent possible would seem to be a promising strategy, given the many issues that remain to be worked out. However, development of hydrogen energy systems seems to be moving slowly.

SECTOR ISSUES AND OUTLOOK

After the Industrial Revolution, energy's role in the economy has become more and more important. Now, with global concern about sustainability, its heavy impacts on the environment are being exposed. These forces increase volatility in the sector and drive the search for better sources and greater energy efficiency. Energy and information are twin systems that drive infrastructure systems and make them smarter. Energy is also interdependent with other infrastructures, especially water. As the energy sector restructures, its capital demands will continue to grow, especially in the electric power sector. Given its strategic importance, the energy sector faces many challenges, including overcoming coal's negative environmental impacts, developing safer nuclear power options, and creating storage devices that work across the spectrum of small to large devices and applications.

Energy Is a Giant Sector with Strong Impacts on the Economy and Environment

The U.S. energy economy is more than a $1-trillion-per-year enterprise. Such a large industry has many dramatic impacts on the economy, and energy use is implicated in our most serious environmental issues.

Energy Use Increases Continually, but Sources Can Be Substituted

Exhibit 6.6 shows projections (based on government estimates) for increased energy use from all basic sources and identifies forces that tend to increase or decrease a source. While increased use of renewable sources seems inevitable, the rest of the list seems problematic in the sense that coal has many pressures against it, while use of natural gas is rising faster. At any rate, the exhibit shows that many forces are at play to increase or decrease the sources.

Energy and the Economy Are Linked in an Ever-Changing Journey

Although it is evident that energy supplies are critical to the economy, how they will be used is undergoing continuing transformation. Whereas the Industrial Revolution required large supplies of coal, the automobile economy required continuing increases in oil imports, and rising standards of living required many new

EXHIBIT 6.6 Drivers of Change in Energy Sectors

	% Change	Forces to Increase Use	Forces to Decrease Use
Renewables	2.0	Desire for clean energy	Cost, public opposition
Coal	1.4	Rising electricity use, industrial development	Environmental impacts, global warming, source substitution
Electric power	1.1	Plug-in vehicles, information technology, rising living standards	Shift to natural gas, global warming, renewables, energy conservation, green buildings
Petroleum	0.4	Population growth, emerging nations	National security, efficient vehicles, high cost
Natural gas	0.2	Lower costs, environmental impacts of coal, abundant supplies	Geopolitics, safety
Nuclear	Unknown	Clean energy and shift from coal and petroleum	Safety, cost, public opposition

electric power plants, the information economy and emphasis on conservation and environmentalism have changed the equation. Now the terms to describe the energy economy will include *conserve, unbundle, deregulate, off the grid,* and *clean energy.*

The Energy Sector Will Experience Continued Change and Volatility

The volatility of the energy sector will always be with us, and energy will continue as a prime force for change among other infrastructure systems. Each subsector is changing, especially electric power, which is being subjected to the most change due to environmental restrictions, possible increased demand for plug-in automobiles, and increasing automation and use of computers. The forecast of 1.1 percent annual demand increase through 2030 masks a greater rate of increase in renewables, which will open opportunities for many new players. The petroleum industry will continue to be a strong force in transportation, but security and dwindling supplies will force the nation to search for alternatives. Natural gas is available in greater supply than petroleum and may be used more extensively in applications ranging from electric power production to direct use in vehicles.

Energy and Information Go Hand in Hand to Make Infrastructure Smarter

As complexity of infrastructure systems increases—from smart buildings, to smart highways and power grids—a key feature is joint use of energy and telecom systems. Every infrastructure system involves a central nervous system to sense demand, make decisions, and send commands. This central system works with distributed devices to activate the controls needed to maintain flows and stocks of energy, water, road artery capacity, and other infrastructure attributes. Therefore, the energy and telecom infrastructure sectors will remain fundamental underpinnings for the other infrastructure sectors.

Energy Conservation Will Continue as a Major Business Sector

Energy conservation and independence will grow in importance. Taking buildings off the grid, for example, is a desirable sustainability and security goal. Energy conservation coupled with renewable sources makes a win-win policy goal.

Energy and Water Interdependencies Will Continue to Be a Concern

Energy needs will place great stress on water systems, but the political focus will be on energy, not water systems. To respond, water policy needs reevaluation because many water management issues are neglected. Headwaters regions are especially vulnerable, and better data and indicators are needed to inform regulatory decisions (Grigg, 2006).

Capital Demands of the Electric Power Industry Will Only Grow Larger
In the past, the electric power industry has placed large demands on the capital markets, and these will only grow. All of the indications are that demands on it will grow, but fuels will be more difficult to obtain and use.

The Natural Gas Industry Will Continue to Be Robust and to Grow
While the negative pressures on coal and petroleum are strong, supplies of the cleaner fuel natural gas have increased, and it is rising in favor among energy sources. Due to economic conditions, near-term demand is expected to remain suppressed and prices low, but expected economic growth should boost industrial consumption of natural gas. Low prices have a dramatic impact on drilling activity and will lower production in the near future. Improvements in technology and well productivity increase the production potential from domestic sources.

While the Coal Industry Faces Global Warming, It Still Has the Greatest Reserves
Given the large U.S. reserves of coal, it will remain a very important basic source of energy for a long time. Coal is produced in greater quantity than other fuels in the United States, and most is used to generate electric power. Therefore, as electricity goes, so goes coal, with the exception of source substitution. So it is important to watch natural gas, renewable, and nuclear as competing sources for electric power generation.

Nuclear Power Is a Wild Card in the Energy Sector
If the United States could solve problems of safety, waste disposal, environmental effects, and public acceptance, nuclear power could become a much more important source for the future. Indications are that interest is rising. With the negative environmental effects of coal-fired plants, policy makers may be ready for a change to nuclear power.

Energy Storage and Battery Technologies Are Technologies to Watch
Energy storage involves technologies that range from hydropower dams, to stored compressed air, to battery designs. These technologies will be used in infrastructure applications for energy management, both from the supply side and the demand side. On the supply side, storage technologies offer us better ways to deliver energy when and where needed. On the demand side, they create new

possibilities for energy-using devices, from hand-held computers to plug-in automobiles.

Hydrogen Energy Is Another Wild Card for the Future

Hydrogen as an energy source has received much attention, but it is a carrier, not a primary energy source. Its future success as an energy carrier will depend on its ability to demonstrate similar or superior attributes to electricity. Development of a market for hydrogen fuel cell vehicles would require major financing by industry and government. Competition with other promising technologies makes use of hydrogen fuel cells a challenge (U.S. Energy Information Administration, 2009a). Hydrogen energy would require new infrastructure systems to support supply lines and all ancillary facilities.

CHAPTER 7

Water and Wastewater Sector

The media reminds us constantly that water is a serious global issue, with problems that range from climate change to intrusion of prescription drugs into our local supplies. The media attention makes us think that water should be a good business, but the water sector involves many complexities that are not easy to recognize. It is a large and diverse sector, but it has a low profile compared to the telecommunications, energy, and transportation sectors. Treated drinking water is sold as a commodity to homes and businesses through a network of publicly owned and privately owned utilities, and wastewater service also can be considered a utility service. The water sector also includes another large collection of water services that are less understood to most citizens. These include irrigation and drainage, operation of dams and reservoirs, control of stormwater and flooding, and environmental water quality management. All of these services affect the multifaceted water business in one way or another.

This chapter addresses the structure, finance, and operations of the water sector. It explains where business opportunities occur and where government is certain to run the show, thus blocking private operators. The chapter also explains how opportunities may change in the future due to drivers that include climate change, environmental sustainability, water scarcity, and vulnerable and aging populations, among others.

THEN AND NOW

Elements of a vital and sustainable future, such as a healthy society and environment, abundant food and energy, and public recreation, depend directly on water infrastructure systems. Safe water led to control of waterborne diseases, such as cholera, typhoid, and dysentery, and water treatment accounted for even more improvement in public health than medical advances. Environmental controls have repaired damaged streams and landscapes to offer new hope for water-based land development and recreation, and irrigation is an essential input for food production around the world. Clean and abundant water for the environment nurtures habitat and enables water-based recreation, including a robust sport fishing industry. Clearly, water management has proved its worth as one issue after another has been faced and resolved over the years. Balancing water use and the environment is essential to a sustainable future and good business.

The environmental writer Sandra Postel (2007) explained how water managers hold the key to sustaining this vital resource:

> As one of the most publicly visible stewards of the earth's water sources, drinking water utilities are uniquely positioned to exert a leadership role in the emerging field of ecologically sustainable water management. In important ways, this field is integrating the traditional goals of water management with those of ecosystem conservation in order to sustain a broader spectrum of the valuable goods and services on which human communities depend.

Now water managers face new problems, such as detectable levels of industrial chemicals and pharmaceuticals in water. Developing countries still have a big health crisis in water services, and at least 1 billion people lack access to safe water supplies and basic sanitation, leading to untold cases of misery and death. The world also faces food and energy shortages, and water is essential to production in both sectors. Irrigated agriculture and an emerging biofuels industry both depend on reliable sources of water to grow crops. The energy industry is a large user of water, especially for cooling of generation plants. Climate change may throw a monkey wrench into the best-laid plans to solve the water problems behind these issues.

Given the many relationships among water, society, and the economy, we would expect the water sector to offer good business and investment opportunities. It does, but they turn up in unexpected ways, which will be described in this chapter. Mainly they occur in a fragmented, government-dominated industry that is only loosely organized and difficult to characterize. As a result of political and regulatory factors, business and investment opportunities in the water sector often look better than they turn out to be. This apparent contradiction was described by Cui and Davis (2008) this way: "Water may be the world's most critical commodity. But it has been a tough market for many investors to tap profitably lately."

They traced a new wave of water investment vehicles that sought to capitalize on rising need for clean water but showed how water-oriented stocks are exposed to economic problems, such as the housing decline. They explained how water is different from other commodities because it can be traded only in regional markets. Although the sector is large, they explained that investors were forced into a small set of opportunities.

While some service firms and equipment suppliers do well in the regulated, politicized, and government-dominated water industry, the industry is fragmented and defies the general characterization that is required to assemble a successful index or water fund.

Water investment indices and funds barely scratch the surface of the industry's activity because it is so dispersed among different subsectors (e.g., water supply and wastewater) and different geographic areas. As a result, an index or fund cannot be very representative of the range of activity stimulated by rising water demands.

Cui and Davis correctly pinpointed the water industry's tight relationship to homebuilding, which is the largest part of U.S. construction spending. Homebuilding generates demand and financing for water infrastructure and services, which total about $80 billion per year. (In 2009, homebuilding fell into the doldrums; how long it will take the field to recover is unknown.) However, this financing does not translate into large demands for equipment and services, compared to the large, mostly local government budgets for labor and operational expenses among water and wastewater utilities.

Another reality of the water industry is that while it is capital intensive, its infrastructure is mostly long lasting, and annual capital investments for renewal are small. For example, some 1 million miles of buried water supply mains in the United States have a replacement value of around $400 billion, but the replacement rate averages about once in 200 years and a large backlog of deferred maintenance is accumulating. As a result of this slow renewal rate, the country experiences about 275,000 damaging water main breaks per year.

Cui and Davis are also correct that water is the world's most critical commodity and that it is tricky to profit from it. Water deserves more attention from economic statisticians and investors. However, after their initial surge of interest, short-run investors are apt to be discouraged by the complex economics and heavy politics of the water sector.

SECTOR STRUCTURE AND SIZE

As an investment sector, water can look seductive because demand for it is certain to grow with population, the supply is limited, and water requires a lot of equipment and services. As a mostly government-run sector, the water industry needs many reforms that would seem to invite privatization and innovative financial strategies. Although these possibilities can seem attractive, the heavily regulated and highly political water sector has disappointed many would-be investors and reformers. One way or the other, the sector is vital to a sustainable future, and it offers many opportunities for improvements through innovative finance.

The facilities and operations for water-related services require a large infrastructure base that includes dams, treatment plants, well fields, pipe networks, pumping stations, and many other components. To operate and support these extensive infrastructure systems requires a workforce that reaches about 1 million, according to my estimates. This includes about 200,000 water supply utility workers, another 175,000 wastewater utility workers, and a large workforce in government, in the other water services, and in supplier and regulator organizations.

Even as an aggregated sector, water is still smaller than the better-known electric power sector. Electric power has much larger revenues than all of the water industry, and its total employment is larger. Employment in the private electric power side is slightly above 400,000, about the same as water, wastewater, and stormwater combined.

Perhaps the low profile of water is because the sector is so fragmented. In any case, its profile is rising because of highly visible social and environmental problems. It seems that water continues to garner media attention, such as the 2009 book *Planet Water: Investing in the World's Most Valuable Resource*. The author covers topics that are similar to those in this chapter: operation of water companies, fragmentation of the industry, social issues, and others (Hoffman, 2009).

The other side of the water coin is its controversy as a human and environmental right. As the book was written, a movie titled *Flow* was released to focus attention on poverty, environmental degradation, and the role of large international water companies, development banks, and other corporate interests (Oscilloscope, 2009). The promotion for the movie claims that it is an investigation into the world water crisis, which experts call the most important political and environmental issue of the twenty-first century. The producer "builds a case against the growing privatization of the world's dwindling fresh water supply with an unflinching focus on politics, pollution, human rights, and the emergence of a domineering world water cartel." "Interviews with scientists and activists intelligently reveal the rapidly building crisis, at both the global and human scale, and the film introduces many of the governmental and corporate culprits behind the water grab, while begging the question 'Can anyone really own water?'" (Oscilloscope, 2009). These claims are discussed in the chapter's concluding section. They seem extreme, but they do point to a series of widely held beliefs that can influence people who lack insight to explain the complexities of the sector.

The water sector has two basic parts: the services provided in urban areas (water supply, wastewater, and stormwater) and all other services, such as environmental water control. A good reason to divide the sector into these parts is that they are managed by different groups. The urban services fall mostly within utilities and public works departments. The other services are run by a diverse group of state agencies, power companies, and other service providers.

Water supply is the most visible urban service, but wastewater is nearly as big, and stormwater expenditures are large and increasing. The other water subsectors (hydroelectricity, irrigation, dams and reservoirs, navigation, flood control, environmental water, and management of groundwater) are large and important but are not as easy to characterize as urban water services. Each of the water subsectors is an industry unto itself, but with the exception of water supply and wastewater, they are niches and embedded in other industries.

While it is a stretch to classify water management as an integrated industry, it is increasingly looking like one, although it remains government dominated and is heavily regulated. Trade of water is limited, but trade of goods and services among the industry's players is robust. These players are based in other industries, such as manufacturing, professional services, and construction, and the water industry is one of their main markets.

A model of the water sector shows utilities and other service providers at the center, government and private sector water management and regulation in the next ring, and support sector activity in the third ring (see Exhibit 7.1). Most utilities are government owned and are regulated by the government, but the support sector offers many business and investment opportunities. Also, a significant number of private water companies are pioneering new businesses as the water sector changes.

Water utilities and service providers can be placed into broad categories, arranged roughly in terms of their economic activity and number of players:*

- **Water supply.** Provides water service to residential, commercial, and industrial users, including self-supply. A \$40 billion industry with about 200,000 employees. It has over 50,000 utilities, but many are very small. Many industries and other entities have separate water services. U.S. Environmental Protection Agency (EPA) estimates show about 105,000 noncommunity water systems, including about 20,000 nontransient systems (e.g., factories or schools) and about 85,000 transient systems (e.g., campgrounds or gas stations).

---

*Estimates are based on Grigg (2007). The employee counts include service providers only, not regulators or support sector employees.

- **Wastewater and water quality.** Collects, treats, and disposes of wastewater and manages water quality in streams and aquifers. A $40 billion industry with about 175,000 employees. Similar in structure to water supply, but the industry has a separate regulatory structure, a separate trade association, and different types of equipment and facilities.
- **Stormwater and flood.** Provides stormwater management, flood control, and floodplain management, and water quality control from runoff. A $20 billion industry with around 50,000 employees. Managed almost entirely by local governments and subject to increasing regulation.
- **Irrigation and drainage.** Manages water for farming and landscaping and disposes of drainage water. Industry size and employment have not been estimated. Concentrated in the arid West but spreading to humid areas and to the landscape industry.
- **Dams and instream flows.** Owns and operates dams and other water-control structures for fish and wildlife, hydropower, recreation, and navigation. Industry size and employment have not been estimated, but the United States has about 75,000 dams large enough to be regulated.
- **Groundwater.** Controls groundwater quantity and quality. Industry size and employment have not been estimated. Service providers are limited in number, but support sector is large due to widespread use of individual wells.

The water industry is heavily regulated by fragmented groups and authorities. Regulators of the water industry fall into various categories:

- Health and safety, such as safe drinking water. Main authority is the Safe Drinking Water Act, and most regulators are in state EPAs or local health departments.
- Water quality to ensure clean streams. Main authority is the Clean Water Act, and most regulators are in state EPAs.
- Water quantity allocation to recognize legal water rights or to issue permits for water use. Main authorities are in state government departments.
- Fish and wildlife protection to require instream flows for fish. Authority is distributed among environmental laws and enforced through state government departments. Authority is weaker than safe drinking water and clean water programs, which have stronger federal mandates.
- Finance to control rates of private water companies. The authority is with state public utility commissions, which only have oversight over private companies. Government water companies are mostly self-regulated for financial operations.

- Service quality to maintain an adequate water pressure. Some regulation for service quality by private water companies occurs in public service commissions but only indirectly for government-owned utilities.

The support sector of the water industry can be divided into parts: suppliers, construction contractors, professional service firms, knowledge sector, advocacy groups, financiers and insurers, and associations. These will be discussed in more detail later in the chapter.

Although the focus of the water sector is on water supply and wastewater, it is well to pay attention to other water-related investments, including flood management. Everyone will remember the more than $100 billion worth of damage done by Hurricane Katrina to New Orleans and its surroundings. This water-related disaster spurred massive relief and rebuilding, with a focus on upgrading the levee system that was supposed to protect the city. Now Houston is considering a $2 to $4 billion "Ike Dike" to protect itself and the energy infrastructure along the gulf coast. Houston experienced some subsidence, or a decline in ground elevation due to settlement and is more vulnerable to floods than in the past. Large projects like this tend to end up in the accounts of the construction industry rather than the water industry, but they are water-related issues (Casselman, 2009).

FINANCIAL FRAMEWORK OF THE SECTOR

The water sector's financial framework is based on revenues for the service providers shown on Exhibit 7.1. Regulators and government agencies are financed mostly from tax rolls, and the support sector generally is supported by purchases from the service providers.

Exhibit 7.2 shows an overview of revenues that originate as fees, purchases, or tax payments from households and businesses. In addition to utilities and industry, the exhibit shows the government sector, which is relatively small, and the household and business sector, which is larger but of undetermined size. The exhibit has considerable detail but can be useful to illustrate how the money flows. Mainly, you can see how the payments from households and businesses ($120 billion per year) flow through the utilities and lead to purchases of products and services from the supply sector. Much of the $120 billion is consumed in salaries and operating costs of the infrastructure providers, but a considerable sum also flows to private sector suppliers.

The utility-based water services are financed by fees and charges, and they purchase goods and services from the support sector. The estimate for this sector is $100 billion, or $40 billion each for water and wastewater

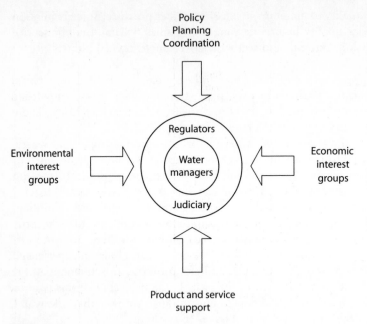

EXHIBIT 7.1 Water Industry Participants

and $20 billion for stormwater nationally. This translates to about $28 per capita per month for a population of 300 million, or about $83 for a family of three in a home. That $83 would cover water supply, wastewater, and stormwater services. The bill will be higher in some regions than others, and it also includes a share toward paying for water services in all commercial, government, and nongovernmental facilities.

A number of industries provide their own water, including electric power utilities, manufacturers, and large farms. Some would be connected to utility systems, and their charges would be reflected in the $100 billion total just discussed. Others would pay for their own stand-alone systems, and these costs would be embedded in their products and services rather than being paid directly by consumers. For smaller systems, the funds would flow as shown in the household and business sector shown on Exhibit 7.2.

The government sector is estimated at $20 billion, mainly at the federal and state levels. It includes resource management, environmental protection, regulatory controls, large-scale flood control, and security. This includes budgets of large agencies, such as the Corps of Engineers and Bureau of Reclamation, as well as the smaller budgets of some federal agencies, such as U.S. Geological Survey, and many state agencies. This sector

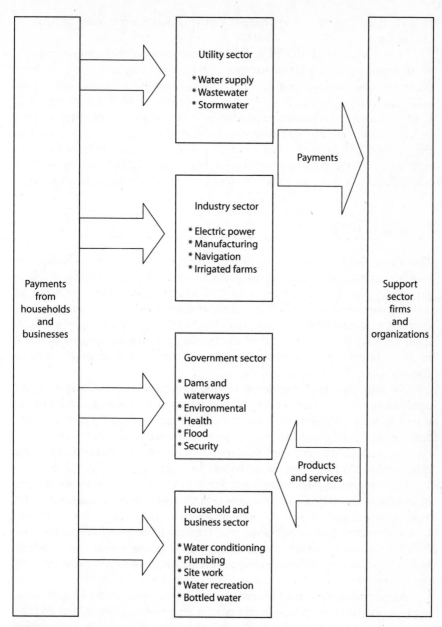

EXHIBIT 7.2 Financial Flows of the Water Sector

receives mostly taxes and appropriations because its services are difficult to charge for.

In the household and business sector, payments from individuals or small businesses are applied toward water system improvements, such as plumbing construction and renewal, site landscaping, water conditioning and purification, bottled water sales, and boating and sport fishing. It is hard to analyze and estimate expenditures in this sector. No doubt the sector is large, however. For example, the Bureau of Labor Statistics estimates that, in 2007, there were some 435,010 plumbers, pipefitters, and steamfitters working at a mean annual average wage of $47,350. This totals over $20 billion in wages and does not include costs of their support systems.

FINANCIAL ISSUES

The water sector is difficult to finance using only user charges because it involves public goods as well as private commodity-type goods. While a private regulated water company can collect, treat, and distribute water as a utility service, it will be subjected to stringent health and environmental controls that can disrupt its profitability. At the same time, water management requires the involvement of numerous government agencies that are financed largely through taxes for services, such as monitoring pollution control and guarding against flooding.

No one expects a revolution in the way the water industry is managed. However, although it has been considered a slow-moving industry, it will undergo change that is driven by its unique drivers (Means, Ospina, and Patrick, 2005). Indicators of change in the sector are water shortages, climate change, demand for high-quality water, environmentalism, aging infrastructure, higher rates, security, and new information technologies.

New water supplies will be needed in growth areas, but they will be hard to find. In 2009, California governor Arnold Schwarzenegger declared a drought emergency due to three years of shortages and low supplies. In spite of emergencies like this, problems of environmentalism and the NIMBY (not-in-my-backyard) syndrome signal that new water supplies will be hard to come by and more efficient use of water and higher rates will be the norm.

Another change is more insistence on higher-quality water for our aging population and consumers who are paying attention to health alerts and the quality of their food and drink. The fact that sales of bottled water rose for many years is an indicator of this trend. Now, new health concerns have slowed this growth. Although environmentalism seems mature as a force, new facets of it continue to influence decision making in the water sector.

New laws and regulations emerge more slowly than they did in the past, but public concern with sustainability creates pressures for water conservation, pollution prevention, and prevention of new water storage and diversion projects.

In the United States, although it is difficult to construct new dams, existing dams are part of our aging infrastructure, which includes other elements such as a million miles of underground water pipes and comparable stocks of wastewater piping. Infrastructure renewal will be a slow-growing issue for all water systems, and management of underground infrastructure will grow in importance. Another element of the infrastructure problem is building plumbing systems, which will receive more focus in the future as a health issue.

Security is also a big issue in the water industry, and both terrorism and natural disasters must be anticipated to protect water systems. Risk management and strengthening security of water systems has been a growing business activity for over a decade.

The size of the water industry seems stable, and it is unlikely that its structure will change much. Continuing industry consolidation will occur gradually, and any enthusiasm for privatization in the water industry and its regulatory and political aspects must be approached with caution. Revenues will probably be level, although per unit costs may rise. The employee count will not increase much, but a new workforce is required to replace retiring baby boomers.

The water industry has a low-tech image, but it uses sophisticated information technologies for data collection, meter reading, and control systems. Like smart highways and smart grids, information technology and controls will be a growth area for water utilities.

Managing the thousands of small water systems will continue to be a challenge, mainly due to lack of funds to pay for managers and for equipment and support services.

BUSINESS PROFILES

The model shown in Exhibit 7.1 includes private sector businesses in three categories: service providers (such as private water companies), professional service firms, and businesses that provide support products and services. The support sector involves many large and small businesses, and often the large businesses are represented by subsidiaries, such as GE Water as part of the larger GE Corporation. The fact that the larger support companies offer services across industries makes it difficult to assemble stock funds from them that are focused primarily on the water business.

Water and wastewater organizations are similar in character. The larger organizations are mostly public utilities, and the smaller ones range across many categories, from private water systems to systems that are managed as adjuncts to other activities. Many entities provide their own water services, including workplaces and hospitals, campgrounds and gas stations, among others. The utilities have source, treatment, and distribution systems and use products and services such as professional services, contracting, equipment, materials and chemicals, and energy. Businesses in the water sector range from ownership and/or operation of utilities to sale of support services and products, and they include many activities of the nongovernmental sector.

The largest water supply utilities are government owned, such as the Chicago Department of Water Management, the Los Angeles Department of Water & Power, and the Massachusetts Water Resources Authority. A few large private companies, such as American Water, also operate, and there are tens of thousands of smaller water utilities, both public and private.

Privately owned water companies can range from public companies listed on a stock exchange (investor-owned water utilities) to small businesses serving only a few water taps. Regardless of size, their business model is to provide water supply (and sometimes also wastewater) services on a regulated monopoly basis. As monopolies, they are regulated in the United States by state public utility commissions, just as private sector electric companies are (Center for Public Integrity, 2008).

In the United States, the private water companies are represented by the National Association of Water Companies, founded in 1895, with some 340 members. The proportion of U.S. water services provided by private water companies has remained close to 15 percent for over 50 years (measured by customers served or volume of water handled). Investor-owned water supply utilities accounted for about 14 percent of water revenues and about 11 percent of water system assets in 1995. Investor ownership of wastewater utilities is less than water supply utilities for several reasons, including federal subsidies of wastewater treatment plants.

American Water

American Water is the largest investor-owned water supply and wastewater company in the United States. It evolved from about 1886, and its story up to the 1990s is told in Cross (1991). The company grew by acquisitions organized by John Ware, the entrepreneur who led the company through its period of greatest growth. It currently offers water and wastewater services to about 15.6 million people in more than 1,600 communities in the United States and Canada. American Water is listed on the New York Stock Exchange, its listing having been restored after an acquisition by RWE and later divesture and initial public offering. RWE sold 39.5 percent of its holdings in 2007 and plans to divest its remaining share to focus on power and gas markets. It still owned some 60 percent of American Water in early 2009 ("RWE CFO Repeats," 2009). American Water had $2.3 billion in revenue in 2008 (Yahoo Finance, 2009).

California Water Service Company

The California Water Service Company is the largest investor-owned water company in the West and the third largest in the nation. It is a subsidiary of the California Water Service Group, which also owns Washington Water Service Company, New Mexico Water Service Company, Hawaii Water Service Company, and CWS Utility Services. The entire group serves about 2 million people in some 100 communities. California Water Service Group (2009) is listed on the New York Stock Exchange and had $410 million in revenue in 2008.

Aqua America, Inc.

Aqua America, Inc. evolved from the Philadelphia Suburban Water Company and adopted its present name in 2004. It operates regulated water or wastewater utilities in Pennsylvania, Ohio, North Carolina, Illinois, Texas, New Jersey, New York, Florida, Indiana, Virginia, Maine, Missouri, and South Carolina. It also provides services through operating contracts. As of the end of 2008, it served approximately 3 million customers and revenue for that year was $642 million (Yahoo Finance, 2009).

Connecticut Water Service, Inc.

Smaller water companies range across the size range, from very small as in a few subdivisions, to larger and well-organized companies, such as Connecticut Water Service Inc. The company has acquired a number of other smaller water companies, such as Crystal Water Company of Danielson, Compilation Tool. Crystal Water Company was acquired in 1999 through a stock trade and began operating as a subsidiary. Connecticut Water Service, Inc. is an investor-owned utility and the holding company for several water companies. It also hosts Connecticut Water Utility Services, Inc., which is an unregulated subsidiary providing water-related services (Business Wire, 1999). The company also operates in real estate and services and rentals, providing services to water and wastewater clients including delivery of emergency drinking water to businesses and residences. As of December 31, 2008, Connecticut Water Service, Inc. served 87,361 customers in 54 towns in Connecticut. Its 2008 revenue was $61 million (Connecticut Water, 2009).

Saur Group

The Saur Group began as one of France's three main water companies. It was acquired in the 1990s then divested later by the Bouygues Group, a diversified French construction and industrial company. Saur's main activity is in France, where it serves some 6,700 communities. A subsidiary, Saur International, focuses on management contracts. With 2,400 employees, Saur International had net sales of €103 million for the fiscal year ended March 31, 2008. Coved is the sanitation subsidiary of the Saur group, and it handles solid wastes and related sanitation work. The Saur group is now held in private equity ownership. The AXA Private Equity (2009) group purchased a share of Saur in 2007 when the PAI investment fund resold it to them, the Séché Environnement industrial group, and the Caisse des dépôts et consignations. The three partners created a holding group to manage this investment, and AXA Private Equity has a 20 percent equity stake in the partnership.

RWE AG

RWE AG (2009) is a German utility corporation that offers electricity, gas, water and wastewater, and waste disposal and recycling services. RWE focuses on Europe and has an integrated business model for electricity and gas as well as the water business. It purchased American Water, but decided to divest it with an initial public offering in 2007. In fiscal 2007, RWE revenue was €42.55 billion, or about $60 billion.

GDF SUEZ

GDF SUEZ (2009) was formed in 1997 by a merger between Compagnie de Suez and the water company Lyonnaise des Eaux. It employs 198,200 people globally and had revenues of €74.3 billion in 2007. It is listed on the Paris stock exchange. GDF SUEZ is engaged in energy, energy services, and environmental businesses, where it offers its drinking water, wastewater treatment, and waste management services. SUEZ ENVIRONNEMENT has 63,400 employees on five continents. It acquired the U.S. water businesses of United Utilities and Aquarion. In 2007, it had revenues of €12 billion or about $17 billion.

United Utilities

United Utilities (2009) is the largest water and wastewater company in the United Kingdom. It was created in 1996 by a merger of Northwest Water plc and Norweb plc. Water and wastewater are its biggest business, but other services include electricity distribution and telecommunications. United Utilities is expanding its operations internationally. Its annual revenue is about $4 billion as of early 2009.

WATER INDUSTRY SUPPORT BUSINESSES

Professional services and equipment and supplies are two businesses that provide critical support to the water industry and sector. Water utilities require a range of professional services, such as engineering, management consulting, hydrology and geology, and environmental science. Also, lawyers, accountants, and other specialists provide business support and advice.

Equipment and supplies form an important avenue for participation of the private sector in the water industry. Areas include equipment and supplies to utilities, businesses, and consumers from the equipment manufacturer, the wholesaler, and the supplier that assembles equipment into systems.

Professional Services

Professional service firms are in many ways a shadow workforce for water utilities. Many of them do work for utilities and local governments that could be done in house. In the 2002 Economic Census, engineering services across all types of work showed revenues of $116 billion and payroll of $50 billion. Total employees were 861,000 (U.S. Bureau of Census, 2002). Data from the next census will be available in 2009 and 2010. The portion of the engineering services devoted to the water sector mirrors roughly the percentage of construction work in that sector, with the exception that water utilities require a good bit of environmental work that may or may not be connected to construction projects.

The engineering firms perform services that include design, consulting studies, construction and remediation, program management, equipment and product manufacture, technology and research and development, laboratory and analytical services, and contract operations.

The larger water engineering firms include CH2M Hill (Denver, CO); Tetra Tech Inc. (Pasadena, CA); Black & Veatch (Overland Park, KS); MWH

(Broomfield, CO); and HDR (Omaha, NE). All of these are employee owned with the exception of Tetra Tech, which is a public-listed company.

Management consulting firms serving the water industry include firms such as EMA, Inc. (Minneapolis, MN) and Raftelis Financial Consultants Inc. (Charlotte, NC), which advises on topics such as human resources and financial management. Larger management consultants, such as Booz Allen Hamilton (McLean, VA), also work in the water industry. Big consulting engineering firms often have subsidiaries that offer management consulting. An example is Black & Veatch's Enterprise Management Solutions.

Closely related to professional services is the knowledge sector of the water industry, which provides education, research, training, outreach, and information services. A broad group of firms, government agencies, associations, universities, and institutes participate. Examples are the Water Research Foundation (Denver, CO), and the Water Environment Research Foundation (Alexandria, VA).

Although water and wastewater utilities require construction and reconstruction for treatment plants, pipes, and related facilities, their total annual construction requirements do not rival residential building or highways and street construction. Local governments operate most systems, and in 2007, construction put in place for their facilities (September 2008 data) was $16.7 billion for water supply and $23.8 billion for sewage and waste disposal (U.S. Census Bureau, 2009c). These totals do not include construction by private parties. Water and wastewater are local services, and it is likely that smaller contractors do most of the work.

No single association represents water industry suppliers, but the Water and Wastewater Equipment Manufacturers Association (WWEMA) represents a range of them and is an identifiable voice of the supplier industry. Other trade associations, such as those for pipe or chemicals, represent sectors of the industry. These associations deal mostly with business issues, which can attract attention of trade policy makers as well. For example, in 2009 the Federation of Canadian Municipalities passed a resolution giving the United States an ultimatum to broker a fair trade deal about Canadian infrastructure projects. The focus was on water and wastewater and sought to prevent trade restrictions against Canada in the stimulus bill. WWEMA had warned Congress of the risks of protectionist measures in the stimulus bill. In 2008, the United States exported $6.18 billion in water and wastewater equipment to Canada (Water and Wastewater Equipment Manufacturers Association, 2009).

Insituform Technologies, Inc.   Much of the water industry's work is completed by utility contractors, which install pumps and pipelines, build treatment plants, and handle other specialty work for water utilities. As an example, Insituform Technologies Inc. was founded in the U.S. in 1971 and was based originally on a technology developed by Eric Wood, a British inventor, who created the Insituform process. In this process, a flexible, resin-saturated tube is placed under water pressure into a sewer through a manhole. The water is heated to cure the resin and create a structurally sound cured-in-place pipe lining. Some 96 percent of Insituform's business is sewer rehabilitation, with operations through partners in several countries as well as the United States. The company is listed as Insituform Technologies Inc. (INSU) and had $537 million in revenues in 2008 (Insituform, 2009).

Equipment and Supplies

Equipment and Supplies business offer products and services including test equipment, chemicals, computers, software, construction machinery, corrosion and leak detection services, pipe, pumps, valves, and assembled treatment units. Smaller-scale suppliers provide plumbing components, water conditioning equipment, landscape equipment and supplies, package treatment plant equipment, septic tanks, and garden center supplies. In addition to supplies, water and wastewater utilities require specialized services, such as pigging, leak detection, lab services, and other maintenance and/or diagnosis services.

Ameron Ameron International Corporation supplies engineered products and materials for the chemical, industrial, energy, transportation, and infrastructure industries. Its Fiberglass-Composite Pipe group provides fiberglass pipes, fittings, and well screens for various industrial uses. Water Transmission provides concrete pipe systems for water supply, wastewater, and stormwater systems. It also sells wind towers and polyvinyl chloride and polyethylene protective materials for infrastructure systems. The Infrastructure Products group provides ready-mix concrete, aggregates, concrete pipe, and box culverts as well as steel poles and traffic signals. The company was founded in 1907 and is headquartered in Pasadena, California. Revenue increased from $549 million in 2006 to $668 million in 2008 (Yahoo Finance, 2009).

Mueller Water Products, Inc. Mueller Water Products, Inc. markets water equipment through three divisions: Mueller Company, U.S. Pipe, and Anvil. Mueller Company manufactures fire hydrants, valves, meters, and various tools and fittings. U.S. Pipe manufactures and sells ductile iron pipe and related products. Anvil also manufactures pipe fittings and related products for mechanical, fire protection, and other piping systems. The company is listed on the New York Stock Exchange as Mueller Water Products, Inc.

(MWA). The company had revenues of $1.86 billion in 2008. It had an initial public offering in 2006, but its stock is sensitive to the housing market (Yahoo Finance, 2009).

Calgon Carbon Corporation   Calgon Carbon Corporation operates in the drinking water, industrial process, environmental, and food markets. Its three lines are Activated Carbon and Service, Equipment, and Consumer. The Activated Carbon and Service segment sells activated carbon to remove organic compounds from water, air, and other liquids and gases and leases and maintains carbon adsorption equipment. The Equipment segment offers treatment systems for air and water. These treat volatile organic compounds, air stripper gases, and landfill emissions as well as wastewater treatment and groundwater remediation. Its 2008 revenue was $400 million, up from $316 million in 2006 (Yahoo Finance.com, 2009).

Dow Chemical Company   The Dow Chemical Company operates across a range of markets for chemicals, plastic materials, agricultural, and other products and services. It serves a number of industries, including manufacturing, building and construction, processing, oil and gas, pulp and paper, and utilities. It had revenues of $57 billion in 2008, up from $49 billion in 2006 (Yahoo Finance, 2009).

American Standard   The household end of the water business is large but seems closer to the home and bath improvements than to the utility industry. American Standard valves and toilets seem to appear in every home. The company's roots date back to before 1900, and the company was incorporated in 1929 as the American Radiator & Standard Sanitary Corporation. It began as a manufacturer of plumbing and heating products and became the world leader in toilets and radiators. Now it has core businesses in air conditioning (after acquiring the Trane Company), plumbing products, and automotive products, and medical diagnostic technologies. The company divested all but the air-conditioning business in 2007 and was renamed Trane. The kitchen and bath division was sold to Bain Capital Partners, LLC, including sale of the American Standard name to Bain for use in water-related products. One of the founders of Bain was Mitt Romney, who ran for the U.S. presidency in 2008. The company has acquired many businesses and has a large portfolio under management (Funding Universe, 2009a).

PRIVATIZATION IN THE WATER SECTOR

Privatization of publicly owned water systems has received a lot of attention, but interest in it has waxed and waned. Water privatization became popular during the Reagan-Thatcher era because most of the United Kingdom's water systems were privatized in that period. However, it seems that many failures and controversial deals put the brakes on new experiments with it. Chapter 12 provides further details on modes of privatization and their results.

While outright privatization is difficult to achieve, as a business line, it can take different forms in water and wastewater operations. These include full sale of government-owned assets to private companies, which occurred in the United Kingdom; contract operation by private companies of government-owned systems (which has occurred in Indianapolis); design-build-operate agreements; and outsourcing of utility support services (such as laboratory services).

Contract operation is a popular method of privatization, both for water supply and wastewater, but it takes on different forms. Private contract operation, along with public ownership, is not subject to financial regulation in the way that private ownership is. While some contract operations have been successful, some contracts have not been renewed, and there are instances in which contracts were terminated early and litigation ensued. Houtsma, deMonsabert, and Gutner (2003) performed a study and found that wastewater contract operations offer good opportunities as well as challenges. Contract operation has proved to be one unbundled water operations activities amenable to outsourcing in some cases.

Build-operate-transfer offers an attractive way for local governments and utilities to partner with the private sector to establish water and wastewater facilities. Two examples in which it has been used are Seattle's water treatment plant and Tampa Bay Water's desalination plant (National Research Council, 2002). It has not yet been used on a widespread basis because of more attractive alternatives and availability of funds, political barriers, and resistance to change (Algarni, Arditi, and Polat, 2007).

Small to medium-size water utilities are the most likely candidates for privatization. However, it involves many business issues that are not apparent at first glance. A private company with the same real costs as a public operator would have to charge higher rates due to tax burdens. Public sector rates may enjoy subsidies and/or be held low for political reasons. Private companies consider that asset transfer is risky and have concerns about competing for contracts. Deferred maintenance and renewal are huge issues for the water services industry. Bidding is costly and competition can be intense. If private companies compete with public entities, they wonder if the playing field is level.

Major conclusions about water privatization from a study by the National Research Council (2002) study are that no arrangement fits all situations and that outsourcing of work is the most common form of privatization. In recent decades, no major U.S. city has sold its utility assets to private companies, but some small water utilities have. The most likely scenario is continued public ownership of water utilities but use of privatization for diverse purposes on a case-by-case basis. In any event, although privatization has proceeded slowly, it has spurred public water agencies to improve their own performance.

INVESTING IN WATER AS A COMMODITY

Like other commodities, raw water can seem like a good investment, but it is risky. In Colorado, for example, buying water rights is well established, but the law works against speculation. An investment group named American Water Development Inc. attempted to export groundwater to Denver in the 1990s, but was unsuccessful after legal challenges.

In 1999, T. Boone Pickens started a Texas company known as Mesa Water. The idea was to use the Ogallala Aquifer to transfer water to communities that need it (Mesa Water Inc., 2009). The eventual success of this venture is unknown at this time. Enron started a water company known as Azurix. This move into public utilities launched a business model to buy water as a commodity and use the Internet as a marketing exchange for trading water. At the time, Enron vice chairperson Rebecca Mark said the company would purchase water assets in Europe and South America. It agreed to buy Wessex Water PLC, a U.K.-based water and wastewater utility, but the business venture proved unsuccessful.

There have been many failures in attempts to speculate in water as a commodity. It appears that without public support and involvement, large water movement projects have a difficult time.

INDUSTRY POLICY AND REGULATION

In many ways, water management is a dichotomy because although water is a local service, policy and regulation take place mostly at the state and federal levels. Because water management is so closely connected to public health and the environment, it is heavily regulated, and there are continuing calls for reform of national water policy.

Although many people call for coherent national water policy, in many ways, there is none because water is so multifaceted. In the 1950s and 1960s, several national commissions studied water policy. Today, however, it is clear that national policy is expressed through legislation such as the Clean Water Act and the Safe Drinking Water Act and their counterparts at the state level. At times in the past, the federal government has had offices of water policy, but most such federal offices are gone now, supplanted by more attention to water policy at the state level.

The water industry's regulators have authorities in health and safety, environment, water use, fish and wildlife protection, and service levels. These diverse areas draw in many agencies and can stop projects by ensnaring them in webs of reviews and government processes. As examples of three types of agencies, the U.S. Environmental Protection Agency (USEPA) develops and administers rules for safe drinking water, wastewater, and related water activities; state environmental protection agencies implement legislation, and USEPA rules and exercise enforcement power; and state public utility commissions regulate rates of private water companies, as they do the rates of electric power utilities.

U.S. Environmental Protection Agency

The USEPA (2009a) is the main water and environmental regulatory office of the federal government. USEPA's programs are carried out in the headquarters office, where an assistant administrator directs the Office of Water. Programs are delivered through 10 regional offices, each of which has a unit dealing with water regulations. USEPA has a number of water laboratories. USEPA maintains extensive statistics about water and wastewater finance and publishes guidance about state revolving loan programs and other avenues of financial assistance. USEPA was the main federal agency that oversaw the original wastewater construction grants program, which dispensed some $50 billion in grants from 1972 to the mid-1980s. These grants provided the subsidies to build much of the existing infrastructure of wastewater plants, which are now aging and needing renewal.

COORDINATION IN THE WATER SECTOR

In a private sector industry, the market coordinates among suppliers and customers, but in an industry with heavy government involvement, such as water, coordination requires direct actions by regulators, public authorities, and industry associations.

Coordination in the water sector is difficult and involves much intergovernmental work that in many cases breaks down into litigation or political strife. A case in point might be the future water supply for the City of Atlanta, Georgia. Having an adequate water supply is a critical issue for economic development anywhere, but in Atlanta, the supply has looked inadequate for over two decades, exacerbated by drought and interstate conflict. Although it seems like an exaggeration, the problem has been referred to as a trillion-dollar issue because so much development is at stake. It is a long story, but millions of dollars have been spent, a compact was passed by Congress, and an enormous number of hours of negotiation among Georgia, Florida, and Atlanta have been completed. According to current participants, when a notice goes out to the parties, copies must go to more than 60 attorneys. Although this is an exceptional case, it illustrates how water issues can become snarled. The point is that if you are considering a water project, be sure to assess the full cost of the coordination required. It may take much longer and involve many more issues than you ever imagined.

A key agency in water coordination is the U.S. Army Corps of Engineers (USACE, the Corps), which issues the dredge-and-fill permit that water projects require. If any federal interest in a proposed project can be shown, the Corps organizes public hearings and may require a full environmental impact statement (EIS). The EIS process can be long and costly, and may result in a failed project. It illustrates again how proponents of water projects must count the cost before making investment decisions.

Army Corps of Engineers

The USACE includes military and civilian parts. Its civilian part has built many dams and maintains water facilities for navigation and related functions. It employs about 34,600 civilian and 650 military men and women who work on planning, designing, building, and operating water resources and other civil works projects; designing and managing the construction of military facilities for the army and air force, and providing design and construction management support for other Defense and federal agencies. The Corps includes a headquarters office that operates some 41 districts organized in 9 divisions, and a group of centers, laboratories, and field activities (U.S. Army Corps of Engineers, 2009).

Mostly, the USACE water offices are districts that employ engineers and water management specialists. A few key offices carry out water-related research and training.

SECTOR ISSUES AND OUTLOOK

The water sector is in some ways an enigma. On one hand, it is essential to economic development, and water shortages and pollution problems seem to promise business opportunities, but, on the other hand, government involvement and political gridlock about water as a social right and as a core environmental issue have defeated many proposals for solutions. Regardless of these dilemmas, it is certain that global water issues will remain in the headlines. Emerging issues such as global climate change, water security, and aging infrastructures will continue to drive investments in this capital-intensive and mostly stable industry.

The "World Water Crisis" Will Remain at Center Stage

The media coverage of the "world water crisis" will continue, as it has for nearly four decades. This can translate into business growth in some areas, such as building infrastructure, but can thwart business ventures in other areas, such as investing in water rights. The water industry has many political and social aspects that can override business principles. It mixes the themes of poverty, human rights, public health, access to safe water, climate change, environmental degradation, privatization, and roles of international corporations and development banks, among others. These valid and compelling concerns have been on the radar screen for a long time and are difficult to fix. Part of the issue is how to lift people from poverty and accelerate international development. Another piece is justice, in this case the obligation and equity involved in providing low-cost and safe water. Another piece is socialism versus capitalism. Then there is the issue of corporate social responsibility. It is a stew of many complex issues, singling out a water company as a culprit or alleging that a soft drink bottler is somehow guilty because it wants to locate a bottle plant in a town somewhere seems nonsensical.

Water Is an Essential Element to a Vital and Sustainable Future

The reasons for media attention to water focus on water's inputs to a healthy society and environment, abundant food and energy, and public recreation. It is not an exaggeration to say that safe water is more important than public health systems to the overall health of people around the world. Water management is good business and proves its value daily as one issue after another is solved.

The Water Industry Is Difficult to Characterize

In spite of its size, the water sector has a low profile compared to most infrastructure sectors, especially electric power and telecom. It is difficult to characterize because it addresses a range of different needs. While some firms and equipment suppliers do well in it, the industry defies the general characterization that is required to assemble a successful index or water fund. Water investment indices and funds barely scratch the surface of the industry's activity because it is so dispersed among different subsectors (such as water supply and wastewater) and locales. As a result, an index or fund cannot be very representative of the range of activity stimulated by rising water demands. The sector is large and diverse, comprising utilities and "water resources," a policy-related term that captures all public responsibilities for water management other than the pure business aspects of utilities.

The Water Industry Is Linked Tightly to the Economy, Especially Homebuilding

Like other infrastructure sectors, the water industry has a tight relationship to homebuilding, which is the largest part of U.S. construction spending. As homebuilding slows, the need for new water connections goes down and suppresses the demands for equipment and services. Water utilities have large labor and operational expenses, compared to their costs for equipment and services.

The Water Industry Is Capital Intensive, but the Investments Last a Long Time

The water industry is capital intensive and its infrastructure is long lasting, so annual capital investments for renewal are small. For example, the million miles of buried water supply mains in the United States have a replacement value of around $400 billion, but the replacement rate averages about once in 200 years. This slow rate of renewal eventually may create a crisis that increases investment, but no one knows exactly how long it will take.

The Water Business Is Mostly Stable but Can Surprise Investors

Due to shortages, aging infrastructure, and its regulated nature, the water business seems stable but promising to investors. Indeed, water agencies will spend hundreds of billions of dollars annually on construction, equipment, supplies, and services. However, many investors have been deceived by the apparent promise of this highly regulated, highly politicized, and government-dominated industry. After an initial surge of interest, investors are apt to be discouraged by the complex economics and heavy politics of the water sector. It is difficult to jump from the world water crisis to a big change in the water business. It seems more likely that the water business will remain steady as a mixed public-private business with areas of growth but dead ends as well.

Water Is a Human and Environmental Right

The most controversial side of water is in human and environmental rights. These lead to government and political intervention in the industry and can throw a monkey wrench into well-developed investment plans. This means that investors must watch out for government involvement in water. Although water can look attractive as an investment, the mostly government-run water industry has disappointed many investors.

Water and sanitation in developing countries has been a high-profile issue for four or more decades and is a key issue in the fight to overcome global poverty.

Water Supply Is the Most Visible Urban Service, but Wastewater Is Nearly as Big

Water supply and wastewater are the closest of the water services to real businesses. Water supply utilities are similar to those offering electric power, and many water and electric utilities are combined. In some cases, particularly those where irrigation water is involved, you may find electric power subsidizing water services.

The Water Industry Is Heavily Regulated

The water industry's regulators have authorities in health and safety, environment, water use, fish and wildlife protection, and service levels. These diverse areas draw in many laws and interest groups and can lay traps for potential investors or reformers.

The Water Industry Has a Large and Expanding Sector of Support Businesses

The support sector of the water industry is large and growing. Its parts include suppliers, construction contractors, professional service firms, knowledge sector, advocacy groups, financiers and insurers, and associations. As the industry seeks to become more integrated, groups find new business opportunities and relationships in different parts of the industry.

Financing the Water Sector Requires Public-Private Cooperation

Part of the water sector is financed through user charges, but water management also requires involvement of government agencies that are financed through taxes. This occurs due to the public purposes of water management and because the cost of water services sometimes exceeds people's ability to pay. This latter reason is especially evident in developing countries, where some privatization experiments have foundered. In spite of these difficulties, future opportunities for privatization in the water sector exist.

Markets for Water Rights as Commodities

Given the increasing scarcity of water, it is tempting to think that it can be sold like a commodity, like oil and gas. Given the social and political aspects of water, this had led more than one company or entrepreneur down a difficult path to failure. Water development is more contentious than other resource issues.

Future Water Issues Will Determine the Shape of the Industry

Forces of change in the water sector include climate change, demand for high-quality water, environmentalism, aging infrastructure, security, and new information technologies. New supplies will be hard to come by, and more efficient use of water and higher rates will be the norm. Insistence on high-quality water for an aging population and consumers who pay attention to health alerts is increasing, and even sales of bottled water are coming under scrutiny. Although environmentalism seems mature, new facets continue to influence the water sector. New laws and regulations are emerging more slowly than they did in the past, but public concern creates pressures for water conservation, pollution prevention, and prevention of new water storage and diversion projects.

Security

Security has become a big issue in the water industry, and both terrorism and natural disasters must be anticipated to protect water systems. New products and services will be needed to modify systems for protection and resilience against a range of threats.

CHAPTER 8

Waste Management Sector

The waste management business is sometimes called environmental services, but it is really about handling residual wastes from economic and social activities. Environmental services are the part of the business that regulates returns of residuals to the environment. A larger part of the business is in collecting, transporting, and processing a diverse stream of wastes. According to the *Economist* (2009a), in this essential but poorly studied business, there "are really only three things you can do with waste: bury it, burn it or recycle it." Each option carries environmental and financial costs and requires careful management.

In this chapter, we discuss the streams of solid wastes and present financial information and business profiles in each category. Waste management is not as large as some of the infrastructure sectors, but it offers a number of attractive investment opportunities.

SECTOR STRUCTURE AND SIZE

Although this chapter about waste management is the last one about the infrastructure sectors, it does not signal that the business is not important. To the contrary, waste management is a large and important part of infrastructure and public services arena. For proof, just imagine all household, commercial, and industrial solid and hazardous waste piling up with no management plan for it.

Waste disposal and its regulatory environment have created a large waste management industry with a number of trade associations. For example, the National Solid Waste Management Association (2008) represents companies that provide services related to solid, hazardous, and medical wastes. Their companies are involved in collection, recycling, and disposal as well as consulting services. Policy issues of the industry include landfills, incineration, and illegal disposal, along with international trade in waste, recycling, hazardous materials, and nuclear waste (Porter, 2002).

NSWMA characterizes the industry in 2001as having about 27,000 private sector companies and government agencies. It estimated that 55 percent were public sector and 45 percent private sector companies. Revenue estimates were for $43.3 billion in 2001 (net of interindustry payments) with 76 percent generated by the private sector. NSWMA estimated employment at 367,800, with 74 percent in the private sector, and a total of 948,000 jobs when you include all indirect induced effects from the industry's activities. The industry is heavily dependent on motorized equipment and uses many vehicles and other equipment types, including those for compaction and processing.

The waste management industry is heavily regulated. In addition to the 1976 Resource Conservation and Recovery Act (RCRA) and the U.S. Environmental Protection Agency (USEPA) regulation, state and local boards apply additional controls. For example, the California Integrated Waste Management Board (2009) oversees permits and promotes recycling. The board's Web site suggests that it is involved in many important activities, but why such a board is needed is controversial in California (Carlton, 2008).

The general categories of wastes are solid wastes, wastewater, and air emissions. Wastewater was discussed in Chapter 7, and air emissions are not managed, other than being subjected to regulatory controls. In this chapter, we discuss the categories of solid wastes.

CATEGORIES OF SOLID WASTES

Solid wastes are managed, and they include separate streams of wastes*:

- Municipal solid wastes
- Nonhazardous industrial wastes
- Hazardous wastes
- Medical wastes
- Radioactive wastes

As the list shows, the need for regulation and possibilities for businesses increase with the complexity of the waste stream. Whereas in the past, garbage collection might have seemed relatively simple, that is not the case any longer. The waste management business is large and significant, and it involves complex science, politics, and economics.

---

*Most information about solid and hazardous wastes comes from the USEPA Web site at www.epa.gov/osw.

Municipal Solid Wastes

According to the USEPA (2009), municipal solid waste comprises trash or garbage and everyday items such as product packaging, grass clippings, furniture, clothing, bottles, food scraps, newspapers, appliances, paint, and batteries. For many years, the United States has produced these items in large quantities. In 2007, for example, it generated more than 254 million tons, or approximately 4.6 pounds of waste per person per day (763 kg/year). Showing the changing consumption patterns, this figure is up from 2.7 pounds/day/person in 1960. Internationally, the average westerner produces over 500 kg per year (Economist, 2009a).

The volumes of materials fill landfills and consume many acres of land. For example, the former Fresh Kills landfill in New York is five square miles, the largest structure in the world (*Economist*, 2009a).

Typical percentages of waste are shown in this list. You can see that paper dominates the waste stream, along with yard trimmings. Residuals from modern shopping and shipping practices include plastics, metals, and related other materials. The percentages are:

Waste	Percent
Paper	32.7
Yard Trimmings	12.8
Food Scraps	12.5
Plastics	12.1
Metals	8.2
Rubber, Leather, and Textiles	7.6
Wood	5.6
Glass	5.3
Other	3.2

The sheer volume of wastes is a growing worldwide problem. Plastic waste is a troublesome problem, especially in oceans, and this is why many grocery stores are moving toward recyclable bags. To cut down on these volumes of wastes, recycling and reuse are encouraged, and at present, some 33.4 percent of municipal solid wastes are recovered, recycled, or composted. Another 12.6 percent is burned at combustion facilities; the other 54 percent is disposed of in landfills.

Incinerators and waste-to-energy schemes seem promising, but they are controversial. Fairfax County, Virginia, has a plant that burns about 1 million tons/year and generates 80 megawatts, about enough for 75,000 homes. Japan and Singapore burn more than 50 percent of their waste.

However, no new incinerators have been sited in the United States since 1995 (*Economist*, 2009a).

Companies promoting waste-to-energy have organized the Energy Recovery Council (2009) as a trade organization for them and owners of facilities. The council members currently own and operate 69 of the 87 U.S. waste-to-energy facilities. Council members include Covanta Energy Corporation, Veolia ES Waste-to-Energy, Inc., and Wheelabrator Technologies Inc.

To cope with the vast quantity of solid wastes requires a large public-private industry that handles collection, transfer, processing, and disposal of wastes. Participants may be private companies or public agencies, and the processes are regulated in several ways.

You would expect the waste management business to generally follow the business cycle. If gross domestic product is growing, so will waste collection revenues grow because they are based more on number of customers than on volume of waste. This seems to be the case with the mainline waste management companies profiled for this chapter. Specialty waste companies, handling medical waste, for example, might grow in spite of a flat economy.

Waste Age (2009) magazine ranks companies participating in the industry. Mostly these waste management companies are involved in collection and transfer, recycling and processing, and landfill management. The rankings are dominated by the largest companies (especially Waste Management Inc. [WMI]), which remain at the top of the list. After WMI, the size of the companies drops off fast, showing how the industry is dominated by smaller companies. The top five, ranked by 2007 revenues, are shown in Exhibit 8.1.

The top five are public, listed companies. The number-six firm, Safety-Kleen Systems, Inc., is privately owned. In 2008, Republic Services spurned an offer from WMI and bought Allied Waste Industries. Now it owns 41 percent of the market (*Economist*, 2009a). Internationally, Veolia and Suez are significant players in the waste management business.

EXHIBIT 8.1   Largest Waste Management Companies

Company	2007 Revenues $ billions	2007 Employment
Waste Management Inc.	13.3	47,400
Allied Waste Industries Inc.	6.1	22,300
Republic Services Inc.	3.2	13,000
Veolia Environmental Services NA	2.0	11,200
Covanta Holding Corp	1.4	3,500

Waste Management Inc. Waste Management Inc. (2009) is headquartered in Houston. It has nearly 20 million residential, industrial, municipal, and commercial customers and operates 354 collection operations, 341 transfer stations, 277 active landfill disposal sites, 108 landfill gas projects, 105 recycling facilities, 16 waste-to-energy plants, and 6 independent power production plants. With such diverse and large-scale facilities, it operates across a spectrum of urban, environmental, and energy policy areas. Some of the interesting things that WMI does are to:

- Recover methane gas from waste in landfills
- Use trucks powered by natural gas
- Recycle millions of tons of commodities
- Operate waste-to-energy plants

WMI has a Wheelabrator Technologies subsidiary that owns or operates 16 plants to process up to 21,000 tons of waste per day and generate more than 650 megawatts of electricity, enough for 600,000 homes per year. WMI had $13.4 billion in revenues in 2008, an amount that was little changed from 2006 and 2007 (Yahoo Finance, 2009).

Covanta Holding Corporation Covanta Holding Corporation focuses on the waste-to-energy business, on waste disposal, renewable energy, and independent power production. At the end of 2008, it was involved with 60 energy generation facilities that use various fuels, including solid waste. It also owns or operates various waste management businesses and has some insurance operations. Covanta had 2008 revenues of $1.67 billion, up from $1.27 billion in 2006 (Yahoo Finance, 2009).

Private Waste Management Companies Many waste management companies are privately owned, especially the smaller ones. An example of a privately owned company is Appalachian Waste Services LLC, which is based in Georgia and operates as a subsidiary of Advanced Disposal Services, Inc, which operates in the Southeast. Advanced Disposal Services was founded in 2000 and is based in Jacksonville, Florida. It is a unit of American International Group Inc's Highstar Capital LP subsidiary. Advanced Disposal owns an 866-acre disposal facility (*Business Week*, 2008).

Consulting Firms: CalRecovery The solid waste business does not support as much consulting work as other environmental areas, such as water and wastewater. One privately owned consulting firm, CalRecovery (2009), performs work in waste management studies, assessments of solid waste systems, resource recovery systems, and marketing studies for materials and energy. It displays in its promotional material an extensive list of books and articles authored by its staff. It also hosts the international journal *Waste Management*, published by Elsevier.

Nonhazardous Industrial Wastes

Nonhazardous industrial wastes form a special category of wastes that includes construction, demolition, and some varieties of medical wastes. This category of wastes does not fit into the waste management business as neatly as solid wastes, hazardous wastes, and some specialty wastes. In the future, however, it might become a bigger part of the materials recycling industry.

This category of wastes comes from some 17 North American Industry Classification System industrial groups that focus on manufacturing. A 1980s estimate was of 7.6 billion tons per year of chemicals, iron and steel, plastics and resin, stone, clay, glass and concrete, pulp and paper, food and related products. Industrial waste volumes of some 30 times those for municipal solid waste seem like order-of-magnitude estimates. Some of the materials from construction and demolition include concrete, wood from buildings, asphalt from roads and roofing shingles, gypsum from drywall, metals, bricks, glass, plastics, salvaged building components, and trees, stumps, earth, and rock from clearing sites (USEPA, 2009).

Hazardous Wastes

Hazardous wastes are a special category with their own legal definition for regulatory purposes. On a global basis, CyclOpe, a French research institute, estimated that the world's largest economies produce among themselves about 150 million tons/year of hazardous wastes (*Economist*, 2009a).

In the United States, some materials are classified as hazardous wastes under the rules of the 1976 RCRA, which also regulates nonhazardous wastes (USEPA, 2009). Hazardous wastes are defined as liquid, solid, contained gas, or sludge wastes that are dangerous or potentially harmful to human health or the environment. They are classified as listed, characteristic, universal, and mixed wastes. Listed wastes come from common manufacturing and industrial processes, from specific industries, and from commercial chemical products. Characteristic wastes do not appear on the lists but exhibit ignitability, corrosivity, reactivity, or toxicity. Universal wastes are batteries, pesticides, mercury-containing equipment, and certain lamps. Mixed wastes contain both radioactive and hazardous waste components.

RCRA has a Subtitle C that establishes a management system for hazardous wastes and provides regulations for facilities that generate, treat, store, or dispose of them. It provides both for reducing the amount of waste generated and for cleaning up old problems. Another important regulatory program is Superfund, which was enacted in 1980 to provide for cleanup of abandoned hazardous waste sites, to establish legal liability, and to create a trust fund for cleanups. The formal name for Superfund is the Comprehensive Environmental Response, Compensation, and Liability Act.

People are very leery of the dangers of hazardous wastes and toxic substances. In the 1960s and 1970s, a series of disasters afflicted the world. Japan saw releases of mercury-laden chemicals into Minamata Bay that killed over 1,000 people. In the United States, the toxic wastes disposed of in Love Canal near Niagara Falls, New York led to birth defects, and the government had to relocate 800 families. In 2008, a collapsed dike in the Tennessee Valley Authority system released toxic sludge with poisonous heavy metals onto 300 acres. For months afterward, the cost for cleanup was running at $1 million per day (*Economist*, 2009a).

Because hazardous wastes are classified into legal categories with strict requirements, the business of handling them is different from the business of handling the larger volume of solid waste. Waste management companies can have departments to handle hazardous wastes and comply with federal regulations as well as local requirements. This business line is likely to have a lower profile than the larger-volume business and might not be as profitable. Nevertheless, hazardous wastes are a significant issue in businesses, and liability over them is likely to remain on the radar screen for decades into the future.

Medical Wastes

Medical waste is a specialty area that is likely to grow as the healthcare industry expands to take care of an aging population. These wastes are regulated through the Medical Waste Tracking Act of 1988. They are generated at hospitals, clinics, physician and dental offices, blood banks, veterinary clinics, and other medical facilities. A few examples are used bandages; culture dishes and other glassware; discarded surgical gloves, needles, and instruments; and body organs.

Stericycle Inc.   Stericycle Inc. (2009) is a provider of medical waste services for hospitals, blood banks, pharmaceutical manufacturers, outpatient clinics, medical and dental offices, care facilities, and pharmacies. In addition to waste collection, processing, and disposal, its services include highly specialized tasks such as infection control and returns management for expired or recalled healthcare products. The company became publicly traded in 1996 and with acquisitions became North America's largest provider of medical waste services in 2000. In 2003 it acquired Bio Systems Sharps

Management service and entered the reusable container management business. It entered the returns business by acquisition and serves in pharmaceutical and medical device recall, trade returns, and retrieval services. The company handled the single largest prescription drug recall event in U.S. history. Stericyle's 2008 revenue was $1.08 billion, up from $790 million in 2006 (Yahoo Finance, 2009).

Radioactive Wastes

Radioactive wastes in gas, liquid, or solid forms are important but are more of a political and regulatory issue than a business issue. They stem from activities that produce or use radioactive materials, such as mining, nuclear power, and other industrial processes. Categories include low-level (contaminated protective clothing, tools, filters, rags, medical tubes, and other items); high-level (used nuclear reactor fuel and other types); and uranium mill tailings. The categories refer to the origin of the wastes, and some low-level waste can be as radioactive as some high-level waste.

Radioactive wastes are a politically charged topic. The problem is complex scientifically and legally, due to the regulatory structure with many stakeholders and regulatory programs. Federal regulators include USEPA, the Nuclear Regulatory Commission, the Department of Energy (DOE), and the Department of Transportation.

The search for a disposal site for radioactive wastes has gone on for decades. DOE began to study Yucca Mountain in Nevada in 1978 as a place to store spent fuel and other solidified high-level wastes. Even earlier, DOE began to plan and develop a Waste Isolation Pilot Plant (WIPP) near Carlsbad, New Mexico. To some people, Yucca Mountain seemed like a safe and risk-free place for nuclear wastes, but continuing concerns have been raised. It would hold up to 77,000 tons of high-level radioactive wastes, which are now at 121 temporary sites in 39 states. The spent fuel and other high-level defense waste would be stored in engineered containers placed in tunnels deep inside the mountain.

The cost estimates have continued to jump, and during the campaign, President Barack Obama stated his opposition to Yucca Mountain unless waste and safety issues were resolved. In 2008, DOE replaced a Bechtel-SAIC joint venture as manager of Yucca Mountain with USA Repository Services, a team involving URS, Shaw Group Inc., and Areva Federal Services. The five-year contract will be for about $2billion. However, President Obama's proposed 2010 budget cuts funds for Yucca Mountain and throws the project into doubt. If the Nuclear Regulatory Commission delays its permit decision, though, the project could remain alive. Meanwhile, the spent nuclear fuel and other high-level wastes remain at their distributed sites around the nation (ENR.com, 2008).

RECYCLING AND THE MATERIALS INDUSTRY

The waste management industry has a stake in the commodity business when recycling is considered. Recycling programs vary in local areas and are sensitive to economic conditions because of fluctuating demand for materials. Recyclers manage commodities such as cardboard, plastic, paper, steel, and aluminum. For example, in the community of Fort Collins, Colorado, haulers are paid for recyclables, which they must collect at no extra charge to homeowners. Their costs are bundled into the charge to collect regular solid wastes. Incentives are provided in the form of rebates for various commodities. However, when market prices for commodities dropped with the economic slowdown, the program ran into trouble. The price for paper dropped from $150 a ton to $15 and for steel from $240 to less than $100 in a few months.

The city's recycling plant is operated at the county landfill through a contract with Recycle America, a subsidiary of Waste Management Inc., which has been in the recycling field since 1971. Some materials, such as bales of cardboard, can go directly to market. Others, as in the case of "single-stream" deliveries of paper and plastics, must be reprocessed at Recycle America's plant in Denver (Duggan, 2008).

After the crash of commodity prices in 2008, recyclers had to rethink their business strategies. For example, Waste Management had set a goal to triple its recycle volume to 20 million tons per year by 2020 but probably will have a $98 million loss in the business in 2009. High commodity prices had distorted the possibilities for recycling as a business. Still, Waste Management plans to continue its emphasis on recycling, and it now has 33 single-stream sorting facilities, with plans to increase the number. Some use technological methods, such as optical scanners, air blasts, and magnets, to separate the wastes (Palmeri, 2009).

Waste-to-energy programs are a form of recycling. Technologies can range from incineration to bioreactors, which offer ways to convert waste to energy by decomposing it. Other technologies include pyrolysis and gasification to produce syngas. Ze-Gen in Massachusetts gasifies waste by injecting it into molten steel. Farm wastes offer to provide a lot of energy through biological processes. The British firm Sterecycle (a different company from Stericyle Inc., which is in the medical waste business) opened an autoclave facility, which is an industrial-size pressure cooker, to produce clean fuel.

The company is financed through private equity. Another firm with the same approach is Graphite Resources (*Economist*, 2009a).

Recycling is a tricky business due to the difficulty of sorting and the rapidly changing commodity prices. Some materials, such as aluminum, are worth the cost of sorting due to market value, but others are not. There is a great deal of interest in promoting recycling. For example, Britain's Waste and Resources Action Programme works to apply market forces to waste minimization. Materials recovery facilities are a growing business line.

Most cities emphasize recycling in the residential sector. Cities have not developed recycling programs for commercial and industrial wastes to the same extent, but the firms can develop their own recycling programs when they are cost effective. In addition to economic benefits, recycling can help the "green image" of businesses.

Recycling of industrial materials has led to creation of an academic field called industrial ecology, which focuses on using the wastes of one process as the inputs to another, as nature does. It incorporates ideas such as recycling, conservation, efficiency, and minimization of wastes. As an example, an industrial park in Denmark has a power station that produces gypsum from electricity generation; the gypsum becomes a resource for an industry that produces plasterboard.

SECTOR ISSUES AND OUTLOOK

Imagine the tremendous quantities of paper, glass, metal, and other materials and substances required for the global economy, and you have a picture of the challenges and opportunities faced by the waste management industry. The environmental impacts of the industry continue to rise on the public's radar screen because waste disposal places large demands on land, water and air systems to assimilate wastes. On one hand, emerging economies such as China and India are demanding more supplies of commodities for manufacturing, construction, and energy production, while mature economies are stressing efficiency and conservation. The pressures created by these forces are leading the waste management industry in new directions that focus on recycling, waste to energy, and industrial ecology.

The Waste Management Industry Handles Enormous Quantities of Materials

Even though the waste management industry is the smallest infrastructure sector on the basis of revenues, it handles enormous quantities and diverse waste materials and offers many investment opportunities. The largest players, such as Waste Management Inc., are public investor-owned companies, but many other smaller companies operate in local markets and in handling of specialty wastes, such as hazardous industrial wastes or medical wastes.

Waste Management Is an Environmental Service

Although waste management is an environmental service, it is mostly about handling large quantities of residuals from economic and social activities. Environmental services regulate the return of residuals to the environment. The environmental impacts of the waste management industry are huge. Collection is energy intensive, and disposal is still handled mostly in local landfills.

Recycling Is a Wave of the Future and Creates a Commodity Business

Recycling always has been a vibrant business for profitable commodities, such as scrap metal and hard-to-get materials or components. It experiences such large swings in demand, however, that it is hard to finance sustainable recycling businesses. Given the obvious need for more recycling, this policy area needs a lot of attention. One area receiving current attention is single-stream recycling that enables collection by fewer trucks and does not require customers to sort and separate waste streams on site.

Waste-to-Energy Programs Will Remain Vibrant but Limited

While waste-to-energy plants would seem to offer good opportunities for efficiency, and they have less environmental impacts than other technologies, especially considering the waste disposal as well as energy, the United States has not built a new incinerator since 1995. The jury remains out as to whether waste will be an attractive fuel for future electricity generation.

Recycling Offers Opportunities for Government Reform and for Businesses

Given the demands for waste disposal, the need for materials, and the environmental impacts of handling wastes, recycling offers many possibilities. The challenges are more in the realm of management and regulation than in technologies, and this industry will continue to be subject to much political and legal control.

Many Waste Management Companies Are Small and Private

The collection side of the waste business and its many niches offer attractive possibilities for new businesses, which can start small but grow. Disposal and waste to energy are large businesses because of the few sites available and the large capital requirements to enter the business.

Nuclear Waste May Rise on the Radar Screen

Given the rising interest in nuclear power, disposal of its waste products may rise on the public radar screen. Although disposal options have been in the news for decades, little movement toward a solution has been achieved. Whether on-site management continues or a large, centralized solution is found remains an unanswered policy question.

CHAPTER 9

Infrastructure and the Construction Industry

S ome analysts see the infrastructure business and the construction industry as one and the same. While the infrastructure business is broader than the construction industry, we can learn about infrastructure from construction, and vice versa. The business of infrastructure ranges from the conception of any built facility to its decommissioning as well as all support systems. Infrastructure is like a life cycle view of the built environment, whereas the focus of the construction industry is logically on the construction process.

This chapter outlines the future of the construction industry to help us examine how it meshes with the trajectory of the infrastructure business. The chapter characterizes the construction industry and explains how it organizes itself to provide and sustain infrastructure as well as how it is affected by economic ups and downs and the demands for buildings and their support systems.

THEN AND NOW

Although the focus of the construction industry is on the building process, a broader view shows that it includes planning, design, finance, marketing, operations, and renewal of facilities. This broad view can lead us to define the construction industry as including everything in the infrastructure business and involving design engineers, suppliers, assemblers, and financiers as well as building contractors.

Despite the fact that its activity has fallen during the financial crisis, global construction is still a giant industry at nearly $6 trillion per year, out of a world economy with a gross domestic product of some $50 to $60 trillion (Tulacz, 2005). Whether the construction industry is all of the infrastructure business or only part of it does not matter much; construction will always be at the center of the infrastructure business. In the past, the construction industry built the infrastructure but left it alone afterward. Now, in some cases, it is involved in more than pure construction, including design, finance, operation, and, in some cases, ownership.

The close link between infrastructure and the construction industry is evident to every construction interest group and policy panel. The construction industry deals with so many issues that many groups have a hand in it, including contractors, suppliers, commodity groups, realtors, bankers, engineers, architects, and others. Construction offers many business opportunities, and effective construction management helps hold cost down and raise the performance of infrastructure.

Developing construction technologies is one of humankind's oldest and proudest achievements. In the thousands of years between early civilization and the frontier days of the United States, when the infrastructure business was about to start, people used construction to build basic systems and to construct great structures, such as the pyramids of Egypt, the Greek city-state, the Roman aqueducts, and the palaces of the ancient Chinese.

In Egypt, the pyramids were mostly built from 2700 B.C. to 2500 B.C. They were of monumental size, as were the temples of Greece. Today's engineers are amazed at how ancient constructors solved the complex technical and management problems involved in producing and moving large stones, among others. During the nineteenth century, engineers utilized the steam engine, water power, canals, railroads, and other advances to organize construction of large projects and cities. The steam engine was the advance that made skyscrapers possible. Whether a project is as old as the pyramids or as new as a modern skyscraper, the construction industry continues to conquer new challenges with brains, money, and effort.

Construction always has attracted entrepreneurs because of its combination of opportunity, risk, and reward. It mixes visionaries, such as James Eads, who had the vision for an 1874 Mississippi River bridge, and entrepreneurs, such as Andrew Carnegie, who supplied steel and money for the bridge. The bridge project was successful as a business venture, but the work was touch and go, and could have been a big setback for Carnegie. The construction technologies were impressive, especially for the time.

Think of the construction industry as a combination of many minor players who build small projects and fewer major players who build large and complex projects. It has been this way from ancient times, when the minor players were building houses and tending farms while the major players of the day were building complex projects, such as ancient temples or even the Roman aqueducts. As the industry evolved, skilled crafts accumulated knowledge and organized guilds, which predated unions that are organized by craft rather than by industry. After the steam engine and birth of electric and diesel power, large-scale construction took on many new possibilities. Technology has continued to evolve such that today's construction site is much more high tech than in the past.

THE CONSTRUCTION INDUSTRY TODAY

The construction industry is gigantic and includes many parts. Along with the financial and real estate industries, it cuts across the sectors of infrastructure. In terms of infrastructure, it designs, builds, and rebuilds it; supplies equipment and services to maintain infrastructure systems; may finance projects; and may operate and/or own infrastructure facilities as well as build them.

Today's nearly $6 trillion per year global construction industry is comprised mostly of spending in the major markets of Europe, North America, and Asia. Total spending is lower in South America and Eastern Europe but is still significant, and, of course, construction is vital to raise living standards in developing countries. With the exception of the oil-rich Middle East, which has seen oil-based construction booms, construction follows gross domestic product (GDP) to some extent. It fluctuates with economic conditions and national statistics of construction put-in-place vary with currency exchange rates.

Statistics of global construction spending are just now becoming available and are not subjected to much independent verification, but they do give us a good picture of the overall level of activity. *ENR* magazine started tracking statistics of the global construction industry in 1998, when it estimated the industry at $3.2 trillion for some 150 countries. *ENR* had 430,000 readers and 2,000 advertisers at that time (Stussman, 1998). In 2004, *ENR* reported that global construction spending was $3.9 trillion, with U.S. spending at about 25 percent of it. After the United States, Japan, China, and the larger European nations, such as Germany and France, were the largest markets (Tulacz, 2005). The fact that after 124 years of publication, ENR has launched this indicator is evidence of the globalization of the construction market. Construction volumes are very sensitive to economic growth. An analysis by IHS Global Insight Construction Services of Lexington, Massachusetts, projected a 3.7 percent decline in 2009, to follow a 1.2 percent decline in 2008. The market in western Europe was projected at $1.8 trillion; in North America, at $1.04 trillion; and in China, at $701 billion (Rubin, 2009).

Exhibit 9.1, which was prepared from these data, shows interesting variations in the construction spending of North America, Asia, and the Middle

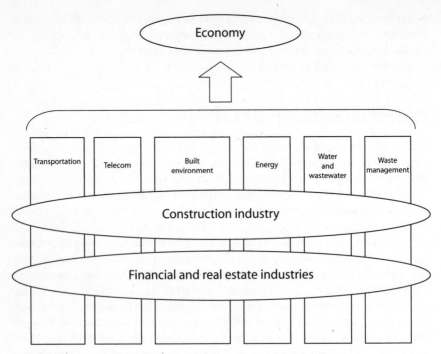

EXHIBIT 9.1 Construction Industry and Infrastructure Sectors

East. North America, dominated by the U.S. market, showed the steepest decline of any region. The housing crisis seems to explain most of that decline. Asia was more stable, probably buoyed by China's continuing robust market. The Middle East shows the most ups-and-downs, being smaller than the other markets and subject to oil price fluctuations and revenues. These numbers will vary with currency fluctuations and are not based on quality-assured statistics, of course.

Although construction falls below 5 percent of GDP and is not as big a share of the economy as categories such as retail trade, information, or finance, it has important multiplier effects. The U.S. construction industry is a separate group in the national economic accounts and by the value-added measure, the total 2008 GDP was $14.3 trillion, of which construction was $582 billion, down from the previous three years. Using this measure, construction is 4.1 percent of GDP. Using the gross output measure, construction accounted for $1.24 trillion (2007 data), or 4.8 percent of GDP (U.S. Bureau of Economic Affairs, 2009a).

Multiplier effects are important in stimulus programs. Although public construction is a smaller category than housing-dominated residential housing, a stimulus program that invests in "shovel-ready" public projects has some capacity to jump-start an economy that is in the doldrums from falling housing starts and weak consumer spending.

In the U.S. market, spending was over $1 trillion per year before the financial crisis. In early 2009, spending had fallen to the range of $970 million. Further details on levels of construction spending are given in Chapter 11.

The constructor side of the industry includes contractors who construct residential, industrial, commercial, and other buildings; heavy and civil engineering construction contractors who build mostly public infrastructure; and specialty trade contractors who perform carpentry, painting, plumbing, and electrical work. In addition to the constructors, the construction industry also involves many design firms, regulators, and suppliers (U.S. Bureau of Labor Statistics, 2009a).

Construction spending in the United States engages some 725,101 business establishments, according to the 2007 Economic Census (U.S. Census Bureau, 2009d). Of these, some 476,290 were specialty trade contractors, another 209,203 were building constructors, and 39,608 were heavy and civil engineering constructors. These firms provided some 7.4 million construction jobs. Most of these are in firms with 250 employees or fewer, and the number of very large firms is relatively small. Some of the largest of these, such as Bechtel, are privately owned, rather than being public, listed companies. The 2007 job count of 7.2 million employees had a payroll of $348 billion for construction workers and their support staffs.

In addition to the organized firms, there are many construction establishments without any employees. In the 2002 Economic Census, there were 2,071,317 mostly self-employed individuals operating small, unincorporated businesses.

A glimpse at the construction job distribution shows where most construction occurs. Exhibit 9.2 displays jobs by category of construction (U.S. Bureau of Labor Statistics, 2009b). From the table, you can see the large fraction employed in residential construction and the many specialty contractors, who can range across the building categories.

Construction spending depends on costs of the factor inputs that include capital, labor, energy, materials, and service inputs. Each of these fluctuates in time and place. *ENR* (2009b) tracks these costs and publishes weekly data for a 20-city national average for construction cost, building cost, materials, skilled labor, and common labor. These data provide clues to trends that affect the commodity markets.

The construction industry requires many products and services as inputs to its building processes, and many groups identify with the industry. For example, asphalt pavement and structural steel are important inputs from the materials and manufacturing industries. A big share of construction spending

EXHIBIT 9.2   Employment in the U.S. Construction Industry, 000s (2006 data)

	Employment	Percent
Construction total	7,689	100.0
Construction of buildings	1,806	23.5
Residential building	1,018	13.2
Nonresidential building construction	789	10.3
Heavy and civil engineering construction	983	12.8
Utility system construction	426	5.5
Highway, street, and bridge construction	349	4.5
Land subdivision	97	1.3
Other heavy and civil engineering construction	112	1.5
Specialty trade contractors	4,900	63.7
Building equipment contractors	2,006	26.1
Foundation, structure, and building exterior contractors	1,132	14.7
Building finishing contractors	1,036	13.5
Other specialty trade contractors	726	9.4

is for intermediate inputs in the form of mechanical, plumbing, electrical, wood, brick, concrete, roofing, landscape, and other supply inputs.

It seems that every group providing construction inputs has its own trade association. The Associated General Contractors of America (AGC) with some 32,000 member firms is a principal voice of the construction industry. There are associations for materials, such as asphalt and concrete; for structural members, such as steel and aluminum; for different kinds of pipe; and for many other inputs.

Trade shows for the construction industry can attract many attendees and exhibits because the industry is so large. For example, the CONEXPO-CON/AGG 2011 show expects 140,000 attendees for its Las Vegas convention. The 2008 show had 2,182 exhibitors with 143,600 attendees. Its organizers include the Association of Equipment Manufacturers (main organizer); National Ready Mixed Concrete Association; National Stone, Sand & Gravel Association; and the AGC (CONEXPO-CON/AGG, 2009).

In the service category, civil engineers and architects identify construction as their major industry. In 2006, architectural and engineering services offered about 1.35 million of some 17 million total jobs in all professional and business services. Consulting engineering companies are a major part of the service sector serving construction. In 2006, some 42,746 of these were reported by U.S. Bureau of Labor Statistics (2009a), mostly in the size range of 1 to 100 employees.

The construction industry also has a number of magazines and trade journals. Many of the industry's sectors or support groups publish a magazine or have a web page. *ENR* (2009c) focuses on the construction industry and devotes a special section in each issue to construction economics, including price data on building commodities and other inputs.

Many research and policy groups study the construction industry. In the U.S. science and policy arena, the National Research Council (2009) has a Board on Infrastructure and the Constructed Environment (BICE). Along with other NRC committees, BICE has been involved in construction industry studies covering topics such as project management, green building, and security. Another construction institute is under the American Society of Civil Engineers, which has a unit that focuses on construction engineering. The construction industry has other research centers, such as the Construction Industry Institute, based at the University of Texas since 1983. The National Institute of Standards and Technology, which used to be the National Bureau of Standards, is a powerful institute in construction because it controls many standards. Also, the American National Standards Institute is important in the same way.

In the United Kingdom, a nongovernmental organization, Constructing Excellence UK (2009), was organized to deliver improved industry performance and a demonstrably better built environment, to serve as a bridge among industry, clients, government, and the research community and to be an umbrella organization for other customers and stakeholders.

ORGANIZATION OF THE INDUSTRY BY FUNCTION AND SECTOR

As shown earlier, the U.S. Census Bureau classifies the construction industry according to whether the activities are for building, heavy and civil engineering construction, or specialty trade construction. Construction of buildings includes residential and remodeling, industrial building, and commercial and institutional buildings. Heavy and civil engineering construction includes a range of projects for utility systems; water well drilling; oil and gas pipelines; industrial process plants; power and communication lines; land subdivision; and highway, street, and bridge construction. Specialty trade contractors include those dealing with foundations and structural, structural steel, precast concrete, framing, masonry, glass and glazing, roofing, siding, building equipment, building finishing, and site preparation. These groups are involved more or less in the infrastructure sectors according to the types of facilities involved.

For example, residential and commercial buildings form the core facilities of the built environment, with streets and utilities providing the support works. Given the types of facilities in each infrastructure sector, we can analyze the construction industry subsectors that are most involved in each one.

In the built environment, the focus on housing and commercial development draws in real estate, bankers, building constructors, architects, engineers, and home improvement companies, among others. This group includes a range of types of companies and trade associations, such as these:

Types of Businesses	Representative Associations
Land development companies	Urban Land Institute
Shopping center development	International Council on Shopping Centers
Architects	American Institute of Architects
Structural engineers	Structural Engineering Institute (ASCE)
Building construction	National Association of Home Builders
Mortgage lending	Mortgage Bankers Association
Home improvement	National Kitchen and Bath Association
Real estate investment trusts	National Association of REITs

In the transportation sector, the focus is on heavy and civil engineering construction, especially on highway, street, and bridge construction. Airports include large quantities of pavement as well as buildings and access facilities. Rail lines and some transit involve special construction methods for their unique needs. Utilities also call on heavy and civil engineering construction, and the construction category of utility contractors focuses on them. Utility contracting is a specialty field of construction. It has its own association, the National Utility Contractors Association. Utility construction can range from process plants, to power and lines, to buried pipelines and more.

Energy sector construction overlaps utility construction but also includes facilities for oil and gas and the coal industry. Waste management resembles the industrial category and is largely a matter of processing facilities and disposal sites. Key associations for these sectors are described elsewhere in the book.

ORGANIZATION BY BUSINESS LINES

The construction industry's businesses are changing and adapting to new opportunities and pressures. Players can enter new business lines through avenues of finance and operations, as well as pure construction. The 700,000 construction firms organize themselves according to what they do (building, heavy and civil engineering construction, and specialty trades), but they also get involved in different ways in the business operations of infrastructure organizations, in roles that range from advice to owners, to operating contracts, to outright ownership.

These roles take on multiple dimensions of planning and design, finance, construction, furnishing equipment, operations and maintenance, and ownership. There are so many possibilities that it is not possible to create a general business model; it is possible, however, to give examples of cooperative business arrangements.

Placing these roles into a matrix of owner and construction industry responsibilities illustrates the range of possibilities. Construction industry firms are meant to include a range of constructors, engineering companies, combination equipment-contractor firms, and other possible arrangements. Some of the roles shown in Exhibit 9.3, such as financing and ownership, can also be assumed by financial sector firms and investors.

As an example of the listed possibilities, consider the process known as build-operate-transfer (BOT). This is more of a project financing method than a project delivery method, but it is also a way for an owner to transfer responsibilities for project development/delivery from itself to a contracting

EXHIBIT 9.3 Owner and Construction Industry Roles

Role	Owners	Construction Industry Firms
Plan and design	Owners direct the process toward the goals of the facility	Architect, planning, and engineering firms mainly do planning and design, but contractors may employ these skill sets
Finance	Owners may arrange financing without participation of the construction industry	Construction industry firms may assist in financing and/or assume risk
Construct	Owners monitor the process and oversee the construction manager	Construction is by construction industry firms
Operate and maintain (O&M)	Owners may assume all O&M work or outsource it	Construction industry firms may perform O&M through contract, as in "contract operations"
Own	Owner may retain all ownership or share it	Construction industry firms may obtain partial or temporary ownership through agreements

entity. In a BOT project, the owner might contract with the firm to undertake all of the tasks shown in Exhibit 9.3 for a period of time, then to have the project infrastructure ownership revert to itself.

A related method, almost the reverse of BOT, is sale-leaseback. The owner might have an infrastructure facility and want to transfer ownership in exchange for capital but not to give up operation. In that case, the investor could obtain ownership of the infrastructure and a guaranteed stream of lease revenues from the original owner. This method might be used in commercial buildings, for example.

Financial management in construction is critical, and the Construction Financial Management Association (CFMA; 2009) has been organized to represent general contractors and subcontractors, developers, construction managers, architects, engineers, owners, and material and equipment suppliers. Associate members are from accounting, insurance, surety, software, legal, and banking. The CFMA has some 7,000 members in 88 chapters in the United States. Members are interested in accounting but also in job cost control, contract life cycles, risk management, and surety relationships. The CFMA works with AGC to organize an annual conference.

PROJECT DELIVERY AND FINANCE

The some 700,000 construction firms in the United States include powerful players that drive change in the industry. If we draw an "iron triangle" of the construction industry—a diagram of companies, government, and interest groups—it would indicate how large contracting companies have influence on federal policy and appropriations for everything from road construction to regulatory reform. Some of these companies have influence at high levels in the government.

In addition to these influential contractors, large engineering companies, developers, bankers, and real estate agents influence construction policy and methods. They track policies ranging from government investments to the details of federal rules, but the one topic they all focus on is improvements in the project delivery process.

The phrase *project delivery process* refers to the set of procedures that comes together to create a finished project. It is more than the construction process because it includes planning, financing, approvals, risk sharing, and control levers, among other arrangements. There are a number of names for the process, including construction management, integrated project delivery, and project management.

Interest in project delivery improvement stems from an apparent decline in productivity in the construction industry, caused by delays, cost overruns, and adversarial relationships among the players. Project delivery can enhance collaboration and smooth out the process for the benefit of all players.

The details of construction project delivery methods are beyond the scope of this discussion, so here we concentrate on their essence as they relate to infrastructure finance.

Think of any project as involving planning, design, construction, approval, O&M, renewal, and decommissioning. Various players are involved and have roles as owner, regulator, financier/investor, builder, and so on. As a simple example, take the construction process for a house. The owner wants to build a house, and the project has three phases: planning, construction, and long-term occupancy (which is the O&M phase for most infrastructure projects).

Planning and construction go together in that they are to prepare the project for use. The owner must secure financing for these stages, normally separately from long-term financing, which may require various inspections and guarantees before the lender is ready to lend on a long-term basis. The owner approaches a financier, probably a savings and loan or regular commercial bank, for a construction loan. The loan will be short term, be interest payments only, probably carry a higher interest rate than the long-term loan, and be subject to certain performance requirements of the owner. The main performance requirement is that the owner obtains a certificate of occupancy. The owner can draw on the principal of the construction loan to pay for the project as it proceeds. The process involves plans, hiring a builder, arranging for inspections and approvals, and eventually occupying the house.

In the simple example of the home construction loan, three basic parties participate: the owner, the builder, and the financier. The owner ultimately must pay for the project; the builder is involved during the construction phase; and the financier uses capital funds as investments to gain a return on investment.

Now consider a more complex project, say a privately owned shopping center, a publicly owned toll road, or a waste-to-energy plant. The requirements are the same: Funds are needed for planning and construction and during the O&M phase. What is different is the level of complexity. Planning may be done with funds on hand, or the infrastructure owner may choose to bundle planning costs in the project construction budget. Then the owner must look for financing for construction phase and the long-term O&M phase.

If we focus on a restricted example, we can examine the case of a toll bridge in which the public agency owner sees the need for the bridge. In a conventional process, it could sell bonds, hire a design engineer, go through construction, and pay off bonds with taxes or tolls.

In newer, public-private deals, the public agency owner also can consider letting the bridge go private or let a concession with a set of terms. Under the private arrangement, it would be up to the private owner and/or operator to raise capital, perform design and construction, and arrange for O&M. The deal could involve ownership reverting to the public after a period of time.

Another option is an actual partnership with split roles. The public owner could offer to private firms the chance to design the bridge and put up a proposal for a build-operate-transfer deal, for example. The selected private firm might dig into its pockets to handle requirements through the bidding phase. It might have to find an investor or use its own capital, taking on roles such as private equity or venture capitalist. The details of the deal would be worked out during the process.

This arrangement illustrates roles of private equity, venture capitalists, and investment bankers, which are discussed in Chapter 12. Private equity means equity capital, not on a public exchange in which investors invest directly in private companies or take public listed companies private. A private equity firm might buy out and privatize a government operation. Venture capital is similar; it provides financing for businesses or enterprises with long-term growth potential that might include taking an equity position. Investment banking is an organized way to perform some of the tasks involved in finding capital for enterprises, such as underwriting debt, issuing equity securities, or facilitating acquisitions.

In the example given, if the deal was done on the basis of splitting up responsibilities, this is like breaking up a company and selling its parts. The part of the deal that offered firms the chance to design the bridge and put up a proposal for a build-operate-transfer deal is like a risk-sharing arrangement or business competition. For the firm to dig into its own pockets is like outsourcing the financing responsibility, in which private equity firms invest on the chance they might get business or ownership. The older method of project delivery is called design-bid-build (DBB). A newer method is "design-build" (DB). It is explained by the Design-Build Institute of America (Design-Build Institute, 2009) as an integrated delivery process, which harkens back to ancient master builders with responsibility for both design and construction. According to the Design-Build Institute, use of design-build is increasing rapidly for nonresidential structures and is nearing 50 percent of the projects while traditional DBB is declining and is now below 50 percent. Another method, called construction management at-risk, is shown as steady with about 10 percent of the projects.

Construction management at-risk is a delivery method in which the construction manager (CM) usually guarantees a finished project within a guaranteed maximum price (GMP). The CM also consults with the owner in the planning and design phases and serves as the general contractor during construction. The CM might be involved early in the planning phase to estimate construction cost and influence the design, based on estimated cost. So, in construction management at-risk, the CM is closely involved with the owner all along the project delivery process and takes on considerable risk in adhering to the GMP.

Project delivery and project finance go hand in hand. For example, in a design-build contract, the subjects of finance and ownership can come up quickly as the owner and the contractor consider the various mutually beneficial possibilities. Issues in project finance can include capitalization of the project, insurance and risk management, and other types of collateral.

If the infrastructure project is entirely private, then project finance can look like a deal in which ownership is shared among partners in, say, an office tower. Equity, risk, and rewards can be shared, and a special organization might be created to isolate the venture from other assets and to manage risk. As in other cases, the partners can consider financing using debt, equity, or cash on hand.

If a public-private partnership (PPP) is involved, other considerations come into play. With the privatization focus in the United Kingdom, a concept called private finance initiative (PFI) has been adopted. PFI also is used in other countries, such as Australia, several other European countries, and Malaysia and Singapore, among others. It is similar to the concept of PPP, which is discussed in more detail in Chapter 12.

CONSTRUCTION COMPANIES

Within the construction industry, there are many possibilities for business arrangements. The best way to illustrate their activities with infrastructure is through examples of firms and their business lines. Given the close connection between infrastructure sectors and construction, examples in other chapters also illustrate the construction industry. (Refer to Vulcan Materials in Chapter 4 and Insituform in Chapter 7.) Vulcan is a materials company that was spun off from a contractor, and Insituform is a utility contractor that has been built around a specific technology: trenchless technology for water and sewer construction.

Large and multifaceted construction companies have long track records of involvement in complex projects across the regions and infrastructure sectors. Some focus on buildings and industrial or commercial sectors, and some focus on heavy and civil engineering construction.

Bechtel Corporation

The largest construction and engineering company by volume in the United States is the Bechtel Corporation, which is involved in many deals around the globe. Bechtel has been around for over a century and has been involved in many deals and countries. As a privately owned company, its activities are harder to track than publicly owned companies. It has always been the subject of controversies and news coverage. Bechtel works on engineering, construction, and project management across the energy, transportation, communications, mining, oil and gas, and government services areas. *ENR* has listed Bechtel as the largest U.S. construction contractor for the past 11 years. Bechtel has some 44,000 employees and had 2008 revenues of $31.4 billion. Types of facilities constructed included airports and seaports, communications networks, defense and aerospace facilities, environmental cleanup projects, fossil and nuclear power plants, mines and smelters, oil and gas field development, pipelines, roads and rail systems, and refineries and petrochemical facilities.

Fluor Corporation

Fluor Corporation is publicly listed and has some 42,000 employees. It had $23 billion in revenues in 2008 working on engineering, procurement, construction management, and project management in oil and gas, petro-chemicals, industrial and infrastructure, transportation, mining, telecommunications, and the building sectors. It has a government segment to provide services to the Departments of Energy, Homeland Security, and Defense. Fluor is a good example of a large and successful construction company with a track record of work for the government (Yahoo Finance, 2009).

Granite Construction Inc.

Granite Construction Inc. focuses on heavy civil construction and construction materials in the United States. The Granite West segment focuses on public sector roads and bridges. It also does site preparation for housing and commercial facilities. The Granite East segment focuses on infrastructure projects, including highways, dams, mass transit, pipelines, waterway locks and dams, and airports. It also does demolition and site work. Granite Construction is also involved in real estate projects and services. It had 2008 revenues of $2.6 billion. Granite is a good example of a company with a strong record in heavy and civil engineering construction in the United States (Yahoo Finance, 2009).

Blount International, Inc.

A construction company may start with a visionary founder who saw an opportunity, as Blount International, Inc. did in 1946. Now it has changed into an equipment manufacturer that serves the construction, utility, environmental, and forestry industries with chain saw accessories and concrete cutting systems, lawn mowers, and industrial and power equipment for timber harvesting and industrial tractors. Winton Blount returned to a family sand and gravel business after World War II, bought four D-7 Caterpillar tractors, and went into the contracting business. The highway boom provided growth and led by the mid-1950s to a diversified construction business. Work in materials led to a spinoff that became Vulcan Materials (see Chapter 4), and they performed construction for NASA and the Department of Defense. In 1962, *ENR* ranked the company at thirty-third largest in the United States. Blount decided to exit government work both because it created cycles in business and he was appointed Postmaster General in 1968. These forces led the company to focus on private work and an acquisitions program as well as a 1972 listing on the American Stock Exchange. The company severed its ties to construction contracting in 1994. It was bought by Lehman Brothers Holdings Inc. in 1999 in a leveraged buyout and split up with some pieces sold off. This left the equipment company of today, which had 2008 revenues of $580 million (Funding Universe, 2009b).

The next few examples are of utility contractors, who have experience with pipes, processing, and the unique requirements of electric power, telecom, natural gas, and water/wastewater.

Quanta Services, Inc.

Quanta Services, Inc. has separate divisions for Infrastructure Services and Dark Fiber. Infrastructure Services provides design, installation, repair, and maintenance of network infrastructure for electric power, gas, telecommunications, and cable television. The Dark Fiber group provides design, procurement, construction, and maintenance for fiber optic facilities and support for licensing for fiber capacity. It has about 14,750 employees and had 2008 revenue of $3.7 billion (Yahoo Finance, 2009).

Henkels & McCoy, Inc.

Henkels & McCoy, Inc. is one of the largest privately held utility contractors, and focuses on the communications, information technology, and utility industries. It has more than 80 offices across the United States. Like many other privately owned construction companies, its origins date back to a visionary founder, with company growth occurring both as a result of opportunity and smart and hard work.

Garney Construction Company

Garney Construction Company (2009) is an employee-owned utility contractor with a focus on water construction. *ENR* rates it first in transmission lines and aqueducts, seventh in water supply, and fourteenth in water treatment. It began in 1961, when Charles Garney left the family plumbing business to start a pipeline and utility construction company. In 2001, Garney Construction acquired Grimm Construction and added to its capabilities in water treatment, pumping, and water storage facilities.

MYR Group

The MYR Group (2009) is a specialty contractor focused on electrical infrastructure (transmission and distribution) and commercial and industrial markets. It has five subsidiaries: the L.E. Myers Co.; Harlan Electric Company; Hawkeye Construction, Inc.; Sturgeon Electric Company, Inc.; and Great Southwestern Construction, Inc. It claims to maintain one of the largest inventories of specialized transmission and distribution equipment in the United States. The transmission and distribution business serves utilities and includes the construction and maintenance of high-voltage transmission lines, substations, and lower-voltage underground and overhead distribution systems. MYR also performs emergency restoration services. Its commercial and industrial group serves construction in the West for airports, hospitals, data centers, commercial, industrial, and transportation management systems. It also provides telecom installation for fiber optic and copper infrastructure for such applications as transmission of voice, data, and video; ramp metering, signalized intersections, and fiber optic traffic management systems; and highway and bridge lighting. Revenue in 2008 was $612 million.

Caterpillar

Caterpillar Inc. is in many ways the icon of the construction equipment business. It produces construction, mining, and forestry machinery with diverse functions. It also has a rail-related business, a logistics services business, and a line of engines for a range of machines. It has a financial products business and offers loans to customers and dealers as well as insurance to customers and dealers. Caterpillar also invests in independent power projects that use its power generation equipment and services. Caterpillar had 2008 revenues of $48.8 billion.

Weyerhaeuser Company

Homebuilding consumes vast amounts of lumber. Weyerhaeuser Company produces trees, manufactures forest products, and builds homes. It owns some 6 million acres of forestland and leases or has licenses on another some 16 million acres. It produces lumber, wood and building products, pulp and paper, and other forest products. The company was established in 1900 and is based in the State of Washington. Weyerhauser had $8 billion in revenue in 2008, down dramatically from $22 billion in 2006. This illustrates how sensitive the company's sales are to homebuilding. At the end of 2008, it had $16.7 billion in assets, down from $26.9 billion in 2006. Of the $16.7 billion, some $10 billion was in property, plant, and equipment (Yahoo Finance, 2009).

The Home Depot, Inc.

Homebuilding and the need for upgrades and renovations led to the emergence of a large home improvement business. The Home Depot, Inc. sells building materials, supplies, and lawn and garden products and provides installation for a range of home improvements and mechanical equipment. As of 2009, it operated some 2,200 retail stores in the United States, Canada, China, and Mexico. In 2008, it had revenue of $71 billion, which was down from $91 billion in 2006 (Yahoo Finance, 2009).

Stantec

Stantec is a large environmental consulting firm with headquarters in Canada. It generally services mining, water resources, commercial, and manufacturing clients, and it has grown through acquisitions. It bought two Canadian firms in 2008 and 2009 to extend its capabilities in environmental management, remediation, and geotechnical engineering services. It employs some 9,000 people in Canada and the United States and had 2008 revenue of $1.1 billion (Yahoo Finance, 2009).

ARCADIS

ARCADIS is an international engineering company in infrastructure, environment and buildings. It has more than 13,500 employees and more than $2 billion in gross revenue. It recently signed an agreement to acquire Malcolm Pirnie, an employee-owned U.S. water and environmental engineering firm. Pirnie has more than 1,700 employees, and 2008 revenues of $392 million. ARCADIS will finance the merger through stock issuance and cash. Financing for the cash payment of $135 million was from financial firms Rabobank, ING, and RBS. Shares to be issued to Pirnie employees have a lockup period of 6 months and incentives to hold them at least 18 months. The combined firm will have a major position in the global water market, a good line of federal government business, and a strong industrial environmental practice (ENR.com, 2009d).

ESRI

Construction in the built environment requires services of many architects, engineers, and other design professionals. They require a range of support products and services, including those in the fast-changing information technology arena. ESRI (2009) is a privately owned company that sells a popular version of geographic information system (GIS) software. Its roots date to its 1969 California founding as Environmental Systems Research Institute, Inc. It started slowly as a land use consulting firm, without the need for venture capital or public investments.

During the 1980s, ESRI developed its GIS software, and in 1981, it held its first user conference. Today, about 14,000 people attend, making it the largest GIS conference in the world. Its first software was named ARC/INFO, to combine computer display of geographic features with database tools to assign attributes to the features. Today, mapping applications on personal digital assistants, laptops, desktops, and the Internet have proliferated. ESRI currently has 2,700 employees in the United States. The company is privately held and debt free and has no plans to go public.

Autodesk, Inc.

Autodesk, Inc. is a software company with four lines: Platform Solutions and Emerging Business and Other; Architecture, Engineering, and Construction; Manufacturing Solutions; and Media and Entertainment. It sells AutoCAD computer-aided design and mapping software that relate to other industrial software applications, such as data management, mechanical design, and three-dimensional modeling for visual effects. These products cut across markets in architecture, engineering and construction, manufacturing, mapping, and entertainment. Autodesk's revenue increased from $1.8 billion in 2006 to $2.3 billion in 2008 (Autodesk Inc., 2009).

Bentley Systems, Inc.

Bentley Systems, Inc. (2009) provides software for infrastructure design and management and serves markets for engineers, architects, contractors, governments, and utilities. Bentley has over 2,800 employees and annual 2008 revenues over $500 million, and it claims to have invested over $1 billion in research, development, and acquisitions since 1993. Bentley is a privately held company. It uses a subscription model for its customer base and signed an interoperability agreement with Autodesk in 2008.

SECTOR ISSUES AND OUTLOOK

The housing bubble that led to the financial crisis exposed the fault lines in the construction industry, which continues to be redefined in a search for greater efficiency and use of capital. The new profile of the construction industry features greater integration among finance and industry players, with engineers, builders, and equipment suppliers becoming more involved in project finance. Digital advances are also creating change in construction, and their influences can be seen all the way from scheduling to organization of job sites. In many ways, the construction industry forms the core of the infrastructure sector, and it serves as a bellwether of further change to come.

The Construction Business Is Volatile
The construction industry is subjected to many economic, technological, and political forces and undergoes constant change. The dramatic falloff in homebuilding has emphasized that in recent years.

The Construction Industry Undergoes Continuing Restructuring
New forms of joint ventures and networks between construction professionals and suppliers lead to innovation and higher efficiency. Large construction businesses will get even bigger as they tackle mega-projects on a global scale.

The Construction Industry Is Being Redefined
The construction industry is involved from the research and development phase through project development and finance. New project delivery methods, such as design-build and many variations of it, are being used to replace the older design-bid-build model.

Technology, Organizational Innovation, and New Products Create Change
Dennis Lenard, former head of Constructing Excellence UK, said that technology, organizational innovation, and new products will make job sites more efficient. Just as in manufacturing, the cooperation of suppliers with product assemblers is moving toward more integration and efficiency. New technologies available to contractors include cranes and machines with greater capabilities, new materials, and new prefabricated components and systems. Management technologies have also evolved, with many types of partnerships and financing arrangements now available.

Constructors think that emerging fields of materials and information technology will have a major impact on them. A few applications are genetically engineered microorganisms to manufacture high-strength building materials, wall membranes of new materials to store and transmit light and heat, and pervasive use of computers in the building environment (Clough, 2000).

Digital Technology Creates Change in Construction Methods

The use of information technology to aid construction has increased by an order of magnitude, all the way from new techniques for surveying and mapping through sophisticated building information modeling systems. Digital technology by the computer and Internet will change planning and project management. With virtual reality, it is possible to use simulation to study all aspects of the construction process. Automation changes the nature of labor inputs to construction.

Construction and Finance Are Increasingly Integrated

Construction and finance businesses are merging because construction involves so much cash flow. The emergence of PPP and PFI are indicators of the changing relationships.

Globalization and Environmental Change Are Important Forces to Construction

The interest in sustainability will also hit the construction industry, as global warming, poverty, and resource use confront it (Hilti, 2005).

Construction Is Important to Global Problems

Looking at the big picture, civil engineers see challenges that will affect construction, including housing the expanding population, fixing the decaying urban infrastructure, recovering from natural disasters and facing climate change, and transporting more people and goods safely and efficiently.

Construction Can Benefit from Stimulus but Suffer Later

Investment in public works could create many jobs (Karp and Frangos, 2008), but it may also create a boom-and-bust scenario for the construction industry.

CHAPTER 10

Investor and Business Opportunities in Infrastructure

The six infrastructure sectors and the construction industry that were discussed in Chapters 3 to 9 offer many opportunities for investors and entrepreneurs. This chapter explains direct avenues for investment, such as stocks and bonds, and information about infrastructure sector indices, which are proliferating due to the rising popularity of infrastructure as an investment category. The chapter also addresses business opportunities that arise for private equity, start-ups, and new markets for infrastructure firms.

The next part of the book addresses how the financial flows of the infrastructure sectors can be used to improve effectiveness of both public and private management approaches. The final chapter addresses government reforms as well as financial issues for the future.

THEN AND NOW

When you think about investments in utilities or an infrastructure business, the image of a staid and slow-moving but reliable investment comes to mind. Compared to some flashy stocks, that may still be the case, but with deregulation and many new forms of infrastructure program delivery, the investment scene has changed a lot.

In many ways, the era of reliable returns from a regulated utility may have just been temporary. Many old timers can recall the days when "telephone" stock was steady as a rock. The company was, in fact, a national monopoly, and it had command of a growing business sector that it could control. Many people can remember someone in their family who had shares of telephone stock and considered it a bedrock investment.

What is known today as AT&T, with the stock symbol T, is only distantly related to the older, regulated company. The only connection is that one of the Baby Bell spinoffs purchased the name and symbol, but the company is not the same. This story is told in a little more detail in Chapter 5.

In ways it is the same with the electric utility business, which has been deregulated to some extent and has more ups-and-downs than you would expect. Even water utilities, long thought to be the most conservative in the utility family, are not as stable as you might expect. A water utility may be involved in mergers and acquisitions and have unexpected forces affecting its bottom line.

Tax-exempt municipal bonds are the traditional route to get steady and attractive returns from infrastructure investments. The $2 trillion plus municipal bond market (based on bonds outstanding) offers a wide selection of types and risks of investments, and it features both a primary and secondary market for bond buyers and traders. In addition, many bond funds are also available.

In spite of market fluctuations, an attractive investment route is to buy stocks or funds of listed infrastructure service providers or suppliers as well as companies engaging in infrastructure public-private partnerships. The diverse infrastructure sector also includes sector funds for real estate, energy, transportation, utilities, and cross-cutting subsectors such as construction. The number of infrastructure-related mutual funds has increased in the last few years, including the newer exchange-traded funds (ETFs).

Private equity firms also can take positions in infrastructure operations, and their activities are increasing with the emergence of new players. Infusing capital from private equity into infrastructure operations brings a new dimension of financing to supplement public funding and/or shareowner plays in infrastructure-related companies. The challenge, as always, is to ensure a level playing field for private investors, government, and the public.

Lending to infrastructure enterprises is done through purchase of bonds and direct loans from banks, especially development banks. Banks and investment funds have important roles in infrastructure financing, and they can purchase mortgage-backed securities as well as to lend directly to infrastructure enterprises through commercial lending. When private equity provides investment funds, it normally takes an ownership stake rather than simply lending to the infrastructure organization.

Still another way to invest in infrastructure is through purchase of real estate or shares of real estate investment trusts (REITs). It might seem like stretching a point to link infrastructure and real estate investments this way because real estate markets are much more visible than investments in public infrastructure. However, as we explain in Chapter 3, much infrastructure expense is embedded in the cost of housing and real estate in the form of impact fees and other fixed costs. In many cases, when you buy real estate, you are buying equity in the infrastructure too. This fact shows how the value of infrastructure that is embedded in real estate can be volatile, just as housing values can be.

For example, the value of existing infrastructure in rapidly growing areas may be increasing due to congestion and increases in demand. This could be a factor to consider in appraising potential real estate investments. However, old infrastructure located in areas with dwindling prospects may not be as valuable and may even be a liability. So, you would not necessarily invest in real estate because of the underlying infrastructure value but because you recognize that the value of existing developments includes sunk cost of infrastructure and can be an asset or a liability. Normally the infrastructure component of development is financed by different methods rather than real estate; the tax-exempt bond market is the main source of funds for much of its capital construction.

BOND MARKET

Infrastructure-related bonds, which are usually tax-exempt municipals, can be bought in the primary or secondary bond markets. Chapter 12 explains how the bonds work, and this section explains how to purchase or trade bonds and gives examples. Part of the explanation in this section is from Municipalbonds.com (2009).

An infrastructure organization that requires funding will issue its bonds through an underwriter, which is a securities dealer who buys the bonds from the issuer and resells them to investors. The underwriter profits from the transaction by buying the bonds at a discount and selling them at an agreed price. Underwriters may be independent firms or divisions of securities firms or investment banks with municipal bond departments to do underwriting, marketing, or trading of municipal securities.

Underwriters may be large international financial firms, such as Bank of America, Goldman Sachs, or J.P. Morgan or they can be smaller regional firms. As an example of large-scale business activity, Bank of America managed 111 issues and $15.4 billion in bonds in the first quarter of 2009 (*Bond Buyer*, 2009). The smaller, regional investment firms might handle issues from the under-$1 million range up to much larger issues. The 2002 Economic Census listed 466 establishments that were engaged in investment banking and securities dealing related to state, provincial, and local notes and bonds. These establishments reported $1.48 billion in revenue in 2002 for their product lines (U.S. Census Bureau, 2002). According to Securities Industry and Financial Markets Association data (see Chapter 12), municipal bond issuance for 2002 was $358 billion, so these numbers indicate that revenues work out to be less than 0.5 percent of bond proceeds.

Actually, the average charge to sell municipal bonds was closer to $6 per $1,000 of face value, or about 0.6 percent. According to Bloomberg.com (2008), banks were increasing their fees due to difficulty in selling bonds in the poor economy. For example, one large infrastructure organization, the Los Angeles Department of Water and Power, was reported to pay an underwriter fee of $6.26 per $1,000 for a $550 million bond issue, or 0.63 percent.

State and local governments issue debt either through bidding processes or negotiated sales. In either case, their underwriters work with traders to set the price of an issue. A new issue also can be sold through private placement, in which issuers sell bonds directly to investors or through an agent. In a competitive sale, underwriters submit sealed bids to the issuer. Notice of the competition normally is published in financial media outlets, such as the *Bond Buyer* (2009), and also sent to potential bidders. For example, in 2009, the State of Arkansas issued $15.3 million in water, waste disposal, and pollution abatement general obligation bonds due in the interval of 2010 to 2043. The winning bid was by Crews & Associates, an investment bank located in Little Rock, Arkansas.

When bonds are sold through negotiated sales, disclosure rules vary among state and local governments. The Government Finance Officers Association has published guidelines for disclosure, but the market is largely unregulated without specific disclosure requirements (Public Bonds, 2009).

Bonds are sold over the counter in the secondary market, normally through bond dealers, banks, and many brokerages. Generally, the minimum bond purchase is $5,000 of par value. Licensed securities dealers own the bonds they sell, and over 2,000 dealers are licensed to sell municipal bonds. The dealer's profit on municipal bonds is in the markup. If you purchase a bond, it will have a maturity date. If you do not hold your bond to maturity, you will be able to sell it in the secondary market, but the market is not as liquid as it is for stocks. The secondary market is where dealers buy bonds at a price in which they profit from a resale. Some bonds also have call dates, in which the issuer can pay the bond back early.

Bond trades are reported to the Municipal Securities Rulemaking Board, and MunicipalBonds.com lists all trades. Bonds have CUSIP numbers (CUSIP represents "Committee on Uniform Securities Identification Procedures" numbers, a 9-digit identification code that enables you to track them.

Major firms such as Morgan Stanley or Schwab have departments to specialize in municipal bonds, but they do not list their inventory unless you have an account. Dealers that post their inventory include, for example, FMSBonds.com, Stoever Glass, Fidelity, George K. Baum, Lebenthal, Stone & Youngberg, Bergen Capital, and Herbert J. Sims. On a given day, for example, FMSBonds, Inc. (2009) of Boca Raton, Florida, was offering 140 bonds for the Denver Convention Center, which were issued in 2006 at a coupon rate of 5.125 percent. The bond was for sale at $82.103, which translates to a current yield of 6.24 percent. It was rated at Baaa3 by Moody's and BBB–by Standard & Poor's (S&P). FMS Bonds also was offering 1,890 Pensacola, Florida, Airport Revenue Bonds, with a coupon rate of 6.25. It was due October 1, 2038, and the first coupon was scheduled for April 1, 2009. Therefore, the offering price was about the same as the coupon rate.

When a bond is issued, the underwriter's goal is to sell all of the issue quickly, which means that large sales to institutional investors are more attractive than small-lot sales to individuals. Therefore, individuals or institutions can buy municipal bonds. Often it is easier for individuals to buy bond funds, such as T. Rowe Price's (2009) municipal funds, although these carry a service fee.

As another example of a fund's bond holdings, the Fidelity (2009) Municipal Income Fund had (as of March 31, 2009) 10.8 percent water, sewer and gas utilities, 9.6 percent transportation, 6.9 percent electric utilities, 3.1 percent industrial revenue/pollution control, and 0.4 percent resource recovery, along with other state and local obligations and miscellaneous other securities. Its top holding was Washington Public Power Systems Nuclear Project #2 with a market value of $62 million. Its second and third top holdings were Atlanta water and wastewater revenue bonds and Texas Turnpike Authority bonds. The Washington Public Power Supply System (WPPSS), which was nicknamed "Whoops," achieved notoriety in the 1980s by defaulting on $2.25 billion in bonds that financed nuclear plant construction that was halted after the Three Mile Island incident. This remains the largest municipal bond default in U.S. history. The organization is now a municipal corporation named Energy Northwest, which operates a single nuclear plant, along with some renewable facilities, and continues to repay debt from the defaulted bonds.

Examples of bonds in its portfolio (including Energy Northwest) for the six categories of infrastructure are:

Built environment	Arizona Health Facilities Authority Revenue Series 2008D
Transportation	New York Metropolitan Transit Authority Revenue Series 2008A
Energy	Energy Northwest Electric Revenue (#3 Project) Series 2002B
Communications	None as bonds in this category usually are by private sector financing
Water	King County Sewer Revenue Series 2002B
Waste management	PA Economic Development Financing Authority Solid Waste Disposal Revenue Series 2004A

In the past, individuals might buy municipal bonds, clip and mail interest coupons, and feel secure about their investments. Today, with many more issues of varying quality and with a volatile economy, they must study the market carefully to assess risk and rates of return based on interest rate fluctuations and management fees. When they purchase shares in a bond fund, they pay additional management fees but may benefit from volume discounts in transaction fees, as compared to buying a few bonds in the over-the-counter market.

The federal tax exemption applies to all tax-exempt municipal bonds, but the tax treatment by state tax authorities varies by state. Therefore, deciding which bonds to buy and hold requires careful study, and financial advisors should consider how tax sensitive an investor is when recommending which bonds or funds to buy.

The 2009 stimulus program included a provision for a "Build America" bond program in which state and local governments can issue taxable bonds and receive a new federal subsidy for part of their borrowing costs. The program was authorized in the American Recovery and Reinvestment Act of 2009, and the subsidy payment can be equal to 35 percent of total coupon interest. The New Jersey Turnpike sold $1.375 billion as the first takers of the new program, and California followed soon afterward with a $6.9 billion issue. New York's Metropolitan Transit Authority was planning a $500 million issue (Cooke, 2009).

Municipal bonds provide tax-free interest and relative safety because municipal bond defaults are rare but not impossible. Moody's Investor's Service (2002) provided a primer on bond defaults. Even if bonds default, the recovery rate is normally high. Bonds have five types of risk: in credit of the issuer, interest rate changes, inflation, currency fluctuation, and liquidity.

In addition to municipal bonds, investors can buy corporate bonds for public companies working in the infrastructure sector. As explained in Chapters 3 to 8, these companies involve players all the way from gigantic GE and Siemens to smaller companies that are barely large enough to be listed on a stock exchange.

STOCKS OF INFRASTRUCTURE COMPANIES

As explained in Chapter 12, bonds represent debt of an organization, and stocks represent ownership in an organization. You can buy ownership through the stocks of private sector infrastructure companies, but normally municipal bond debt is issued only by publicly owned agencies. There are some exceptions, such as industrial development bonds, in which private companies can participate in tax-exempt debt. As mentioned, you also can buy corporate bonds of infrastructure-related companies.

Private companies that offer stock can be infrastructure service providers, companies that use infrastructure to deliver services, and suppliers of goods and services to infrastructure organizations. Examples in each category are presented next.

> **Companies that own infrastructure:** investor-owned electric utilities; natural gas transmission companies; railroad companies; REITs
>
> **Service companies that use infrastructure:** airline companies; electric generators using other transmission infrastructure; trucking firms; shipping companies using ports
>
> **Suppliers of goods and services:** manufacturers of water supply pipe (goods); coal companies (goods/commodities); construction contractors (services); consulting firms (services).

Some of these are regulated, for-profit businesses, which you would expect to have stable business and income. Examples include electric power, natural gas, and water utilities. Others, such as airline companies, are regulated but have volatile profits because business volume fluctuates and they are not regulated for rates of return in the way utilities are. Still others may provide goods and services to infrastructure businesses but also sell in other sectors. There are many examples of firms in this category, including construction contractors and giant conglomerates, such as GE. Where conglomerates are concerned, it is difficult to figure out business trends for all company products. This is one reason why analysis of companies in the infrastructure sector can be tricky.

While it is not our purpose to give investment advice, this chapter and earlier ones provide a great deal of information that may be useful to investors. Appendix B provides a list of the companies that were mentioned in Chapters 3 to 9, and the next sections summarize information about them and relate it to the overall picture of infrastructure as a business sector.

Homebuilders, Home Improvement, REITs, and Bank Stocks

The real estate and housing construction sectors are large and have been shown to be volatile during the financial crisis. They also link closely to banking and to the home improvement sector. The economic accounts for these sectors fall into different North American Industry Classification System categories, but across the board, stocks in these categories showed their sensitivity to the housing market during the crisis beginning in about 2008.

The financial crisis ushered in an extraordinary period in the economic history of the homebuilding industry, and the numbers showed it. Pulte Homes, the nation's largest homebuilder, saw its revenue fall from $14.7 billion in 2005 to $6.3 billion in 2008. Weyerhauser's revenues fell from $18.8 billion to $8.0 billion in the same four-year period. As you would expect, Home Depot, with its focus on home improvement, did not drop as much, but revenues fell from $77.0 to $71.2 billion (Yahoo Finance, 2009).

In the commercial sector, Simon Property Group, which focuses on newer commercial properties, saw its revenues increase from $3.3 billion to $3.8 billion in the three-year period through 2008, and it continued paying a dividend. Its balance sheet showed the value of its property, plant, and equipment level at close to $19 billion and a decline in stockholder equity from $3.8 billion to $2.5 billion. Of course, how real estate is valued on the books is a question for all companies in this volatile time.

General Growth Properties showed rising revenue through 2008, but it had to enter bankruptcy reorganization in 2009. It owns the local, older mall in the author's town, as well as a number of others. These older malls have generally had difficulty attracting sales and stable retailers. Other signs about commercial real estate, especially falling consumer spending and falling popularity of traditional malls, indicate that continued adjustments will occur in this sector. *Time* magazine's March 23, 2009, story about "recycling malls" as a major trend is an indicator of the financial issues among owners of older shopping centers.

When the house price bubble burst, it led to sharp drops in house prices and exposed many weak residential loans. This led to severe stress in the financial system and the need for large government bailouts to banks. Although they are government-sponsored enterprises, Fannie Mae and Freddie Mac (explained in Chapter 3) both suffered steep losses and required bailout funds. Fannie Mae (2009) reported continued losses in early 2009 and had a net worth deficit of almost $19 billion as of March 31, 2009. It submitted a request for that amount in bailout funds through its government conservator, the director of the Federal Housing Finance Agency. Freddie Mac (2009) had a net worth deficit of $6.0 billion for the same date and also applied for Treasury funds to get it past the hump. Stocks of both Fannie Mae and Freddie Mac fell from as high as $77 for Fannie and $73 for Freddie in late 2004 to less than $1 in early 2009.

The rates of recovery of the housing market and its financial support system will determine future prospects for stock investments in the built environment. The declines in home prices and new home starts have been the most precipitous in decades, and the stress on the banking system was unprecedented since the Great Depression. Commercial lending has also been under stress, with similar gaps between loans outstanding and property values. Forecasters are mixed in their guesses for the next year or two, which should signal the future for this volatile sector.

Transportation Stocks

Stocks in the transportation sector come from diverse business sectors, and the overall investment opportunities in transportation are difficult to characterize. The Dow Jones Transportation Average (DJTA) tracks companies that deliver transportation-related services and does not include much about infrastructure itself, except for rail companies that are included. Transportation service providers, such as package delivery and freight rail, are closely linked to the consumer economy and very sensitive to retail sales. Business conditions affect the health of the freight business, from movement of shipping containers to individual packages from Internet shopping. If the objective of infrastructure investments is to lower risk and ensure reliable returns, these are not the stocks to choose.

The infrastructure side of transportation is heavily dependent on public heavy construction, especially for highway renovation and improvement. Highways, with their public construction emphasis, might act as a flywheel to carry construction spending ahead, even if housing remains in the doldrums.

The passenger travel side of transportation also will fluctuate with the economy because airline business travel is sensitive to economic activity. However, passenger ridership on public transit might increase. Less passenger travel via automobiles means less gasoline sales; therefore, it also means fewer tax collections to pay for highway improvements and therefore less construction funding.

Highway construction draws in groups of contractors, suppliers, and engineers to plan and build new or renovated roads, bridges, and interchanges. The projects can take years and cost billions of dollars. For example, the total cost of the "Big Dig" project in Boston was around $15 billion, even before interest cost is added. As another example, the TREX project, a 17-mile interstate upgrade through Denver, was completed in 2006 at a cost of $1.67 billion.

ENR (2009a) magazine's top 400 contractors showed $281 billion in revenue, of which $38 billion was in transportation. The top construction category by revenue was building construction, at $170 billion. None of the large publicly listed companies on the list specializes in road building. The two largest contractors on the list, Bechtel (privately owned) and Fluor (public company), specialize in industrial and petrochemical construction.

Turner, the third largest (privately owned), specializes in buildings. The highest-ranked company with a large stake in transportation is the privately owned Walsh Group, based in Chicago. The first company on the list that does almost all transportation work is Flatiron Construction at number 50. It is a privately owned company based in Longmont, Colorado, with $1.26 billion in 2008 revenue.

The conclusion is that it is hard to find stock investments in contractors that will be sensitive to road building. However, suppliers such as Vulcan Materials will be sensitive to it. Also, transportation and the new smart roads business is stimulating work for other categories of listed companies, such as the engineering companies URS, AECOM, and Iteris, Inc., which is in the instrumentation and controls market.

Although it is difficult to find publicly listed construction companies that engage mostly in transportation, infrastructure funds are tracking contractors and concessionaires seeking design-build-operate deals for roads. An example is Abertis Infraestructuras, S.A., a Spanish firm seeking work in the United States (see Chapter 4).

In air transportation, the airlines have had problems for a number of years due to fuel costs, terrorism, and the financial crisis, and their stocks have been volatile. United Airlines emerged from bankruptcy in 2006, and Frontier entered it in 2008. Southwest Airlines increased its revenues from 2006 through 2008 but saw net income drop due to rising fuel costs.

The performance of freight railroads has been more stable than airlines through the crisis. For example, Burlington Northern Santa Fe saw revenues rise from 2006 through 2008, with net income rising slightly to $2.1 billion in 2008. Its largest competitor, Union Pacific, had similar results.

Reflecting the varying definitions of infrastructure, funds in the sector sometimes include oil and gas transportation companies in their portfolios (see Chapter 4). Therefore, if you want to invest in an infrastructure fund, you must check to see what basket of companies is included. In many cases, the fund will have only a few holdings and may be more volatile than broader-based funds.

Telecommunications Stocks

Due to the rapid change in the telecommunications sector, telecom stocks exhibit different behavior from other infrastructure-related stocks. Deregulation and changing technologies have neutralized any past monopoly advantages, and changing customer expectations create rapid change in customer demands and preferences.

Telecom stocks have been through deregulation and the technology stock boom-and-bust that occurred from about 1995 to 2001. Stocks of some major telecom companies did not fall as far as some dot-com stocks, but others did. Verizon fell from its 1999 highs in the $60 dollar range to just under $30, and the new AT&T's experience was similar, falling from the high $50 range to about $20. Qwest had large losses and debt load problems, and fell from a high of over $60 to nearly as low as $1 per share. Level 3 Communications fell from its high of about $130 to recent levels near $1 per share.

None of the niches of the telcom industry retains a monopoly provider advantage today. Although telecom can be considered part of the infrastructure sector, its stocks require a different approach to analysis from those in the other infrastructure categories.

Energy Stocks

The energy sector is so large and has so many investment channels that it is hard to characterize. Its investment opportunities range from the generation and production side through delivery of energy services to customers. It also includes energy storage, transmission, and mitigation of environmental effects. A key feature of its sector is its link to nonrenewable natural resources of oil, gas, and coal. Given the wide range of oil and gas prices and the fickle nature of natural resources ownership, energy stocks will be volatile.

The generation and production side involves oil and gas companies, ranging from giant Exxon Mobil through small players in exploration and production. It also includes coal companies with their high level of risk about climate change and difficulty in producing clean coal. Peabody Energy (explained in Chapter 6) stock, for example, rose rapidly from 2004 into 2006, then fell about 50 percent, only to rise again to a higher peak within two years and then to fall again some 75 percent from its peak.

The climate change issue also leads to questions about investments in technologies such as carbon dioxide sequestration because any solution to the coal dilemma could open the floodgates to its greater use.

The fastest-moving part of electric power generation is in renewables, especially wind energy. As in the cases of other alternative energy sources, such as oil shale and solar, prospects for wind energy can wax and wane with government policy and subsidies.

Energy storage involves technologies that range from using compressed air to store wind-generated energy through use of information technology to facilitate rapid transfer of power across the grid in a form of virtual storage. Energy storage also uses battery technology, which is critical to enable plug-in vehicles and to transform the transportation system to move the nation away from dependence on imported oil.

Energy transmission includes pipeline companies that appear in several of infrastructure funds and also can involve electricity transmission and even transportation of coal, which is an important business for freight rail.

Although utility investments used to seem stable (remember the utilities in a Monopoly game?), with unbundling and deregulation, they may no longer have the advantage of selling a monopoly commodity at regulated prices. Stock in a company like Duke Energy, for example, can experience pressure from energy supply, climate change, and national regulatory policy, such as hydroelectric regulatory decisions. Stock of the Southern Company has been more stable, mostly rising from about 1990 to the present. Even with this pattern, however Southern stock has experienced fluctuations of as much as 35 percent in short periods (e.g., March to May 2001).

Water Stocks

Given the fragmentation of the water industry (see Chapter 7), it is difficult to assemble a diverse basket of stocks of companies that concentrates on the water industry. You can find listed private utilities, such as American Water, the largest private water company in the nation, but other companies may not devote themselves exclusively to the water industry. A case in point is GE Water, which is part of a much bigger family of subsidiaries. In 2008, total GE revenues were $181 billion, distributed among energy infrastructure ($38.6 billion); technology infrastructure ($46.3 billion); NBC Universal ($17.0 billion); capital finance ($67.0 billion); and consumer and industrial ($11.7 billion). GE Water & Process Technologies is part of the Energy Infrastructure group (Yahoo Finance, 2009).

Still, investment advisors and funds assemble baskets of water stocks in attempts to identify firms that will profit from the highly publicized global water crisis. Examples are the water stock lists published by *U.S. Water News* (2009) through its *Water Investment News*; Water-Stocks .com (2009), a Web site for water news and investment advice; and TechKNOWLEDGEy Strategic Group (2009).

Palisades Indexes LLC (2009) is an index preparation company with a water index, which is discussed later in the chapter. The index tracks companies that provide potable water and water treatment, and that offer products and services related to water consumption. It is the basis for Invesco's PowerShares (2009) Water Resources Portfolio fund, which generally tracks the Palisades Water Index.

Generally speaking, the companies identified in these indices comprise private water utilities, suppliers, contractors, and consultants. Some of the companies are so large that only small parts of them fit in the water arena. The top holdings of the PFW Water A (PFWAX) fund include Energy Recovery, Inc. (desalting), Cantel Medical Corporation (healthcare), Southwest Water Company (water and wastewater), NALCO Holding Company (water treatment), Mueller Water Products (pipe and fittings), Consolidated

Water Co. Ltd. (water supplier), Glacier Water Services (water from vending machines), AMERON Inc. (pipe, fittings, etc.), Watts Water Tech A (water safety and control), and Pentair Inc. (industrial products). The fund's major sector weights are 39 percent for industrial materials, 24 percent for utilities, and 22 percent for business services.

So, in spite of the hype about a world water crisis, it is difficult to see a clear focus in the fragmented water business. Compared to some of the volatile sectors, stocks in the water utilities seem more stable. For example, California Water Service Company Stock has shown steady growth from about $15 in 1992 to the $35 to $45 range in 2009. Based on appreciation alone, this represents an annual increase of about 6 percent. Veolia Environnement, however, fell from a high of $65 in 2008 to below $16 in early 2009. It operates several businesses in international markets and is subject to many more forces than California Water Service Company, which is a regulated U.S. utility.

Waste Management Stocks

Given the narrow focus of the waste management business, it not easy to assemble a diverse portfolio of companies devoted to it. Also, stocks and funds in the waste management sector may be labeled as "environmental." This labeling tends to confuse the underlying issues in the waste management business, which really does offer interesting possibilities. The sector includes many smaller, nonlisted companies and is not very integrated among collection, processing, and disposal operations.

Alacra (2009) publishes a list of public companies in the waste management sector. The largest company, Waste Management Inc., with annual revenues in the $13 billion range, traded consistently in the range of $20 to $40 per share between 2001 and 2009, although it did show volatility when it had a sharp run-up from $10 to $50 between 1995 and 1998, followed by a sharp, one-year decline back to about $14. Covanta Holding Corporation, focusing on waste to energy, traded at below $1 per share in 2003, followed by a run-up to $28 in 2008, then a decline to about $14 in mid-2009. Its revenue increased from $1.27 billion in 2006 to $1.67 in 2008.

Other waste management companies with high-market capitalization include Veolia Environnement, Republic Services, Inc., Stericycle, Inc., and Kimmins Corporation. Veolia was mentioned previously as it also participates in the water industry. Republic had a stable eight-year rise from about $7 to about $34 in 2008, then exhibited sudden instability in late 2008 before reaching the $22 level in early 2009. Among these stocks, Stericycle, operating in the medical wastes arena, has exhibited the most stability, rising steadily from the $2 range in 1997 to over $60 in 2008, with a decline back to the $50 range in 2009 but exhibiting little of the instability shown by other stocks during the financial meltdown. It had substantial revenue and income growth from 2006 to 2008.

Construction Company Stocks

The construction industry cuts across the infrastructure categories. Although many of the largest companies are privately owned, the sector offers a wide range of investment opportunities. Public companies include contractors, such as Fluor Corporation, Granite Construction, Chicago Bridge and Iron, and the Jacobs Engineering Group; suppliers, such as Lafarge, Cemex, and NCI Building Systems; and equipment manufacturers, such as the bellwether Caterpillar company. Construction has been a volatile investment sector, especially considering its heavy emphasis on building construction, which tumbled so far during the financial meltdown.

INFRASTRUCTURE FUNDS

Although investment funds for parts of the infrastructure sector have been around for a long time, especially those for real estate, utilities, and transportation, new funds and new groupings are becoming available. As a rationale for its new fund, started in 2008, Preqin (2009) explained that the global unlisted infrastructure market had grown from a niche sector of the private equity market into a major asset category on its own.

According to our classification of infrastructure, any fund that invests in real estate, energy, transportation, communications, water, or environmental services is an infrastructure fund. The newer funds, as well as newer indices, target all or parts of the infrastructure spectrum. This section describes a sample of funds and their investment choices. Although they are discussed by infrastructure categories, most funds do not fit exclusively into one category.

Funds that fit into our built environment category center on real estate and construction, both of which are sectors in the US BEA's national gross domestic product economic accounts. There are many real estate funds, which tend to own different flavors of REITs. There are far fewer construction-related funds, and they tend to be considered technology or cyclical funds. To illustrate the alignment of these funds, stock holdings in two real estate funds and one construction fund are presented next (Yahoo Finance, 2009).

Fidelity Advisor Real Estate A and T. Rowe Price Real Estate Advisor had 44 and 47 total holdings respectively. Their main holdings were:

Simon Property Group, Inc. (REIT in retail properties)

Public Storage (REIT in self-storage)

Ventas, Inc. (REIT in senior housing and healthcare)

Highwoods Properties, Vornado Realty Trust (REITs in integrated properties)

AvalonBay Communities, Inc. (REIT in multifamily communities)

Equity Residential (REIT, apartments)

Regency Centers Corporation (REIT in upscale shopping centers)

Fidelity Select Construction & Housing had 42 holdings, with top holdings being Home Depot, Inc. (home improvements); Lowe's Companies Inc. (home improvements); Sherwin-Williams Company (Home improvements, paint); Equity Residential (REIT in apartments); and Fluor Corporation (construction, broad-based).

Transportation funds tend to mirror the stocks in the Dow-Jones Transportation Average and are thus transportation *service* funds more than they are transportation *infrastructure* funds. Two funds show a mixture of transportation service providers: Fidelity Select Transport Fund and Rydex Transportation A. Their top holdings include:

United Parcel Service and Fedex Corporation (package delivery)

Union Pacific, Norfolk Southern Corporation, Burlington Northern Santa Fe, C S X Corporation, and Canadian National Railway (railroads)

UAL Corporation New and Delta Air Lines New (airlines)

Expeditors International and C.H. Robinson Worldwide, Inc. (freight coordination)

Telecommunications funds range across the categories explained in Chapter 5, which were local phone, long distance, wireless, and Internet services. In some cases they mix media stocks with telecom stocks. Two funds, iShares Dow Jones US Telecom (an index fund) and Fidelity Select Telecommunications, had top holdings in:

AT&T Inc. (telecom)

Embarq Corporation (telecom and logistics)

Leucadia National Corp. (integrated with some telecom)

MetroPCS Communications Inc. (wireless)

Verizon (telecom)

Windstream Corporation (rural telecom)

Sprint Nextel (telecom)

Global Crossing Ltd. (Internet based)

Cbeyond, Inc. (Internet-based communications services to small businesses)

Our energy infrastructure category focuses on electric power and natural gas, but the broader energy sector also focuses on natural resources and energy generators and their basic sources of oil, gas, coal, nuclear, and renewables. In the past, the energy industry has focused on oil, gas, and coal companies; today's interest in renewables is changing the picture rapidly.

The side of energy expressed through utility funds also has been around for a long time. In fact, the Dow Jones Utilities Average (DJUA) dates back to 1929, when utilities were removed from the Dow Jones Industrial Average (DJIA). The DJUA originally included AT&T, but that company was removed in 1938 and added to the DJIA. Today, the DJUA lists 15 utility companies, mainly in the electric power and natural gas industries.

Fund companies normally include utilities as one of the fund sectors. For example, Fidelity Select Utilities Portfolio and Vanguard Energy Fund Investor Shares have holdings in:

Exelon Corporation and PG & E Corporation (diversified utilities)

Dominion Resources, Inc. and Entergy Corporation (primarily electric power)

Sempra Energy (energy services holding)

ExxonMobil Corporation, Chevron Corporation, and ConocoPhillips (oil and gas)

Weatherford International, Inc. (oil and gas equipment and services)

Like the other sectors, water funds are also proliferating. For example, First Trust ISE Water Index Fund and PowerShares Global Water Portfolio have major holdings in:

Nalco Holding Company, Kemira Oyj, Kurita Water Industries Ltd., and Hyflux Ltd (water treatment, chemicals, processes)

Millipore Corporation (bioscience and pharmaceutical)

Flowserve Corporation (flow control equipment)

Roper Industries, Inc. (energy systems and controls)

Aqua America, Inc. (water utility)

Pentair, Inc., ITT Corporation, Crane Company, and Idex Corporation (manufacturing)

Veolia Environnement ADR and Suez Environnement Company (environmental services)

Arcadis NV (consulting services)

Valmont Industries, Inc. (irrigation and other equipment)

As explained earlier, it is a challenge to assemble a broad-based water fund. In some cases, the actual water portfolios in these funds are relatively small because companies they might hold, such as GE or ITT Corporation, are engaged in many other businesses, and water is a minor part of their business activity.

Waste management funds normally are found in the category of environmental funds, where you also might have solid waste companies, green businesses, and socially responsible businesses. The funds that invest in green or socially responsible businesses might not hold waste management companies. Instead, they might buy firms that are certified to be easy on the environment in one way or another.

One fund that invests in waste management businesses is an exchange-traded fund, Market Vectors Environmental Services (EVX). Its holdings include: Republic Services, Inc. A; Stericycle, Inc.; Waste Management, Inc.; Veolia Environnement ADR; Nalco Holding Company; Clean Harbors, Inc.; Waste Connections, Inc.; Calgon Carbon Corporation; Shaw Group; and Covanta Holding Corporation.

FourWinds Capital Management is also setting up a waste-industry fund that will also target recycling. It specializes in commodities and natural resources across energy, metals, agriculture, timber, water, waste, and alternative energy (Cobley, 2008).

Newer broad-based funds that are considered infrastructure funds contain mixtures of companies in the other categories. Analysis shows that while they are involved in infrastructure, much of their holdings is in the energy sector. For example, two funds, Kensington Global Infrastructure and iShares S&P Global Infrastructure fund include:

TransCanada Corporation (energy pipelines)

Williams Companies, Inc. (natural gas production, transmission)

Suez (utilities and environment)

Abertis Infraestructuras, S.A., Iberdrola, and Atlantia (toll roads)

Vinci (construction, toll roads)

El Paso Corporation (natural gas)

Two other funds, Macquarie Global Infrastructure Total Return and First American Global Infrastructure, hold stocks of a variety of infrastructure-related companies:

BAA plc (airports)

Magellan Midstream Partners LP (transportation, storage and distribution of refined petroleum)

Transurban Group (advanced electronic toll roads)

Kinder Morgan Energy Partners L.P. (liquids and natural gas pipelines)

Enbridge Energy Partners L.P. (transportation of crude oil)

National Grid plc and United Utilities Group plc (utilities)

East Japan Railway Co. (railroad)

Kinder Morgan Management (energy storage and transmission)

Covanta (energy and waste management)

INFRASTRUCTURE INDICES

Funds and indices are related in the sense that each is based on a basket of stocks. Market averages or indices are indicators of the price levels of baskets of stocks, and organizing them is as complex as the analysis of industry classifications (see Chapter 2).

The traditional indexing approach has been to classify stocks in broad-based groups, such as "industrial" or "technology" stocks. The DJIA and S&P 500 are such broad-based indices. If stocks are focused in a narrow sector, such as "utilities," the index measures a specific industry or niche.

Before the days of computers, sector indices included the DJTA and DJUA. They are averages and not indices in the sense that the stocks are not weighted, as they are in the DJIA.

In any of the indices or averages, you see mixtures of types of economic activity. As a broad index, the DJIA companies include four in finance, one giant retailer (Walmart), a healthcare company, a consumer products company, an entertainment giant (Disney), three food and two pharmaceutical companies, a chemical company, a home improvement company, a metals company, six manufacturers, two oil and gas companies, and six telecom and computer companies. While it is called "industrial," it is not concentrated at all on basic manufacturers.

The DJTA focuses on transportation services. Its 20 companies include: five trucking, four airlines, four railroads, three delivery services, two marine transport companies, and one each of transportation services and business support services. It does not include any data on transportation infrastructure other than within the railroads group, where the infrastructure is almost all in the private sector.

The DJTA signals movement of goods. In mid-2009, it was up for the year. According to a concept named Dow Theory, if the industrials and transports move in tandem, it is evidence that a bull market is ahead. Dow Theory is based on the idea that many market signals are implicit in movements of the indices. Of course, this is just theory, and it can go the other way. A measure that is implicit in the DJTA is number of railroad cars being loaded with commodities such as coal and with manufacturing equipment. Car loadings were down nearly 20 percent compared to a year earlier, according to the Association of American Railroads (2009). Loadings have fluctuated even as transport stocks rose, so the data are uncertain (Gongloff, 2009).

The DJUA has 14 stocks representing electric and gas utilities and companies, so this index is fairly narrow when the full utility industry is considered.

With the proliferation of computers and as infrastructure has become more attractive as a sector, new indices have been created. One new set is by Dow Jones Brookfield (2009), which offers a family of infrastructure indices organized by sector (airports, communications, diversified, master limited partnerships, oil and gas storage and transportation, ports, toll roads, transmission and distribution, and water) and by region (America, Asia/Pacific, Europe, Global ex-U.S. infrastructure).

The indices vary in their concentration on sectors. For example, Global Infrastructure is 30 percent oil and gas storage and transmission; 27 percent transmission and distribution; 14 percent communications; 11 percent toll roads; 9 percent water; and the other 8 percent airports, ports, and diversified. Toll Roads Infrastructure is 70 percent infrastructure and at least 50 percent toll roads. It includes: Abertis Infraestructuras S.A.; Atlantia S.p.A; Transurban Group; Macquarie Infrastructure Group; Brisa-Autoestradas de Portugal S.A.; Zhejiang Expressway Co., Ltd.; Macquarie Korea Infrastructure Fund; Cintra Concesiones de Infraestructuras de Transporte; Jiangsu Expressway Co. Ltd.; and ConnectEast Group. Countries represented include Spain, Italy, Portugal, China, South Korea, and Australia. Water Infrastructure is a subset of Global Infrastructure and includes all utilities: United Utilities Group PLC; Severn Trent PLC; Aqua America, Inc.; Pennon Group, PLC; Northumbrian Water, PLC; Companhia de Saneamento Basico do Estado de Sao Paulo; American Water Works Co.; California Water Services Co.; and American States Water Company.

The range of business activities of the companies listed includes those that own or operate infrastructure assets. The assets include airports, toll roads, ports, and communication facilities (broadcast/mobile towers, satellites, fiber optic/copper, and cable, but not including telecom services). The transmission and distribution fund includes ownership, leasing, concession, or management of assets but not revenues from generation, exploration, and production of energy. The water fund includes water-related infrastructure, including water distribution, wastewater management, and purification/desalination. This fund has to include revenues from sale of water services because it is rare to see assets separated from service delivery.

Another set of indices by the Macquarie Global Infrastructure Index Series (MGII) is managed by FTSE (2009), a global index firm. The series includes: Macquarie Global Infrastructure Index, Macquarie Global Infrastructure 100 Index, Macquarie Global Infrastructure Hedged Index, regional indices, and sector indices. Its sector indices include oil and gas pipelines, transportation services, telecommunications equipment and electricity, and gas and water utilities. FTSE is jointly owned by *The Financial Times* and the London Stock Exchange and manages a number of Indices for equity, bond, and other asset classes. Dow Jones and FTSE offer the Industry Classification Benchmark, which contains over 60,000 companies and 65,000 securities worldwide.

As explained earlier, it is difficult in some industries to create baskets of stocks. Utilities might be an exception, because you can include only electric and gas utilities if you choose, as in the DJUA. However, if you label an index "infrastructure," you can have such a broad mix that it is not clear what sector you are tracking. This fragmentation of infrastructure sectors was explained in Chapter 2.

COMMODITY MARKETS

Commodity markets are not part of capital markets in the sense that you raise capital by borrowing money or floating new issues in the commodity markets, but they are important in the sense that many infrastructure-related materials are traded there. Examples include oil, energy futures, timber, and industrial materials. In addition to raw and processed materials, new infrastructure-related trading commodities could include weather and emissions rights, as in carbon emissions.

Some 80 percent of global commodity trading is done on a dozen of some 20 major commodity exchanges, such as the Chicago Board of Trade. The basic function of a commodity exchange is to enable producers and users of commodities to hedge their price risks. The speculator is critical to make the system work through futures contracts (Commodities Resource Corporation, 2009).

MORTGAGE-BACKED SECURITIES

Mortgage-backed securities relate to infrastructure investments, but they are aimed more at residential housing than at its supporting infrastructure. As we explained in Chapter 3, mortgages are purchased by government and private entities from banks and other lenders and assembled into pools, which are "securitized" and sold as bonds or other forms of securities. Most are issued by government agencies or government-sponsored enterprises, such as Fannie Mae, Ginnie Mae, and Freddie Mac, but brokerage firms, banks, and homebuilders also securitize mortgages as "private-label" mortgage securities.

If you purchase shares of the government-sponsored enterprises or brokers, or if you purchase the mortgage-backed bonds directly, you are investing in infrastructure-related securities. Commercial mortgage-backed securities also exist. Private-label mortgage-backed securities are complex and fell into disrepute during the financial crisis. The American Securitization Forum (2009) has instituted Project RESTART that seeks to reduce opacity with new disclosure and reporting practices. The forum is an independent part of the Securities Industry and Financial Markets Association.

PRIVATE EQUITY AND INFRASTRUCTURE

Private equity stakes in infrastructure deals are increasing. According to Palter, Walder, and Westlake (2008), the 20 largest private equity infrastructure funds now have $130 billion under management, and most is from new entrants after 2006.

Private equity companies may acquire direct ownership in infrastructure organizations or may bid on infrastructure opportunities and form companies to manage them. They focus on gaining new assets in emerging markets or improving operation of existing projects to get better returns.

- Examples of private equity action that were discussed at the 2009 Dow Jones Infrastructure Summit in New York City include: Goldman Sachs' (2009) Infrastructure Investment Group is interested in larger investments in areas with established legal, political, and regulatory frameworks.
- The Carlyle Group (2009) purchased Synagro Technologies, Inc. in 2007. Synagro is the largest recycler of organic, nonhazardous waste and wastewater residuals in the United States It also has investments in energy and power, automotive and transportation, and technology.

- RREEF Infrastructure (2009), part of the Deutsche Bank, invests in the transport, communications and utilities sectors as well as in specialist sectors such as forestry, social infrastructure, and corporate infrastructure operations. It has been involved in the Melbourne Airport privatization, a German motorway service operator, Peel Ports in the United Kingdom, the A5 Ostregion Austrian Toll Road, and Maher Terminals in the Ports of New York and New Jersey.
- The Australia-based Macquarie Group (2009) has a number of infrastructure funds in the United States. The Macquarie Infrastructure Company is listed on the New York Stock Exchange. Its business lines include airport services, airport parking, gas production and distribution, district energy, and bulk liquid storage.

THE INFRASTRUCTURE SUPPORT SECTOR

The support groups come in a wide variety of industries, and their products cut across the categories. This list of product and service categories is typical, and firms offer their wares in single sectors such transportation, or across the sectors, such as in water and energy.

- Consultants
- Information technology
- Measuring devices
- Control devices
- Pipe and fitting manufacturers
- Chemicals and commodities
- Contractors

INFRASTRUCTURE INVESTMENT MEDIA

The same financial media that cover the economy in general are good sources of information about infrastructure investments, but niche media services have sprung up to focus on the infrastructure sectors. Each sector has its own media, such as the *Water Investment Newsletter*, and some industry-wide publications have developed.

One of these is *Infrastructure Investor* magazine (2009), which defines *infrastructure* as the man-made facilities that ensure any economy can operate to be segmented into transportation (rail, roads, and airports), utilities (energy generation and distribution, water and wastewater processing and telecommunications), and social infrastructure (schools, hospitals, and state housing). This is not inconsistent with definitions we reviewed in Chapter 1, but it leaves out buildings. The magazine explains how infrastructure was mainly a government concern until private sector participation increased in the last decade. It focuses on financing and purchase of assets by syndicates. The magazine started in London in 2001 in a financial media group, Euromoney Institutional Investor PLC, and it grew to focus on alternative assets. *Infrastructure Investor* is one of five magazines the company publishes.

Another infrastructure finance magazine is *Project Finance* (2009), which originally was named *Infrastructure Finance*. It focuses on financing arrangements and deals in the infrastructure sector. The *Infrastructure Journal* (2009) is another financial journal with a focus on the public-private partnerships and private finance initiative (PFI) deals in infrastructure today.

CORRUPTION IN THE INFRASTRUCTURE BUSINESS

Perhaps it is the large size of construction contracts or the lucrative nature of infrastructure concessions, but the business seems to foment corruption in some places. This introduces important considerations when considering investments or infrastructure business management.

This is not a new problem. For example, in nineteenth-century United States, the Crédit Mobilier scandal of 1872–1873 involved illegal manipulation of construction contracts for the Union Pacific Railroad and reached to the highest levels of the government.

The Union Pacific's major stockholders had created a company named Crédit Mobilier of America to siphon off construction profits and to trade stock to politicians in return for their favors. The company name was chosen because it sounded good, not because a French financial house was involved. The Central Pacific and the Union Pacific railroads had been awarded contracts to build a transcontinental railroad line, and Crédit Mobilier was contracted to construct the Union Pacific portion. The company overcharged the railroad for construction costs. Congressional investigations found that that company payments in cash and stock to politicians had induced generous congressional land grants and government loans (American Public Works Association, 1976).

If you fast forward about a century, you can find that a sitting vice president of the United States, Spiro Agnew, was forced to resign because while a county executive, governor of Maryland, and vice president, he had accepted bribes from the construction industry.

Corruption is a difficult problem in other countries as well, especially those in the developing world. The World Bank has organized a set of good government and anticorruption programs and indicators to fight corruption.

INTERNATIONAL SPENDING PLANS

Although U.S. infrastructure needs are large, global demands for infrastructure expansion are larger as many countries seek to upgrade systems to serve growing populations, rising standards of living, and backlogs. Dzierwa (2009) summarized the global situation, and concluded that substantial opportunities were emerging. His evidence was a series of international trips and reports by consultants, policy groups, and investment bankers. One report was from Britain's Foresight Programme, which has focused attention on infrastructure and recently completed studies on intelligent infrastructure and coastal defense against floods.

Dzierwa reported that global infrastructure needs are at levels of $32 trillion to $41 trillion for the next 20 to25 years. Drivers are demographics, globalization, government policies, and a desire of nations to upgrade infrastructure for entry to the European Union (e.g., as in Poland). Countries and regions studied include Mexico, Canada, the Middle East (Dubai, Qatar, Saudi Arabia), BRIC countries (Brazil, Russia, India, China), and Latin America. Projects similar to Boston's Big Dig are coming and include, for example, repairs to London's water system. Electricity use in China, India, and Latin America is forecast to grow at 4 to 5 percent per year. (Note that Chapter 6 reports U.S. use is growing at closer to 1 percent per year.)

Dzierwa thought that even though some corruption must be overcome, the political will exists to undertake the infrastructure projects and that beneficiaries will include companies such as those we mentioned or profiled (Caterpillar, AECOM, Jacobs) and also Manitowoc Co. (U.S., cranes); CEMEX and S.A.B. de C.V. (Mexico, cement and materials); Lafarge (France, materials); and Leighton Holdings (Australia, construction). Commodities such as copper and steel will be in increasing demand to fuel the construction. Dzierwa also saw port operators as having a rosier future, including Hamburger Hafen (Germany), DP World (Dubai), and Mundra Port in India.

INVESTMENT ISSUES AND OUTLOOK

On the surface, investor opportunities in infrastructure would focus on listed stocks and bonds, but the sector also offers other possibilities by considering how economic trends impact infrastructure supply businesses. For example, the housing crisis dampened homebuilding but did not affect home improvement businesses as much, and pressures in the energy sector are creating many possibilities for innovation in batteries. The overall infrastructure arena is so large and diverse that it is difficult to characterize it into stock index categories, but the mixture of construction, transportation, energy, and utilities offers investor perspectives that differ starkly from consumer-related trends. On an overall basis, the sector offers investments and business opportunities that span the range of risk from the relative safety of bonds to the volatility of emerging businesses, such as in the telecom sector.

Not All Infrastructure Investments Are Staid Utility Stocks

Although the infrastructure sectors offer attractive investment opportunities, many of the stocks or funds exhibit risk that occurs in volatile sectors. So, while stereotype of a utility stock that hardly ever changes and pays a good dividend year after year is not evident in today's market, the infrastructure arena does offer some attributes that might lead to attractive but stable investments.

The Built Environment Offers Infrastructure-Related Investment Opportunities

The most familiar infrastructure-related investment is purchase of real estate, but the adage that most people's main investment is their home seems weaker with the collapse of the housing bubble. In the built environment, a comparison between private and public construction shows that private construction goes up and down with more volatility than public construction. During the meltdown, residential homebuilding went into a deep freeze compared to public construction, which has longer horizons and is more affected by government spending. When homebuilding comes back up, it may create a new boom of unexpected proportions.

Transportation Infrastructure Is a Diverse Field of Investments

The transportation field has hot spots that range across the modes from smart roads to rail expansion. New opportunities to solve the capital crisis by innovative contracting and concessions for private toll road operators following the European model merit our attention.

The Energy Sector Mixes Natural Resources, Utilities, and Infrastructure

Energy and infrastructure exhibit many interfaces, ranging from how the built environment and our transportation systems are powered to use of infrastructure, such as rail and pipelines, to transport fuels. Hot issues to track include clean coal, plug-in vehicles, renewables, and more traditional sources, such as hydropower. The energy arena still has some of the stable companies that provide predictable regulated services and receive revenues based mostly on decisions by government commissions.

Recycling and Specialty Wastes Are Areas to Watch

In waste management, success of Stericyle shows that niche markets may be attractive, as compared to the massive scale of Waste Management, Inc. and the diverse experiences of European players, such as Veolia Environnement. Recycling is a key to a green future, which seems high on the priority lists of many government policy makers.

Globalization Opens New Avenues for Investors from All Countries

Globalization is leading to the internationalization of U.S. infrastructure, as seen in foreign companies' interest in selling rail cars, building systems, and getting concessions to run transportation systems. Investments by Spanish companies and Australia's Macquarie Bank are two examples.

Infrastructure Investments Have Moved toward the Field of Action

By leaving the quieter fields of government operation, the infrastructure sector aligns with strong social and economic forces that create demand. Examples might be the vulnerable aging population, concern about global warming, fear about the economy, terrorism, and the need to do something about increasing traffic congestion. Infrastructure management relates to these areas in many ways, such as the increase in medical waste exhibited in the rise of Stericycle stock. Should a solution to carbon dioxide and energy production be developed, it would have a tremendous effect on market prospects. The threat of terrorism has led to steady spending on security upgrades in several infrastructure sectors and protection against it is especially important to telecommunications (cybersecurity) and the energy and water fields as well as to protecting the built environment. Traffic congestion is another tough problem, and it has spawned a new industry of smart roads and vehicles.

Government Stimulus Will Not Necessarily Help Infrastructure Stocks

The some $800 billion U.S. government stimulus program did not channel enough new business to infrastructure-related companies to provide much of a rise in stock prices. In fact, the government has been criticized for how long the program took to show any effects and to stimulate much construction activity and new jobs. Yet it must be remembered that, during the Great Depression, it took a long time for construction stimulus programs, such as the Public Works Administration, to show substantive effects.

Tax-Exempt Municipal Bonds Will Continue to Be the Main Way to Invest in Infrastructure

Tax-exempt bonds have proved their worth in providing funds for infrastructure projects, and the default rates have been low. As investors search for safe but attractive investment channels, tax-exempts will continue to be attractive.

Infrastructure Stocks and Funds Remain Attractive

In spite of the wide-ranging infrastructure market in general and the limited availability of "pure" infrastructure stocks, the combination of energy, utilities, construction, real estate, and environmental stocks offers a wide range of choice in stocks and funds.

Private Equity Will Increase Its Activities in Infrastructure

Private equity may blow hot and cold in its interest in infrastructure investments, but the business fundamentals of the infrastructure sectors seem to promise stability and good returns. Infrastructure operations can be expected to remain and perhaps increase in the portfolios of private equity.

Infrastructure Indices Are Difficult to Assemble

It is always difficult to assemble representative indices, and the investor must study them to know what is being represented. Infrastructure is an especially difficult sector to represent because its definition can be vague and what it includes can vary substantially.

Investments in Regulated Businesses Remain Available

Given the mixture of types of organizations in the infrastructure field, one way to analyze the sectors is to pick out the companies that still offer regulated service. Although regulation has changed much in the past few decades, there are still regulated entities in electric power, natural gas, water supply, waste collection, airports, and rail. Through careful analysis, you can find stocks in regulated businesses with performance that should be more or less stable.

Financing Infrastructure

CHAPTER 11

A Scorecard for Infrastructure Performance

Most of us like to see the big picture of something before we delve into the details. This chapter draws from the sector discussions in Chapters 3 to 8 to summarize the financial statistics of infrastructure in the form of a composite scorecard with operating revenues and the condition and value of fixed assets. It draws on the Infrastructure Report Card of the American Society of Civil Engineers (ASCE, 2009a) but presents the metrics and indicators in a more comprehensive format. Given the composite view of the scorecard, it is focused more on infrastructure policy issues than it is on investment opportunities. These policy issues rely on a wide range of financial information, such as the aggregated investment needs or the deferred depreciation of a sector. This macro-level information gets translated eventually into micro-level decisions by infrastructure sector managers.

TRACKING INFRASTRUCTURE PERFORMANCE

Infrastructure can be difficult to characterize because it is a composite of diverse sectors, but unless it can be characterized and measured, evaluating its policies, funds, or sector indices is difficult. To illustrate the problem, think about the wide differences between the services of using a telephone (requiring telecommunications infrastructure) and having household waste collected and sent to solid waste disposal facilities. At a general level, these services can be considered similar (as utility services), but there is a wide difference between communication and waste disposal as service types.

Although the infrastructure sector is diverse and hard to characterize, we still need to look at it in a composite view. Requirements range from having valid sector indices for stock investments to looking at the government's obligation to invest in infrastructure. In other words, since the infrastructure business has such a high profile, we need indicators for its performance and condition. These indicators should focus on the reasons that infrastructure deserves separate attention as a sector.

Chapters 3 to 10 built on a conceptual model of the infrastructure sector to present the public and private aspects and finances of each of its subsectors. The financial picture shows a composite sector with a mixed bag of public and private enterprises. Some include massive investments in heavy fixed assets (e.g., highways) and others are more focused on equipment, new technologies, and operations (e.g., transit). Some of the finances are public sector taxes (e.g., transit taxes and subsidies), and some are in the private sector (e.g., rail company revenues).

Infrastructure finance also addresses national economic issues that include, for example, effects of the housing bubble, effects of gas prices on travel, electricity's effects on global warming, the crisis in water, disposal of nuclear wastes, massive aging infrastructures, and the war on terror. Each of these issues adds cost to infrastructure and affects its bottom line in one way or another. Some of them are high-profile, global issues and are addressed in Chapter 15.

Given the heavily public nature of infrastructure systems, with many instances of monopolies, performance reporting does not lend itself to the standard financial bottom line. Some metrics for infrastructure finance are similar to corporate annual reporting and draw from financial accounting methods, but there are important differences between infrastructure and corporate performance.

The basic performance of business corporations is measured by revenues, costs, and profit—the financial bottom line. How well a business uses its assets can be derived from the income statement and balance sheet, and the performance of an industry can be measured by aggregated financial results. In contrast, the performance of an infrastructure organization cannot be measured by financial results alone, nor is it possible to measure how well an organization uses its assets from financial statements alone. This is true because infrastructure organizations have mixed public and private purposes with aspects of both social services and private goods and services. Nor is it possible to track the performance of an infrastructure industry very well using only financials. Not only are the objectives more diffuse than those of private sector businesses, the infrastructure sectors are diverse within themselves. For example, the transportation sector includes public and private systems, road, rail, transit, and air.

Another problem in measuring infrastructure performance is the mixed public-private picture in ownership and operation of facilities (see Chapter 2). This disparity in ownership also blurs the question of who pays for the services and when subsidies are appropriate, in spite of the fact that much infrastructure is operated by private sector companies. No wonder it is difficult to compute bottom lines using only financials.

Effective ways to measure infrastructure performance and cost are needed because public governing boards must make investment and other decisions and, in some cases, must provide performance information to regulatory agencies. Even when public subsidies are received, as for example in the case of the State Drinking Water Revolving Fund, performance and cost information are required. This fund is based on a Congressionally-mandated program that provides replenishment funding for state revolving funds.

An infrastructure scorecard for a single category, such as highways, can focus on performance, condition, and cost information from one sector. However, an infrastructure scorecard is by definition a composite because infrastructure itself is a composite sector. Therefore, a grade for a single category in the ASCE Report Card is like the grade for one subject in school, whereas the overall report card is like the grades for all the subjects in one place. The grade for one infrastructure sector is like a grade in one specific subject. But this single grade hides important information, and sometimes the teacher makes comments to enable parents to understand the grade better. Those comments are like the indicators for infrastructure sectors, such as revenues, fixed assets, condition, and performance levels. This more detailed information is somewhat like the standardized school testing that is done today, such as is required by the No Child Left Behind program. This education program is founded on principles of standards-based reform and the idea that setting high standards and measurable goals can improve outcomes in education. Infrastructure is not as far along as education in performance measurement.

Thus, the goal of an infrastructure scorecard should be to present useful and broad-based information on performance and use of assets. To compile a scorecard, these questions should be answered:

- Which systems are to be measured?
- What are the performance standards?
- How well do the systems perform?
- How much do they cost?
- How ready are they to perform?

WHAT SYSTEMS TO MEASURE?

To get around the ambiguity in what to include, we defined in Chapter 1 a list of six categories of infrastructure, and most include several subcategories. To drill into the categories requires that transportation be divided into highways, transit, rail, and aviation. We could divide the other categories as well, but that leads to too much detail. There are differences between water and wastewater, for example, but the four transportation categories are even more distinct. The choice of the categories to report is, however, somewhat arbitrary, and this difficulty arises because infrastructure definitions vary from one list to another.

The next list, which was introduced in Chapter 2, is used to compile the scorecard:

- Built environment
- Highways and streets
- Mass transit
- Rail transportation
- Aviation
- Communications
- Energy (including electric power and natural gas)
- Water (including drinking water and wastewater)
- Waste management

WHAT ARE THE PERFORMANCE STANDARDS?

Because infrastructure serves public needs, policy and budget analysts have sought performance standards and yardsticks for a long time. However, setting the performance standards for a composite service like infrastructure or one of its sectors is a challenge, compared to the simpler task of setting them for a piece of equipment.

During the 1990s, infrastructure performance was studied by a National Research Council (NRC; 1995) committee, which defined it as "the degree to which infrastructure provides the services that the community expects of it" and that it is "a function of effectiveness, reliability, and cost." While these concepts represent the committee's attempt to be precise, they can sound vague, compared to the "bottom line" of financial results. The NRC committee is a high-level group that thought about the issues at the general level but stopped short of proposing specific measures for the individual sectors.

The problem is not that we do not know what each category of infrastructure is supposed to do. Each one has goals, customers, and regulatory performance requirements. For example, Interstate Highways have capacities, users, and performance standards established by the government through legislation and rule development. The problem is that when you add everything up, it becomes complex. In fact, if you look at, say, highways, you find that the Federal Highway Administration already has extensive studies of highway statistics and performance.

It is much easier to set specific indicators for systems at the local level. Local public works departments do have performance indicators, usually linked to the budget process and expressing simple measures of a limited range of goals. For example, the City of Corvallis Oregon (2009), divides its measures into general categories according to the Corvallis council's values: cost efficiency, community involvement, sustainability, and diversity. In the category of cost efficiency, the indicators and measures are:

- Maintain street sweeping costs in lower third of comparator cities (street sweeping expenditures per linear mile swept)
- Maintain facility maintenance costs in lower third of comparator cities (custodial expenditures per square foot for administrative/office spaces)
- Maintain transit costs below national average of $2.70 (costs per transit ride)
- Have utility rates that contribute to Corvallis being an attractive place to live (average monthly utility bill, compared to other mid-Willamette Valley providers)
- Efficient treatment of wastewater (full time equivalent employee count per million gallons of wastewater treated in lower third of comparator cities)
- Efficient treatment of water (full time equivalent employee count per million gallons of water treated in lower third of comparator cities)
- Maximize budget available for infrastructure improvements (project design and construction management as a percentage of construction costs)
- Efficiently review development proposals (average development review division full time equivalent employee count hours per construction project plan review)

Additional indicators used by the city to indicate community involvement, sustainability, and diversity are:

- Achieve an average 78 percent rating of excellent or good for street, water, sewer, and storm drainage services (citizen rating from the Citizen Attitude Survey)
- Be in the upper third of comparator cities for alternative fuels usage (percentage of vehicles and heavy equipment using alternative fuels)
- Remain below national average of 10 percent annually for water loss in the distribution system (percent of water loss in the distribution system)

- Achieve an annual increase in targeted categories of transit ridership over the previous year (number of rides categorized as seniors, youth, or with a disability in the annual transit survey)

These are valid and useful indicators, but they only scratch the surface of measuring the full performance of the infrastructure systems. To build a comprehensive set of indicators, you can start from what each infrastructure system is supposed to do and create simple baseline indicators. For example, as road systems should enable safe and efficient transportation of people and goods, indicators on accidents and travel time can be developed. These help, but the dilemma is that choice of simple performance metrics may mask essential issues. Yet if we compile sets of statistics, they can become so complex that only experts understand them. Still, compiling a few basic indicators like this is the only way to start.

The issue of trade-offs presents one of the biggest barriers to creating a meaningful scorecard. You can measure a deficit in "needed investment," but you must be sure that the "need" is valid and cannot be met by trade-offs. For example, the trade-off between more capacity and less demand for roads involves, among other things, a choice between truck or rail freight. Say a group of engineers says that $500 billion is needed to improve highways to meet demand. Another interest group may call that a political statement rather than an unbiased professional assessment and claim that the need is bogus and can be met by shifting freight demand to rail. The interest group might not acknowledge that it is very difficult to shift the demand and refuse to accept the professional needs assessment.

One of the most frequent areas of disagreement about trade-offs is demand projections based on population. The service could be road trips or drinking water or others. If the public agency extrapolates current demand to the future on the basis of expected population growth, the opposition will call it self-fulfilling prophecy and will demand proof that alternatives have not been considered. Sometimes opposition of this kind seems more like anti-growth or "We are not opposed to growth, as long as it isn't here." These ideas go together with NIMBY (not in my backyard) and BANANA (build absolutely nothing anywhere near anything) opposition to infrastructure projects.

Measuring how well infrastructure performs can help assess trade-offs. Performance criteria must include multiple measures, especially for effectiveness and cost. To address effectiveness, the different points of view must be considered. For example, corporations and environmentalists may have different views of where to put wind farms. On the cost side, any infrastructure will have social and environmental costs to go along with the financial ledger.

Because it is not possible to derive one overarching purpose for each infrastructure system, the best we can do is to start with broad goals that state the highest purpose of each category and add the caveat of achieving that purpose at minimum economic, social, and environmental cost. Examples are:

- **Built environment.** Enable healthy economic and social activity.
- **Transportation (roads, transit, rail, aviation).** Enable mobility of people and goods.
- **Communications.** Enable accessible and efficient communications to support economic and social activity.
- **Energy.** Supply required energy.
- **Water and wastewater.** Supply clean and safe water and manage wastewater.
- **Waste management.** Collect and manage waste.

These broad goals sound obvious, but they are actually minimalist. For example, the water and wastewater goal can have added to it additional statements about protecting the environment. They are also too general to measure by specific sets of metrics. They contain words that can be interpreted differently, such as *healthy, mobility, accessible and efficient,* and *required*. The meanings of these terms and their metrics are not exact. They are subject to interpretation, which leads to practical difficulties in measuring performance.

Getting around these difficulties requires a suite of performance measures for each infrastructure category because each system has complex performance requirements. These suites of measures should take into account the different dimensions of the NRC's categories of effectiveness, reliability, and cost.

As an example, we may know the percentage of drinking water systems that operate without any violations during any given year. However, measuring the overall effectiveness of supplying water requires many more metrics. Sets of these have been developed by researchers, and they reach into such detail as to become overwhelming.

As another example, statistics on traffic congestion on Interstate Highways show demand-to-capacity ratios, but they do not give information on trade-offs between truck and rail. Since these trade-offs are price sensitive and do not depend on command-and-control decisions, how can you assess the trade-offs?

An infrastructure scorecard must present the main issues in succinct form; otherwise, the information will not be relevant or will be too complex to grasp. Handling suites of complex measures within a simple presentation requires us to aggregate judgments of the multiple dimensions of infrastructure performance. So, the answer to the question of what to measure is, unfortunately, "it depends." What it depends on is a matter of local decision. The assembly of infrastructure performance reports remains as much a work of art as it is a science.

HOW MUCH DO THEY COST?

While it is difficult to know what to measure and how to set the standards, more progress has been made in the area of cost estimation of infrastructure needs and performance. In the field of economics, this need to measure performance has devolved to the method of cost effectiveness, in which you set the performance standards and find the minimum cost program to achieve them. This method at least eliminates the variable of the goals and standards, but it also makes outcomes less comprehensive. It is like the difference between efficiency and effectiveness in that you can be efficient at the wrong thing.

The full costs (and benefits) of infrastructure systems should be measured by the triple bottom line—that is, in economic, social, and environmental categories. Financial costs fit within the economic category, and more data are available for financial than for social or environmental costs. It is still difficult to measure the full financial cost of infrastructure, however, and many questions arise, such as cost of capital, cost of inefficiencies, and costs incurred due to monopoly constraints. Social and environmental costs are even vaguer and difficult to measure, other than through use of descriptive language.

As a result of measurement challenges, the cost of infrastructure usually is reported in terms of financial cost of service, which assumes that service levels are known and fixed. This rigid approach focuses on efficiency and discloses the costs to provide the service, but it leaves unanswered questions about effectiveness, equity, and the possibility of trade-offs. Even determining the cost of service can involve large uncertainties because reliable estimates of capital costs are difficult to obtain.

HOW READY ARE THEY TO PERFORM?

The readiness to serve of infrastructure systems is measured by facility condition, which is usually rated by government needs studies and interest group scorecards, such as the ASCE Infrastructure Report Card. Let us consider the government needs studies first.

During the 1980s, an apparent infrastructure "crisis" developed. Although investments were short of needs, the crisis was media-driven and seemed to start with a 1981 book entitled *America in Ruins: Beyond the Public Works Pork Barrel* by Pat Choate and Susan Walter (1981). Choate is an economist and ran for U.S. Vice President on the 1996 Independent ticket with Ross Perot. He has recently written a new book, *Dangerous Business: The Risks of Globalization to America.*

The media picked up on the infrastructure crisis theme, and several cover stories appeared in the early 1980s. The huge price tags came from adding together long-term needs in all categories. These popularized media stories led to studies by the Congressional Budget Office, the Joint Economic Committee, and a special commission named the National Council on Public Works Improvement (NCPWI; 1988), which created the concept of the report card used by the ASCE for its infrastructure report. During the 1990s, the U.S. Army Corps of Engineers also performed a national infrastructure study.

Given today's needs studies for highways, transit, airports, and water systems, an investment requirement of $2 to $3 trillion over 20 years is not at all out of the question. If you add in needed private investment for rail, airlines, and private energy systems, the total needs will grow. You might say that we have a better handle on these issues than we did in the 1980s.

The needs studies have now become into ongoing assessment programs, such as the Condition and Performance Report for transportation (see Chapter 4). The U.S. Environmental Protection Agency (USEPA) also prepares regular updates of needs for water and wastewater facilities. The authorities for these are in the Clean Water Act and the Safe Drinking Water Act, which serve to institutionalize the studies. Other sectors have their own needs studies, although they are not always packaged within federal programs such as we see for highways and water/wastewater.

Although the condition of infrastructure is difficult to measure, the ASCE Report Card gained traction with the media when it was introduced in 1998, 10 years hiatus after the National Council on Public Works Improvement report. The ASCE report is modeled after the council's report, but the grades assigned by ASCE are much lower than those in 1988. This disparity might be caused by the fact that the council's report was not dominated by engineers, whereas ASCE's report was prepared by engineers alone.

ASCE's methodology is based on expert opinion among engineers, supplemented by data from surveys and reports. For each scorecard, the society assembles a panel of national experts, surveys additional groups of engineers, and studies reports about infrastructure. Grades are assigned on the basis of condition and capacity and funding versus need. Initial grades are assigned on the basis of raw ratings, such as "77 percent of roads are in good condition or better." These grades are adjusted by the panel of experts on the basis of trends such as funding and risk, such as consequences of failure of a critical infrastructure (ASCE, 2009b).

The assessments consider existing or near-future (up to three years) condition, particularly where projects to improve conditions are funded or in design. They consider existing and future capacity compared to demand. To garner this information, ASCE looks at master plans, funding plans, and capital improvement programs. They also consider operations and maintenance issues, such as funding for facility maintenance and how failures contribute to noncompliance. Security and safety are considered in each category. Ratings are based on equal weights for condition, capacity, operate and maintain, and safety and security (ASCE California Section, 2009).

Exhibit 11.1 shows the grades from the ASCE 2009 Report Card, compared to the original 1988 grades.

Given the low grades in the 2009 report, it is tempting to ask whether this is just a public relations stunt, or if the poor grades actually represent a failing performance, After all, you would normally not graduate from school with an average below a C. To gain insight into the grades, let us consider roads, for example, at D–. Does ASCE really mean that the nation's roads and highways are not meeting a minimum basic need and at least passing with a C?

ASCE's explanations of the grade for roads are:

- Americans spend 4.2 billion hours a year stuck in traffic at a cost of $78.2 billion a year.
- Roadway conditions are a significant factor in about one-third of traffic fatalities.
- Poor road conditions cost U.S. motorists $67 billion a year in repairs and operating costs.
- Thirty-three percent of America's major roads are in poor or mediocre condition, and 36 percent of the nation's major urban highways are congested.
- The current spending level of $70.3 billion for highway capital improvements is well below the estimated $186 billion needed annually to substantially improve the nation's highways.

These seem to be valid statistics and arguments about the need for improved roads, but the D– grade also seems to be based on undefined

EXHIBIT 11.1 Grades from Infrastructure Report Cards

Category	NCPWI 1988	ASCE 2009	Examples of Deficiencies Cited in 2009 Report Card
Aviation	B−	D	Need to upgrade airports, modernize outdated air traffic control system
Bridges	Not available	C	Need to modernize more than 26% of bridges that are structurally deficient or functionally obsolete
Drinking water	B−	D−	Funds needed for aging facilities, to repair leaking pipes, to comply with regulations, and to respond to growth in demand
Energy	Not available	D+	Funds needed to meet increasing demand for electricity and to upgrade transmission and distribution facilities
Hazardous waste	D	D	Many cities have brownfield sites awaiting cleanup, but funding for cleanup of worst toxic waste sites has declined
Rail	Not available	C−	Modernization is required to resolve freight bottlenecks and meet increase in passenger rail demand
Roads	C+	D−	Funding required to reduce congestion and improve road conditions to keep up with rising demand
Solid waste	C−	C+	Funding needed to upgrade landfills, accommodate large volumes of waste, and promote recycling
Transit	C−	D	Funding needed for buses, rail cars, and transit facilities and rails
Wastewater	C	D−	Funding needed to upgrade aging systems that discharge untreated wastewater into surface waters

standards for hours stuck in traffic, fatalities caused by road conditions, annual cost of repairs and operating, and percent of roads in poor condition or congested. Even the phrases *stuck, road conditions, cost of repairs,* and *poor condition* should be defined better. You can almost imagine a lawyer cross-examining the report card team and finding a lot of missing information about standards on which the grades are based. It is hard to escape the conclusion that while the ASCE Report Card presents valuable information and conclusions, the standards against which it bases the grades are not entirely clear.

FINANCIAL AND ECONOMIC DATA
ON INFRASTRUCTURE

It is clear that preparing an infrastructure scorecard is not an easy task. Answers to the questions posed earlier might be given this way:

- Systems are to be measured—can be determined.
- Goals and standards of performance—mostly determined in legislation.
- Performance—hard to measure, but many statistics are available.
- Cost—known fairly well.
- Ready to perform in the future—it depends (see previous discussion on the ASCE Report Card).

This logic tells us that the issue of trade-offs is a main challenge in creating a meaningful scorecard. You can see it in the government needs studies and in the ASCE Report Card, neither of which is taken seriously enough by decision makers or the public to stimulate full funding. In addition to trade-offs in modes (such as truck or rail freight), we must face trade-offs in time and consider future patterns in issues such as commuting versus telecommuting.

Looking again at the questions tells us that we can measure the past but are not sure what to do in the future when, in extreme cases, old infrastructures may even become obsolete. An example of this might be a developing country that never had an effective telephone system but leapfrogs into the future with wireless cell phones. A needs assessment or report card on the telephone system would be meaningless.

Our yardsticks for infrastructure depend on the future being similar to the past, and trade-offs may render that assumption invalid. Still, we have to start somewhere, so in the next sections we review the aggregated data that provide some insight into the measurement of today's infrastructure condition and performance.

Infrastructure in the Gross Domestic Product

If infrastructure was a gross domestic product (GDP) category, then policy makers could study the national economic accounts to decide how to use it to raise productivity. Unfortunately, infrastructure sectors do not align with the GDP accounts, which are based on the North American Industrial Classification System (NAICS) (U.S. Census Bureau, 2009e). GDP accounts do not measure infrastructure directly, but they measure it indirectly in industry and government accounts.

Codes in the NAICS that measure most infrastructure activities are for utilities, construction, transportation, and government (public administration). Other categories that have some relationship to infrastructure are for information; real estate; professional, scientific, and technical services; waste management and remediation; and manufacturing. Infrastructure sectors cut across these GDP codes and cannot be mapped onto them easily, which presents a problem to those creating infrastructure stock indices. The construction and utilities categories align best with infrastructure, but transportation omits road spending, which is mainly in the government category.

As shown by 2007 data, the GDP (gross outputs) gives some signals about levels of infrastructure activity:

- **Utilities.** GDP levels for power generation and supply, natural gas distribution, and water, sewage, and other systems were $336 billion, $115 billion, and $10 billion respectively. This $461 billion total omits government utility activities, which are substantial, especially in electric power and water.
- **Construction.** GDP level was $1.25 trillion, which was not that far from construction spending levels.
- **Telecommunications.** GDP level was $580 billion, which seems in the ballpark for industry revenues.
- **Transportation.** GDP levels were $150 billion for air transportation, $70 billion for rail, $36 billion for water, and $274 billion for truck transportation. The numbers are in the same ranges as industry revenues, but the total omits spending on roads, airports, private cars, and transit.
- **Government.** GDP levels were $1.71 trillion for state and local general government and $869 billion for federal general government. Detailed study is needed of the Census of Governments, which is prepared by the U.S. Census Bureau, to derive infrastructure-related government expenditures, but data on "state and local enterprises" summed up to $233 billion, which includes electric power and other utilities. Data on them as separate accounts are most likely available from the U.S. Census Bureau.

Electric power and natural gas GDP gross output levels are not far from revenues of the industries (see Chapter 6), but water and sewage GDP estimates omit most activity in the government sector and are not close to the revenues reported in Chapter 7. Although construction GDP is of the same order of magnitude as construction spending, GDP data recognize the greater contributions of commercial buildings than those of residential structures, which dominate construction spending. In the construction

EXHIBIT 11.2 State and Local Capital Spending

Sector	2005 Spending $ billions	% Capital	% Local	% State
Roads	124,604	55.9	38.5	61.5
Air	17,962	51.9	92.2	7.8
Sewerage	36,600	38.7	97.0	3.0
Solid waste	21,469	9.3	85.2	14.8
Water supply	45,799	31.4	99.3	0.7
Transit	44,310	31.3	79.5	20.5

category, architectural and engineering services are also large in the GDP, at $278 billion.

While GDP data do not measure infrastructure spending directly, other government statistics do. The U.S. Census Bureau (2009f) reports state and local public works spending and reveals the relative magnitudes of government infrastructure activity (see Exhibit 11.2).

Capital Stock Data for Infrastructure

The capital stock of infrastructure is measured by the fixed asset data. As shown in Exhibit 11.3, in 2006, private and public fixed assets in the United States were valued at $40.6 trillion, and of these, 42 percent were in residential housing.

EXHIBIT 11.3 U.S. Fixed Assets, 2006

Category of Spending	$ trillions
Total U.S. fixed assets, $ trillions	40.6
Private fixed assets	31.8
Nonresidential structures	9.7
Residential	17.1
Government fixed assets	8.7
Structures	7.5
Federal fixed assets	1.8
Defense fixed assets	1.1
State and local fixed assets	6.9

Source: U.S. Bureau of Census, 2009g

EXHIBIT 11.4 Government Fixed Asset Data, 2007

Category	$ trillions
All government structures	8.31
Highways and streets	2.63
Transportation (includes transit)	0.53
State and local sewer	0.53
State and local water supply	0.38
Power	0.24

Details of the fixed assets are shown by data from more recent lookup tables of the U.S. Bureau of Economic Affairs (2009b). Exhibit 11.4 presents government fixed assets in 2007.

Highways and streets dominate government fixed asset structures, while electric power is low because it is accounted for in both the private sector and government categories.

Exhibit 11.5 presents comparable fixed asset data for private sector systems U.S. Bureau of Economic Affairs (2009b).

Construction Spending

Construction spending data reveal the rates of change of capital stock and provide an independent check on rates of change of the infrastructure inventory. The data normally show about 70 percent private spending and 30 percent public spending, but private spending is more variable and dipped sharply during the financial crisis. Construction spending for public infrastructure has a flywheel effect, which can be maintained for government work that is ordered as part of a stimulus package. On the

EXHIBIT 11.5 Private Sector Fixed Asset Data ($ trillions)

Category	$ trillions
Utilities	0.33
Air	0.06
Water transportation	0.01
Rail	0.29
Transit and ground passenger transportation	0.02
Pipeline transportation	0.11

EXHIBIT 11.6 Construction Spending, 2008 Data

Category	Total Spending ($ billions)	% of Total Spending	Public-Private Split, %
All construction	1,074.8	100.0	29–71
All private construction	766.9	71.4	Not available
All public construction	307.8	28.6	Not available
All residential	363.5	33.8	2–98
All nonresidential	711.3	66.2	42–58
Highway and street	80.5	7.5	100–0
Power	71.2	6.6	16–84
Transportation	35.2	3.3	71–29
Sewage and waste disposal	25.7	2.4	98–2
Communication	24.9	2.3	1–99
Water supply	16.9	1.6	96–4

Source: U.S. Bureau of Census, 2009c

private side, it can be more like a seesaw, such as for the ups and downs of housing starts. During the financial crisis, contractors flocked to public spending as private spending fell, thus causing competition to rise and bids to fall.

During 2003 to 2006, annual increases in total construction spending varied in the 5 to 11 percent range, but 2007 and 2008 saw declines of 3 and 5 percent due to lower economic activity. Exhibit 11.6 from 2008 construction spending shows key infrastructure categories.

The exhibit illustrates that 71.4 percent of spending was private, and residential construction was 33.8 percent of the total. Thus, when housing starts drop, all construction spending is affected. Of the public and private nonresidential categories combined, some 36 percent is for the infrastructure categories shown. Other nonresidential categories include commercial, lodging, office, heath care, religious, education, and amusement facilities. The biggest infrastructure category is highway and street construction, which is essentially 100 percent public. The categories most dominated by the private sector are power and communications.

Construction spending data for private infrastructure are augmented by the U.S. Bureau of Census's (2009h) Annual Capital Expenditures Survey, which is based on samples of companies. The 2007 data showed total expenditures at $1.3 trillion for all private capital spending for structures and equipment. Data for infrastructure categories are shown in Exhibit 11.7, which displays the split in spending on structures and equipment:

EXHIBIT 11.7 Private Sector Capital Spending Data ($ billions)

Category	Total	Equipment	Structures	% Structures
Utilities	83.6	45.1	38.5	0.46
Electric power	72.2	39.1	33.0	0.46
Natural gas (distribution only)	8.6	5.4	3.3	0.38
Water, sewage, and other systems	2.8	0.6	2.2	0.78
Air transportation	13.6	12.8	0.7	0.06
Rail transportation	11.0	2.9	8.2	0.74
Water transportation	3.4	2.6	0.8	0.24
Transit and ground passengers	2.4	2.3	0.1	0.04
Pipeline (except natural gas)	5.8	1.8	4.0	0.69
Pipeline (natural gas)	10.6	3.4	7.2	0.68
Wired telecommunications	35.2	25.9	9.3	0.26
Wireless telecommunications	22.2	15.0	7.3	0.33
Waste management	4.4	3.2	1.2	0.27

These data show clearly how some infrastructure categories spend heavily on structures (rail, water and sewage, pipeline) and others spend relatively more on equipment (air, transit). Along with data for construction spending, these data also reveal rates of expansion and renewal of infrastructure stock.

INFRASTRUCTURE SCORECARD

We explained earlier that an infrastructure scorecard must be complex to represent multiple indicators for the composite sector. Drawing from the data in the last few chapters, we prepared such a scorecard to:

- Identify the sectors and their main goals.
- Explain the public-private split.
- Estimate the sector revenues.
- Estimate the sector fixed asset level.
- Present condition information for the sector infrastructure.

The scorecard, presented in Exhibit 11.8, is condensed and requires the explanatory notes given beneath it. Fixed asset data were removed from the exhibit and added to Note 5.

EXHIBIT 11.8 Composite Infrastructure Scorecard

Sector and Goals	Public-Private	Annual Revenue Estimate	Condition[1]
Roads. Passenger & freight mobility[2]	Public: roads; private: vehicles	$148 billion[3]	ASCE grade D−
Transit. Passenger mobility[2]	Public: most fixed transit; private: most paratransit	$40 billion (fixed transit)	ASCE grade D
Rail. Passenger & freight mobility[2]	Private: rails and equipment	$60 billion[4]	ASCE grade C−
Aviation. Passenger & freight mobility[2]	Public: airports and Advanced Train Control System; private: aircraft	$143 billion	ASCE grade D
Telecom. Accessible/ efficient communication	Private	$600 billion[5]	Not reported
Energy. Required electricity & natural gas	Public-private split	$500 billion	ASCE grade D+
Water. Safe water/ wastewater management	Mostly public; many private water companies	$175 billion	ASCE grade D−
Waste management. Collect & manage waste	Public-private collection; most disposal public	$50 billion	ASCE grade C+

[1] Condition information can be augmented by needs estimates. For roads and bridges, the S. Department of Transportation Federal Highway Administration estimates that about $120 billion per year are needed in the cost-to-improve scenario. For transit, the comparable estimate is $22 billion per year. USEPA 20-year needs estimates for water and wastewater are $335 billion (2007) and $203 billion (2004) respectively, or a total of about $27 billion per year. Other categories involve complex mixtures of public and private capital needs, and comprehensive estimates are not available.

[2] Mobility for roads is intercity and intracity. For rail and air, it is intercity. For transit, it is mostly intracity.

[3] Expenditures by three levels of government.

[4] Rail revenues are about $54 billion per year for freight rail. Seven of some 550 companies receive 93 percent of revenue (2006 statistics from the U.S. Federal Rail Administration. Passenger rail: Amtrak revenue was about $2.5 billion in 2008.

[5] Global telecom revenue estimates are $1.7 trillion. U.S. GDP for 2007 shows $600 billion gross output for telecommunications (U.S. Bureau of Economic Affairs, 2009a).

[6] Fixed assets are difficult to summarize. Government fixed assets for roads were $2.6 trillion, and annual capital spending for structures was $80 billion. Government fixed assets for other transportation were $0.5 trillion, but transit and airport assets have not been separated out. Most of $64 billion in aviation capital is in private sector equipment. Private rail fixed assets are $300 billion. Broadcasting and communications had fixed assets of about $1.0 trillion, but telecommunications were not separated. Fixed assets at $680 billion are combined public and private power and natural gas (distribution only). Water and wastewater at $900 billion includes public and private. Waste management fixed assets were not determined, but most assets are in landfills and equipment.

EXHIBIT 11.9 Revenues of Infrastructure Sectors

Sector	Approximate Annual Revenues ($ billions)
Telecom	600
Energy	500
Water	175
Roads	150
Aviation	140
Rail	60
Waste management	50
Transit	40

The scorecard places light on three important attributes of infrastructure: revenues, public/private split, and condition. Fixed asset data can be added, but it makes the scorecard much more complex.

There are big differences among the infrastructure sectors in revenues, public/private split, condition, and fixed asset levels. These enable us to look closely at how the sectors differ. The annual revenue estimates are order of magnitude only, and the values used are shown in Exhibit 11.9.

These data show how telecom and energy are the "99-pound gorillas" of the infrastructure sectors. Road infrastructure would be much larger if vehicle operating costs were included in the system, and energy would be larger than telecom if the petroleum and coal industries were included. Since revenues of the coal industry are included mostly in the electric power costs, it would be double-counting simply to add the numbers.

On the basis of economic versus social uses, Exhibit 11.10 shows telecom, energy, and transportation as having very high importance to the economy. Water and waste management, along with transit, have higher social purposes, comparatively speaking. Rail and aviation are shown with high focus on the economy, whereas transit, water, and waste management are shown having more social (and in some cases, environmental) focus.

On the basis of fixed assets, Exhibit 11.11 shows how some sectors are structures intensive and others are equipment intensive. Energy, water, roads, and rail have high ratios of structures to equipment, and these services tend to own their own infrastructures. In the case of roads, if the operating costs of vehicles were included, the category would become the largest infrastructure sector by far and the ratio of equipment to structures would rise. Telecom, aviation, transit, and waste have higher ratios of equipment to

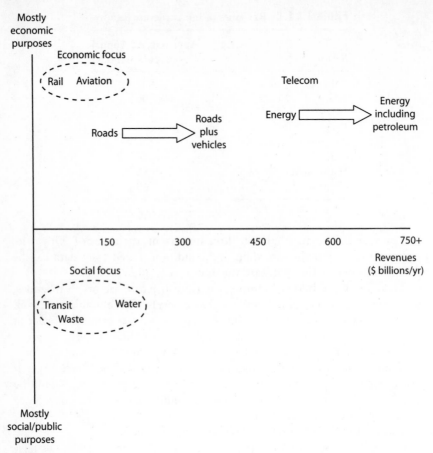

EXHIBIT 11.10 Infrastructure by Revenues and Economic-Social Purposes

structures. These services operate over infrastructures that often are owned by other parties, even telecom, which includes a large data transfer business element.

By looking at these two exhibits, we can derive a classification of infrastructure sectors by size (revenues), by economic versus social purposes, and by the intensity of fixed assets as equipment or structures. This information goes a long way toward answering questions about how to charge for private versus public goods and about why some infrastructure sectors need more frequent infusions of capital funding than others do.

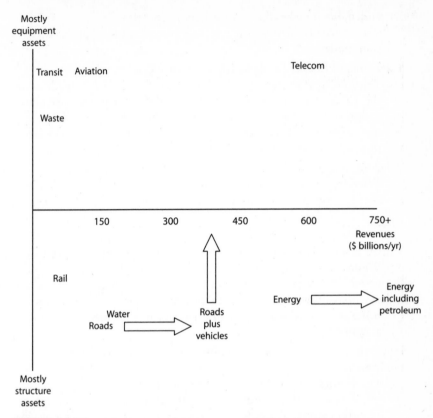

EXHIBIT 11.11 Infrastructure by Revenues and Fixed Asset Levels

SUMMARY

Although it is difficult to assemble a single scorecard for infrastructure performance, both government and professional groups keep trying to do so because the complexity must be reduced if the public is to be able to grasp the investment needs. The differences among the infrastructure sectors will block any single measure from working across all of them, but a common framework can be used.

Revenues, Public-Private Profile, and Condition Provide an Infrastructure Scorecard

The scores tell us the size of the sectors, the degree of political involvement, and the investment needs. Fixed asset data can be added, but it makes the scorecard more complex. The scorecard does not indicate trade-offs that are available, such as among transportation modes.

Telecom and Energy Lead the Infrastructure Categories

Telecom and energy are the largest infrastructure categories on the basis of revenues. The fixed assets of the road infrastructure are greatest, and it would be the largest sector by revenues if vehicle operating costs were included in the system. Energy would be larger than telecom if the petroleum and coal industries were included.

Telecom, Energy, and Transportation Are Economic Drivers

Telecom, energy, and transportation are very important to the economy. Energy powers it, telecom provides paths for information flow, and transportation handles flows of passengers and freight across the modes.

Water, Waste Management, and Transit Have High Social Purposes

While all infrastructure categories are critical to society, transit, water, and waste management have especially high social and environmental values. For this reason, they are more likely to receive subsidies than the infrastructure categories that focus on economic systems.

Infrastructure Categories Vary in Intensity of Structures versus Equipment

The sectors that are high in structures are energy, water, roads, and rail. These tend to require more capital investment, although the capital might last longer in some sectors than in others. The services with high ratios of equipment to structures include telecom, aviation, transit, and waste management. In some cases, the infrastructures are owned by different entities than those that own the equipment.

Setting Infrastructure Performance Indicators Is a Worthy Challenge

Setting performance standards for infrastructure services or sectors is challenging but worthwhile because the systems have multiple economic, social, and environmental goals. Each agency must set its own goals and indicators, but frameworks and guidance are available.

Infrastructure Report Cards Are Useful but More Information Is Needed

The 1980s infrastructure "crisis" led to today's ASCE Infrastructure Report Card, which receives publicity each time it is released. The Report Card presents valuable information, but clearer standards are needed to judge the effectiveness of its ratings.

CHAPTER 12

Financial Models for Infrastructure Organizations

The macro-level view of infrastructure on the scorecard in Chapter 11 helps our understanding of the big picture, but we still need to know how things work at the ground level. The big picture showed the sectors, their sizes, and their public-private split; how they meet economic versus social needs; and how their fixed assets are distributed. These metrics provide us with a quantitative understanding of the components of the infrastructure sector model presented in Chapter 2. At the micro-level, individual agencies and private sector organizations fit within these parameters by focusing on specific businesses that provide required public services. Depending on the sector, these services require fixed assets in the form of structures and equipment and, in some cases, labor-intensive operations, particularly for maintenance of fixed assets.

This chapter explains the details of infrastructure finance through the use of a general management model with variables that explain the different types of operations among the sectors. Although the model is simple, it accommodates public or private sector delivery of services, and it enables you to evaluate the operating characteristics of the different infrastructure sectors.

The management model focuses on organizational issues, such as type of organization and public service offered and the extent to which the government is involved. It leads to a simple financial model, which is introduced to explain financing mechanisms, as opposed to organizational and operational features. You can see from this model how revenues flow into infrastructure organizations from different sources, depending on the sector.

The remainder of the chapter builds on the models to explain how capital and operational needs are financed, how government works to improve its performance in infrastructure operations, and how the infrastructure sectors use forms of privatization and managed competition to involve the private sector.

GENERAL MANAGEMENT MODEL

The services addressed by the management model include energy, transportation, drinking water, waste management, and several others. They involve different types of organizations and operations, and the models for managing and financing infrastructure systems apply at the organizational level, where basic business decisions are made. The models offer a common platform to understand capital and operating financing in each sector and enable us to see nuances in funding principles for the different services.

The organizations that are explained in the chapter range across public and private providers and the infrastructure sectors. Examples of these organizations include:

- State transportation departments
- General government streets departments
- Private regulated monopoly utilities (energy and water sectors)
- Private regulated companies, nonmonopoly (telecom)
- Toll road authorities
- Mass transit providers
- Railroad companies
- Airline companies
- Waste management companies

The simple management model shown on Exhibit 12.1 is based on the industry integration model introduced in Chapter 2 and features four variables that change among the sectors: type of organization, type of service, form of payment, and government involvement. The simplicity of the model may be deceptive because many variations of these arrangements occur.

The variable of type of organization can represent a public or private sector infrastructure provider in any of the sectors. For the most part, these are monopolies or highly regulated entities with only a few closely controlled providers in any market. As explained in Chapter 2, the model must differentiate the organizations managing the infrastructure from those delivering services to customers. For example, the way that road networks are managed is quite different from intercity rail.

Another set of variables comprises type of service and form of payment, by fee, capital charge, or tax subsidy. This set of variables captures whether

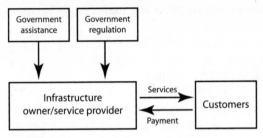

EXHIBIT 12.1 Management Model for Infrastructure Services

the service involves a public or private good and whether it can be charged for as a commodity or not. Chapter 14 explains these issues in more detail.

Other variables explain government involvement as a regulator and as a financial supporter. Sometimes government roles get mixed, and an official can be a regulator and a helper at the same time, taking on the "good cop" and "bad cop" roles simultaneously.

The variables in the management model enable us to use it to identify different arrangements among sectors, organization types, service types, financing mechanisms, and government roles. These variables turn out to be the same ones that are used to classify goods as public or utility goods (see Chapter 14) and include questions such as type of providing organization, why the services are needed, whether they are optional or essential, the extent to which they benefit the general public or only individuals, whether their use can be measured and rationed, and whether the provider is a natural monopoly.

The general case of infrastructure-based services is the monopoly government or private sector provider; in some cases (such as airlines and waste collectors), only a few competitors exist in a given market segment. Both government assistance and government regulation are usually at play in these cases.

Chapter 2 identified the infrastructure owners and service providers in each category and showed how:

- In the built environment, the buildings and facilities are operated and maintained by owners and property managers.
- Highways and streets are owned by state and local governments, along with road and bridge authorities. The owners operate and maintain the infrastructure, but vehicle operators provide transportation on it.
- Mass transit agencies use buses, light and heavy rail systems, and bus rapid transit systems that belong to transit agencies and companies.

- Rail transportation occurs on rail infrastructure, which is owned and operated by rail companies.
- Aviation occurs by private airline companies operating from publicly owned airports and controlled through a government air traffic control system.
- Communications infrastructure includes cables and wireless systems, which are owned by telecom companies.
- Energy is provided via electric power and natural gas infrastructures that are owned and operated by generation, transmission, and distribution companies and utilities.
- Water and wastewater infrastructures are owned and operated by government utilities and private water companies.
- Waste management services are provided by local governments and waste companies that utilize government- and privately owned landfills, incinerators, and processing plants.

The management model leads to the varying financing mechanisms that occur in each infrastructure sector, which depend on ownership and operating arrangements.

GENERAL FINANCING MODEL

It is important to distinguish capital and operations because different financing mechanisms are used for them. A general financing model will illustrate the capital and operating structures of the service provider organizations and distinguish the infrastructure management function from the service delivery function. For example, in the top box of Exhibit 12.2, the infrastructure provider might be the local government airport authority and the service provider might be the airlines.

The model applies to the case of an enterprise operation without subsidies. If subsidies are provided to the organization, they add to its finances but are not based on user payments for services. They are a form of general assistance to compensate for the fact that user charges are not adequate to pay for all of the needs met by the service.

The top part of the exhibit explains capital flows and the bottom part explains operations. The capital base of organizations enables the operations, which are the basis for the services provided. Customers pay for services, and their payments support operational costs and the costs of capital, whether paid for by debt, ongoing contributions, or return on stock investments. Later in the chapter, we explain how debt financing is called "pay as you use" and ongoing contributions are called "pay as you go."

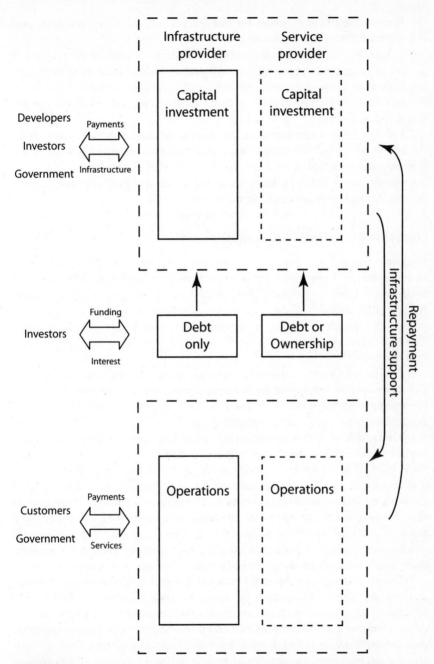

EXHIBIT 12.2 Infrastructure Enterprise Financing Model Showing Capital and Operations

Investors purchase debt, in the case of bonds, or they purchase ownership, in the case of stocks of private sector companies. As we explain later, there are important differences in how debt or ownership is repaid or rewarded in capital financing of infrastructure. Investors in debt financing securities are repaid with interest and return of principal; investors in ownership positions receive returns in the form of dividends and/or stock appreciation.

Exhibit 12.2 is the basis for the discussion in the next section. Refer to the top of the exhibit to follow capital sources and to the bottom to see how revenues for operations work. In the middle of the exhibit, investors provide the funds for debt financing. Repayment of capital is provided from revenues collected from operations.

Financing Operations and Capital Needs

Infrastructure organizations require funds for ongoing operations and funds to expand and renew their physical facilities and equipment. Government and private business infrastructure providers have the same basic choices for access to capital funding, except that government cannot issue stock and private businesses lack some tools related to taxes and/or special charges. The basic choices are to pay from reserves, to borrow, or to pay from current revenues.

Details of capital financing methods are discussed in Chapter 13. For government infrastructure organizations, most financing is via the tax-exempt municipal bond market. For-profit companies can issue corporate bonds or stock for investment capital.

To pay for growth and expansion, a form of growth-pays-its-own-way capital financing has gained in popularity for government organizations. As explained in Chapter 2, in this method of infrastructure finance, land and facility developers pay impact fees or construct and contribute capital facilities to government organizations. Developers and new customers in this arrangement might pay for all infrastructure expansion, whereas capital renewal projects would be financed by current customers. In the case of private sector systems, investors usually contribute capital and get a return on it, the rate of which is regulated by public utility commissions.

The basic choice of methods to finance ongoing operations is between fees for services or tax-supported subsidies, as discussed in Chapter 14. In a pure enterprise, such as an electric power utility, fees can support most operations, with the possible exception of emergencies and hardship cases, which might be supported by donations, intergovernmental transfers, or internal subsidies approved by regulators. Other infrastructure sectors rely on mixtures of fees and tax revenues. For example, roads and bridges are financed by local, state, and federal tax revenues and, to a minor extent, toll charges. As another example, a publicly owned landfill might be financed from property taxes and fees for use. Some services are supported entirely by tax revenues because you cannot assign private benefit to them, only diffused public benefits. An example of this service might be flood control.

SECTOR FINANCING MODELS

To illustrate the range of financing arrangements in infrastructure, two sectors are illustrated: one shows operation of a road transportation system, with its social contract between the public and private sector and another shows enterprise operation of a utility offering sale of a commodity (electric power).

Road Transportation

The financing model for road transportation is shown in Exhibit 12.3, which illustrates the social contract between the infrastructure providers (mostly state and local governments) and the infrastructure users (owners of cars, trucks, buses, and other vehicles). At the top of the exhibit, you see the main capital investments in roads, bridges, and associated structures. This is the infrastructure that has a fixed asset value of nearly $3 trillion in the United States and that requires a minimum of $80 billion in capital funding each year. Vehicle owners are paying for capital investments in their vehicles, and tax revenues are paying for capital needs in the road system. Equity investors have only a small role here, as they might invest in businesses that operate toll roads or own commercial vehicles, which earn a return on investment. The infrastructure that vehicle owners, tax authorities, and equity investors get comprises the roads and bridges that enable travel and the equipment used by travelers. The services received in the form of transportation of passengers and freight are shown at the bottom of the exhibit.

The social contract arises because the service (transportation of passengers and freight) is provided by private owners who use the publicly owned infrastructure. In Chapter 4, we explained how, on an annual basis, the expenditures by these private owners are on the order of 10 times those of the governments that build and maintain the roads. The policy question for government is: How much more funding should be required from road users to support the infrastructure? Given the ratio of 10 that is evident here, it seems surprising that government would be unwilling to raise the gas tax, but for political reasons it has refused to do so. Therefore, the

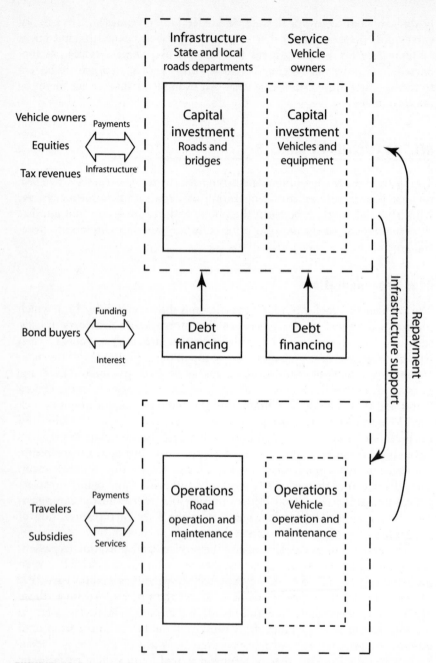

EXHIBIT 12.3   Road Transportation Financing Model

government continually searches for creative ways to provide road funding without raising taxes.

Anecdotally, this is the same issue facing government in other sectors with a high degree of public goods, such as basic healthcare. There are three basic options for the future of healthcare in the nation: raise taxes, cut services, or cut costs. Among these, the only bright light is to increase choice of healthcare options by giving the consumer more decision-making power. It is the same in road transportation: By adding choices, such as to pay tolls for single drivers in high-occupancy vehicle lanes, problems may be solved without raising taxes.

At the bottom of the exhibit you see travelers paying fees for operation of vehicles and tax subsidies paying for operations and maintenance of the road system. This reveals how the same tax sources are used to capitalize and to maintain road systems. The top and bottom of the diagram correspond to capital budgets (top) and operating budgets (bottom) of infrastructure organizations.

Electric Power

Electric power financing is shown in Exhibit 12.4, which illustrates the situation in which public company, government, and subsidized cooperatives provide electricity service to a range of customers. The top of the exhibit shows capital investments in electric power generation, transmission, and distribution systems. These are the systems that will require so much capital investment in the years ahead (see Chapter 4). In the case of electric power, the normal situation is that a utility owns most of its own infrastructure, so the right side of the exhibit showing service providers converges with the left side, which represents infrastructure owners. The exceptions are those utilities that purchase power from others, which is a widespread practice now, especially after the deregulation of generation and transmission that occurred in the last decade. *Investors* as shown are direct investors, such as private equity groups. *Equities* represent stock ownership in investor-owned electric utilities, and *tax revenues* refer to situations in which public power authorities have access to tax streams, such as property or sales taxes.

Bond buyers for electric power could purchase tax-exempt bonds, in the case of public power, or buy corporate bonds, in the case of investor-owned utilities. Sometimes investor-owned utilities can gain access to tax advantages, but usually they operate at arm's length from government sources. In the lower part of the exhibit, operations are financed mostly by customer payments and subsidies apply only in limited situations, such as rural cooperative systems receiving federal subsidies in the form of low-interest loans, for example.

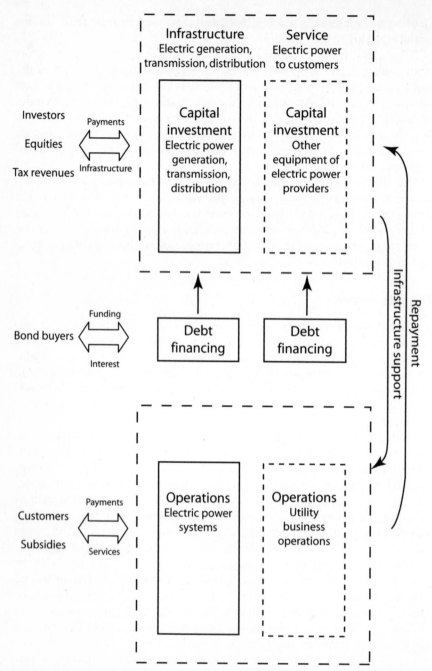

EXHIBIT 12.4 Electric Power Financing Model

HOW GOVERNMENTS CAN IMPROVE
INFRASTRUCTURE PERFORMANCE

As we explained in Chapter 1, the choice between government and business providers of infrastructure-related services is not always clear. Experience shows that three forms of ownership and management are used: pure government, pure privatization, and mixed approaches.

In the case of pure government management approaches, the tools of public administration can be used to increase efficiency. These are constantly changing with innovative approaches to improve performance. Although government management always will have the potential for inefficiencies, in some cases it can turn in impressive performance.

Without forced accountability, government operations tend to become more inefficient over time. This is due to human behavior, lack of competition, and other institutional factors. The tendency for government to grow, whether it needs to or not, was explained in a humorous essay by the British economist Cyril Parkinson (1955), who wrote: "Work expands so as to fill the time available for its completion." Parkinson explained further that in government, the number of employees grows because an official wants to multiply subordinates instead of rivals and officials make work for each other. His studies showed that the number of employees in a bureaucracy increased by 5 to 7 percent per year without any change in work required.

When you combine bureaucratic trends with people's reluctance to pay government fees and taxes, it is easy to see how government can become inefficient and out of touch. Responses to this dilemma include new political leadership, reorganizations, consolidations, and other interventions. Privatization might be an answer for some cases, but it may not serve all categories of the public interest. Therefore, there is a continuing search for ways to make government more effective and efficient.

Public administration has developed programs and tools, such as government executive institutes, to make public enterprises and agencies more effective. The federal government has a Government Performance and Results Act that is intended to increase performance measurement and accountability. It continually looks for ways to make government more focused on results (U.S. Government Accountability Office [GAO, 2005]).

During the fiscal crisis, large and small government entities have felt stress, and there is a widespread search for greater efficiency in delivering services. This features new experiments with eliminating, outsourcing or collaborating on services and puts a spotlight on the role of government as a service provider.

Osborne and Gaebler (1992) wrote *Reinvention of Government* to offer prescriptions to make government more effective. This was followed in 2004 by *The Price of Government*, which introduced a way to budget and manage by performance, rather than just program (Osborne and Hutchinson, 2004). Together, these works contain two main ideas: to make budgeting more effective through a process called "budgeting for outcomes" and to unbundle services and programs to find those that can be opened to competition (reinventing government). The budget method takes the concept of performance budgeting further and opens the way for managed competition between the public and private sectors.

Budgeting for Outcomes

Government inefficiency can be seen in the standard budget process in which agencies may volunteer a few cuts and pad their costs to protect against inevitable cuts. Responses to this range from across-the-board cuts to constitutional tax limit proposals. These cause other problems and may impact services negatively. There is always a need to cut unneeded programs and concentrate revenues on areas of greatest need.

Citizens want value for their money, but they do not want to cut spending in areas that are vital to them. This situation calls for a combination of setting priorities and increasing efficiency through the budget process. *The Price of Government* approach poses five questions to shape the budget process:

1. Is the real problem short or long term?
2. How much are citizens willing to spend?
3. What results do citizens want for their money?
4. How much will government spend to produce each of these results?
5. How best can that money be spent to achieve each of the core results?

The answers to these questions should lead to a budget process that helps government to get a grip on the problem, set the price of government, set priorities of government, allocate available resources across priorities, and develop a purchasing plan for each result. Strategies to implement this approach include review processes outside the budget process, consolidation of funding streams, "rightsizing," buying services competitively, rewarding performance, and smarter customer service.

These ideals give government infrastructure agencies a benchmark target, but the budgeting process can be contentious because many different objectives are at play. It is not easy to zero out traditional agencies and start over again by having them compete with other agencies and/or the private sector. Still, this approach offers fresh thinking about budgeting and a way to break through the conventional thinking that sometimes creates gridlock in reform efforts.

Managed Competition

Managed competition has the same general goals as budgeting for outcomes, and it can organize competition between the public and private sectors by unbundling services to create a system that allows services to be delivered by government, the private sector, or a mixture of the two. For example, the City of Charlotte, North Carolina, introduced a managed competition system in the 1990s as a planned approach for service delivery. In their approach, private sector firms were invited to compete against the public sector to supply services. This was part of Charlotte's strategy to balance limited revenues against escalating costs and demands for services. The main achievement of managed competition in Charlotte was to develop a culture in which government is run like a business; city staff recognized that if the city was to compete successfully, changes were necessary (Greenough et al., 1999).

In the budgeting for outcomes process or in managed competition, many issues must be faced. One important issue is to ensure a level playing field to encourage private sector firms to compete against government departments. Doing this requires both a valid set of accounts and public sector willingness to identify costs fairly and expertly so that the true costs of individual services can be identified.

Privatization

Privatization, in which a public entity turns over operation or ownership of all or part of a government enterprise to a private company, became trendy about 1980. Its attraction is the claimed increase in productivity through competition rather than government processes that involve politicians or civil servants. Privatization can reduce costs and promote private sector responses to consumer preferences. The opposite of privatization is government takeover, such as seizing a company and converting it to government ownership and operation.

With the U.S. takeover of businesses in 2009, especially finance and automobiles, it seems that the pendulum has swung the other way from privatization. Time will tell whether the government is able to extract itself from the businesses in which it has taken a stake.

The 1980s interest in infrastructure privatization was fueled by the elections of conservatives Ronald Reagan and Margaret Thatcher and by the fall of the Berlin Wall and the opening of socialist countries to more economic competition. In Asia, emerging nations needed new economic models, and South Korea, Malaysia, and China developed models for privatization. Many experiments have been tried; some have been successful, and some have not been. It seems safe to say that by the end of the 1980s, most governments had embraced the concept that private sector involvement in running infrastructure systems was a good thing.

During the 1980s, the visible examples were privatization of industries at national levels, such as the sell-off in Britain of state-owned enterprises. The Thatcher government made the sale of public-owned companies as a high priority, and the companies to be sold accounted for more than 10 percent of the gross domestic product. The companies had consumed billions of dollars in subsidies since World War II and had damaged British competitiveness, according to the Thatcher government. An example cited was the National Coal Board, a high-cost producer whose major customer was the national electricity industry, a monopoly that passed along the cost as high energy costs. By 1983, the Thatcher government had sold all or part of British Aerospace, Cable and Wireless, Amersham International, Britoil, and Associated British Ports (Brown, 1983).

Privatization continued in Britain, and British Telecom was privatized in 1984. The electricity industry was privatized beginning in 1989, and the British Water Industry and the British Airports Authority were privatized in the 1980s. British Gas became a private company in 1996. British Rail was also privatized in stages during the 1990s. Today, privatization is an accepted method to offer infrastructure services in the United Kingdom.

Developing countries are likely to have networks of state enterprises to provide services, but often these enterprises have poor service delivery records. Rather than being taken over by local firms, these state companies might be targets for buyout or contract operation by large, international firms.

Privatization can take on different forms, depending on how facilities are financed and operated:

- Complete private ownership and management, in which the private entity builds or buys the facility and operates it under a service contract with a government entity.
- Private financing of construction and leaseback to the government entity. Capitalization is by the private investor with operation by the government.
- Contract operations by the private firm, which has complete responsibility for operations.

Arrangements are limited only by the imagination of the parties involved. They can include lease-purchase, sale and leaseback, and other cooperative deals.

Examples of Privatization   In the nineteenth-century United States, private roads and bridges were built even before the government took over the roads network. Today *privatization* means to convert government roads to private ownership or operation, and the private sector can also construct new roads and/or bridges (see Chapter 4). An example of road privatization is the lease of the Chicago Skyway, which was the first long-term lease of an existing toll road in the United States.

The 7.8-mile toll road was leased in 2005 through a concession agreement to Cintra/Macquarie, a private equity operator. Cintra/Macquarie bid $1.83 billion for the 99-year concession. The other two bidders came in much lower, one at about $700 million (Vinci Concessions, a French and Canadian group) and the other at about $500 million (Abertis Infraestructuras). The concession operates through the Skyway Concession Company, LLC, which has responsibility for all operating and maintenance costs in exchange for all toll and concession revenue (U.S. Federal Highway Administration, 2009d).

Transit privatization is not used much in the United States because it requires subsidies and a heavy dose of political decision making. However, it occurs frequently in Latin America. According to the International Transit Studies Program, an ongoing activity of the U.S. Transportation Research Board, transit agencies in Buenos Aires, Argentina; Montevideo, Uruguay; and Porto Alegre, Curitiba, and Sao Paulo, Brazil have let operating concessions to private companies, which are regulated by government agencies (Lee, 1999).

The privatization of British Rail offers a good case study in the rail infrastructure sector. It is a long story, and the privatization process was controversial and contentious. To summarize, after developments that occurred following the landmark Railways Act of 1993, the organization was to be broken up into many different operating units. The infrastructure is now owned and operated by a company named Network Rail, which provides the network infrastructure for the passenger and freight operating companies, which were spun off. Regulation is by an Office of Rail Regulation, similar in design to other regulatory authorities for privatized companies.

This division of British Rail into an infrastructure company (Network Rail) and operating companies follows the model of this chapter, in which organizational variables distinguish between whether it is infrastructure or services that are to be managed.

The U.S. Government Accountability Office (formerly General Accounting Office, or GAO, 1996) studied airport privatization during the 1990s and found ongoing efforts in some 50 countries. In the study, the initiatives were in early stages, but the experience in the United Kingdom had been in place long enough to provide useful results. There, privately owned airports had generated attractive profits because of growth in passenger traffic and concession revenues, in spite of government regulation of fees and owner infrastructure costs.

In the United States, there has been interest in privatization of commercial airports, but the issue has been too contentious to move very far, and funding has been difficult during the financial crisis. A high-profile effort to lease out Chicago's Midway Airport has failed so far, but new proposals are sure to be developed, if not in Chicago then in other cities.

As with the electric power industry, water supply utilities can be owned either publicly or privately. However, turning over ownership of a water supply utility can be a contentious experience, as the City of Cochabama, Bolivia, learned when its privatization attempt was reversed after civil disturbances. Even in U.S. cities, such as Atlanta, privatization of water supply is controversial and can lead to unexpected consequences, such as labor unrest and higher rates.

On the wastewater side, the United States has a good bit of experience with operating concessions, in which private operators run treatment plants and answer to regulators. Internationally, large private companies such as Veolia Environnement and United Water, are seeking and obtaining operating concessions (see Chapter 7).

Assessment of Privatization After studying a number of case studies in the water sector, I prepared an exhibit to align the arguments for and against privatization of water services. The arguments were long and complex, but they fell into the five categories shown in the first column of Exhibit 12.5. The arguments extend easily to forms of transportation, energy, and waste management, but they do not work too well in the telecommunications sector. As you examine the arguments, you can see that how they compare to each other will depend on case-by-case situations. For example, in a case of a highly effective public agency, as compared to a poorly run private company, the public sector argument will prevail. Although Exhibit 12.5 is not perfect, it presents a way to align the different viewpoints about privatization.

PUBLIC-PRIVATE PARTNERSHIPS

Given the controversies over privatization, the more general concept of public-private partnerships (PPP) have gained in popularity. For example, project delivery and finance methods such as design-build and build-operate-transfer enable government to take advantage of the capital and expertise of the private sector while securing public benefits of infrastructure systems. These methods were discussed in Chapter 9 because they are so important to the construction industry.

Use of PPPs is increasing. The U.S. Federal Highway Administration's (2009e) "Public-Private Partnerships Toolkit for Highways" provides

EXHIBIT 12.5 Arguments for and against Privatization

Criterion	For Privatization	Against Privatization
Ideology	Water is an economic good and ought to be managed by the private sector; smaller government is better.	Water is a public good and ought to be managed by government; government is needed to resist excesses of private sector.
Efficiency	The private sector is more competent than the public sector. Cost savings occur in construction, procurement, hiring and training and tax obligations.	The public sector is efficient; cost savings in privatization are fictional; tax benefits are a shell game; negative aspects of long-term contracts; potential for rate increases.
Social impacts	Government is not reliable, and people do not always trust it.	Loss of political control; loss of jobs; loss of public benefits of water.
Risk reduction	Private firm will guarantee performance.	Effective management by government minimizes risk.
Capital generation	Access to capital in private markets; government debt limits not imposed.	The public sector should generate capital for infrastructure.

advice. It emphasizes innovative financing mechanisms to provide flexibility in project delivery, such as private activity bonds, which give private developers and operators access to the tax-exempt bond market, and the Transportation Infrastructure Finance and Innovation Act credit program (see Chapter 4), which leverages co-investment by providing supplemental and subordinate capital.

The World Bank (2009a) has also adopted the PPP model as a tool to solve infrastructure problems. It offers toolkits across the sectors, including for concessions, selection of advisors, and dealing with labor as well as in the sectors for highways, ports, solid waste, telecommunications (focus on regulation), urban bus service, and water and sanitation.

Other donor organizations have joined the World Bank in a group called the Public-Private Infrastructure Partnership Facility (2009b), whose goal is to "eliminate poverty and achieve sustainable development through public-private partnerships in infrastructure." As a result of these efforts, many more resources are available today to promote and evaluate private sector involvement than when privatization became trendy in the 1980s.

There are many examples around the world of PPP in action. The outsourcing of an operations contract for transit in New Orleans is an example. The city's Regional Transit Authority plans to hire a subsidiary of Veolia Environnement with a contract worth potentially $600 million in a decade to finance, manage, and operate the system. It can be a win-win deal and save the authority some 30 percent of its costs. Risks include the financial soundness of the private operator and the political sensitivity that might arise. These kinds of issues have delayed or stopped deals to privatize Chicago's Midway Airport and construction of a new tunnel to the Port of Miami. The New Orleans deal is unusual because big-city transit agencies in the United States normally do not outsource so much control. Savannah, Georgia, is negotiating a similar contract with Veolia, and in the Phoenix, Arizona, region, a light rail line of Valley Metro is operated by private contractor Alternate Concepts Inc. The authority already outsources bus services. The transit authority in Houston, Texas, awarded a $1.5 billion build-operate-transfer contract to Parsons Corporation for light rail lines, and Dallas and Fort Worth are looking for a private partner to finance, build, maintain, and operate a future rail system. In Los Angeles, California, the Metropolitan Transportation Authority contracts service on some bus lines but has no plans for further contracting because of labor agreements. New Orleans's unionized bus drivers will become Veolia employees and preserve their labor agreements (Conkey, 2009b).

REGULATION

Behind all schemes to reinvent government, privatize, or have mixed competition lie the subjects of monopoly, competition, and antitrust. Early on, it was discovered that infrastructure often involves a monopoly or some restraint on free competition and requires oversight. The history and role of regulation in infrastructure financing is discussed in Chapter 13. Regulatory controls, along with political decision making, will continue to be wild cards in the evaluation of private sector involvement in infrastructure.

SUMMARY

Models for infrastructure management and finance provide a useful framework to compare performance and results across the sectors. The management model shows how to consider organizational and process variables, and the financial model shows the flows of capital and operating funds. These models can be used to simplify complex discussions and help keep policy makers on the same page when comparing approaches and assessing proposed solutions.

A Management Model Shows Organizational and Operational Arrangements

A model of organization illustrates the similarities and differences among infrastructure sectors. Variables in the management model are type of organization, type of service, form of payment, and degree and mode of government involvement. These control the financing mechanisms for each infrastructure sector.

A Financial Model Explains Revenues, Costs, and Assets of Infrastructure Systems

The financial model shows capital and operating aspects of infrastructure organizations with explanations for the infrastructure management function and the service delivery function. It can be used for both enterprise payments and tax subsidies, where they are used.

"Growth Pays Its Own Way" Is a Viable but Variable Source of Infrastructure Financing

The growth-pays-its-own-way method enables local governments to assign capital costs to the beneficiaries of infrastructure projects. The method can create an effective way to embed the cost of infrastructure in the cost of buildings, but it fluctuates with building construction activity level. For privately owned infrastructure systems, investors contribute capital and get a regulated rate of return on it.

Road Infrastructure Finance Depends on the Gas Tax and Needs Reform

The some $80 billion per year spent on road infrastructure is not adequate to maintain and improve the vast U.S. road system, and the gas tax is inadequate to finance even this level of maintenance. New methods to finance the system are essential if conditions are to improve or even stay the same.

Private Passenger and Freight Transportation Expenditures Are Much Larger than Infrastructure Investments

When viewing road transportation as a system, it is important to consider both infrastructure and vehicle operating costs. On an annual basis, the expenditures by private vehicle owners are on the order of 10 times those of the governments that build and maintain the roads.

Electric Power Places a Major Call in U.S. Capital Resources

Public company, government, and subsidized cooperatives require major capital investments to maintain and improve their systems.

As electric power changes and absorbs new demands, these capital requirements will increase.

Governments Can Improve Infrastructure Performance through Creative Management

The three levels of government can bring to bear new tools of public administration, which include improved budgeting and unbundling services and programs to open some to competition between the public and private sectors.

Managed Competition Can Help Government Run Like a Business

Citizens want lower taxes, but they do not want to give up essential services, so running government enterprises like businesses is a win-win proposition. Managed competition can help government run its infrastructure enterprises like businesses.

Privatization as a Form of Public-Private Cooperation Can Work in Many Cases

Privatization in different forms fits into the spectrum of public-private partnerships and is a viable alternative for operation and ownership of some infrastructure systems. It cannot be used across the board as a panacea for all government inefficiencies, but it has attractive possibilities in selected situations.

Public-Private Partnerships Are an Umbrella under Which to Organize New Arrangements

Public-private partnerships are trendy, but the term is only the tip of the iceberg and must be translated into specific applications across the range of infrastructure services.

CHAPTER 13

Capital Markets for Infrastructure

Given their heavy reliance on structures and equipment, infrastructure agencies require substantial and continuing funding from the capital markets. Capital demands for electric power are among the highest of all industries, and other capital-intensive sectors, such as highways, also absorb large amounts of capital funding every year, albeit from different sources.

This chapter explains the functioning of the capital markets that serve the infrastructure sectors. It begins by summarizing the capital requirements of the infrastructure sectors and then explains capital flows from bonds, loans, government grants, current revenues, private equity, and development fees. The chapter provides an overall picture of the capital structure of the infrastructure sectors and provides details of how the individual sources of capital work.

CAPITAL REQUIREMENTS OF SECTORS

The infrastructure sectors differ widely in their requirements for capital investments. Sectors with a high ratio of structures to equipment, such as water supply utilities, require most of their funding for long-lived assets, such as pipelines, which in some cases last 100 years or more. In other structures-heavy sectors, especially highways, more frequent funding doses for renewal and reinvestment are required because the structures (especially road pavements) wear out more quickly. Still other sectors, such as transit and airlines, invest more in equipment than in structures and tend to have higher percentages of operating expenses than the capital-intensive sectors; they also require replacement capital when equipment wears out.

Regardless of the capital split between structures or equipment, all infrastructure sectors use the capital markets heavily. Public agencies focus on the tax-exempt bond markets; private infrastructure companies, such as electric power utilities, use corporate bonds, cash, and equity. Of course, the private sector suppliers of infrastructure providers utilize the same sources of capital funds as other businesses.

Capital spending by public agencies normally is channeled through the processes of comprehensive planning, programming, and budgeting. Capital budgeting is a critical process for all three levels of government, especially at the level of local government, where infrastructure enterprises are mostly found. In the budget processes at the local government level, it is easy to see why "all politics are local."

It is important to understand the local capital budgeting process because it determines most of the investments at the local level, where most infrastructure spending occurs. At the local level, integrated plans are called comprehensive plans, policy plans, and by other names, such as Vision 2020 for Metropolis, or something similar. The infrastructure manager's job is to translate the broad outlines of these plans into specific infrastructure programs and to make the shift from the planning world to the engineering and financial worlds.

Capital planning begins with integrated planning and moves through a process of:

- Dividing up plans for infrastructure sectors or city zones
- Sector planning, such as the master streets plan
- Deriving the broad capital improvement plan
- Isolating projects or systems for further planning
- Dividing projects into subprojects or incremental stages
- Detailed planning for the subprojects
- Programming subprojects for years of construction
- Gaining approval for the capital improvement program
- Determining methods to finance the capital budget
- Publishing the capital improvement plan in the entity's capital programs and budgets

State governments have capital budgets, but at the national level, it has not been possible to organize a coherent capital budgeting process because the politics of budgeting are so complex and contentious. Nevertheless, the topic of a national capital budget continues to be studied (President's Commission to Study Capital Budgeting, 1999). Currently, federal finances are tilted heavily toward deficit spending, of which a good bit has gone to capital spending for the stimulus package. Although this part of the budget is not considered a capital budget per se, the federal government maintains records of the split between ongoing and capital expenses.

CAPITAL FLOWS OF INFRASTRUCTURE

The general flow of infrastructure capital funding is illustrated by Exhibit 13.1, which shows how financial assets provide funding for the capital markets, which in turn provide funding for the sectors of infrastructure as well as for other capital needs of business and individuals. Investment funds come from financial assets that are managed by individuals, banks, investment companies, and other financial institutions. They flow as capital sources in the forms of mortgage lending, bonds, stock purchases, loans, fees, grants, and private equity stakes. The capital investments go to the infrastructure sectors, which generate services that benefit individuals, businesses, and government and therefore benefit financial assets by making the economy more productive.

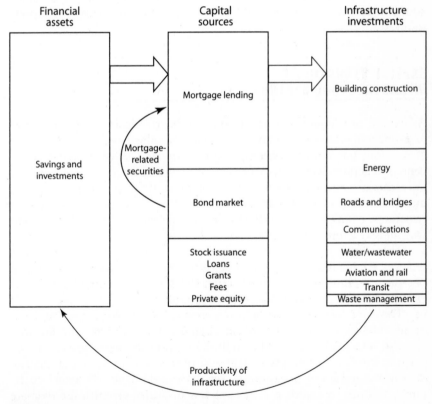

EXHIBIT 13.1   Capital Flows for Infrastructure

Of course, a view like Exhibit 13.1 seems to suggest that the supply of capital is fixed. However, the financial assets shown on the figure fluctuate greatly, and capital to invest in U.S. infrastructure systems does not necessarily have to come from U.S. investors. At any rate, the balance sheet of households maintained by the Federal Reserve Bank (2009b) shows household real estate at $17.9 trillion and all net worth at $50.4 trillion as of the end of the first quarter of 2009. The net worth figure includes nonprofit corporations as well. The value of wealth declined from a high of $62.6 trillion in 2007, reflecting the fall-off in real estate values and stocks.

The more effective the infrastructure, the greater its productivity will be in enhancing financial assets. So, as the model shows, it is rather obvious that investments in infrastructure are a win-win proposition only as long as they improve productivity of the economy. That is, if they improve productivity and produce profits that increase wealth, then more capital is available to invest in infrastructure. If investments in infrastructure are to no avail—that is, if they are spent on useless white elephants—then they add nothing to the wealth and do not improve productivity and prospects to invest more in infrastructure.

CAPITAL STRUCTURE OF INFRASTRUCTURE SECTORS

As we saw in Chapter 11, U.S. fixed assets, or the depreciated cumulative investment in infrastructure and equipment, are valued at about $40 trillion. Nearly four-fifths of the fixed assets are in private residential and nonresidential structures and equipment. The rest (some 21 percent) are in public infrastructure and equipment, which comprise the capital base of public infrastructure systems. Of this public side of fixed assets, most comprises structures, mainly roads and bridges, which are the backbone of the highway infrastructure.

These fixed assets are replenished by construction for expansion or renewal. Each infrastructure sector has different needs, according to its type of structures, rates of renewal, and related factors. These capital needs were explained in Chapters 3 to 8 and are summarized here.

The capital needs of the built environment are driven by construction of new homes. Commercial, industrial, and public buildings and facilities are also important, but single-family homes are the main driver. As we explained in Chapter 3, residential housing accounts for more than half of all private fixed assets and absorbs a big share of the capital flowing into the public and private building market. A few measures give the approximate

EXHIBIT 13.2 Building Construction Put in Place (in $ millions)

	January 2007	January 2009
Residential	573,253	294,695
Educational	89,005	103,644
Commercial	82,447	71,397
Office	61,184	65,803
Health care	41,309	45,526
Lodging	21,624	30,368
Religious	7,913	6,903
Total	876,735	618,336

Source: U.S. Census Bureau , 2009c

size of the total capital flows for construction in the built environment. For example, Exhibit 13.2 presents the building rates for construction put in place, as summarized in Chapter 9. These data illustrate that capital flows into building construction are on the order of $600 to $900 billion per year, depending on the rates of construction. Almost all of the $258 billion decline in construction from 2007 to 2009 can be attributed to the fall-off in residential building. Some categories, such as schools, increased in construction spending.

As explained in Chapter 4, total 2006 expenditures for roads and bridges were $161 billion, and funding was 21, 51, and 29 percent from federal, state, and local sources, respectively. About half this amount, or some $80 billion, was for capital expenses, and this is consistent with the figure for construction put in place for highways and streets at $80.5 billion (2008 data).

Also explained in Chapter 4 is that transit expenses for capital are smaller, at $13.3 billion for 2006. Transit capital expenses include significant amounts for equipment as well as structures.

Data on aviation and rail capital expenditures are lumped into the transportation category of the North American Industry Classification System (omitting roads). In 2008, construction for this transportation category was $35.2 billion. This includes airports and all associated public spending as well as private spending on structures. Both air and rail also have significant capital costs for equipment. Private capital spending for air and rail in 2007 was a total of $24.6 billion, with $12.8 billion for air equipment and $2.9 billion for rail equipment. Private sector structures for the two categories were $700 million for air and $8.2 billion for rail, which shows how much more dependent on structures rail is than aviation.

Communications construction in 2008 was $24.9 billion. Reports for capital expenditures in 2007 were $57.4 billion total, $40.9 billion in equipment and $16.6 billion for structures. As Chapter 5 explains, these are all private expenditures.

Construction spending for 2008 in the energy sector was $71.2 billion. On the private side, capital investments in 2007 were $72.2 billion for electric power ($29.1 billion for equipment and $33.0 billion for structures) and $8.6 billion for natural gas distribution ($5.4 billion equipment and $3.3 billion structures). Capital spending for government energy enterprises has not been broken out of the totals but would add significantly to them. As an estimate of total capital spending, it seems reasonable to assume about $100 billion per year for electric power and $12 billion for natural gas. Both figures include equipment and structures.

In the water sector, construction in 2008 was $16.9 billion for water and $25.7 billion for wastewater. On the private side, data show that in 2007, capital spending was $2.8 billion, including $600 million for equipment and $2.2 billion for structures.

Waste management construction on the public side is not broken out separately. Private capital spending in 2007 was $4.4 billion, including $3.2 billion for equipment and $1.2 billion for structures.

Overall capital spending in the sectors varies greatly from year to year, and precise estimates of average spending are not available. However, based on the data just reported, Exhibit 13.3 tabulates current levels of approximate spending to show relative capital needs of the infrastructure sectors.

In these figures, aviation and rail were estimated by taking transportation construction at $35 billion less transit and water transportation construction (estimated at $15 billion), plus $15 billion for aviation and rail equipment.

EXHIBIT 13.3 Estimates of Average Capital Spending for Infrastructure Sectors ($ billions)

Building construction	$750
Energy	112
Roads and bridges	80
Communications	55
Water and wastewater	45
Aviation and rail	35
Transit	13
Waste management	5

As you can see from the exhibit, building construction, which is dominated by housing, dwarfs the rest of nation's capital spending. This explains why when homebuilding sneezes, the rest of the construction industry catches a cold. The table also shows that although the fixed asset value of roads and bridges is much larger than those of energy or communications, capital spending for energy is much larger. This validates for the often-repeated mantra that the electric power industry absorbs more capital than any other industry.

SOURCES OF CAPITAL

This section summarizes sources of capital for the infrastructure sectors. Each sector has individual characteristics and accesses the capital markets in different ways. However, capital sources such as bonds, equities, and payment of fees apply to most categories.

Infrastructure Bonds

Of all capital sources, bonds are the most-recognized way to finance the investment needs of infrastructure. As a concept, bonds are nearly as old as stocks, and state loan stocks were used as far back as the fifteenth century (Brown, 2006). In 2009, total U.S. bond indebtedness was over $33 trillion, or more than $100,000 per capita. As explained later, this figure includes a number of different bond types.

The reason why municipal bonds are so popular is that they offer an effective way to raise capital when needed and a payback method that uses current revenues to service debt on the basis of pay as you use the infrastructure facilities. To understand why municipal bonds are so important, it is useful to understand the difference between pay-as-you-use and pay-as-you-go financing.

To illustrate with a familiar example, assume you purchase and use an automobile for five years. Your cost of ownership will be computed as the total cost of the capital and operating expenses. If you had saved up and purchased the car with cash from your bank account, you would have paid the capital before you used the car. If instead, you borrow the money to buy the car and pay it back over the five-year period, you are paying for the capital as you use the car. It is the same with bonds and infrastructure. If an infrastructure agency saves money from current customers to pay for future infrastructure, then past customers are paying for facilities to be used by future customers. Following this reasoning, use of bonds for infrastructure financing has held up in the legal arena and is sanctioned by federal law and policy.

Infrastructure organizations routinely turn to bonds to finance capital needs, and they usually rely on tax-exempt municipal bonds. Revenue bonds are the most common type used by infrastructure enterprises such as water and sewer agencies, but general obligation bonds also are used frequently to secure debt by the tax base rather than the revenues of an enterprise.

Bonds are offered by the infrastructure management authority to finance projects such as water treatment or road construction. Bond issues are handled by investment bankers or underwriters, who will market their services to groups attending meetings of the Government Finance Officer's Association and other infrastructure professional associations.

All types of bonds involve borrowing with a promise to repay with interest. The municipal bond category is most relevant to infrastructure managers. Data on the bond market is compiled by the Securities Industry and Financial Markets Association (SIFMA), which was formed by a merger of the Securities Industry Association and the Bond Market Association. SIFMA (2009a) represents more than 650 member firms around the world and provides explanations of the types of bonds and related securities. The next list provides a summary of the categories most prevalent in the infrastructure sector.

> **Municipal Bonds.** Debt obligations issued by states, cities, counties, and other governmental entities to provide capital to construct buildings and infrastructure and undertake other public interest projects. Tax exemptions vary. Some bonds are exempt at the federal level but not in all states. One category of municipal bonds is taxable at the federal level.

> **Zero-Coupon Municipal Bonds.** Introduced in 1982, these bonds have no periodic interest payments, but the investor receives the principal plus interest compounded semiannually at maturity. They are sold at a discount from the face amount.

> **AAA-Rated Insured Municipal Bonds.** Insured bonds seem to retain more market value than uninsured bonds in economic downturns, but insurance does not guarantee a bond price. Government regulation through state insurance departments provides oversight of municipal bond insurance.

> **GSE Debt Securities.** Government-sponsored enterprises (GSEs) are created by Congress to fund loans to categories of borrowers such as homeowners and students. The government seeks to aid these groups to borrow at affordable rates. All of the different GSEs

have public purposes; they include the Federal National Mortgage Association (Fannie Mae) and Federal Home Loan Mortgage Corporation (Freddie Mac). GSE debt is sponsored but not guaranteed by the federal government. Normally, being sponsored means the government initiated the agency but expected it to function then as a self-supported business enterprise.

Corporate Bonds. Corporate bonds are issued to raise capital by private and public corporations. Unlike stocks, they do not extend ownership in the issuing corporation.

Fixed-Rate Capital Securities. Developed in the early 1990s for income-oriented investors, fixed-rate capital securities combine features of corporate debt securities and preferred stock.

Mortgage Securities. Mortgage securities represent ownership interest in mortgage loans created when loans are packaged or pooled for sale to investors. Investors may purchase these securities when they are issued or in a secondary market. The basis for the securities is a participation certificate to represent ownership in a pool of mortgage loans. The may be pooled again to create collateral for a collateralized mortgage obligation or related types of mortgage-backed security, such as real estate mortgage investment conduits.

Several other categories of bonds or related debt instruments include U.S. Treasury securities, which are obligations of the federal government issued to finance national spending; asset-backed securities, bonds, or notes backed by financial assets such as receivables other than mortgage loans; fixed-income exchange-traded funds; callable securities; high-yield bonds issued by organizations without investment-grade ratings; and certificates of deposit.

Exhibit 13.4 shows bond indebtedness of the United States as of the end of 2008.

As with fixed assets and construction spending, the mortgage portion of the portfolio is the greatest. Corporate debt is next, followed by Treasury-backed bonds. Municipal bonds are near the end of the list, but still amount to over $2.5 trillion, with nearly $400 billion new issues in 2008. All these categories of bonds are involved to some extent in infrastructure, but municipal bonds are of most interest and will be discussed in more detail.

For the most part, municipal bonds are tax exempt and offer a subsidy from the federal government and sometimes from state governments. Because they offer tax exemption, they carry a lower interest rate than taxable bonds. The subsidy for municipal bonds was affirmed in an 1895 Supreme

EXHIBIT 13.4 U.S. Bond Debt and New Issues, $ billions

Type of Mortgage Debt	Total	2008 Issues
Mortgage related[1]	8,897.3	1,339.7
Corporate debt	6,280.6	706.2
Treasury backed[2]	5,912.2	1,037.3
Money markets[3]	3,791.1	Not available
Federal agency securities	3,247.4	1,114.9
Municipal bonds	2,690.1	391.3
Asset backed[4]	2,671.8	137.2
Total	33,490.5	4,726.6

Source: 2009b data, from SIFMA, 2009
[1]Includes all mortgage-backed securities such as those backed by Fannie Mae and other collateralized mortgage obligations.
[2]Interest bearing marketable public debt.
[3]Includes commercial paper, bankers acceptances, and large time deposits.
[4]Includes auto, credit card, HEL, manufacturing, student loan, and other. (CDOs are included.)

Court case and codified in the Revenue Act of 1913 (Summers and Noland, 2008; U.S. Internal Revenue Service, 2009).

Tax exempt bonds may be issued as government bonds or private activity bonds. Examples of government bonds are for highways, government office buildings, and water and sewer facilities built by state and local governments. Private activity bonds might be for an industrial development project sanctioned by a government but carried out by a private entity, and they may be taxable.

Municipal bonds are mainly issued as general obligation or revenue bonds. General obligation (GO) bonds are backed by the taxing authority of the government organization and are used for projects with community-wide benefits, such as public buildings, public schools, streets and bridges and economic development programs. As an example of GO bond offerings, the City of Austin, Texas (2009), has an Affordable Housing Corporation that issues bonds for projects proposed by developers. This enables the city to use its access to capital to promote the socially desirable goal of affordable housing.

In 2006, Austin voters approved $55 million in GO bonds for affordable housing; the city was to receive funds from the bond sale proceeds over seven years. Then the Austin City Council approved the allocation of bond funds through its own decisions, through a time-sensitive fast-track and competitive process. Revenue bonds are issued by a range of government authorities and are repaid from revenues of an enterprise rather than by the full faith and credit of the local government that issues them. These bonds are used for such purposes as toll roads, water and wastewater, electric power, solid waste, parking garages, airports, housing, hospitals, street lighting, stadiums, and many other community projects. Projects funded by revenue bonds are supposed to serve only those who pay for the services, but GO bonds finance general projects with community-wide benefits. Therefore, GO bonds are aligned with public purposes, whereas revenue bonds are aligned with enterprises.

Typical bond increments are $5,000 units, and maturity periods may be 20 to 30 years, in many cases. Bonds with staggered maturity dates are called serial bonds. Income from municipal enterprises pays for operational expenses first, then revenue bond debt service. Revenue bonds are not backed by taxing power, as general obligation bonds are, and thus are somewhat riskier and have higher interest rates.

As an example of a revenue bond issue, Atlanta, Georgia, issued about $1.5 billion in airport general revenue bonds for its Hartsfield-Jackson International Airport. The airport has net revenues to secure the bonds, and the Fitch bond rating company affirmed the A+ rating. The airport is consistently one of the world's busiest in terms of enplanements, and the Atlanta area has a strong economy. The rating takes into account the performance of the airport plus factors relating to continued growth, such as the outlook for Delta Airlines, which is headquartered in Atlanta (Reuters, 2009a). As an example of an industrial revenue bond, Wisconsin has a program with more than $200 million available to offer low-interest loans to small manufacturers with expansion projects. The Wisconsin Department of Commerce (2009) grants bonding authority to municipalities, which issue the bonds for the businesses. This is a way to use tax exemption in selected cases to promote jobs and economic development.

Risk Measurement   Utilities and infrastructure organizations are generally safe investments, but risk of default is present. The risk was evident during the financial crisis, when state and local governments began to see all sources of tax revenues decline. Sales taxes declined sharply toward the end of 2008, and a group of 41 states that reported tax revenue saw a 12.8 percent decline in total tax receipts in the first two months of 2009, compared to a year earlier. State governments depend on personal and corporate income taxes, sales taxes, and property taxes, and all were in decline (Dougherty, 2009).

In the 1970s, New York City had a default caused by financing its ongoing operations with bond revenues. In 1983, a default occurred on $2.5 billion in bonds of the Washington Public Power Supply System, which were used to finance nuclear power. In the 1990s, Orange County, California, faced a crisis brought on by a tax limitation initiative in the state (Public Bonds, 2009). In 2006, the Eurotunnel authority restructured its debt to avoid bankruptcy (Eurotunnel, 2006; Sakoui, 2006). Sewer bonds of Jefferson County, Alabama, were given "junk" status in 2008, and the county was facing bankruptcy in 2009 (*Birmingham News*, 2009).

Rating agencies, such as Standard and Poor's Corporation, Moody's Investor's Service, Inc., and Fitch, assess municipal bond risk. However, unlike listed stocks, the municipal bond market is not well publicized, and no regulator has oversight over all of the industry. The Municipal Securities Rule-making Board regulates part of the market and the bankers and others who sell the bonds, but it does not regulate the bond issuers. Disclosure requirements of corporate bonds do not apply to municipal issuers; the Government Accounting Standards Board issues guidelines but lacks enforcement power. The pay-to-play aspect of the bond market means that lawyers, advisors, and asset managers can win business by donating to bond campaigns, contributing to charity, or paying for entertainment (Levitt, 2009).

Given the significant risk attached to municipal bonds, underwriters have looked for ways to transfer part of that risk back to issuers. In 2009, a new form of municipal bond sought to do that by transferring risk back to the selling authority by allowing lenders to pull money out at any time. There is a weekly auction with rates based on a short-term municipal debt index; if lenders want to pull out, borrowers have 7 to 12 months to refinance or raise cash to repay. Money market funds also pick up risk as the bond seller might be unable to cover the bonds quickly. This approach changes the past bond insurance arrangement, in which the seller paid a higher rate and the banks provided a safety net in case the bond issuer lacked funds to pay the interest on the bonds. The seller backs this form of municipal bond and gets a lower rate, but risk has also been transferred to the money markets. As an example, Morgan Stanley issued $133 million in 2009 for the Regional Transportation Authority of Illinois (Copeland and Rappaport, 2009).

Cities had a harder time issuing debt as the financial crisis took hold. Reports from state bond authorities, such as the New York Transitional Finance Authority, the Maine Municipal Bond Bank, and the Montana Facility Finance Authority, signaled that cities were cutting back on projects and that it will be more difficult to raise capital. Some of the structured-finance bond products that lowered costs but added risks were discarded, and there was a return to older forms of more-structured bond markets (Walsh, 2008). Municipal Market Advisors (2009) is an advisory service that tracks these trends.

Municipal bonds vary a good bit, and no comprehensive database characterizes them statistically. Therefore, to demonstrate at least part of their range, examples for several infrastructure categories are given next.

Roads State transportation departments issue bonds for various purposes. Their revenue streams typically include income taxes, fees, federal grants, and other sources. Innovative financing schemes, such as the Transportation Infrastructure Finance and Innovation Act, are designed to help them with their revenue streams and keep construction going (see Chapter 4). An example of state transportation borrowing is the 2009 issue by the Delaware Department of Transportation, which sold $105.3 million of Delaware Transportation Authority bonds as Transportation System Senior Revenue Bonds, 2009 Series A. These were underwritten by J.P. Morgan Securities, Inc. and the true interest cost, a technical term that embodies all bond servicing costs, was 3.96 percent. The bonds were rated as AA+ by Standard & Poor's and Aa3 by Moody's Investors Services. Both agencies reported a "stable" outlook for the bonds. The bond sale allows the department to keep projects moving even though revenues from traditional sources such as tolls and motor vehicle fees have dropped (*Delaware Business Ledger*, 2009).

Transit The Dallas Area Rapid Transit Authority issued a $1 billion revenue bond sale on June 16, 2009. The bonds will finance extensions to the light rail system in Dallas, including a line to the Dallas–Fort Worth International Airport. The bonds included a $750 million Build America Bond component (see explanation later in this section). In addition to system revenues, the bonds will be backed by a dedicated 1 percent sales tax to be collected across a broad area of Dallas. This will help make the bonds more attractive and overcome the problem of inadequate farebox revenues typical of transit agencies. The bonds were handled by a group led by Siebert Brandford Shank & Company and several comanagers. The bond issue was fast-tracked to enable stimulus projects to proceed, and the package was assembled to make it attractive to institutional investors and for secondary market buyers (Williamson, 2009).

Airports The John Wayne Airport (2009) in Orange County, California, is issuing Series 2009 revenue bonds and received a Standard & Poor's rating of AA- with a stable outlook. The county-owned airport will issue up to $250 million in revenue bonds to support the Airport Improvement Program. The bonds will come in a Series A for governmental purposes and a Series B for private activity. The County General Fund will not be pledged, and the debt will be repaid by airport net revenues and facility charge revenues.

Water Supply and Wastewater Normally, water supply and wastewater bonds are issued by local governments and pay for construction of treatment plants, pipelines, and other infrastructure. In the case of California, however, everything seems to be at a larger scale. Governor Arnold Schwarzenegger and Senator Dianne Feinstein teamed up in 2008 to develop a $9.3 billion bond proposal with a number of water projects: to increase water storage, to improve water conveyance, to restore the delta ecosystem, and to increase use of conservation and water efficiency. The proposal for these bonds could go before voters in 2010, depending on resolution of other state funding issues.

Solid Wastes   As we have shown earlier, solid waste management is the smallest infrastructure service in terms of capital needs, but it still can require large capital infusions. For example, in 2008, Palm Beach County, Florida, county commissioners acting as the Solid Waste Authority (SWA) approved a $315 million bond issue. The funds were to pay for projects that include $200 million for improvements to the North County Resource Recovery Facility (Sorentrue, 2008). The SWA has an integrated system with recycling, composting, waste to energy, landfill, and hazardous waste collection as well as five transfer stations. The facilities were financed mostly by $420 million in revenue bonds in 1984 and 1986 and subsequent issues.

Bonds are not always held to maturity and may be bought and sold on the secondary bond market. A feature of bond trading is that if interest rates go up, prices of bonds tend to come down because when bonds are sold initially, they have a fixed interest rate. Thus, if you pay the par value and keep the bond to maturity, you will receive the designated rate of interest through the life of the bond. However, the interest rate at par reflects the cost of money at the time the bond is issued. If the interest rate goes down, the bond is more valuable because it earns more interest. If the interest rate goes up, the bond is worth less because it earns less than the prevailing rate of interest.

Owners of municipal securities can sell their bonds in the secondary market through a bank or dealer registered to trade municipal securities, which are traded in the over-the-counter market. To buy municipal bonds on the secondary market, you can look up prices in financial news sources for widely traded securities. You also can get price quotes from municipal securities brokers. Dealers trade securities at a net cost, which includes their profit on the transaction (FMS Bonds, Inc., 2009).

The financial crisis beginning in 2007 and its accompanying stimulus packages have opened the way for new approaches to bond lending. Build America Bonds are authorized by the federal stimulus plan and carry either a 35 percent rebate on interest costs to the bond issuers or a tax credit to investors. Therefore, they might involve a higher tax cost than a tax-exempt bond, but the 35 percent credit turns it into a lower borrowing rate. The New Jersey Turnpike Authority issued $1.38 billion in 3A (Moody's) bonds, and several other agencies were lining up to issue them as well. The New

Jersey bonds provided an annual return well above the baseline treasury rate (Rosenberg, 2009).

Stock Market

Private sector infrastructure companies have the same choices for raising capital as other public companies have. They can offer ownership through stock offerings or debt obligations for bond issues. Public companies are spread across the infrastructure sectors and include electric power and natural gas, telecommunications, some categories of transportation, private water companies, and waste management.

Large public utility companies are more apt to offer debt than to issue new stock. However, many smaller companies on the supplier side of the infrastructure business find stock issues attractive as a way to raise capital and as an exit strategy for company founders. Thus, the stock market is more active as a way for suppliers and fast-moving sectors, such as energy and telecommunications, to raise capital than it is for older, more established utilities.

An example of an initial public offering (IPO) by an infrastructure-related company is when American Water was spun off in 2008 from the German utility RWE, which sought to raise about $1.6 billion by selling 64 million shares at the $24 to $26 range. The purpose was to exchange stock for cash that would return to RWE, which would still own the major share of the now-listed company. When the IPO occurred, it raised a less-than-expected $1.25 billion, computed as some 58 million shares at $21.50 per share). As of mid-2009, its parent, RWE Aqua Holdings GMBH, still owned over 96 million shares, or some 60 percent of the 160 million shares outstanding (Reuters, 2009b).

One of the world's largest recent infrastructure IPOs was in 2008 by China Railway Construction Corp., which is a state-owned railroad builder that will be listed on the Hong Kong and Shanghai exchanges (Gopalan, 2008). The company was established in 1948 and was the railway building and maintenance division of the People's Liberation Army. It is now under the state-owned Assets Supervision and Administration Commission and has built many railways, highways, airports, and water and power plant projects. China seems on the verge of the world's largest 2009 IPO at $5.93 billion for the China State Construction Engineering Corporation, a giant Chinese homebuilding firm (Hong and Poon, 2009).

Another example of a U.S. infrastructure-related IPO is Government Properties Income Trust, which owns properties leased to federal and state government tenants. This real estate investment trust proposed to raise $210 million in 2009 through sale of 10 million shares (Gelsi, 2008).

IPOs among large infrastructure-related companies are rare; they are more common among subsidiaries and suppliers. For example, a U.S. natural gas partnership, Williams Pipeline Partners, raised $325 million in 2009 for a 54.6 percent limited partnership interest in Williams Companies, Inc., a natural gas transportation and storage business.

An example of a secondary stock offering in the electric power industry occurred when American Electric Power issued 60 million shares in early 2009 to raise $1.5 billion for the purpose of repaying existing indebtedness (Trading Markets.com, 2009).

Another 2009 secondary offering was by IESI-BFC Ltd. for 13 million shares to raise $141 million, which was accompanied by the company's intent to become listed on the New York Stock Exchange. IESI-BFC is a Canadian waste management company, with operations also in the United States (Reuters, 2009c).

Private Equity

Private equity, or ownership through securities not listed on a public exchange, also can be used to capitalize infrastructure enterprises (Maxwell, 2007). Examples of this approach might include the entrepreneur who uses venture capital to start a small private water company or to purchase a waste management company. Venture capitalists could buy toll roads or other large-scale facilities, but so far most concessions are for operating them rather than turning over ownership (see Chapter 4).

Bank Loans and Mortgage Lending

Lending as a source of infrastructure capital comes in three basic forms: the mortgage market, which funds much of residential and commercial construction, commercial lending, and development banking.

Mortgage lending, the backbone of finance for residential construction and much of commercial construction, was explained in Chapter 3. The *U.S. Statistical Abstract* showed for 2007 that a total of $14.6 trillion in mortgage debt was outstanding, of which $11.1 trillion was for homes and $2.5 trillion for commercial properties. The data are from the Board of Governors of the Federal Reserve Bank System (2009a).

Although much of the financial crisis was caused by securitizing high-risk home mortgages, commercial mortgages add to the total risk level. For example, in 2009, a number of pension funds with investments in commercial real estate found themselves exposed. An example is a fund for police and firefighters in Springfield, Missouri, that invested in a pooled real estate fund management by Prudential Real Estate Investors, a unit of the insurance giant Prudential. The fund backed a Manhattan office building that fell short of occupancy and rental goals, thus lowering the value of the fund by a large margin (Troianovski, 2009).

For-profit or government infrastructure providers have the same access to commercial bank loans as other businesses do. On the basis of their credit ratings, they can receive short- or long-term loans for activities such as construction, ongoing operations, or other needs. Some commercial lending for infrastructure providers occurs, but it is not a main source of their capital. Private supplier companies, including those that seek concessions to own or operate infrastructure facilities, are more likely to apply for commercial loans.

Development bank lending for infrastructure is a main source of capital in some sectors and regions. Development banks comprise a range of lending institutions with loan conditions that vary from near-commercial terms to those that practically amount to grants with very permissive repayment requirements.

At one end of the spectrum of development bank activities are the lending agencies at the level of state government. The Drinking Water State Revolving Fund, established under the 1996 Amendments to the Safe Drinking Water Act and subsidized by federal appropriations, is an example. It lends money for restricted purposes of promoting safe drinking water. Another example is the State Infrastructure Bank Pilot Program established under the National Highway System Designation Act of 1995, which appropriated funds and authorized states to use federal aid funds to capitalize pilot banks. The design of the bank programs varies among the states, from ambitious, as in California, to modest programs in smaller states.

The California Infrastructure and Economic Development Bank is a general-purpose financing authority providing funding from \$250,000 to \$10 million for project categories that include roads and streets, drainage, water supply and flood control, schools, environmental improvements, parks and recreation, ports, transit, wastewater, solid waste, defense conversion, public safety facilities, and power and communications (California Infrastructure and Economic Development Bank, 2009).

At the national or international levels, many larger development banks provide funds for infrastructure financing. Examples include the World Bank, the InterAmerican Development Bank, the Asian Development Bank, and the African Development Bank. Infrastructure is a principal concern of these banks because it is so closely aligned with poverty-reduction programs. World Bank (2009c) lending in 2007 was, for example, 20 percent in transportation and another 12 percent in water and sanitation; other lending occurred in related areas, such as public administration and finance.

The World Bank (2009b) announced in 2009 its intention to invest $45 billion as part of the global recovery fund. The World Bank president, Robert Zoellick, said: "Investments in infrastructure can provide the platform for job creation, sustainable economic growth and overcoming poverty, and help jump start a recovery from the crisis. . . . The Latin American and Asian crisis showed how countries can suffer from a decline in infrastructure, leaving a weaker foundation for long-term economic growth that hits the poorest the hardest."

In addition to these funds, which amount to $15 billion more than the previous three years' investment, the World Bank's private sector arm, International Finance Corporation, will contribute up to $300 million in equity for private projects or public-private partnerships.

Government Grants

Government grants for infrastructure are sometimes called "intergovern-mental revenue," meaning that one level or agency of government passes money through to another one. Examples of these range from programmatic grants, such as the cost-shared grants used to build wastewater treatment plants in the 1970s and 1980s, to various earmarks and grants from other special legislation. As an example, the City of Fort Collins, Colorado, is pursuing a grant to build a mass transit corridor and received part of its funding through the Federal Transit Administration.

Current Revenues, Development Fees, and Taxes

When current revenues are used for capital, they are called "pay as you go." They are basically a savings account or sinking fund set up to finance capital needs when they occur in the future. The reason why "pay as you use" using bonds often is preferred is that the actual users pay for the capital costs rather than today's users paying for tomorrow's needs.

Impact fees were introduced in Chapter 3 as a method to promote the philosophy of growth paying its own way. In the publicly owned in-frastructure setting, they are straightforward ways to assign costs to the actual users of the infrastructure through up-front charges. The case of an investor-owned utility illustrates a different approach, however; here in-vestors and ratepayers pay the cost of infrastructure expansion and renewal. Since rate increases for them are authorized by public utility commissions on the basis of invested capital, it makes more sense for the utilities to use investment capital rather than customer charges (or contributed capital) to pay for connection costs.

At the local level, sales and property taxes are widely used to finance infrastructure. Income tax revenues are used by state governments, which often use these revenues to finance parts of their road systems and/or replenish local development and infrastructure banks.

Government also can be creative by using tax relief powers, such as tax-increment financing (TIF) to help with capital costs. For example, in 2009, the Colorado Legislature is considering a bill to grant future sales tax revenues up to $50 million per year to developers of a facility to serve as a racetrack and the venue for the National Western Stock Show. The tax rebates would be used to retire bonds, and other recreational facilities might qualify, such as for the Winter Olympics, for example (Fender and Illescas, 2009).

TIF financing has been used in the United States for over 50 years. It is now attracting attention in the United Kingdom as a possible financing strategy to jump-start older areas that seek redevelopment. A development in Edinburgh by Forth Ports, a docks company, seemed to be going nowhere. The city guesses that $800 million is needed for infrastructure. In the past, that sum might have been extracted from developer contributions or a U.K. version of the U.S. impact fee. With the economy down, that source is out of reach, so Edinburgh may test out the TIF approach with a square-kilometer project with $80 million in infrastructure investments. This is large enough for some 2,200 houses and associated commercial developments, and the financial planner estimates that in 30 years it will pull in over $400 million in property taxes. This approach has caught the attention of the Chancellor of the Exchequer, who thinks it might work on a national basis, with rebates to localities. Examples of potential projects include a science city in Newcastle and rail schemes in the West Midlands. TIFs are controversial. Some people consider them successful, but others think they are just a way to increase public debt (*Economist*, 2009b).

INVESTMENT BANKING

Investment banks are key players in infrastructure finance. They manage the issuance of stocks and bonds and trade in securities. Some investment banks are oriented toward a specialty activity, such as bond trading. As explained in Chapter 9, investment banks can be large firms, such as Bank of America, Goldman Sachs, and J.P. Morgan, or smaller firms that specialize in niches or local issues. Some of the larger firms have changed dramatically recently. Merrill Lynch was acquired by Bank of America, and Smith Barney, which was the center of Citigroup's wealth management business, agreed to a joint venture that gave Morgan Stanley a 51 percent stake in it in exchange for $2.75 billion. Morgan Stanley has the right to buy the rest of the firm over the next five years. The venture is expected to bring in revenue of $14 billion by managing some $1.7 trillion in client assets (Bruno, 2009).

SUMMARY

The infrastructure sector attracts a large share of the nation's investment capital, especially when building construction is included in its definition. Most funds flow through the mortgage markets and their secondary forms in the bond markets. The energy, transportation, and telecom sectors are the largest and require most of the capital, although from different sources and in different forms. Water and wastewater require less capital but they still occupy important positions in the bond markets. Waste management, with its heavy concentration of smaller firms and agencies, is the smallest of the sectors.

Building Construction Dominates the Infrastructure Capital Markets

As it does other economic metrics, building construction dominates the infrastructure-related capital markets, with most funds flowing through the mortgage markets. Energy, especially electric power, also has large capital needs. Most electricity providers are private sector companies that utilize corporate bonds and commercial lending as well as cash flows for their capital needs. Telecommunications is similar to energy, except that it is essentially a 100 percent private sector operation.

Transportation Draws Capital from Government and the Private Sector

In the transportation sector, roads and bridges are financed mostly from government sources, principally the gas tax, which is sensitive to gasoline use. Aviation and rail are mainly in the private sector and thus turn to corporate funding sources more than public sources. The exception is airports, which are mostly owned by local governments and funded through a mixture of fees, taxes, and intergovernmental revenues. Transit and passenger rail are the cases in transportation where government subsidies are needed to augment user charges.

Water and Wastewater Capital Draws Mostly from the Bond Market

Water and wastewater are funded heavily by government entities, so the tax-exempt market is used to a great extent. Waste management is a closely related environmental service, but it involves many private companies, most of which are unlisted and left to raise their own capital through corporate channels.

Capital-Intensive Infrastructure Requires Large Flows of Capital

Infrastructure systems require large amounts of capital for structures and equipment. Electric power uses the most capital, mainly from private sources, and highways are close behind, using mainly government funding.

Public Infrastructure Capital Planning Is through Planning and Budget Processes

The planning and budget processes for most public infrastructure are dominated by local government politics. Therefore, the value-based choices of local elected leaders are important in identifying infrastructure patterns such as roads, land developments, and other capital improvements.

The Debate over a National Capital Budget Is Over

In the past, there were calls for a national capital budget, but today there are no serious thoughts about dividing the federal budget process into two parts like local budgets. The federal budget process is too complex and has too many macroeconomic implications for such an approach.

The Bond Market Remains the Most Important Infrastructure Capital Source

Bonds are effective to raise capital and offer a logical payback method based on pay-as-you-use financing. The deep recession of 2008 and 2009 showed that revenue bonds are not risk free and are vulnerable to the financial problems of local governments.

Government Grants for Infrastructure Address Public Purposes

Although some categories of infrastructure can be financed as enterprises through user fees, it will always be necessary to finance facilities that serve public purposes through government grants and fund allocations from tax revenues.

Private Equity Is Becoming More Involved in Infrastructure Finance

Investment banks and private equity sources are finding infrastructure investments increasingly attractive. As infrastructure systems become more diverse and complex, the opportunities—and risks—for private equity increase. Not only does private equity invest, it sometimes takes on operating roles as well.

CHAPTER 14

Revenues for the Infrastructure Sectors

The financial model in Chapter 12 showed how user fees flow to infrastructure organizations under the pure enterprise concept of self-support through fees for services. In the case in which services have public purposes and are difficult to charge for on a full-cost basis, the model shows that tax revenues may be used in the form of subsidies. This method moves away from an economic demand management model to a political choice model of payment. Examples are some forms of transit, environmental conservation, and providing lifeline services to low-income people. In addition to customer-generated revenues and tax subsidies, the financing plans for infrastructure organizations can include mixtures of other fees, tax revenues, intergovernmental transfers, and internal subsidies. In addition, capital sources are tapped for investment funds, on the basis of both debt and ownership, as explained in Chapter 13.

This chapter explains how these revenue streams can be used for operations and to retire debt from capital investments. The chapter enables us to assess the reliability of the revenue streams and to judge the institutional stability of infrastructure management organizations. For example, if an organization relies entirely on user charges that are sensitive to economic shocks, it will have less capacity to service debt than an organization with multiple streams of more reliable revenues.

FLOW OF REVENUES

Exhibit 14.1 shows the flows of revenues to support an infrastructure system, which provides the capital base for delivery of public services. It can be used to follow the discussion in the chapter. The exhibit shows the capital base of an infrastructure system that supports the operations and the services

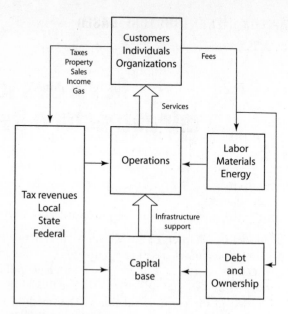

EXHIBIT 14.1 Infrastructure Revenue Model

they deliver to customers. Customers pay fees, which are distributed back to the organization to pay for both operational and capital expenses. An example of the system shown might be a bus transit system, where the right side of the exhibit shows the flow of bus fares that pay drivers' and mechanics' salaries, fuel, and related costs. The debt would pay for bus equipment, maintenance facilities, and other capital structures and equipment.

On the left side of the exhibit, the same customers pay a range of taxes, which are filtered through the financial system to convert income, property, sales, and other taxes into government revenues. In the case of the transit example, sales and property taxes might flow directly to a transit district, whereas any federal grants would originate from income tax and gas tax revenues.

Taxes to subsidize infrastructure systems in this way range from gas tax payments, which are an indirect form of fees for service when used to build roads, to redistribution of individual and corporate income taxes. In the top box on the exhibit, an individual customer would be a home or small business, for example. An organizational customer can be an industry with a water tap to supply its network, a military base, or even partner units inside a government unit. For example, in a large city, the parks department can be a customer of the water department.

RATE-SETTING FOR INFRASTRUCTURE-BASED SERVICES

Rate-setting is used to set fees for utility-type services delivered through enterprises in which the cost of service can be quantified. An enterprise is defined as a self-supporting service organization. In the case of public entities, special funds are designated as enterprise funds to separate revenues and costs for the activities involved. Electric power, natural gas distribution, and water supply are examples of services in which enterprise financing is prevalent. Rate principles also can be applied to other services, such as wastewater, storm drainage, and even road maintenance, by identifying the service supplied and charging accordingly.

If the systems serve distributed public purposes, they may merit full or partial subsidies to spread charges across taxpayers. A service may be individual, such as basic water service, but also may be required for public purposes, such as street cleaning and water supply for low-income housing. Sewerage serves individuals and provides benefits to communities. Although these functions can be subsidized, they also can be charged out by identifying the correct internal customers. For example, residential telephone service benefits individuals but also knits communities together in functions such as emergency response. Therefore, if a phone company is forced to provide service for emergency use, it seems proper that it might charge the community a fee for that service, and the community might pay for this general benefit from tax revenues. Another example is a water department requiring reserve capacity for firefighting. The benefits would be general, and it seems appropriate that the community would pay for this from general revenues rather than charging on the basis of daily water use.

The legality and feasibility of various charges and tax subsidies are matters of state law and local politics. State law is administered through public utility commissions for privately owned systems and through local boards for publicly owned systems. Sometimes the legality of a charge is in question, and the matters are resolved through the courts. For example, after a tax-limit law is passed in a state, such as California's 1970s Proposition 13, a local government might decide to bypass the tax limitation by charging a fee for a service, such as street maintenance. A key legal question might be whether the benefits of the service can be associated closely enough with individuals and properties to justify a fee rather than to pay for the service by community-wide tax revenues. Using this theory, fees for storm drainage have been applied successfully in many communities, while in others the service is financed through taxes.

Public versus Private Services

These questions about services, benefits, and appropriate charges have led to theories for rate-setting that consider:

- The types of public goods or services and why they are needed
- Whether they are optional or essential
- The extent to which they benefit the general public or only individuals
- Whether their use can be measured and rationed
- Whether the provider is a natural monopoly

The theory for whether an infrastructure service can be delivered as an enterprise is still evolving and deals squarely with the issues raised in Chapter 1 about the difference between a public and a private good. A classification of public and private services has emerged, and three categories represent the range of choices (Mushkin, 1972):

1. Public utility–type goods that offer essential public services and can be measured and priced. Examples include water supply, electric power, gas supply, and transit use.
2. Private goods that have important public purposes but can be offered by private firms. Examples include wastewater, solid waste collection, and toll roads and bridges.
3. Services in which public purposes dominate and one use of the service does not diminish its availability to others. Examples include water quality management, air pollution control, and highway use.

Although attitudes about public and private purposes can change and alter the classification of infrastructure across the categories of public and private goods, the next list presents current thinking.

- Residential housing, commercial buildings, manufacturing facilities, and other facilities are mostly private goods. Exceptions are found in public buildings that serve everyone and in subsidized public housing.
- Electric power and natural gas are commodities that are almost purely in the category of private goods. Minimum quantities to sustain life and safety usually are considered public goods.
- Water systems range across the public and private categories. Some services, such as domestic water supply, can be commodities in the same sense as electric power. Other services, such as environmental water quality, are public goods. Even domestic water supply has a social and public good attribute.

- Transportation systems range across private and public purposes. Highways, airports, and transit have mixed benefits. They have attributes of private goods, but the social purposes of transit and the emergency aspects of highways and rail are public goods. Air travel is mostly a private good. Freight shipping has become an important part of a new logistics-based economy and is mostly a private good.
- Communication systems serving the public are almost all private goods. A few services, such as weather and emergency radio, benefit the public at large.
- Solid waste collection and disposal are mixed public and private goods because, while people can recycle and reduce waste, not everyone can do it. Public good services, such as hazardous materials management, may require subsidies to get people to use them.

The arguments about public and private charges can be summarized this way (Vaughn, 1983):

Social benefits. Services bring social benefits that cannot be measured and charged for.

Income distribution. Tax payments for services redistribute income to those who cannot afford vital services.

Economic development. Public facilities and services attract economic development, and tax revenues to help finance services.

Earmarking. Dedicating tax revenues to services (a form of user charges) reduces budget flexibility and reallocation during times of changing priorities.

Coordination. Managing individual services with dedicated user charges inhibits coordination of public services.

Common Principles for Rates

Although rate-setting takes on different features unique to the infrastructure systems, a common set of principles for rates applies across most sectors (Vaughn, 1983).

User pays. Fees should be levied on the beneficiaries of the services.

Efficiency and equity. Fees should provide both economic efficiency and equity. (*Efficiency* means no waste, the public gets what it pays for, and rations use of service; *equity* ensures justice and fairness in access and cost of service.)

Marginal cost pricing. Prices or fees should be set at the marginal or incremental cost of providing the service, not the average cost. (This is an efficiency principle and must be balanced with equity considerations.)

Peak load pricing. Peak load pricing should be used to manage demand.

Access. Access to services should be provided for low-income residents where burdens will result from marginal cost pricing.

Responsiveness. User fees should be responsive to inflation and to economic growth.

If fees are set to recover the "cost of service," the rate study determines the needed facilities and operations, how much they cost, and how to allocate the costs across customer classes using an equitable scheme. If the utility is regulated by a public utility commission, then the decisions are reviewed and approved by third parties. In many cases, the regulation is by a political oversight body, such as the elected board of a city government or special district.

While rate-setting principles seem rational, some groups oppose rates to charge for public services. This opposition shows that infrastructure finance is not a purely economic topic but also has a large component of political choice that focuses on equity. The question of equity is dependent on the point of view. If your political philosophy is fiscally conservative, you may see the need to charge for all public services. If you are a social liberal, you may believe that public services should be free (and thus charged for by taxes) so that everyone has access. These arguments focus on the obligation of government to provide services more uniformly and not only on the basis of a charge.

Once on a trip to Finland, I arrived at the airport in the City of Tampere and was surprised to learn that the carts to move luggage were free, but you had to pay to use the airport toilets. In my airport, you pay for the carts but the toilets are free. Differences like this can be hard to explain, but they illustrate the range of choice.

Comparison of Rates across the United States

Rates for use of infrastructure and public services vary across the nation. Generally, but not always, they will vary with cost of housing. For example, for electric power, as of the end of 2008, Wyoming had the lowest rate at $.057 per kilowatt-hour, and Hawaii had the highest rate, at $.258. The national average was $.097. New England has the highest regional rates, at $.161, and rates are lowest in the central parts of the nation. Data are published in the Electric Power Monthly report by the U.S. Energy Information Administration (Nebraska Energy Office, 2009).

Natural gas prices also vary, with Hawaii having the highest residential cost at $.448 per 1,000 cubic feet in 2008. Alaska was lowest, at $.0872, and Utah next, at $.090 (U.S. Energy Information Administration, 2009b).

Water, wastewater, and solid waste charges are not tabulated by any central information source, and they tend to vary among localities as well as between regions. One city might have water charges at $3 per 1,000 gallons and another at $7, depending on capital costs that need to be amortized and/or a city's decision to promote conservation through its rate structure.

Impact fees, which were discussed in Chapter 3, also vary with location. Some areas do not use them at all, but in other regions, such as California, they can add $20,000 and more to the cost of each residential dwelling.

RATE REGULATION

The regulation of charges for infrastructure services varies sharply among the categories, reflecting the differences between the services. Regulation emerged in the late nineteenth century as a tool to prevent abuse of monopoly power and to replace attempts to coordinate and pool services to achieve fairness for all.

Use of structures in the built environment is generally not subject to rate regulation, with the rare exception of rent control. Rent control is a complex subject that is mostly beyond the scope of this discussion, but it has some aspects that relate to infrastructure services. Mainly, rent control has implications for the dynamism of urban areas and rates and types of renewal, which can influence demand for infrastructure services such as transit, energy, and waste management. When imposed, rent control might have an objective such as to prevent profiteering on rental housing during a shortage, but it can quickly lead to additional shortages, given its dampening effect on incentives of owners to invest in improvements. Rent control might be imposed on lots in a mobile home park to prevent arbitrary increases that force tenants to move or sell their mobile homes.

Charges for use of highways and streets occur only in the case of toll roads, which are mostly in the public sector and not normally regulated for rates. Toll road regulation becomes an issue when public roads are privatized or public-private partnerships are organized to improve mobility. In the United States, only a few toll road concessions are in operation, but more are likely to be approved in the future. An example of a privately owned toll road is the Dulles Greenway, which is part of the access road system to Dulles Airport, which serves the Washington, DC, area. Dulles Airport was completed in 1962. Its original access road was built as part of the project and is now the Dulles Toll Road, operated by the Virginia Department of Transportation. The Dulles Greenway is a privately owned 14-mile toll road that connects to the Dulles Toll Road. It is the first private toll road in Virginia since 1816. The greenway was dedicated in 1995 as a private venture now regulated by the Virginia State Corporation Commission. It is not considered a monopoly (and therefore not a utility) because untolled routes are available (Dulles Greenway, 2009; *Toll Road News*, 2007). As more toll roads are built, the method to regulate rates will receive more attention. Two basic approaches are available: the rate of return on invested capital and a contract-based concession approach (Poole, 2008).

State public utility commissions regulate some forms of privately owned mass transit, electric power and natural gas distribution, and water systems. Facilities with interstate services, such as rail transportation, aviation, and communications, are regulated also by the federal government. Otherwise, most infrastructure regulation is political and exercised by local (and sometimes state) boards and commissions.

Regulation is important; if an investment is attractive because it is supposed to be in a stable and regulated industry, then potential investors should know all aspects of the regulatory process. The principle behind this presumed stability is that the investors are entitled to a reasonable rate of return on their investments in assets to deliver monopoly public services.

According to Rodgers (1979), the concept of regulation is attributed to early church thinking about a "just price" as opposed to "natural price" between willing buyers and sellers. The just price would avoid exploitation when sellers had an advantage, such as during a food shortage. Regulation goes back Roman edicts and to control of monopoly guilds during the Middle Ages. English common law recognized that certain occupations, such as ferrymen, had a duty to serve the public, and this doctrine was transplanted to America for common carriers over land and water. Common carriers are businesses that offer transportation to the public and require a license, and principles of their regulation extend to other public services.

An important Supreme Court ruling of 1824 in *Gibbons v. Ogden* broadened application of the Commerce Clause of the Constitution and opened the way to regulate more than just trade between states. The need to regulate railroad charges through public commissions emerged soon afterward, and these led much later to government regulation of other public services through state public utility commissions.

The 1870s Granger movement, in which farmers rose in protest against exploitation, led to rate regulation of railroads and grain elevators in several states during the severe depression. In 1877, the Supreme Court held in *Munn v. Illinois* that when private property is affected with a public interest (meaning that, in addition to supplying consumer goods it furnishes an essential product or service), the owner must submit to controls. This case laid the foundation for modern regulation. The 1887 Act to Regulate Commerce led to the establishment of the Interstate Commerce Commission, which hosted the first convention in 1889 of what was to become the National Association of Regulatory Utility Commissioners. It began as the National Association of Railroad Commissioners in 1901, and by 1907, several states had established regulatory authority over electric, gas, telephone, telegraph, and water companies.

The earliest forms of regulation focused on railroad competition due to the rapid development of competing railroads and the need to prevent chaos in the industry and to protect customers. Early railroad owners worked with bankers and each other to find solutions, leading to today's models for regulation.

Nowadays, rate of return regulation is mostly controlled by state public utility commissions (PUCs), which have diverse histories. For example, Colorado's PUC dates back to the 1885 office of Railroad Commissioner. This office was abolished and reestablished in 1907 as a rate-regulating body with the power to fine violators. Another PUC was created in 1913 to regulate street lighting and telephone service. It absorbed the Railroad Commission functions and expanded its definition of common carriers to add trucks and automobiles. Its scope has fluctuated over the years. Air travel was regulated in 1969 and deregulated by federal law in 1978. Fixed utility regulation (electric, gas, water, and telecommunications) has also varied. Rural electric cooperatives sought regulation in 1961 and then rejected it in 1983. State legislation also ended PUC jurisdiction over municipal utility services outside of city limits. After the 1980s telephone breakup, the Colorado PUC started to regulate new long-distance service in the state. Today, it has some jurisdiction over hundreds of fixed utilities and more than 10,000 motor carriers (Colorado Department of Regulatory Agencies, 2009).

The National Association of Regulatory Utility Commissioners (2009) coordinates state PUCs and sponsors the National Regulatory Research Institute (2009) to promote effective regulation in the public interest. It publishes a matrix to display the services it offers in industry areas that include electricity, gas, telecommunications, water, and multi-utility issues.

While PUC regulation is the model for many utilities, local government control of other infrastructure services leads to a regulatory model based on political choice. This model can be seen most clearly in water and wastewater services, which are regulated by the U.S. Environmental Protection Agency for health and environmental goals. In almost all cases when utilities are publicly owned, rate regulation is purely a local choice. Local elected leaders must take the public interest into account when making rate decisions.

The elected leaders represent businesses, individuals, and nongovernmental organizations and must balance health and the environment and the need to sustain the economy.

For infrastructure services that go beyond state borders, federal regulation applies. Examples include the Interstate Commerce Commission for rail transportation, the Federal Aviation Administration for aviation, the Federal Communication Commission for telecommunication, and the Federal Energy Regulatory Commission for electric power and natural gas.

REVENUE AND COST OF SERVICE ANALYSIS

Analysis of needed revenues and the cost to provide infrastructure services is performed by rate studies. For example, in the water supply sector, rate-setting is the American Water Works Association's most popular seminar and is attended by water utility managers, rate analysts, accounting and budget staff, board members, attorneys, and other planners. They attend because financials in the industry change constantly due to escalating costs, shifting regulatory and environmental forces, and public demands. Topics covered in the three-day seminar include revenue requirements, cost of service while promoting community objectives, contemporary rate structures, capital budgeting and financing, classifying and allocating costs, and avoiding rate shock (American Water Works Association, 2009).

The procedures for cost-of-service rate studies are well established because courts have ruled that the studies provide a fair way to allocate costs to users of services. For example, an often-cited court case is *Federal Power Commission v. Natural Gas Pipeline Company* (1942). Chief Justice Stone wrote:

> *The establishment of a rate for a regulated industry often includes two steps of a different character, one of which may appropriately precede the other. The first is the adjustment of a general revenue level to the demands of a fair return. The second is the adjustment of a rate schedule conforming to that level, so as to eliminate discrimination and unfairness from its details.*

This has led to a set of procedures that include estimating the funds needed to support capital and operations; assigning the costs to infrastructure functions needed to provide the services; assigning each functional cost to components of cost; and allocating each cost component to each customer class based on its proportion of use. It can be difficult for small utilities to perform these studies, and they may need assistance from consultants or from advisory services, such as the University of Tennessee's Institute for

Public Service, which offers a guide for local officials on how to conduct a rate study and increase their rates (Young and Rollins, 2008).

Consulting firms often perform rate studies for infrastructure organizations. For example, Utility Financial Solutions (2009) in Michigan specializes in cost of service, unbundling studies, pricing, and special financial analysis for electric, water, wastewater, and telecommunications organizations. It works for the American Public Power Association, which includes many smaller electric utilities. By the same token, Raftelis Financial Consultants (2009) work for small public water companies. It seems that the more fragmented industries, such as public power and private water supply, require more training in rate-setting because more small management entities are involved.

TAX REVENUES AND SUBSIDIES

Services with a high proportion of public good attributes tend to be financed more by taxes, whereas those with more private good attributes can be priced out with user charges. The main taxes that fund infrastructure at the local level are the property tax and the sales tax. Property taxes are levied against residential, commercial, industrial, agricultural, and vacant land properties as well as on natural resources, mines, oil, and gas. The property tax is an ad valorem tax because it is calculated according to the value of the property. Given that approach, it is easy to see that property taxes are sensitive to urban vitality and to the cost of housing.

States have different formulas to calculate the ad valorem tax. In Colorado, for example, the state sets a multiplier to apply against the assessed market value so that taxes are maintained in line with revenue needs and not too burdensome on property owners. A government with taxing power on properties collects revenue calculated as the mill levy times the assessed valuation times the multiplier. The tax revenue would then be distributed according to the legally determined formulas among school districts, city and county governments, fire districts, and other government entities. Tax increment financing is a way to use a development district to capture the part of property taxes that occurs from growth (see Chapter 3).

Sales taxes are a way to obtain revenues from those who have current income and to redistribute it to public purposes. Sales tax formulas vary by locality, with different rates and different categories of taxable items. For example, in Colorado, sales taxes are levied by state and local governments, but food is taxed at a lower rate than other retail goods. This policy recognizes the need for subsistence for all income levels.

Although most infrastructure is managed at the local levels, state government revenue also is used for a great deal of infrastructure, especially road systems. State governments also manage water systems, parks, buildings, and, in some cases, even electric power systems. At the state government level, revenue sources include individual and corporate income taxes, property taxes, sales taxes, gas taxes, and miscellaneous taxes (U.S. Census Bureau, 2007).

State government finance is a high-profile issue in large states, such as California and New York. It deals with many mandates, from both the federal and the state governments themselves. In Colorado, for example, there are so many budget mandates for required programs that state legislators have few. The main discretionary categories are highways and higher education, both of which have experienced large fluctuations in tax support. Cutting funds from transportation tends to shift emphasis toward use of toll roads and away from publicly financed higher education toward higher tuition fees and models that resemble private universities.

From the previous discussion of public and private purposes, you can see which services are more likely to receive tax revenues. Services with a high ratio of private good attributes included residential and commercial property, water supply, electric power, natural gas, telecom, air travel, freight rail, toll roads, and solid waste collection. Not surprisingly, these services are mostly paid for by users.

Services in which the private good attribute is low include water and air quality management, flood control, use of open highways, and various environmental services. These are apt to be funded entirely with tax revenues.

In between these categories you find services such as transit, public housing, wastewater management, and hazardous material management, which might collect some fees but also receive subsidies.

Grants or intergovernmental revenue are an important part of the financing of local infrastructure and were discussed in Chapter 13 as capital transfers. If the funds are used for operations, as they can be used to some extent for transit, then they also apply to the ongoing revenue base.

Infrastructure services may receive payments from other parts of general government and vice versa. It can be difficult to discern whether this is a matter of hidden subsides or a matter of levying correct charges on users. Two forms of hidden subsidies are prevalent. One is the payment in lieu of taxes, and the other is to treat an infrastructure enterprise as an internal customer and charge for services such as accounting, fleet services, and others.

In states with tax limitation laws in effect, such internal charges can mask rising costs of governments. For example, they may shift the cost of government from taxes to utility customers who pay fees above the cost of service, which are then transferred to pay other costs of government.

Subsidies going in the other direction—where general government subsidizes infrastructure—are not as common and mainly involve allocation of tax revenue to infrastructure departments.

INFRASTRUCTURE REVENUE BY SECTOR

Although infrastructure revenues vary by sector, in one way or another, they all come from customers, either in the form of direct charges for use or as transfers from one group to another through tax mechanisms.

Most of the built environment is in private ownership, and revenues are based on rents and charges. Residential properties are financed by direct users, except in the case of subsidized housing. Commercial real estate is funded by revenues that flow through their management companies. Publicly owned facilities usually are financed from current revenues and taxes. Bonds may be used to finance construction, with payback from revenues over a stream of time.

In the case of public recreation and exhibition facilities, such as stadiums, arenas, and convention centers, the financial plan can involve a complex mixture of use fees, sales taxes, and various other charges. Policy makers may have to walk a fine line between charging enough to pay for the facilities and keeping charges low enough to attract good programs. If a convention or large entertainment event can be attracted, in some cases, the multiplier effect in the form of sales taxes and stimulation to businesses can justify subsidies.

Transportation finance varies by the modes. The Highway Trust Fund and related state programs finance roads and bridges. Transit revenues are from user charges and tax subsidies that might come from all three levels of government. Intercity rail is financed by user charges and fees for freight. Some passenger rail receives federal subsidies. Airports are financed by user charges and also receive federal funding assistance.

Of all public services, electric power and natural gas are the closest to true utilities, and user charges can be used for operating expenses or to retire debt. Water supply also can be charged according to use. Wastewater rates are more difficult to levy on users, but wastewater has become established as a utility, after a period of government subsidy for capital construction.

Solid waste collection services are readily privatized and can be financed entirely by user fees. Disposal of wastes can be financed by user charges as well, but recycling and management of some hazardous materials may require subsidies.

SUMMARY

Whether infrastructure services are delivered through private or public channels, rates for service continue to be important as the main financing mechanism. It is also important to maintain the balance between enterprise financing through rates and public subsidies for services with important social purposes, especially during times of economic challenge, such as during periods of financial crisis. The methods to charge for services vary widely among the infrastructure categories, and many equity and efficiency issues remain to be resolved.

Regulated Rate-Setting Continues as an Important Financing Mechanism

Regulated rates for utility-type services delivered through enterprises will continue as an important source of infrastructure financing. Regulation is becoming more complex due to deregulation, unbundling, and changes in federal laws as well as societal values.

Government Subsidies Are Used to Finance Public Purposes

Infrastructure services with public purposes require subsidies to spread charges across taxpayers. Public purposes, such as maintaining transit systems, become more visible during economic hard times as cities see the need to focus on the basic needs of their citizens.

Rate Analysis Methods Are Well Established

Methods for rate studies are well established, especially in the electric power and water supply fields, where they are informed by procedures of public utility commissions and their accountants.

Theories for Rate-Setting Address Attributes of Infrastructure Services

Rate-setting theories consider attributes of infrastructure-related services and address the variables shown earlier in the management model. The theories are still evolving, as is our understanding of the best balance between the private and public sectors.

Rate Regulation Varies among Infrastructure Categories

While rate regulation has many uses, in practice, it is applied differently across the organizational models of the infrastructure sectors. No single formula will work consistently, and the use of rate structures to shape demand requires insightful analysis that considers the triple bottom line in each sector.

Rates for Infrastructure-Related Services Vary across the Nation

Rates for electric power and natural gas vary widely across the nation. Other services have variable rates as well but are not as dependent on energy sources. Impact fees vary with location and are higher in the fastest-growing states.

PART Three

Toward the Future

CHAPTER 15

Opportunities and Risks
for Infrastructure

Now that we have looked at infrastructure from different perspectives, we see even better how vital it is, that it offers many avenues for private sector involvement, and that it requires wise and insightful approaches to public policy.

This final chapter explains the opportunities and risks of infrastructure as policy issues. The policy question for infrastructure and its sectors has three parts: How can we use infrastructure services to advance society (economic question)? How can we deliver equitable services (social question)? And how do we sustain the natural environment? Infrastructure finance as it relates to the private sector has many interfaces with these public policy questions, and these interfaces illustrate the many places where the public and private sectors can cooperate in advancing infrastructure.

INFRASTRUCTURE AS A POLICY SECTOR

It is clear that infrastructure systems are the foundation for public services that are essential to the economy and necessary for a good life. Keeping these systems functional and secure is paramount among the nation's policy needs. Addressing infrastructure as a sector focuses on a cluster of national needs. It shows how if we are successful at innovation in infrastructure systems, we can solve problems such as energy cost and security, better mobility on roads, high-speed trains, more effective and convenient air travel, and housing a growing population.

In explaining how infrastructure takes aim at these critical issues, this book addressed many topics, including how infrastructure is hard to define and classify, why it is difficult to measure its productivity and needs, how its finances work, and how much it costs.

Financial structures of the infrastructure sectors and how they can be used to improve public sector services were also included in the discussion. Public and private sector managers can use financial tools to assess efficiency in use of public funds and policy choices that leverage private sector capabilities to bolster government infrastructure programs.

Financial tools such as capital budgeting and revenue analysis tell us how much of each type of public facility to provide, who pays for it, when they pay, and how they pay. These questions are answered separately for the built environment, energy, transportation, communications, water, and waste management systems. All of these sectors require large capital investments, but some invest more in structures while others invest more in equipment and spend more on operations.

Performance of infrastructure systems cannot be evaluated purely on financial bottom-line results. It takes little imagination to picture how buildings, energy, transportation, communications, water, and waste management support both the economy and society. As a composite of dynamic public-private businesses, infrastructure systems require scorecards to show triple-bottom-line performance that also measures how "green" they are.

Investing in infrastructure systems offers many opportunities for businesses and individuals to profit from a productive sector of the economy, but the sums involved are so large and the stakes so high that a comprehensive approach is needed to assess the risks and payoffs. As we have shown, the sums required for both capital and operating costs are in the range of $1 trillion for annual construction spending and nearly as high for operating costs. These figures are dominated by the high costs of residential housing, but costs in other categories are hundreds of billions of dollars annually.

INFRASTRUCTURE POLICY ELEMENTS

Infrastructure policy starts with affordability questions that address social and economic needs. Paramount among these needs is fueling a vibrant economy so that social needs can be met. These social needs are concerned directly with the problem of poverty and basic human needs for energy and public health, and they extend to affordable housing and empowerment for work and life through public transportation systems.

In an increasingly crowded world, environmental sustainability rises on our list of policy priorities. Infrastructure has tremendous power both to degrade sustainability and to enhance it. Sustainability topics in the world of infrastructure include green building, response to global warming, recycling of wastes, and more.

The policy questions for infrastructure performance align with a triple-bottom-line accounting framework to measure economic, social, and environmental outcomes. They require policies for the quantity and mix of infrastructure and for the distribution of responsibilities among the public and private sectors.

At the highest policy level, infrastructure requires a composite approach because it is not one unified system but a combination of systems and sectors. However, infrastructure policy at this level is abstract, and policy must be studied at the level of specific sectors, such as transportation and energy.

The question of how much national income and wealth should go to infrastructure addresses trade-offs such as those between guns and butter. Infrastructure is enormously expensive with its large-scale fixed assets. High levels of deferred investment create a third deficit in the nation, to go along with the national debt and Social Security shortfalls. A central example is the sheer magnitude of the problem of managing over 4 million miles of roadway in the United States. Infrastructure finance is a key policy tool to face up to these responsibilities.

Debate over infrastructure finance was summarized by Gramlich (2001), who wrote that while is not clear how infrastructure investments affect the economy at the margin, they have been important historically as government subsidies or regulation helped open bottlenecks and influence private investment. Examples given were the Interstate Highway System and the Internet, both of which were breakthrough developments. Another important role for government is to ensure that public infrastructure is properly managed and maintained and that industries are competitive.

The mix of infrastructure involves micro-level and macro-level questions that range from the national issue of trade-offs between truck or rail freight to local questions of cars or transit in urban areas. Even in a stable sector like water supply, trade-offs occur between choices of fixed infrastructure, such as large water pipes, and more nimble choices, such as dual-water systems for potable and industrial water.

Infrastructure is big business and has a major role in the economy. Business models open up avenues to innovate for greater public sector productivity and to make infrastructure businesses more attractive. Already, infrastructure business is global; the U.S. infrastructure market looks attractive to companies from around the world. Private equity has definitely noticed the action in the infrastructure arena, and we will see more private sector involvement in the future.

Each sector of infrastructure faces issues of operational efficiency and aging of physical assets. In addition to these ongoing concerns, the sectors also face transformational issues, such as shifts to new modes of transportation or sources of energy. The next section lists issues from each sector; after that we list cross-cutting and transformational issues.

SECTOR ISSUES

The following list of sector issues is not exhaustive, but it represents issues that should be added to the common problems of aging infrastructure and low operational efficiency. Some of the transformational issues are carried to the next section for discussion.

The major issue of the built environment is to create an effective, equitable, and secure housing finance system. In addition, urban policy should address many issues of land use development, brownfields, revitalization of old areas, control of sprawl, and other infrastructure-related policies. President Obama announced an urban policy plan during the 2008 election that included, in addition to renewal and revitalization, a section on strengthening the core infrastructure. In addition to attention to transportation, water, and other systems, it promised a National Infrastructure Reinvestment Bank to pump capital into transportation systems.

In the transportation sector, the major needs are to:

- Improve the balance among modes to promote mobility and energy efficiency
- Finance the high cost of roads
- Promote intelligent road systems
- Provide incentives for transit and rail
- Provide robust airport, air traffic control systems, and airline companies
- Support development of the Internet-based logistics economy

Our national energy policy seeks to reduce dependence on imported oil and increase energy security. Sources of basic energy should be diversified. In addition, capital is needed to meet expanding energy requirements. A smart grid is needed to support emerging technologies, such as plug-in vehicles. Incentives for energy conservation are needed, and global warming should be addressed with strategies such as clean coal.

In the telecommunications sector, the government should clear the way for private initiatives while improving security and promoting effective regulation. Also, communication systems for public use and emergencies should be provided.

In the case of water and wastewater systems, aging infrastructure is mentioned explicitly because of the large proportion of buried assets in the industry. Decentralization of water and wastewater organizations and consolidation of small systems should be promoted. Water conservation should be encouraged, and policies to ensure water industry revenues so as to support economic and social needs should be encouraged.

Rate structures and management plans to promote waste recycling and to handle diverse streams of high-tech and consumer waste are needed.

TRANSFORMATIONAL ISSUES

Transformational issues rise to the surface because they are associated with rapid change, have interdependencies with other infrastructure categories, and maybe have scales that extend beyond our national borders.

Critical Infrastructure Security

The term *critical infrastructure* emerged in the 1990s with President Clinton's Executive Order 13010 that created the Commission on Critical Infrastructure Protection. Critical infrastructure includes, in addition to the systems addressed in this book, economic and political systems such as agriculture and food, public health, emergency services, defense industrial base, postal and shipping, and banking and finance. Key industries, such as the chemical industry and hazardous materials, and important facilities, such as national monuments and icons and nuclear power plants, are also included.

The buildup to today's security issues accelerated after World War II, when cushions of time and distance that protected the United States diminished. During the 1950s, intercontinental ballistic missiles threatened the nation. Under the Federal Civil Defense Act of 1950, the Defense Civil Preparedness Agency was born. After about 1989, the world changed with more dangerous geopolitics and an increase in large-scale natural disasters. Terrorism became a big factor in national security. The commission found that certain national infrastructures are so vital that their incapacity or destruction would have a debilitating impact on the defense or economic security of the United States.

The Department of Homeland Security was formed in 2003 to provide a home for agencies such as the Federal Emergency Management Agency and the Federal Bureau of Investigation. It developed a National Infrastructure Protection Plan to plan for protection of the diverse categories of critical infrastructure. The *Wiley Handbook of Science and Technology for Homeland Security* was published to explain issues of homeland security, including critical infrastructure protection (Voeller, 2008).

Global Warming, the Environment, and Infrastructure

Global warming and other environmental challenges have impacts that range across the categories of infrastructure systems. Given our heavy reliance on electric power and because the primary basic energy source, coal, is the main culprit in carbon dioxide emissions, our energy infrastructure faces enormous challenges. Auto emissions are a big factor in greenhouse gas emissions as well, and some solutions, such as plug-in vehicles, will add to the load on electric networks.

The push for sustainability is expressed in green buildings, which would be high in energy and water efficiency and have low carbon footprints. Water efficiency can reduce excessive withdrawals and improve resilience of surface and groundwater sources. Recycling and waste minimization can go a long way toward decreasing the load on natural resources.

Housing Finance System

The need for an effective, equitable, and secure housing finance system was introduced as a sector issue, along with the need for improved urban policies. As Chapter 3 explained, expanding the levels of homeownership is a long-term national goal with many payoffs. A high rate of homeownership indicates that wealth is not concentrated in the hands of the few. Homeownership in the United States increased continually until the mortgage crisis beginning in 2007, when many defaults occurred. Now the challenge is to rebuild an effective housing finance system with the necessary opportunities, checks, and balances.

A housing finance system provides access to credit for potential homebuyers who can afford the minimum payment levels. It cannot compensate for situations in which homeowners are not able to service their debts, so it must operate in tandem with a healthy economy and robust employment policy.

Housing purchases are linked closely to infrastructure development both through demand for infrastructure and through paying for it by impact fees. Additionally, homeowners pay property taxes and utility charges, which recycle through infrastructure organizations and government and are used to service bond debt. Therefore, a robust housing market, supported by an effective housing finance system, is a key plank to support the health of local infrastructure systems.

Energy Security and Diversification of Sources

Energy security is about ensuring supplies and protecting the nation against shocks caused by problems such as oil embargos, terrorism, sabotage, and devastating natural disasters. Security is one of the planks of energy policy, which also includes development of new supplies, energy conservation, diversification of sources, and the solution of environmental problems raised by energy production and use.

The United States has been working earnestly on energy policy for decades and currently has many incentives in place for clean energy and conservation. Energy policy is connected to every category of infrastructure, beginning with the largest energy users in the built environment and transportation systems. The built environment represents energy use for residential, commercial, and industrial users, all of which consume large quantities of electric power and natural gas. Transportation relies mostly on petroleum and may begin to shift to higher levels of electricity use.

Although the details vary, there seems to be a national consensus on the needed elements of energy policy. For example, oilman T. Boone Pickens (2009) has presented an energy security plan with job creation that occurs by generating up to 22 percent of electricity from wind, adding solar capacity, improving the backbone electrical grid, using domestic natural gas to replace imported oil, and providing incentives for conservation.

Mobility for the Economy and Society

Mobility in the transportation system is an integrated measure of access, efficiency, and effectiveness. It means that passengers and freight can be transported readily from origin to destination without delays, excessive costs, or negative external effects, such as on the environment. It requires choices among efficient, safe, and accessible travel modes that use roads, rail, air, and water facilities.

Given the high capital costs of developing roads, airports, rail systems, and waterways, transportation has always required public-private approaches that provide incentives to modernize systems and balance access and use. The sector issues of financing the high cost of roads, making effective trade-offs between roads and rail, developing workable strategic plans for rail and air travel, and facilitating the Internet-based logistics economy are part of the bigger picture of the quest for mobility.

These plans are evolving. For example, in April 2009, President Obama released a strategic rail plan. It identified $8 billion in the American Recovery and Reinvestment Act and a $1 billion-per-year budget request for five years for a high-speed passenger rail system. It mentioned 10 high-speed rail corridors for possible federal funding. The existing corridor from Washington to Boston also can compete for funds to improve its high-speed rail service. The president stated that high-speed rail can reduce dependence on foreign oil, lower carbon emissions, foster economic development, and provide more choices for travelers. Also, it would generate many construction jobs and permanent jobs for rail employees (U.S. Department of Transportation, 2009).

Materials, Recycling, Natural Resources Use

With the exception of national issues such as nuclear wastes, solid waste management is focused on local services. The overall need to minimize waste streams and preserve natural resources is widely embraced, but it is often difficult to provide the right incentives. As an example of a strategic approach, the California Integrated Waste Management Board has as its purpose to meet mandates in the state's Integrated Waste Management Act for reducing waste generation, diverting materials from landfills, recovering resources for their highest and best uses, combating illegal dumping, and remediating illegal sites. These goals are toward a sustainable California, where resources are conserved, greenhouse gases are reduced, bioenergy and biofuels are produced in the state, and the natural environment is preserved (California Integrated Waste Management Board, 2009).

Smart and Secure Systems

Emergence of microelectronics, computers, and the Internet have provided the capability to network infrastructure systems in new ways. This development was labeled "Smart Roads, Smart Bridges, Smart Grids" in a *Wall Street Journal* special report (Totty, 2009). The development of smart systems offers opportunities to use resources better and improve performance of high-cost fixed assets, but it carries the risk that hackers or even accidents can create large-scale systemic disruptions. Ways to use the power of information systems to achieve the promised benefits while mitigating these risks must be developed.

Balancing Private and Public Sector Involvement

The balance between public and private sector involvement in infrastructure is a central political issue facing the nation. Providing infrastructure services has never been a complete government monopoly. Moreover, with today's massive financial deficits and overwhelming public obligations, there is a need to shift burdens as much as possible to the private sector. As explained earlier in the book, there will always be a need to direct part of the infrastructure effort toward social needs in which the beneficiaries cannot pay for services and to invest tax funds in public goods that must be financed from the tax base.

Private equity and privatization policies can open opportunities for greatly enhanced services and productivity, but the playing field has to be level and the conditions must be attractive if private sector involvement is to succeed.

As the infrastructure story has unfolded, it became clear how closely financing public systems and services is linked to the national macroeconomic picture. Government support for infrastructure requires healthy revenues from taxpayers, and policies to use the treasury to leverage productive infrastructure systems require continuing tune-ups. These methods focus on tax-exempt securities as the principal mechanism for state and local borrowing, but national financial policies also can use the tax system and direct investments as mechanisms to stimulate innovation in infrastructure.

Management Models

Infrastructure systems and services are fundamental parts of the economy and national wealth. To manage them in the future, older models must give way to newer ones that are flexible, adaptive, nimble, and sustainable. The pendulum has swung between private sector and public sector models, and now the United States has moved to mixed models that embrace privatization and manage competition among the public and private sectors. While these evolving public-private models differ by sector, they feature reinventing government with smaller and more efficient approaches, new public-private mechanisms, market-based solutions, unbundling and deregulation of services, and innovative financial approaches.

In almost every management scenario, finance and organization are the central issues and tools to provide solutions. Financial needs, both capital and operating, of infrastructure must be studied individually by sector. The financial study should ask: What is this system? Why is it necessary? What function does it serve? How is it provided? How are capital and operating costs financed?

Meeting future infrastructure needs in a different world challenges us as a society. Can we really address the triple bottom line and use infrastructure policy to stimulate business, meet social needs, and sustain the environment? Tools available range from new smart technologies, through financial incentives for the private sector, and extend all the way to comprehensive new management models across the infrastructure sectors.

Balancing Financing of Public and Private Goods

Regulated rates for utility-type services delivered through enterprises continue to be an important source of infrastructure financing. Rate-setting theories consider attributes of infrastructure-related services and address the variables shown earlier in the management model. The theories are still evolving, as is our understanding of the best balance between the private and public sectors. Methods for rate studies are well established, especially in the electric power and water supply fields, where they are informed by procedures of public utility commissions and their accountants. While rate regulation has many uses, in practice, it is applied differently across the organizational models of the infrastructure sectors. Rates for electric power and natural gas vary widely across the nation. Other services have variable rates as well but are not as dependent on energy sources. Impact fees vary with location and are higher in the fastest-growing states.

Government subsidies still must be used to finance public purposes, and infrastructure services with public purposes require subsidies to spread charges across taxpayers.

Addressing Global Infrastructure Issues

The topics covered in the book are at the root of basic human needs. Strategically speaking, they are core issues for the planet. Given the many books about climate change, green building, sustainability, and related topics, it is no surprise that energy, transportation, housing, clean water, and the other infrastructure topics are high on many radar screens.

In his recent book *Hot, Flat, and Crowded*, Thomas Friedman (2008) took on five issues that relate directly to infrastructure: energy supply and demand, corruption of political systems in petroleum-producing countries (which he calls "petro-dictatorship"), climate change, energy poverty, and biodiversity loss. These topics appear mainly in our discussions about problems and opportunities in the energy infrastructure sector. Friedman sees them as caused by global warming, globalization, and growing competition for resources. He argues that these five issues will determine future peace, security, economic growth, and human rights.

The complexity of these issues illustrates what we have to face in finding the right public-private balance and in facing up to public responsibilities, such as addressing poverty, rather than pursuing only the "American lifestyle," as Friedman puts it. Increasing responsibility in use of resources and in providing equitable services is the only way to avoid the resource and poverty crises he describes.

Friedman argues for a more sustainable growth model, led by the United States. This would help reduce our dependence on foreign oil and avoid the ridiculous situation in which our wasteful lifestyles help dictators and terrorists. The other side of the energy coin is what Friedman calls "energy poverty": the situation in which 1.6 billion people lack access to electricity.

This is another dimension to the problem of infrastructure poverty that we discuss throughout the book, especially in Chapter 7: the lack of access to water and sanitation.

In Friedman's eyes, America must lead in the development of a new green economy if it is to maintain its global competitive edge. He pushes the new technologies of clean energy, energy efficiency, and an ethic of conservation that are discussed here in Chapter 6.

To achieve this, Friedman explains how institutional improvements are needed in government policies, regulations, and research and tax incentives. His argument that the current utility incentive system rewards them for selling more energy is widely held. For example, by using a smart grid, you could put the incentive to conserve in the hands of the consumer. Much of this is possible now, in the utility practice of time-of-day pricing. Other ways to use pricing would show consumers the true cost of burning fossil fuels. He argues for electric cars, which also seem to be on the way.

Friedman also discusses the need to promote biodiversity. This is part of the need to promote a green future but is linked to much more than the energy economy.

Friedman takes special aim at the United States and China, because we are mega-countries that can determine a lot of the future. His message to China: Do not take the same dirty-energy path the West has taken. Good advice. He points out that democratic America may take a long time deciding but then stick to its policy; command-and-control China may decide quickly but not implement. Friedman's points line up with those in this book in the sense that how we approach energy (and other infrastructures that relate directly to energy) will be critical to our future.

The quality of life and our future success in solving national problems will depend greatly on how effectively we develop and manage our infrastructure systems. In turn, these depend on both public sector management and private sector investment. Thus, investors, public sector managers, and policy makers have critical roles in forging new forms of public-private cooperation to make government efficient and responsive. As this cooperation strikes a balance between economic advancement, social equity, and environmental sustainability, it will create exciting new opportunities across the infrastructure sectors.

Data Sources

The data sources listed have been used in the book. The list is not exhaustive as most data categories involve many topics. The list can serve as a starting point for further research.

Data Category	Source	Web Site
ASCE Infrastructure Report Card	American Society of Civil Engineers, *Report Card for America's Infrastructure*	www.asce.org/reportcard/ 2009
Bond data	Securities Industry and Financial Markets Association, "Outstanding U.S. Bond Market Debt	www.sifma.org/research/ research.aspx?ID=10806
Telecommunications	Federal Communications Commission	www.fcc.gov
Construction spending	U.S. Census Bureau, "Construction Spending"	www.census.gov/const/ www/c30index.html
Electric power industry finances	Edison Electric Institute, "Industry Financial Performance"	www.eei.org
Energy statistics	U.S. Energy Information Administration, "Official Energy Statistics of the U.S. Government"	www.eia.doe.gov
Financial data in *Statistical Abstract*	U.S. Census Bureau, *2009 Statistical Abstract*	www.census.gov/ compendia/statab
Fixed assets	U.S. Bureau of Economic Affairs, "Fixed Assets"	www.bea.gov
Gross domestic product	U.S. Bureau of Economic Affairs, "Gross Domestic Product"	www.bea.gov

(Continued)

Data Category	Source	Web Site
Highway and transit investment needs	U.S. Federal Highway Administration, "Status of the Nation's Highways, Bridges, and Transit"	www.fhwa.dot.gov/policy/2006cpr/index.htm
Highway statistics	U.S. Federal Highway Administration, "Highway Statistics"	www.fhwa.dot.gov/policy/ohpi/qfroad.cfm
House price data	Federal Housing Finance Agency, "U.S. Monthly House Price Index Estimates"	www.fhfa.gov
Housing starts	U.S. Census Bureau, "New Residential Construction"	www.census.gov/const/www/newresconstindex.html
Housing stock, values, cost, price	U.S. Census Bureau, "American Housing Survey"	www.census.gov/hhes/www/housing/ahs/ahs.html
North American Industrial Classification System codes	U.S. Census Bureau, "North American Industrial Classification System"	www.census.gov/eos/www/naics
Natural gas industry statistics	Natural Gas Supply Association, "Industry and Market Structure"	www.NaturalGas.org
Solid waste industry statistics	National Solid Waste Management Association, "The Solid Waste Industry"	http://www.environmentalistseveryday.org/
Transit ridership	American Public Transit Association, *2008 Public Transportation Fact Book*	www.apta.com
Transportation statistics	U.S. Bureau of Transportation Statistics	www.transtats.bts.gov
Waste Age 100	*Waste Age*	http://wasteage.com
Wastewater industry statistics	U.S. Environmental Protection Agency, "Clean Watersheds Needs Survey"	www.epa.gov/owm/mtb/cwns/index.htm
Water supply industry statistics	U.S. Environmental Protection Agency, "Public Drinking Water Systems"	www.epa.gov/safewater/pws/index.html
Wealth data	Board of Governors of the Federal Reserve System, "Flow of Funds Accounts of the United States"	www.federalreserve.gov/releases/z1

Infrastructure Companies

T his list of infrastructure-related companies discussed in the book is not meant to offer any investment advice but shows the range of economic activity in the infrastructure sector. If no stock symbol is shown, the company is not publicly listed.

Company (Stock Symbol)	Sector	Business Type	Chapter
Abertis Infraestructuras, S.A. (ABS.MC)	Transportation	Contractor	4
Advanced Disposal Services, Inc.	Waste	Waste management	8
AECOM (ACM)	Transportation	Services	4
Allegiant Travel Company (ALGT)	Transportation	Air travel	4
American Standard	Water	Home improvement	7
American Water (AWK)	Water	Water utility	7
Ameron (AMN)	Water	Supplier	7
Amtrak	Transportation	Rail	4
Aqua America (WTR)	Water	Water utility	7
ARCADIS (ARCAD: EURONEXT)	Construction	Consultant	9
AT&T (T)	Telecom	Telecom	5
Autodesk, Inc. (ADSK)	Construction	Information technology	9
Bechtel Corp.	Construction	Contractor	9
Bentley Systems, Inc.	Construction	Information technology	9
Blount International Inc. (BLT)	Construction	Equipment	9
Boeing, Inc. (BA)	Transportation	Equipment	4
Broadwind Energy	Energy	Wind power	6

(Continued)

Company (Stock Symbol)	Sector	Business Type	Chapter
Burlington Northern Santa Fe Corporation (BNI)	Transportation	Rail	4
Calgon Carbon Corporation (CCC)	Water	Chemicals	7
California Water Service Company (CWT)	Water	Water utility	7
CalRecovery	Waste	Waste management	8
Canadian National Railway (CNR.TO)	Transportation	Rail	4
Caterpillar (CAT)	Construction	Equipment	9
CEMEX, S.A.B. de C.V. (CX)	Transportation	Cement	4
Connecticut Water Service Inc. (CTS)	Water	Water utility	7
Conrail, CSX, Norfolk Southern Corporation (NSC)	Transportation	Rail	4
Covanta, Inc. (CVA)	Waste	Waste management	8
Dow Chemical (DOW)	Water	Chemicals	7
Dubai World	Transportation	Ports	4
Duke Energy (DUK)	Energy	Utility	6
El Paso Corporation (EP)	Energy	Gas corporation	6
Energen (EGN)	Energy	Utility	6
Energy East Corporation	Energy	Utility	6
ESRI	Construction	Information technology	3, 9
Exelon (EXC)	Energy	Utility	6
Exxon Mobil Corp. (XOM)	Energy	Oil and gas	6
Fannie Mae (FNM)	Built	Banking	3
Fluor Corporation (FLR)	Construction	Contractor	9
Freddie Mac (FRE)	Built	Banking	3
Garney Construction Company	Construction	Contractor	9
GDF SUEZ (GDSZF)	Water	Water utility	7
GE Water	Water	Equipment	7
General Growth Properties, Inc. (GGP)	Built	Real estate investment trust	3
Granite Construction Inc. (GVA)	Construction	Contractor	9
GSA	Built	Real estate investment trust	3
Henkels & McCoy Inc.	Construction	Contractor	9
Iberdrola (IBE.MC)	Energy	Contractor	4
Insituform Technologies Inc. (INSU)	Water	Contractor	7
Iteris, Inc. (ITI)	Transportation	Equipment	4
Johnson Controls, Inc. (JCI)	Energy	Equipment	6

Level 3 (LVLT)	Telecom	Fiber cable	
Mueller Water Products, Inc.	Water	Equipment	7
MYR Group (MYRG)	Construction	Contractor	9
NAHB	Built	Real estate investment trust	3
Pacific Gas and Electric (PCG)	Energy	Utility	6
Peabody Energy Company (BTU)	Energy	Coal	6
Pepco Holdings Inc. (PHI)	Energy	Utility	6
Public housing agencies	Built	Real estate investment trust	3
Pulte Homes Inc. (PHM)	Built	Homebuilder	3
Quanta Services Inc. (PWR)	Construction	Contractor	9
Qwest (Q)	Telecom	Telecom	5
RWE AG (RWNFF)	Energy	Utility	7
Saur Group	Water	Water utility	7
School districts	Built	Real estate investment trust	3
Sempra Energy (SRE)	Energy	Utility	6
Siemens (SI)	Transportation	Equipment	4
Simon Property Group (SPG)	Built	Real estate investment trust	3
Southern Company (SO)	Energy	Utility	6
Stantec (TSX:STN)	Construction	Consultant	9
Stericycle Inc. (SRCL)	Waste	Waste management	8
Telvent Corporation (TLVT)	Transportation	Equipment	4
The Home Depot Inc. (HD)	Built	Home improvement	3
UAL Corporation (UAUA)	Transportation	Airline	4
United Utilities (UUGWF)	Water	Water utility	7
URS (URS)	Transportation	Consultant	4
Veolia Environmental Services	Water	Utility	8
Vulcan materials (VMC)	Transportation	Aggregates	4
Waste Management Inc. (WM)	Waste	Waste management	8
Weyerhaeuser Company (WY)	Construction	Lumber	9
Wind Capital Group	Energy	Wind energy	6
Xcel Energy (XEL)	Energy	Utility	6

Acronyms

This list of acronyms includes public agencies and infrastructure associations that are profiled in the text, as well as common financial terms. (For corporate and public companies, see Appendix B.) Federal agencies are generally given by their main initials, such as EPA, rather than USEPA. Alternates are listed in parentheses. In some cases, such as USGS, the agency is always designated with the "US" and is listed that way here.

AAAE	American Association of Airport Executives
AAR	American Association of Railroads
AASHTO	American Association of State Highway & Transportation Officials
ADA	Americans with Disabilities Act
AGC	Associated General Contractors
AIA	American Institute of Architects
AMEX	American Stock Exchange
Amtrak	National Railroad Passenger Corporation
ANSI	American National Standards Institute
APPA	American Public Power Association
APTA	American Public Transit Association
APWA	American Public Works Association
ARM	Adjustable rate mortgage
ARPANET	Advanced Research Projects Agency network
ARRA	American Recovery and Reinvestment Act
ASCE	American Society of Civil Engineers
AT&T	American Telephone and Telegraph
ATA	Air Transport Association of America
ATC	Air traffic control
AWDI	American Water Development Inc.
AWWA	American Water Works Association
BEA (USBEA)	Bureau of Economic Affairs

BFO	Budgeting for outcomes
BICE	Board for Infrastructure and Constructed Environment of the National Research Council
BKWH	Billion kilowatt-hours
BOC (USBOC)	Bureau of Census,
BOT	Build-operate-transfer
BTU	British thermal unit
CAPEX	Capital expenditures
CBO (USCBO)	Congressional Budget Office
CDO	Collateralized debt obligation
CFMA	Construction Financial Management Association
CIP	Capital improvement program
CM	Construction manager
CMBS	Commercial mortgage-backed security
CMO	Collateralized mortgage obligation
COFI	Cost of Funds Index
CONEXPO	Construction and materials trade show (w/CON/AGG)
DB	Design-build
DBB	Design-bid-build
DBI	Design-Build Institute of America
DHS (USDHS)	U.S. Department of Homeland Security
DistribuTECH	Trade show of electricity transmission and distribution equipment
DJIA	Dow Jones Industrial Average
DJTA	Dow Jones Transportation Average
DJUA	Dow Jones Utility Average
DOE (USDOE)	Department of Energy
DOJ (USDOJ)	US Department of Justice
DOT (USDOT)	Department of Transportation
EEI	Edison Electric Institute
EIS	Environmental Impact Statement
ENR	*Engineering News-Record* magazine
EPA (USEPA)	Environmental Protection Agency
ETF	Exchange traded fund
FAA (USFAA)	Federal Aviation Administration
FCC (USFCC)	Federal Communication Commission
FDIC	Federal Deposit Insurance Corporation
FHA	Federal Housing Administration
FHFA	Federal Housing Finance Agency
FHLMC	Federal Home Loan Mortgage Corporation (Freddie Mac)

FHWA (USFHWA)	Federal Highway Administration
FNMA	Federal National Mortgage Association (Fannie Mae)
FRA (USFRA)	Federal Rail Administration
FSLIC	Federal Savings and Loan Insurance Corporation
FTA (USFTA)	Federal Transit Administration
GAO (USGAO)	Government Accountability Office
GDP	Gross domestic product
GFOA	Government Finance Officers Association
GGP	General Growth Properties
GIS	Geographical information system
GMP	Guaranteed Maximum Price
GNMA	Government National Mortgage Association (Ginnie Mae)
GO	General obligation bond
GSA (USGSA)	General Services Administration
GSE	Government-sponsored enterprise
HAZMAT	Hazardous materials
HEL	Home equity loan
HOV	High-occupancy vehicle lane
IATA	International Air Transportation Association
IEEE	Institute of Electrical and Electronics Engineers
IPO	Initial public offering
IRS (USIRS)	Internal Revenue Service
ISTEA	Intermodal Surface Transportation Efficiency Act
KW	Kilowatt
KWH	Kilowatt-hour
LEED	Leadership in Energy and Environmental Design
LLC	Limited liability corporation
mbbls/day	Million barrels per day
MBS	Mortgage-backed securities
MRF	Materials recovery facilities
MTA	Metropolitan Transit Authority (NY)
NAHB	National Association of Homebuilders
NAICS	North American Industrial Classification System
NARUC	National Association of Regulatory Utility Commissioners
Nasdaq	National Association of Securities Dealers Automated Quotations
NAWC	National Association of Water Companies
NIMBY	Not in my backyard
NIST	National Institute of Standards and Technology

NRC   National Research Council
NRECA   National Rural Electric Cooperative Association
NSF   National Science Foundation
NSF   National Sanitation Foundation
NSWMA   National Solid Waste Management Association
NUCA   National Utility Contractors Association
NYSE   New York Stock Exchange
OFHEO   Office of Federal Housing Enterprise Oversight
OMB (USOMB)   Office of Management and Budget
PFI   Private Finance Initiative
PHADA   Public Housing Authorities Director's Association
PILOT   Payment in lieu of taxes
PPP   Public-private partnerships
PUC   State public utility commission
RCRA   Resource Conservation and Recovery Act
REIT   Real Estate Investment Trust
S&L   Savings and loans bank
S&P   Standard & Poor's
SAFETEA-LU   Safe, Accountable, Flexible, Efficient Transportation
                           Equity Act
SIFMA   Securities Industry and Financial Markets
                           Association
TBL   Triple bottom line
TCF   Thousand cubic feet
TEA   Transportation Equity Act
TEA-21   Transportation Equity Act for the 21st Century
TIC   True interest cost
TIF   Tax-increment financing
TIFIA   Transportation Infrastructure Finance and
                           Innovation Act
TRB   Transportation Research Board of the National
                           Research Council
TSA (USTSA)   Transportation Security Administration
TVA   Tennessee Valley Authority
UAE   United Arab Emirates
ULI   Urban Land Institute
URISA   Urban and Regional Information Systems
                           Association
USACE   U.S. Army Corps of Engineers
USDA   U.S. Department of Agriculture
USEIA   U.S. Energy Information Administration
USFERC   Federal Energy Regulatory Commission

USGS	U.S. Geological Survey
USHUD	Housing and Urban Development Department
VA (USVA)	Veteran's Administration
VoIP	Voice over Internet Protocol
WASTEC	Waste Equipment Technology Association
WasteExpo	Trade show for waste management and recycling
WEF	Water Environment Federation
WIPP	Waste Isolation Pilot Plant

References

Abertis Infraestructuras, S.A. 2009. "Corporation Information." http://www.abertis.com/. Accessed May 14, 2009.

AECOM. 2009. "About Us." http://www.aecom.com/. Accessed May 24, 2009.

Alacra. 2009. "Industry: Waste Management." http://www.alacra.com/. Accessed May 29, 2009.

Algarni, A.M., D. Arditi, and G. Polat. 2007. "Build-Operate-Transfer in Infrastructure Projects in the United States." *ASCE Journal of Construction Engineering and Management.* 133, no. 10, (October 2007) 728–735.

American Association of State Highway & Transportation Officials. 2009. "Innovative Finance." http://www.innovativefinance.org/. Accessed June 29, 2009.

American Bus Association. 2009. "About ABA." http://www.buses.org/. Accessed March 14, 2009.

American Gas Association. 2009. "Statistics." http://www.aga.org/. Accessed March 16, 2009.

American Public Power Association. 2009. "Electric Power Statistics." http://www.appanet.org/aboutpublic/index.cfm?ItemNumber=2691. Accessed October 11, 2009.

American Public Transit Association. 2009. "2008 Public Transportation Fact Book." *Historical Ridership Trends.* http://www.apta.com/. Accessed March 14, 2009.

American Public Works Association. 1976. *History of Public Works in the United States: 1776–1976.* Ed. Ellis L. Armstrong. Chicago: American Public Works Association, 1976.

American Securitization Forum. 2009. "About the ASF." http://www.americansecuritization.com/. Accessed May 17, 2009.

American Society of Civil Engineers. 2009a. "Report Card for America's Infrastructure." http://www.asce.org/reportcard/2009/. Accessed March 20, 2009.

American Society of Civil Engineers. 2009b. "Report Card for America's Infrastructure: Methodology." http://www.asce.org/reportcard/2005/page.cfm?id=92. Accessed March 28, 2009.

American Society of Civil Engineers California Section. 2009. "Methodology for California Infrastructure Report Card." http://www.ascecareportcard.org/Data_Specific/Methodology/California_Infrastructure_Report_Card_Methodolgy_Final2.doc. Accessed March 28, 2009.

American Water Works Association. 2009. "Financial Management: Cost of Service Rate-Making." www.awwa.org. Accessed April 24, 2009.

American Wind Energy Association. 2009. "Board of Directors." http://www.awea.org. Accessed May 22, 2009.

Amtrak. 2008. "Amtrak National Facts." http://www.amtrak.com. Accessed December 14, 2008.

Association of American Railroads. 2009. "Railroad Statistics." http://www.aar.org/Homepage.aspx. Accessed October 8, 2009.

Autodesk Inc. 2009. *Company.* http://usa.autodesk.com/. Accessed October 8, 2009.

AXA Private Equity. 2009. "Infrastructure Investment: Saur." http://www.axaprivateequity.com/. Accessed June 4, 2009.

Bechtel. 2009. "Corporate Overview." http://www.bechtel.com/overview.html. Accessed July 6, 2009.

Bentley Systems Inc. 2009. "Corporate." http://www.bentley.com/en-US/. Accessed October 8, 2009.

Birmingham News. 2009. "Key Decisions About Jefferson County Sewer System to Be Made by Others." http://www.al.com/. Accessed April 19, 2009.

Bloomberg.com. 2008. "Municipal Bond Fees Rising at Fastest Pace Since 1981." http://www.bloomberg.com. December 12, 2008. Accessed May 14, 2009.

Boeing Company. 2009. "About Us." http://www.boeing.com. Accessed May 25, 2009.

Bond Buyer. 2009. "About Us." http://www.bondbuyer.com/. Accessed May 14, 2009.

Boyd, L., and L. Pritcher. 2007. "Brief History of the U.S. Passenger Rail Industry." http://scriptorium.lib.duke.edu/adaccess/rails-history.html. Accessed March 14, 2009.

Broadwind Energy. 2009. "Companies." http://www.broadwindenergy.com/. Accessed October 5, 2009.

Brown, A.C. 1983. "For Sale: Pieces of the Public Sector." *Fortune.* October 31.

Brown, P. 2006. *An Introduction to the Bond Markets.* Hoboken, NJ: John Wiley & Sons.

Bruno, J.B. 2009. "Official: Morgan Stanley Smith Barney." *Wall Street Journal.* June 2, C6.

Business Week. 2008. "Appalachian Waste Services LLC." http://investing.businessweek.com/research/stocks/private/snapshot.asp?privcapId=43031772. Accessed November 15, 2008.

Business Wire. 1999. "Connecticut Water Service, Inc. Completes $7.4 million Acquisition of Crystal Water Utilities Corporation." Sept 30. http://www.businesswire.com/portal/site/home/. Accessed November 21, 2008.

California Infrastructure and Economic Development Bank. 2009. "Infrastructure State Revolving Fund Program." http://www.ibank.ca.gov/Programs/infrastructure.html. Accessed April 21, 2009.

California Integrated Waste Management Board. 2009. "Strategic Directives." http://www.ciwmb.ca.gov/BoardInfo/StrategicPlan/.

California Legislative Analysts Office. 2009. "2009–2010 Budget Analysis Series: Transportation." http://www.lao.ca.gov. Accessed May 25, 2009.

California Water Service Group. 2009. "About Cal Water." http://www.calwater.com/. Accessed October 6, 2009.

CalRecovery. 2009. "Services." http://www.calrecovery.com/. Accessed October 7, 2009.

Carey, S. 2009. "For Allegiant, Getaways Mean Profits." *Wall Street Journal*. February 18, B1,4.

Carlton, J. 2008. "Targeting the Wasteful, Activists Seek End to California's Water Board." *Wall Street Journal*. December 26, A5.

Carlyle Group. 2009. "Portfolio." http://www.carlyle.com/Portfolio/item10016.html.

Casselman, B. 2009. "Planning the 'Ike Dike' Defense." *Wall Street Journal*. June 4, A3.

Catan, T., and D. Gautheier-Villars. 2009. "Europe Listens for U.S. Train Whistle." *Wall Street Journal*. May 29, B1,2.

Center for Public Integrity. 2008. "The Water Barons." http://projects.publicintegrity.org/. Accessed November 14, 2008.

Chaker, A.M. 2009. "Planes, Trains...and Buses?" June 18. *Wall Street Journal Online*. http://online.wsj.com/article/SB124528126290225307.html. Accessed October 5, 2009.

Chicago Public Schools. 2009. "Popular Annual Financial Report." http://www.cps.edu. Accessed May 12, 2009.

Choate, P., and S. Walter. 1981. "America in Ruins: Beyond the Public Works Pork Barrel." Council of State Planning Agencies, Washington.

City of Austin Housing Finance Corporation. 2009. "General Obligation Bonds." http://www.ci.austin.tx.us/ahfc/gobonds.htm. Accessed June 26, 2009.

City of Corvallis. 2009. "City Manager's Office Performance Indicators." http://www.ci.corvallis.or.us/downloads/cmo/Performance_Indicators.pdf. Accessed July 1, 2009.

City of Dallas, Texas. 2007. "Needs Inventory." http://www.dallascityhall.com. Accessed May 5, 2009.

Clough, G.W. 2000. "Civil Engineering in the New Millennium." *New Millennium Colloquium of Civil and Environmental Engineering*, MIT. March 19 to 21, 2000.

Cobley, M. 2008. "FourWinds to Diversify With Private Equity Deals." www.efinancialnews.com/homepage/content/2450067107. Accessed July 7, 2009.

Colorado Department of Regulatory Agencies. 2009. "History of the Public Utilities Commission." http://www.dora.state.co.us/PUC/About/AboutHistory.htm.

Colorado Department of Transportation. 2008. "Proposed Budget for Fiscal Year 2009–2010." Denver.

Commodities Resource Corporation. 2009. "Commodity Primer." http://www.commodity.com/?setPage=primer. Accessed July 12, 2009.

CONEXPO-CON/AGG 2011. 2009. "Attendees Overview." http://www.conexpoconagg.com. Accessed June 28, 2009.

Conkey, Christopher. 2009a. "U.S. Highway Fund Low on Cash Again." *Wall Street Journal*. June 3, A4.

———. 2009b. "Highway Upgrade Goes Private." *Wall Street Journal*. March 9, A3.

Connecticut Water. 2009. "About Us." http://www.ctwater.com/. Accessed October 6, 2009.

Conrail. 2009. "A Brief History of Conrail." http://www.conrail.com/history.htm. Accessed March 14, 2009.

Constructing Excellence UK. 2009. "About Us." http://www.constructingexcellence .org.uk/. Accessed July 4, 2009.

Construction Financial Management Association. 2009. "About Us." http://www .cfma.org/about/about.asp. Accessed July 7, 2009.

Cooke, J.R. 2009. *California Sells Record $6.9 Billion in Build America Bond Deal*. http://www.Bloomberg.com. Accessed May 18, 2009.

Copeland, R., and L. Rappaport. 2009. "New Security Shifts Risk to Borrower." *Wall Street Journal Online*. June 15.

Corkery, M. 2009. "Three Pulte Directors Rejected in Vote." *Wall Street Journal*. May 18, B6.

Cross, G. 1991. *A Dynasty of Water: The Story of American Water Works Company*. Vorhees, NJ: American Water Works Company.

Cui, C., and A. Davis. 2008. "Water's Slippery Seduction: Investors Flood Sector Amid Economic Falloff, Limited Opportunities." *Wall Street Journal*. March 29, P. B1.

Delaware Business Ledger. 2009. "State Transportation Bond Sale Successful." June 8. http://www.ledgerdelaware.com. Accessed June 26, 2009.

Design-Build Institute of America. 2009. "What is Design-Build?" http://www.dbia .org. Accessed July 6, 2009.

Digital Wire. 2008. "China to spend $730.6 Bln on Railways to 2020." ENR.com. Accessed December 21, 2008.

Dougherty, C. 2009. "Sales Tax Revenue Falls at Fastest Pace in Years." *Wall Street Journal*. April 15, A4.

Dow-Jones Brookfield. 2009. "Dow-Jones Brookfield Infrastructure Indices." http://www.djindexes.com/brookfield/?go=literature-center. Accessed May 25, 2009.

Duggan, K. 2008. "Recycling in its Own Slowdown." *Coloradoan*. December 22, A1, 2.

Duke Energy. 2009. "Our Company." http://www.duke-energy.com/. Accessed October 5, 2009.

Dulles Greenway. 2009. "Corporate Overview & SCC Governance." http:// dullesgreenway.com/corporate-overview-scc-governance.html. Accessed April 25, 2009.

Duncan Associates. 2009. "Impact fees." www.Impactfees.com. Accessed February 26, 2009.

Dzierwa, J. 2009. "Infrastructure: A Global Opportunity for Investors." *U.S. Global Investors*. www.usfunds.com.

Economist. 2007. "Pocket World in Figures." *Economist*, London.

Economist. 2008. "Infrastructure: The Cracks Are Showing." June 28, 36.

Economist. 2009a. "Talking rubbish: Special Report on Waste." *Economist*, http:// www.economist.com/specialreports/displaystory.cfm?story_id=13135413

———. 2009b. "Regenerating Cities: TIFs and Urban Development." *Economist*, Accessed June 27, 62.

Edison Electric Institute. 2008. "Key Facts about the Electric Power Industry." Washington. http://www.eei.org. Accessed November 23, 2008.

Edison Electric Institute. 2009. "Industry Financial Performance." 2007. http://www
.eei.org. Accessed March 15, 2009.

Einhorn, B. 2009. "Looking for Life After Laptops." *Business Week*. June 1.
P. 43.

El Paso Corporation. 2009. "Profile." http://www.elpaso.com/. Accessed October 5,
2009.

Energen. 2009. "About Energen." http://www.energen.com/. Accessed October 5,
2009.

Energy East Corporation. 2009. "About Energy East." http://energyeast.com/. Accessed October 5, 2009.

Energy Recovery Council. 2009. "About Us." http://www.wte.org/about. Accessed
July 1, 2009.

ENR. 2009. "Missouri Sports Nation's First Private Commercial Airport." Accessed
May 11. 262(15): 15.

ENR.com 2008. "Yucca Mountain." Accessed November 25, 2008.

———. 2009a. "Fontainebleau Las Vegas files for Chapter 11." Accessed June 10,
2009.

———. 2009b. "ENR Top Lists." http://enr.construction.com/toplists/default.asp.
Accessed October 12, 2009.

———. 2009c. "Construction Economics." http://www.enr.com/features/conEco/
subs/default.asp. Accessed July 7, 2009.

———. 2009d. "ARCADIS Sets Buyout of Malcolm Pirnie." June 25. http://enr
.construction.com. Accessed July 5, 2009.

ESRI. 2009. "About ESRI." http://www.esri.com/. Accessed July 7, 2009.

Eurotunnel. 2006. "Eurotunnel to convert elements of debt into bonds." http://www
.eurotunnel.com. Accessed October 10, 2009.

Exelon Corporation. 2009. "About Exelon." http://www.exeloncorp.com/. Accessed October 5, 2009.

Fannie Mae. 2009. "Fannie Mae Reports First-Quarter 2009 Results." http://www
.fanniemae.com. Accessed May 26, 2009.

Federal Home Loan Financing Agency. 2009. "U.S. Monthly House Price Index Estimates, December 23, 2008." http://www.fhfa.gov/. Accessed May 10,
2009.

Federal Power Commission vs. Natural Gas Pipeline Company. "1941315
U.S. Supreme Court 575." 1942. http://caselaw.lp.findlaw.com/cgi-bin/getcase
.pl?court=us&vol=315&invol=575. Accessed October 12, 2009.

Federal Reserve Bank. 2009a. "Mortgage Debt Outstanding." http://www
.federalreserve.gov/. Accessed May 11, 2009.

———. 2009b. "Flow of Funds Accounts of The United States." Z1. June 11, 2009.
Table B100. Balance Sheet of Households and Nonprofit Organizations.

Fender, J., and C. Illescas. 2009. "Rounding Corner on Giving Tax Break." *Denver
Post*. A1, 4.

Fidelity.com. 2009. "Fidelity Municipal Income Fund." http://personal.fidelity.com.
Accessed May 15, 2009.

FMSBonds Inc. 2009. "Bond Basics." http://www.fmsbonds.com/. Accessed April
19, 2009.

Forrester, J. 1969. "Urban Dynamics." MIT Press. Cambridge, MA.

Freddie Mac. 2009. "Freddie Mac Releases First Quarter 2009 Financial Results." http://www.freddiemac.com. Accessed May 26, 2009.

Friedman, Thomas L. 2008. *Hot, Flat, and Crowded: Why We need a Green Revolution– and How It Can Renew America*. New York: Farrar, Straus and Giroux.

FTSE. 2009. "Macquarie Global Infrastructure Index Series." http://www.ftse.com. Accessed May 26, 2009.

Funding Universe. 2009a. "American Standard Companies, Inc." http://www .fundinguniverse.com. Accessed October 6, 2009.

———. 2009b. "Blount International Inc." http://www.fundinguniverse.com. Accessed July 7, 2009.

Garney Construction Company. 2009. "About Us." http://www.garney.com/. Accessed July 7, 2009.

GDF Suez. 2009. *Group.* http://www.gdfsuez.com/. Accessed October 6, 2009.

Gelinas, N. 2005. "It's Time to Privatize Gotham's Buses: Striking TWU Workers Show the Danger of a Single Monopoly System." *City Journal.* http://www.city-journal.org/. Accessed December 13, 2008.

Gelsi, S. 2008. "Williams Pipeline Partners IPO Ekes Out Gain." January 18, 2008. http://www.marketwatch.com. Accessed May 31, 2009.

Glaeser, E.L., Kahn, M.E., and J. Rappaport. 2008. "Why Do The Poor Live in Cities? The Role of Public Transportation." *Journal of Urban Economics.* Elsevier. 63(1): 1–24.

Goldman Sachs Infrastructure Investment Group. 2009. "About Us." http://www2 .goldmansachs.com.

Gongloff, M. 2009. "Are Transports Falsely Flashing Bullishness?" *Wall Street Journal.* June 12, C1.

Gopalan, N. 2008. "China Railway $5.4 Billion IPO To Be World's Biggest This Year." *Wall Street Journal Online.* Accessed February 25, 2008.

Gramlich, E.M. 2001. "Infrastructure and Economic Development." Speech at the Texas Trade Corridors New Economy Conference, San Antonio, Texas, August 3, 2001. www.federalreserve.gov/boarddocs/speeches/2001/20010803/default.htm. Accessed December 21, 2008.

Greenough, G., T. Eggum, U.G. Ford III, N.S. Grigg, and E. Sizer. 1999. "Public Works Delivery Systems in North America: Private and Public Approaches, Including Managed Competition." *Public Works Management and Policy* 4, No. 1, (July 1999): 41–49.

Greyhound Lines Inc. 2009. "About Greyhound." http://www.greyhound.com. Accessed March 14, 2009.

Grigg, N.S. 2006. "Water Management Requirements for a New Energy Policy." Hydrology Days Presentation. Colorado State University. March.

———. 2007. "Water Sector Structure, Size and Demographics." *Journal Water Resources Planning and Management.* ASCE No. 133, (January/February): 60–66.

Grigg, N., and M. Bryson. 1975. "Interactive Simulation for Water Dynamics." *Journal of the Urban Planning and Development Division*, ASCE, May.

Hilti Inc. 2005. "The Future of Construction: Interview With An Expert." (2005 Annual Report). http://www.hilti.com/. Accessed July 5, 2009.

Hoffman, S. 2009. *Planet Water: Investing in the World's Most Valuable Resource.* Hoboken, NJ: John Wiley & Sons, Inc. Hoboken.

Hong, S., and T. Poon. 2009. "China State Expected to Take IPO Crown." *Wall Street Journal Online.* July 13.

Houtsma, J., S. deMonsabert, and S. Gutner. 2003. "U.S. Wastewater Contract Operations: Contract Details and Views of Contracting." European Regional Science Association. 2003 Congress. Jyväskylä, Finland.

Infrastructure Australia. 2008. "A Report to the Council of Australian Governments." December. http://www.infrastructureaustralia.gov.au/publications .aspx. Accessed October 5, 2009.

Infrastructure Investor. 2009. "About Us." http://www.infrastructureinvestor.com/ Pages.aspx?pageID=1759&ccID=7826. Accessed July 13, 2009.

Infrastructure Journal. 2009. "About Us." http://www.ijonline.com. Accessed July 13, 2009.

Insight Research Corporation. 2009. "About Us." http://www.insight-corp.com.

Insituform. 2009. "Income Statement." http://www.insituform.com/. Accessed May 23, 2009.

International Air Transport Association. 2009. "Grim Prospects—Deep Recession, Bigger Losses." http://www.iata.org/. Accessed May 21, 2009.

Invesco PowerShares. 2009. "Water Resources Portfolio Fund." http://www.invesco powershares.com/products/overview.aspx?ticker=Pho. Accessed July 13, 2009.

InvestorWords. 2009. www.investorwords.com. Accessed January 25, 2009.

John Wayne Airport. 2009. "County of Orange/John Wayne Airport Bond Ratings Announced." http://www.ocair.com. Accessed June 26, 2009.

Karp, Jonathan, and Frangos, Alex. 2008. "Construction Industry Is Poised for a Rebound." *Wall Street Journal.* November 25, A3.

Katz, D., and T. Bolema. 2003. "A brief history of telecom regulation." *Mackinac Center for Public Policy.* http://www.mackinac.org/. Accessed March 17, 2009.

Lacayo, R. 2009. "#4 Reinstating the Interstate." *Time.* March 23, 173(11): 52.

Lee, D.A. 1999. "Models of Government Regulation of Privatized Transit Systems in Five Latin American Cities." *Transportation Quarterly.* 53(1).

Leib, J. 2008. "Rail Group Lays Out Options." *Denver Post.* December 17, 5B.

Levitt, A. Jr. 2009. "Muni Bonds Need Better Oversight." *Wall Street Journal.* May 9–10, A15:108.

Lindenberger, M. 2009. "Private Toll Roads, Free Highways Merge First in Tarrant Project." *Dallas Morning News.* January 30.

Lui, H.F., and P. Emrath. 2008. "The Direct Impact of Home Building and Remodeling on the U.S. Economy." HousingEconomics.com. NAHB. http://www .nahb.org. Accessed November 26, 2008.

Macquarie Infrastructure Company. 2009. "About Us." http://www.macquarie. com/mic.

Mandel, M. 2009. "Innovation Interrupted." *Business Week.* June 15: 34–40.

Matthews, R. "Railroads Seek Tax Aid." 2007. *Wall Street Journal.* January 20–21, A4.

Maxwell, R. 2007. *Private Equity Funds: A Practical Guide for Investors.* Hoboken, NJ: John Wiley & Sons.

McDonald, D.J. and D.L. Thornton. 2008. "A Primer on the Mortgage Market and Mortgage Finance." *Federal Reserve Bank of St. Louis Review*. 90, No. 1 (Jan/Feb 2008): 31–45.

Means, E.G. III, L. Ospina, and R. Patrick. 2005. "Ten Top Trends and Their Implications for Water Utilities." *Journal, AWWA*. 97, No. 7: 64–75.

Mesa Water Inc. 2009. "Mesa Water History." http://www.mesawater.com. Accessed October 6, 2009.

Metropolitan Transit Authority. 2009. "Public Transportation For the New York Region." http://www.mta.info/mta/network.htm. Accessed May 21, 2009.

Moody's Investor's Service. 2002. *Moody's U.S. Municipal Bond Rating Scale*. New York.

Municipal Market Advisors. 2009. "About Us." http://www.mma-research.com/. Accessed July 8, 2009.

Municipalbonds.com. 2009. "How to Buy Municipal Bonds." http://www.municipal bonds.com. Accessed June 26, 2009.

Mushkin, S., ed., *Public Prices for Private Goods*, The Urban Institute, Washington, 1972.

MYR Group, Inc. 2009. "About Us." http://www.myrgroup.com/. Accessed October 8, 2009.

National Association of Homebuilders. 2009a. "About NAHB." http://www.nahb .org/. Accessed June 20, 2009.

———. 2009b. "Housing Starts." http://www.nahb.org. Accessed June 2, 2009.

National Association of Regulatory Utility Commissioners. 2009. "About Us." http://www.naruc.org/news/. Accessed April 25, 2009.

National Council on Public Works Improvement. 1988. *Fragile Foundations: A Report on America's Public Works*. Washington, DC.

National Low Income Housing Coalition. 2009. "About Us." http://www.nlihc .org/template/index.cfm. Accessed October 5, 2009.

National Regulatory Research Institute. 2009. "About Us." http://nrri2.org/index .php. Accessed April 25, 2009.

National Research Council. 1995. *Measuring and Improving Infrastructure Performance*. Washington, DC: NAE Press.

National Research Council. 2002. "Privatization of Water Services in the United States: An Assessment of Issues and Experiences." *National Research Council*. Washington, DC.

National Research Council. 2009. "Board on Infrastructure and the Constructed Environment." http://sites.nationalacademies.org/deps/BICE/index.htm. Accessed June 28, 2009.

National Solid Waste Management Association. 2008. "The Solid Waste Industry" http://wastec.isproductions.net/webmodules/webarticles/anmviewer.asp?a=464. Accessed November 15, 2008.

National Surface Transportation Infrastructure Financing Commission. 2008. "The Path Forward: Funding and Financing Our Surface Transportation System (Interim Report)." February. USDOT. http://transportationcommission.dot.gov

Nebraska Energy Office. 2009. "Electricity Rate Comparison by State." http://www .neo.ne.gov/statshtml/115.htm. Accessed April 28, 2009.

New Jersey Turnpike Authority. 2009. "About Us." http://www.state.nj.us/turnpike/ 2007-NJTA-Annual-Report.pdf. Accessed May 25, 2009.

New Zealand Ministry of Economic Development. 2005. "Sustainable Infrastructure: A Policy Framework."

Obama, B. 2008. "Barack Obama and Joe Biden: Supporting Urban Prosperity." http://www.barackobama.com/pdf/issues/UrbanFactSheet.pdf. Accessed May 7, 2009.

Osborne, D., and Hutchinson, P. 2004. *The Price of Government: Getting the Results We Need in an Age of Permanent Fiscal Crisis*. New York: Basic Books.

Osborne, D., and T. Gaebler. 1992. *Reinventing Government: How The Entrepreneurial Spirit Is Transforming the Public Sector*. Reading, MA: Addison-Wesley.

Oscilloscope. 2009. "About the Film." http://www.flowthefilm.com. Accessed May 31, 2009.

Pacific Gas and Electric Company. 2009. "About Us." http://www.pgecorp.com/. Accessed October 5, 2009.

Palisades Indexes LLC. 2009. http://www.palisadesindexes.com/waterindexes.html. Accessed July 13, 2009.

Palmeri, C. 2009. "Digging for New Ways to Profit from Trash." *Business Week*. May 25, 57.

Palter, R.N., J. Walder, and S. Westlake. 2008. "How Investors Can Get More out of Infrastructure." *McKinsey Quarterly*. February.

Parkinson, C.N. 1955. "Parkinson's Law." *The Economist*. November.

Parliamentary Information Management Committee. 2009. "Briefing: The UK's Critical National Infrastructure." November 27, 2006. http://www.pitcom.org.uk. Accessed January 3, 2009.

Peltz, J. 2009. "Stalemate Stalls WTC Projects." *The Daily Reporter*. August 4. http://dailyreporter.com/blog/tag/new-york/. Accessed October 5, 2009.

Pepco Holdings Inc. 2009. "About PHI." http://www.pepcoholdings.com/. Accessed October 5, 2009.

Pickens, T. B. 2008. "PickensPlan." http://www.pickensplan.com/theplan/. Accessed May 7, 2009.

Poole, R. 2008. "Public Utility Regulation for Toll Roads?" *The Reason Foundation*. http://www.reason.org/news/show/1003154.html. September 30. Accessed April 25, 2009.

Porter, R.C. 2002. "The Economics of Waste." *Resources for the Future*. Washington, DC.

Postel, S. 2007. "Aquatic Ecosystem Protection and Drinking Water Utilities." *Journal AWWA*. 99(2) 52–63.

Poudre School District. 2009. "PSD 2000 Bond & Mill Levy Accountability." http://www.psdschools.org. Accessed May 12, 2009.

Preqin. 2009. "About Us." http://www.preqin.com/. Accessed May 26, 2009.

President's Commission to Study Capital Budgeting. 1999. "Report." http://clinton3.nara.gov/pcscb/report_pcscb.html. Accessed June 9, 2009.

Project Finance Magazine. 2009. "Home Page." http://www.projectfinancemagazine.com/. Accessed October 8, 2009.

Public Bonds. 2009. "Bond Basics." http://www.publicbonds.org. Accessed May 14, 2009.

Public Housing Authorities Director's Association. 2009. "About PHADA." http://www.phada.org. Accessed May 24, 2009.

Pulte Homes. 2009. "Pulte Homes History." http://www.pulte.com/. Accessed May 13, 2009.

Raabe, S. 2009. "Qwest Poised for Total Sale?" *Denver Post.* April 3, 8B.

Raftelis Financial Consultants. 2009. "Who We Are." http://www.raftelis.com/. Accessed July 13, 2009.

Real Estate Developer.com. 2009. "Commercial Real Estate Developers in the 20th Century." http://www.realestatedeveloper.com. Accessed May 13, 2009.

Reason Foundation. 2009. "Transportation and Tolls." http://www.reason.org/transportation/. Accessed March 15, 2009.

Reuters. 2009a. "Fitch Affirms Atlanta Airport's GARBs at 'A+' & PFC Sub Liens at 'A'; Outlook Stable." http://www.reuters.com/article/pressRelease/idUS 162791+05-Jun-2009+BW20090605. Accessed June 26, 2009.

———. 2009b. "American Water Works IPO Raises Less Than Expected." April 23. http://uk.reuters.com. Accessed May 31, 2009.

———. 2009c. "Company Profile For IESI-BFC Ltd." http://in.reuters.com. Accessed June 1, 2009.

Rodgers, P. 1979. "The NARUC Was There: A History of the National Association of Regulatory Utility Commissioners." National Association of Regulatory Utility Commissioners. 1979. Washington, DC.

Rosenberg, S. 2009. "Flow of Build America Bonds Starts Strong." *Wall Street Journal.* April 21, C3.

Roth, A. 2008. "Chicago Rail Deal Advances, but Time Crunch Looms." *Wall Street Journal.* December 26, A3.

———. 2009. "Railway Keeps Its Furloughed at Hand." *Wall Street Journal.* May 18, B1:2.

RREEF Alternative Investments. 2009. "Business Overview." https://www.rreef.com. Accessed May 17, 2009.

Rubin, D.K. 2009. "Construction Spending Hits New Global Low." *ENR.* Accessed April 8, 2009.

RWE AG. 2009. "Investor Relations." http://www.rwe.com/web/cms/de/8/rwe/. Accessed October 6, 2009.

Sakoui, A. 2006. "Eurotunnel Discloses Debt Plan." *Wall Street Journal.* June 1, B7.

Sempra Energy. 2009. "About Us." http://www.sempra.com/. Accessed October 5, 2009.

Sharma, A., and D. Cimilluca. 2009. "Qwest Seeks to Sell Piece of Its Network." *Wall Street Journal.* April 2, B1.

Siemens. 2009. "About Us." http://www.usa.siemens.com. Accessed May 25, 2009.

SIFMA. 2009a. "About Us." http://www.investinginbonds.com/. Accessed April 19, 2009.

———. 2009b. "Outstanding U.S. Bond Market Debt, $ Billions." http://www.sifma .org/uploadedFiles/Research/Statistics/SIFMA_USBondMarketOutstanding.pdf Accessed April 19, 2009.

Simon Property Group, Inc. 2009. "About Us." http://www.simon.com/. Accessed May 24, 2009.

Smith, R. 2008. "Surprise Drop in Power Use Delivers Jolt to Utilities." *Wall Street Journal*, November 21, B1.

Sorentrue, J. 2008. "Palm Beach County OKs $315 Million Bond Deal." October 22. *Palm Beach Post*. http://www.palmbeachpost.com. Accessed June 26, 2009.

Southern Company. 2009. "About Us." http://www.southerncompany.com/. Accessed October 5, 2009.

Stericycle Inc. 2009. "About Us." http://www.stericycle.com/. Accessed October 7, 2009.

Stussman, H. 1998. "Update." *ENR*. December 7, 5.

Summers, G.F., and T.R. Noland. 2008. "An Introduction to the U.S. Municipal Bond Market." *International Journal on Governmental Financial Management*. VIII(2):145–161.

T. Rowe Price. 2009. "Domestic Bond Funds." http://individual.troweprice.com. Accessed May 14, 2009.

TechKNOWLEDGEy Strategic Group. 2009. "About TSG." http://www.techstrategy.com/. Accessed October 8, 2009.

Toll Road News. 2009. "Airports Authority Takeover of Dulles Toll Road Threatened by Critical USDOT Report." July 28. http://www.tollroadsnews.com/node/3044.

Totty, M. 2009. "Smart Roads, Smart Bridges, Smart Grids." *Wall Street Journal*. February 17, R1, R3.

Trading Markets.com. 2009. "American Electric Power Prices Public Offering of Common Stock." http://www.tradingmarkets.com/.site/news/Stock%20News/2255257/. Accessed April 19, 2009.

Troianovski, A. 2009. "Big-City Skyscraper Burns Ozark Town." *Wall Street Journal*. June 4, A1:12.

Tulacz, G. 2005. "World Construction Spending Nears $4 Trillion for 2004." *ENR*. January 3–10, 254(1):12–13.

U.S. Army Corps of Engineers. 2009. "The Engineer of the Army." http://www.hqda.army.mil/daen/. Accessed October 6, 2009.

U.S. Army. 2009. "Military Construction (MILCON) Program." http://www.army.mil. Accessed May 24, 2009.

U.S. Bureau of Economic Affairs. 2009a. "Gross-Domestic-Product-(GDP)-by-Industry Data." http://www.bea.gov/industry/gdpbyind_data.htm. Accessed June 28, 2009.

———. 2009b. "Table 2.1. Current-Cost Net Stock of Private Fixed Assets, Equipment and Software, and Structures by Type. Table 7.1B. Current-Cost Net Stock of Government Fixed Assets." http://www.bea.gov/. Accessed June 20, 2009.

U.S. Bureau of Labor Statistics. 2009a. "Career Guide to Industries. 2008-2009 Edition." http://www.bls.gov/oco/cg/cgs003.htm/. Accessed June 28, 2009.

———. 2009b. "Current Employment Statistics." http://www.bls.gov/ces/. Accessed October 11, 2009.

U.S. Bureau of Transportation Statistics. 2009a. "Freight in America: Shipment Characteristics by Mode of Transportation for 2002." http://www.bts.gov. Accessed March 14, 2009.

———. 2009b. "Top 25 U.S. Ports by Cargo Vessel Type and Calls," 2000. http://www.bts.gov. Accessed March 14, 2009.

U.S. Census Bureau. 2002. "2002 Economic Census." http://www.census.gov/econ/census02/. Accessed October 11, 2009.

———. 2007. "State Government Tax Collections: 2005." http://www.census.gov/govs/statetax/0534ncstax.html. Accessed February 18, 2007.

———. 2008. "American Housing Survey." http://www.census.gov/hhes/www/housing/ahs/ahs.html. Accessed November 26, 2008.

———. 2009a. "Urban and Rural Definitions and Data." http://www.census.gov. Accessed May 10, 2009.

———. 2009b. "State Interim Population Projections by Age and Sex: 2004–2030." http://www.census.gov. Accessed June 20, 2009.

———. 2009c. "Construction Spending." http://www.census.gov/const/www/c30index.html. Accessed April 22, 2009.

———. 2009d. "2007 Economic Census." March 17. http://factfinder.census.gov. Accessed June 28, 2009.

———. 2009e. "2002 NAICS Codes and Titles." http://www.census.gov/epcd/naics02/naicod02.htm. Accessed October 8, 2009.

———. 2009f. "Annual Capital Expenditures Survey." http://www.census.gov/csd/ace/. Accessed July 8, 2009.

———. 2009g. "The 2009 Statistical Abstract. Table 701. Net Stock of Fixed Reproducible Tangible Wealth." http://www.census.gov/compendia/statab/. Accessed October 12, 2009.

———. 2009h. "State and Local Government Finance Data." http://www.census.gov/govs/www/estimate02.html. Accessed July 8, 2009.

U.S. Congressional Budget Office. 1983. *Public Works Infrastructure: Policy Considerations for the 1980's*. April. Washington, DC.

U.S. Department of Homeland Security. 2009. "National Infrastructure Protection Plan." http://www.dhs.gov/files/programs/editorial_0827.shtm. Accessed October 5, 2009.

U.S. Department of Housing and Urban Development. 2008a. *Evolution of the U.S. Housing Finance System: a Historical Survey and Lessons for Emerging Mortgage Markets*. November 26. Washington, DC.

———. 2008b. "The Federal Housing Administration (FHA)." http://www.hud.gov/offices/hsg/fhahistory.cfm. Accessed November 24, 2008.

———. 2008c. "Affordable Housing." http://www.hud.gov/offices/cpd/affordablehousing/index.cfm. Accessed November 28, 2008.

———. 2009. "Solutions That Support Affordable Housing." Regulatory Barriers Clearinghouse. http://www.huduser.org/rbc/search/rbcdetails.asp?DocId=916. Accessed May 12, 2009.

U.S. Department of Transportation. 2009. "Vision for a New Era in Rail Entails Clean, Energy-Efficient Option for Travelers." http://www.fra.dot.gov/us/press-releases/226.

U.S. Energy Information Administration. 2009a. "Energy Basics 101." http://www.eia.doe.gov/basics/energybasics101.html. Accessed October 5, 2009.

———. 2009b. "Natural Gas Prices." http://tonto.eia.doe.gov/. Accessed April 28, 2009.

———. 2009c. "Annual Europe Brent Spot Prices." http://tonto.eia.doe.gov/dnav/pet/hist/rbrteA.htm. Accessed May 21, 2009.

———. 2009d. "Coal Production." *1949–2007*. Accessed March 26, 2009.

———. 2009e. "Nuclear." http://www.eia.doe.gov/fuelnuclear.html. Accessed October 5, 2009.

U.S. Environmental Protection Agency. 2009. "Wastes." http://www.epa.gov/osw/. Accessed March 6, 2009.

———. 2009a. "About EPA." http://www.epa.gov/. Accessed October 11, 2009.

U.S. Federal Communications Commission. 2009. "About the FCC." http://www.fcc .gov/. Accessed March 28, 2009.

U.S. Federal Highway Administration. 2009a. "Highway Statistics." *Office of Highway Policy Information.* http://www.fhwa.dot.gov/policy/ohpi/qfroad.htm. Accessed March 14, 2009.

———. 2009b. "Dwight D. Eisenhower National System of Interstate and Defense Highways." http://www.fhwa.dot.gov/programadmin/interstate.cfm. Accessed October 5, 2009.

———. 2009c. "Status of the Nation's Highways, Bridges, and Transit: 2006 Conditions and Performance." http://www.fhwa.dot.gov/policy/2006cpr/index.htm. Accessed March 14, 2009.

———. 2009d. "PPP Case Studies: Chicago Skyway." http://www.fhwa.dot.gov/ PPP/case_studies_chicago.htm. Accessed June 26, 2009.

———. 2009e. "Public-Private Partnerships Toolkit for Highways." http://www. ppptoolkit.fhwa.dot.gov/about.aspx. Accessed May 31, 2009.

U.S. Federal Rail Administration. 2009. "A Vision for High-Speed Rail in America: Highlights of Strategic Plan." http://www.fra.dot.gov. Accessed May 13, 2009.

U.S. General Services Administration. 2009. "About Us." http://www.gsa.gov. Accessed May 24, 2009.

U.S. Government Accountability Office. 2005. "Results-Oriented Government: Practices That Can Help Enhance and Sustain Collaboration among Federal Agencies." GAO-06–15, October 21, 2005.

U.S. Green Building Council. 2009. "LEED Rating Systems." http://www.usgbc.org. Accessed June 23, 2009.

U.S. Internal Revenue Service. 2009. "Basic Tax Exempt Bond Training – Phase I." http://www.irs.gov/. Accessed April 19, 2009.

U.S. Nuclear Energy Institute. 2009. "Reliable and Affordable Energy." http://www.nei.org. Accessed May 22, 2009.

U.S. Water News. 2009. "Home Page." http://www.uswaternews.com/homepage. html. Accessed October 8, 2009.

United Utilities. 2009. "About United Utilities." http://www.unitedutilities.com/. Accessed October 6, 2009.

Urban Land Institute. 2009. "Connecting the Global Real Estate Community." http://www.uli.org/. Accessed June 20, 2009.

URS Corporation. 2009. "About Us." http://www.urscorp.com. Accessed May 25, 2009.

Utility Financial Solutions. 2009. "Who is UFS?" http://www.ufsweb.com/. Accessed July 13, 2009.

Vaughan, R.J. 1983. "Rebuilding America, Vol 2." *Financing Public Works in the 1980's.* Council of State Planning Agencies. Washington, DC.

Voeller, J.G, ED. 2008. *Wiley Handbook of Science and Technology for Homeland Security*. Hoboken, NJ: John Wiley & Sons, Inc.

Vulcan Materials Company. 2009. "Investor Relations." http://www.vulcan materials.com.

Wall Street Journal Business. 2009. "RWE CFO Repeats Co Still Aims to Fully Divest American Water." February 26. http://online.wsj.com. Accessed March 8, 2009.

Walsh, M.W. 2008. "Under Strain, Cities Are Cutting Back Projects." *New York Times*. September 30.

Wasik, J.F. 2006. *The Merchant of Power: Sam Insull, Thomas Edison, and the Creation of the Modern Metropolis*. New York: Palgrave MacMillan.

Waste Age. 2007. "Waste Age 100." http://wasteage.com/. Accessed June 8, 2009.

Waste Management Inc. 2009. "About Us." http://www.wm.com/. Accessed October 7, 2009.

Water and Wastewater Equipment Manufacturers Association. 2009. "Canadian Municipalities Resolve to Fight Buy American." http://www.wwema.org/?postID=22. Accessed October 6, 2009.

Water-Stocks.com. 2009. "Home Page." http://www.water-stocks.com/Water-Stocks/. Accessed October 8, 2009.

Weisman, J., and B. Graham. 2006. "Dubai Firm to Sell U.S. Port Operations." *Washington Post*. March 10, A1.

Williamson, R. 2009. "Dallas Area Rapid Transit Deal Boosted by BABs." *The Bond Buyer*. June 16. http://www.bondbuyer.com. Accessed June 26, 2009.

Wind Capital Group. 2009. "About Us." http://www.windcapitalgroup.com/Home.aspx. Accessed October 5, 2009.

Wisconsin Department of Commerce. 2009. "Wisconsin's Industrial Revenue Bond Program." http://commerce.wi.gov/BD/BD-IRB.html. Accessed June 26, 2009.

Wood, D. 2009. "Spanish-Led Group Secures $1.8-Bil in P3 Funds For Fla. Express Lanes." Enr.com. March 5. http://enr.construction.com. Accessed May 13, 2009.

World Bank. 2009a. "Privatization toolkits." http://rru.worldbank.org/Toolkits/. Accessed May 31, 2009.

———. 2009b. "World Bank to Invest $45 billion in Infrastructure to Help Create Jobs and Speed Crisis Recovery." http://web.worldbank.org. Accessed April 23, 2009.

———. 2009c. "Our Focus: By Sector." http://web.worldbank.org. Accessed April 21, 2009.

Xcel Energy. 2009. "Company." http://xcelenergy.com. Accessed October 5, 2009.

Yahoo Finance. 2009. http://finance.yahoo.com/. Accessed June 8, 2009.

Young, B., and S. Rollins. 2008. *How Any City Can Conduct a Utility Rate Study and Successfully Increase Rates*. University of Tennessee. Institute for Public Service. http://www.mtas.tennessee.edu.

About the Author

Neil S. Grigg is a professor in the department of civil and environmental engineering at Colorado State University, where his work focuses on infrastructure management and security and on water resources and environmental management. He graduated from the U.S. Military Academy and has graduate degrees in civil engineering from Auburn and Colorado State. He is an experienced municipal consultant and was cofounder of a Denver-area consulting firm, which enabled him to study financing of consulting firms, how they grow through acquisitions, and how their owners capture equity through being acquired. As a state government official in North Carolina, Neil was able to view infrastructure finance from the stance of a regulator. There he had responsibility for natural resources agencies, air and water quality regulation, and oversight for construction grants.

In his volunteer work, he has been a member of the water and transportation boards for the City of Fort Collins and of the national boards of the American Public Works Association and the Board on Infrastructure and the Constructed Environment of the National Research Council. He observed issues in other countries as an international consultant with United Nations and national agencies and local universities. This gave him a perspective of different systems for managing infrastructure, which have been incorporated into his courses at Colorado State.

Neil has held several university management positions in which he had budget authority and financial responsibility. He has served for over 20 years in a U.S. Supreme Court appointment as the River Master of the Pecos River. Since 2000, he had worked closely with the water utility industry on studies of emergency management, infrastructure condition assessment, risk modeling, workforce development, and integrated management strategies. He serves on several infrastructure-related editorial advisory boards, including the *Journal of the American Water Works Association*. His recent books include *Total Water Management: Leadership Practices for a Sustainable Future*; and *Water and Wastewater Workforce: Planning, Design, and Action for Organizational Excellence* (both published by the American Water Works Association).

Index